797,885 Books

are available to read at

Forgotten Books

www.ForgottenBooks.com

Forgotten Books' App
Available for mobile, tablet & eReader

ISBN 978-1-332-76394-8
PIBN 10244991

This book is a reproduction of an important historical work. Forgotten Books uses state-of-the-art technology to digitally reconstruct the work, preserving the original format whilst repairing imperfections present in the aged copy. In rare cases, an imperfection in the original, such as a blemish or missing page, may be replicated in our edition. We do, however, repair the vast majority of imperfections successfully; any imperfections that remain are intentionally left to preserve the state of such historical works.

Forgotten Books is a registered trademark of FB &c Ltd.
Copyright © 2015 FB &c Ltd.
FB &c Ltd, Dalton House, 60 Windsor Avenue, London, SW19 2RR.
Company number 08720141. Registered in England and Wales.

For support please visit www.forgottenbooks.com

1 MONTH OF FREE READING

at

www.ForgottenBooks.com

By purchasing this book you are eligible for one month membership to ForgottenBooks.com, giving you unlimited access to our entire collection of over 700,000 titles via our web site and mobile apps.

To claim your free month visit:
www.forgottenbooks.com/free244991

ˣ Offer is valid for 45 days from date of purchase. Terms and conditions apply.

English
Français
Deutsche
Italiano
Español
Português

www.forgottenbooks.com

Mythology Photography **Fiction** Fishing Christianity **Art** Cooking Essays Buddhism Freemasonry Medicine **Biology** Music **Ancient Egypt** Evolution Carpentry Physics Dance Geology **Mathematics** Fitness Shakespeare **Folklore** Yoga Marketing **Confidence** Immortality Biographies Poetry **Psychology** Witchcraft Electronics Chemistry History **Law** Accounting **Philosophy** Anthropology Alchemy Drama Quantum Mechanics Atheism Sexual Health **Ancient History Entrepreneurship** Languages Sport Paleontology Needlework Islam **Metaphysics** Investment Archaeology Parenting Statistics Criminology **Motivational**

OF THE

DAYS OF THE REFORMATION,

CHIEFLY FROM THE MANUSCRIPTS OF

JOHN FOXE THE MARTYROLOGIST;

WITH TWO

CONTEMPORARY BIOGRAPHIES OF ARCHBISHOP CRANMER.

"GOD is never better served than in adversity. Wealth maketh us wantons;
peace breedeth pride. We have quite forgotten *Mariana tempora.*"
Edmund Bicknoll's Sword against Swearers and Blasphemers, 1561.

EDITED BY

JOHN GOUGH NICHOLS, F.S.A.

PRINTED FOR THE CAMDEN SOCIETY.

M.DCCC.LIX.

590.* A few, however, were separated from the rest; but, having found their way into the collection of the Marquess of Lansdowne, are now, like the others, in our national museum. These are now interspersed in the Lansdowne collection (Nos. 335, 388, 389, 819, 1045, and possibly others, for others of the Lansdowne MSS. belonged to Strype).

A learned and judicious gentleman, already named, well known for the attention which he has for many years bestowed upon ecclesiastical history, as well as for the peculiar advantages which he has enjoyed of access to some of its most important sources, has not long since circulated among his friends a few pages bearing the title of NOTES UPON STRYPE;† repeating the arguments which he had written some ten or twelve years before, in recommendation of a new edition of Strype's works, at the request of a London publisher.

It will (Dr. Maitland remarks) be admitted by all who are in any degree acquainted with it, that there is no period of our history which is more interesting than that of the Reformation. And this, not merely considered in an ecclesiastical, but in a political and philosophical point of view; and as bearing on our constitution, our laws, habits, modes of thought and action,— on the whole history of our country since that time, and our own state and circumstances at the present day. Neither will it be denied, that for anything like familiar acquaintance with this period, we are incomparably more indebted to Strype, than to any other man. The industry and integrity with which, during a long course of years, he devoted himself to the collection of materials

---

* It is in this volume that the narrative of William Maldon occurs, which, having been observed too late for the text of this volume, is placed at the end of the Appendix. There is a remarkable passage at its commencement, showing Foxe's habits in soliciting materials for his work. In the same volume is also preserved a contemporary narrative (but imperfect) of the murder of the Hartgills by Charles Lord Stourton: this is introduced by Strype, but with several errors, in his Ecclesiastical Memorials, vol. iii. and is reprinted by Sir R. C. Hoare in his Modern Wiltshire, Hundred of Mere, p. 153.

† Octavo, pp. 15, dated *Gloucester, Feb.* 22, 1858.

for the history of those times, entitle him to our warmest gratitude; and the treasure of facts and documents which he collected, whether considered in respect of its bulk, or of its interest and importance, is altogether unrivalled.

After bestowing upon Strype this well-merited eulogy, Dr. Maitland proceeds to lament that the works of that laborious compiler are less familiar than they ought to be to English readers; that they are presented in a very uncomfortable, unreadable state, or kept from circulation by their costly price; that, whether in the old unwieldy folios, or in the twenty-five octavo volumes reprinted by the Clarendon Press, they are individually unfurnished with indexes; and though, in the latter respect, there is a general index to the whole series, yet it is unreasonable and absurd to require the purchaser of any one of the works to buy an index to the whole, itself forming two thick volumes; whilst the total cost of the series is an expense which few students will be disposed to incur at one time.*

Such are some of Dr. Maitland's objections against the works of Strype in their present state: but the more important charge which he brings against them is, that they are full of errors of transcription and the press, of which he exhibits many examples that very materially affect the meaning of the documents and quotations introduced.

On these grounds Dr. Maitland recommends that the labours of a careful revision should be bestowed upon the works of Strype, and that they should be again issued in an amended state.†

---

* The price of the Oxford edition, in 27 vols. (including the General Index) is now reduced from 14*l.* to 7*l.* 13*s.*

† There have been two modern attempts to republish Strype, the Memorials of Cranmer having been edited anonymously for the Ecclesiastical History Society in 1848, and by Philip Edward Barnes, esq. B.A. for Mr. Routledge, in 1853. On both occasions it was proposed that Strype's other works should follow, but no more made their appearance. Indeed, the Ecclesiastical History Society broke down after having published only two volumes out of three.

On the other side of the question it might be alleged, and perhaps with equal truth, that not any one of Strype's works is in itself complete as respects any particular period or transaction; that most subjects of which he treats are discussed in more than one of his books,* and that therefore a General Index is the best, and indeed the only satisfactory, key to them; and consequently, in order to make them really what could be wished, the whole should be recast into a chronological narrative, or at least the *disjecta membra* of certain important transactions should be brought together, and properly connected.

On the whole, the more the subject is considered, the more evident it appears that it is not merely revision, but a remoulding and rewriting, that the works of Strype require. Whilst on the one hand his documents undoubtedly ought to be collated, and should never be again reprinted without collation, because they are imperfect and incorrect;† so, on the other, his narrative ought to be remodelled, not because it is often prejudiced or intentionally unfair, but because it is frequently confused in arrangement, imperfect in information, and now obsolete in style.

In many places where Strype has reported, in his own terms, a story of the sixteenth century, his language is now really more old-fashioned and unlike our own, than the plain but effective

* The history of Foxe's Actes and Monuments affords an example, among scores of others. That work, and the various editions of it which appeared during the reign of Elizabeth, form a subject which is treated of by Strype in some half-dozen different places.

† "I do not mean to reflect on Strype, whose integrity and good faith are beyond all doubt: but to the question whether the documents and extracts, as they stand in his works, are in fact accurate copies of their originals, only one answer can be given. They are NOT. . . . . In many cases,—and sometimes in documents of great importance, whereof one would desire to have correct copies,—there is, as the words now stand, nothing but obvious nonsense." (Notes on Strype, by the Rev. S. R. Maitland, D.D. p. 6.)

phraseology of his original. Of this circumstance the present volume will afford frequent proofs.

Whether Strype will yet obtain an editor so patient and so devoted as Dr. Maitland has imagined, may now be doubted; but it must be generally admitted that it would be only a well-deserved testimony to the past labours and merits of the industrious historian in question, as to his more eminent predecessors, that any future Ecclesiastical History of England, on a large and comprehensive scale, whether accomplished by university, society, or individuals, should acknowlege upon its title-page that it was "founded on the works of Foxe, Burnet, Strype," &c.

By printing "The Diary of Henry Machyn" in its integrity the Camden Society has already made public one of the most curious sources of Strype's information; and the present volume may be regarded as a further instalment towards a critical edition of the documents employed by Strype. There are few historical students who will not prefer to read the *ipsissima verba* of the actors and sufferers in the perilous days of the Reformation rather than any modern version of their histories; and, though most of the writers in the present volume are shockingly astray from any recognised standard of orthography, yet it is well that at least one edition of their narratives should be printed as they themselves penned them.

If the assertion of Doctor Johnson, that "those relations are commonly of most value in which the writer tells his own story," be admitted to be just, and one of general acceptation, then the amount of autobiography contained in the present volume will be greatly in its favour.

Archdeacon Louthe,* the writer of the first paper, relates his

---

* Among the letters transcribed in Foxe's copy-book, which is now bound up in the Harl. MS. 417, at fol. 102 v. is the following, which is attributed to John Aylmer, bishop of London, in a side-note written by Strype; but I think it much more probable that it was written by our friend John Louthe, the archdeacon of Nottingham:—

anecdotes as of matters in which he had a personal concern, and of which he might say with the poet, *Quorum pars magna fui.* The narratives of John Davis, Thomas Hancock, Edward Underhill, Thomas Mowntayne, and William Maldon were all written by themselves; and the justification of the conduct of Thomas Thackham towards Julins Palmer also proceeded from his own pen.

In several instances the accuracy of Foxe's book is brought into question. Archdeacon Louthe offers a determined defence of the martyrologist upon that point, and it is on that account that I have placed his papers foremost in the present collection.

He attributes the outcry that had been raised against Foxe's work entirely to the malice of the mortified papists, and alludes especially to the attack which had proceeded from Louvaine, under the name of Alan Cope, but really written,* as was supposed, by Nicholas

---

"Salutem in Christo. Accepimus Reginam Scotorum paralysi graviter laborare, vel ad desperationem, et aliis nonnullis torqueri morbis. Rex ipse, optimæ spei adolescens, parliamenti autoritate decrevit de unâ religione confirmandâ et papisticâ e finibus suis exterminandâ, ita ut quisque missam auditurus primo moneatur, secundo bona ipsius fisco adjudicentur, si tertio peccaverit solum vertere cogatur. Hæc ad te scripsi, tum ut hujus boni participem faciam; tum ut a te preces cum lachrymis Christo nostro fundantur, et nos beare, et suum evangelium propagare pergat. Quæ concedat optimus Jhesus noster, quem non minus tibi familiarem existimo quàm est amicus quisque amico. Ora, ora, mi frater, nam plurimum apud Christum tuas valere preces non dubito.

"Tui amantiss. JOHANNES LOND."

Strype has introduced this letter in his Life of Bishop Aylmer, p. 43, (Oxford edition, p. 24,) and assigned it to about the year 1578. If the bishop of London addressed the martyrologist in these terms, they are certainly very extraordinary proof of the high estimation in which he was held by a prelate in so eminent a position; but I am inclined rather to think that they came from the enthusiastic and highly intolerant John Louthe—who yet did not choose to appear exactly *in propriâ personâ,* but signed JOHANNES LOUD, not LOND. as printed by Strype, and as it had been before by Foxe (see p. 14).

Harpsfield. But Louthe's own anecdotes furnish some proofs of the inexact reports to which Foxe was unavoidably subject, particularly when the reminiscences of years long past were revived.

The third article, that relating to Edward Horne, was purposely written to correct some imperfect information in " the Booke of Martyrs," and yet it seems never to have been brought into its proper place.

The " Defence of Thomas Thackham " is a direct expostulation with Foxe in regard to some statements respecting Julins Palmer in which Thackham's name had been introduced. His protestations, however, appear to have obtained little credit with Foxe's original informants, in consequence of the opinion they had formed of his insincerity. Though Thackham's arguments are excessively prolix, and too tedious to be desirable as a whole, the portions I have extracted will be found to contain some remarkable passages, and some very curious examples of Elizabethan phraseology.

Foxe, though a very laborious, was never a careful author. He admits this himself in the reply which he made to Alan Cope with respect to the story of Sir John Oldcastle lord Cobham: " I heare what you will saie, I should have taken more leisure, and done it better. I graunt and confesse my fault; such is my vice, I cannot sit all the daie (M. Cope,) fining and minsing my letters, and combing my head, and smoothing myself all the daie at the glasse of Cicero. Yet notwithstanding, doing what I can, and doing my good will, me thinkes I should not be reprehended."

The contents of the present volume certainly prove that Foxe, though always busy, was not fond of revising his writings. Several of the papers preserved among his Manuscripts were, like that of Horne, communicated to him for the express purpose of correcting his great work, were preserved by him for that purpose, and yet were never brought to their destined use.

I deem it perfectly unnecessary, however, to attempt any formal defence of Foxe's honesty and veracity. I believe him to have been truth-seeking,* but liable to mistakes in an age of difficult communication, and perhaps occasionally subjected to intentional misinformation.† The violence of his invective too often overshoots its object, and the coarseness of his abuse is necessarily offensive in the ears of a more refined age. In that respect he too much resembles his friend and associate Bale, who may very probably have been the author of some of the comments, particularly in the sidenotes, of the Book of Martyrs, that are so much in his style. It must also be admitted that in his remarks on the conduct and sufferings of those from whom he differed in matters of faith and discipline, Foxe too constantly discovers a merciless and unsympathising spirit, as well as a jocularity towards holy things which is both ill-timed and profane.

The Rev. Dr. Maitland, in his various essays‡ on Foxe's great work, has not only taken just exception to the tone and spirit in which its author wrote, but has shown some instances of what must

---

* See in p. 17, note, his own admission, "Although I deny not," &c.

† I am not myself aware of any proved instance of this; but it is thus stated, and judiciously commented upon, by Granger, in his Biographical History of England: "The same has been said of Foxe which was afterwards said of Burnet; that several persons furnished him with accounts of pretended facts, with a view of ruining the credit of his whole performance. But the author does not stand in need of this apology; as it was impossible in human nature to avoid many errors in so voluminous a work, a great part of which consists of anecdotes."

‡ A Review of Fox's History of the Waldenses. 1837. 8vo.

Six Letters on Fox's Actes and Monuments. 1837.

Six more Letters. 1841.

Notes on the contributions of the Rev. George Townsend to the new edition of Fox's Martyrology: Part 1. On the memoir of Fox ascribed to his Son; Part 2. Puritan Thaumaturgy; Part 3. Historical authority of Fox. 1842. 8vo.

Essays on subjects connected with the Reformation in England. **Reprinted, with additions, from the British Magazine. 1849. 8vo.**

be condemned as culpable carelessness in the treatment of historical evidence, and imperfect skill in learning and scholarship. All this Dr. Maitland has demonstrated with such minuteness and perseverance as might have been deemed unnecessary, or excessive, had not the advocates of the martyrologist, in a spirit of blind and injudicious partisanship, assumed undue weight for his historical authority. The proposition of the Convocation of 1571, that "the Monuments of the Martyrs" should be placed for public perusal in the houses of bishops, deans, and dignitaries, and in cathedral churches—which last expression has been grossly exaggerated into "all parish churches,"—in company with the Holy Bible and other like books pertaining to religion, seems to have exalted the Actes and Monuments of John Foxe, in the estimation of his over-zealous admirers, to a rank scarcely inferior to that of the Acts of the Apostles..

It can now no longer be disputed that as a general history of the Church, in its earlier ages, Foxe's work has been shown to be partial and prejudiced in spirit, imperfect and inaccurate in execution; but it is when approaching his own times—if allowance be still made for the prejudices and partiality which of course continue—that the book becomes most valuable as a record of the doings and sufferings, a mirror of the opinions, passions, and manners of the people of England. For the early annals of the Church there are other authors to be preferred, both of antecedent and of subsequent date; but for familiar pictures of public and private struggles for conscience sake, it is probably unequalled in any country or language. It is the Chronicle of the days of the Reformation, the BOOK OF MARTYRS upon which the intense interest of their own and many subsequent generations was concentrated.

John Foxe had set himself the task of writing a History of the Church in Latin, and he thought it derogatory to his character as a scholar to appear in any other language.* It was the demand of the English public—or, if there was then no literary public in England, of John Day his London publisher, supported, no doubt, by Bishop Grindal and other influential persons,—that, even against the author's will, produced the English edition, and it was the zeal and enthusiasm of a Protestant people that made it so successful. Foxe had given his work in its original language the title of *Commentarii*, and in its English form that of "The Actes and Monuments of the Church;" † it was the English people themselves that called it *The Book of Martyrs*. This popular title in itself

* This appears in his dedication addressed to Queen Elizabeth, in which he apologises that "the story being written in the popular tongue serveth not so greatly for your own peculiar reading, nor for such as be learned;" and again in his letter sent with a copy of the first edition to the President and Fellows of Magdalen College, Oxford:—" Hoc unum dolet, Latinè non esse scriptum opus, quo vel ad plures emanare fructus historia, vel vobis jucundior ejus posset lectio. Atque equidem hoc multo maluissem, sed huc me adegit communis patriæ ac multitudinis ædificandæ respectus, cui et vos ipsos id idem redonare æquum est." We have also Foxe's own statement that the translation of his Latin book into English was not made by himself, but executed by others whilst he was occupied in further researches into episcopal registers.

† The title of "*Actes and Monuments*" appears to have been borrowed from the book entitled *Actiones et Monimenta Martyrum*, printed by Jean Crespin, at Geneva, in 1560. Grindal, to whom Foxe was chiefly indebted for the materials relating to the Marian persecution, speaks in his letter to Foxe dated Strasburgh, 19 Dec. 1558, of their projected work as *Historia Martyrum*. It is therefore contrary to what might have been expected that the word Martyrs did not appear on the English title-page. But, although it did not, there are many proofs that the work was from a very early time recognised as *The Book of Martyrs*. It is so called by Thackham at p. 93 of the present volume, and by Deighton in p. 69. Archdeacon Louthe, in p. 15, styles it "the booke of Actes and Monumentes of Martyres." When directed to be placed in cathedral churches, &c. in 1571, it was called "Monumenta Martyrum."

shows that the portions of the work which really fastened themselves upon the public mind, were not its early historical details, whether faithfully or partially related, but its heart-stirring narratives of events of more recent occurrence, which came home to the sympathies and the passions of those who had shared or witnessed their transaction and their effects.*

For a similar reason the autograph Narratives of some of the sufferers still appeal to us with a more than ordinary degree of interest. Nor are they altogether merely the details of private doings and sufferings. They are connected, indirectly, with many of the most important national events, as will at once be perceived on turning over the leaves of this volume, or by looking down its Table of Contents.

In order to render its illustrative notes more complete, I have trespassed on the time and attention of many of my friends.

To the Rev. James Raine,† of York, I am indebted for a copy of

---

* Foxe himself looked forward to this sort of personal interest that would be taken in his work—" Neque non juvabit et illud nostrorum fortasse animos, quum multi in his historiæ monumentis suos reperient, alii parentes, alii filios, nonnulli uxores, pars maritos, quidam cognatos aut affines, plurimi vicinos aut amicos: de quibus hic legere aliquid, velutique loquentes audire, pro suo quisque affectu avebit." (Dedication of the Commentarii to the Duke of Norfolk, dated at Basle, September 1, 1559.) And yet he seems to have expected that all his readers should understand Latin.

† In how different a position, unfortunately for literary and biographical research, are the records of the two archiepiscopal courts at present placed! While those of the province of York have been liberally thrown open, and to a certain extent made public by the aid of the Surtees Society, those of the province of Canterbury, by the arrangements of the new Courts of Probate and Divorce, have become more rigidly closed than ever. No other copies or notes are permitted than those which are made by the official scribes, and are officially authenticated. Above a certain date, when the handwriting becomes especially

the will of Archdeacon Louthe. The Rev. W. H. Gunner and the Rev. Mackenzie Walcott have both assisted me in illustrating Louthe's biographical anecdotes by extracts from the records of Winchester College. The Right Hon. Lord Monson has obliged me with many valuable suggestions in my endeavours to trace the domestic history of Anne Askew, but which have been rewarded with less success than I was willing to anticipate.

To William Hobbs, F.S.A. of Reading, I owe some information respecting Thomas Thackham, and particularly the patent for the mastership of Reading school which is printed in the Appendix.

But the most important contribution I have received is that of Morice's Anecdotes of Archbishop Cranmer, communicated by the Rev. J. E. B. Mayor, and which led me to introduce the preceding paper, entitled "The Life and Death of Archbishop Cranmer" Both of these articles I fully expect will be regarded as adding materially to the value and interest of the present volume, as they

plain and legible, and free from the pothooks and hangers of modern legal penmanship, the fees for transcription are unreasonably doubled, as if in especial despite to historical inquiry. It will scarcely be credited that the brief will of John Petit, which occupies fourteen lines of the present volume, cost, with the formal record of probate (for we must take the husk with the kernel), the sum of five shillings.

At the recent change of the Ecclesiastical Courts a great opportunity for the propagation of historical knowledge was suffered to pass by. The proper course would have been to have relieved the Will Office by removing its records of a date anterior to the year 1700, to the Public Record Office, or to the British Museum.

Can it not still be arranged that literary inquirers should be allowed to take *unauthenticated* copies or extracts, when furnished for that purpose with a certificate from H. M. Keeper of Public Records? Some such concession may, perhaps, yet be made, when the new buildings of the Prerogative Office are completed.

show the principal sources of one of the most important portions of Foxe's work.

The Rev. W. D. Macray, of Oxford, has examined for me the Ashmolean MS. 861, and has ascertained that it contains extracts from the same Journal, kept by Anthony Anthony, which was quoted by Bishop Burnet with respect to Queen Anne Boleyne, as mentioned in the note in p. 305; and also in regard to the racking of Anne Askew. Though the passages relating to the latter subject have not been recovered, yet the Ashmolean extracts are sufficient to prove that the document which (as I have remarked) was ignored by Mr. Jardine once existed, if it is not now to be found, and that it proceeded from a contemporary writer whose testimony is entitled to some respect and consideration.

By the use of the unpublished sheets of the "Athenæ Cantabrigienses," with which I have been favoured by their authors, Charles Henry Cooper, Esq. F.S.A., and his son, Mr. Thompson Cooper, I have had the gratification to be the first of a long line of editors that will have to acknowledge their continual obligations to a work which is as elaborate and careful in its execution as it is important and comprehensive in its design.

It was my intention to have included in this preface some account of the origin, formation, and literary history of Foxe's great work; but, in pursuing this intention, I have found the materials grow upon my hands to an extent exceeding the limits to which it is

* Morice's paper was communicated by archbishop Parker to Foxe before the preparation of his second edition in 1570, (not 1576, as misdated in p. 234,) in the Index to which the reader's particular attention is directed to it by the following singular entry :—

"Thomas Cranmer made Archbyshop of Canterbury 1200. His storye is worthe the reading, and begynneth 2032."

It lasts from that page to p. 2072.

necessary that I should here confine myself. I must therefore defer "The Literary History of the Book of Martyrs" to some other occasion. I have only further to apologise for a slight error that has been more than once repeated in the present volume. There were nine standard editions of the ACTES AND MONUMENTS, which were published in the years 1563, 1570, 1576, 1583, 1596-7, 1610, 1631-2, 1641, and 1684. All of them, except the last, are now more or less scarce books; and two, those of 1570 and 1583, are not at present in the library of the British Museum. It arose from this circumstance that I have in several places termed the edition of 1576 the second edition instead of the third. By the kindness of Mr. George Offor I have since seen a copy of the edition of 1570.

NARRATIVES

OF THE

DAYS OF THE REFORMATION.

I.

THE REMINISCENCES OF JOHN LOUDE OR LOUTHE,
ARCHDEACON OF NOTTINGHAM,

ADDRESSED TO JOHN FOXE IN 1579.

JOHN LOUDE, Louthe, or Lowth, as the name was more commonly written, claimed descent from several families of importance. His grandfather Thomas Louthe esquire was of Castle Hedingham in Essex, Cretingham in Suffolk, and Sawtrey Beaumys in the county of Huntingdon, and had married Anne, daughter and heir of Thomas Mulso[a] of Cretingham; Lionel Louthe,[b] father of Thomas, had married Katharine Dudley, of the family of Sutton alias Dudley, barons of parliament and knights of the Garter; and Roger Louthe,[c] father of Lionel, is said (by John Loude) to have married " Mary of Henawd," a cousin of Lionel earl of Ulster, and duke of Clarence, son of king Edward the Third. Queen Philippa, the mother of that prince, was a princess of Hainault; but who " Mary of Henawd" may have been it would perhaps be

---

[a] Called sir Edmund Mulso by John Loude, but see the note, p. 4.

[b] Lionel Louthe died Nov. 30, 1471, leaving his widow Katharine possessed of the manor of Bealmes in Sawtrey: see an abstract of his inquisition post mortem in the Appendix. His name occurs as a feoffee in 22 Hen. VI. in Collectanea Topogr. et Geneal. iv. 136.

vain to inquire.[a] Possibly this part of the Loude genealogy partakes of imagination, suggested by the Christian name Lionel. The other alliances, however, are confirmed [b] by the coats of arms which were found in the manor-house of Sawtrey when Nicholas Charles made his Visitation of Huntingdonshire in the year 1613. From that book (already printed for the Camden Society) the following is an extract, with the names of some of the coats of arms supplied:—

In Laurence Farron's howse at Sawtrey in the hall wyndowes.

These 3 in the north wyndowe of the hall.

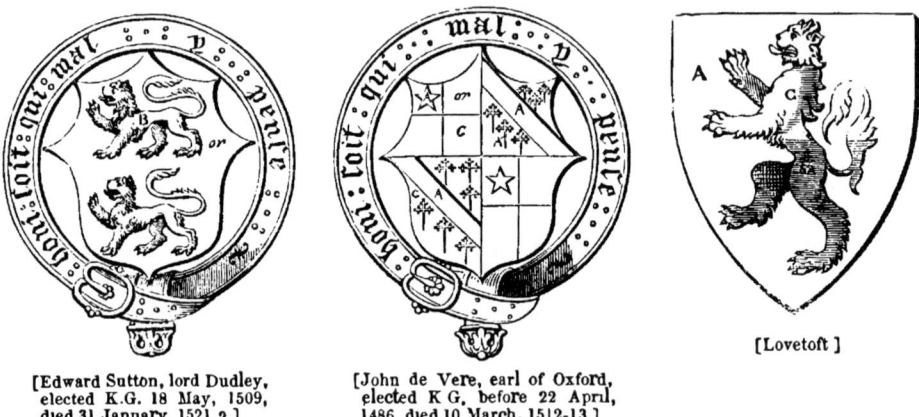

[Edward Sutton, lord Dudley, elected K.G. 18 May, 1509, died 31 January, 1521-2.]

[John de Vere, earl of Oxford, elected K G. before 22 April, 1486, died 10 March, 1512-13.]

[Lovetoft]

These 6 escocheons stand in the south wyndowes of the hall aforesaid.

[Louthe=Stukeley.] [Louthe=Mulso.] [Louthe=Dudley.]

---

[a] See, however, some further remarks in the Appendix.

[b] The arms of Edward lord Dudley, K.G., were evidently set up as those of a kinsman of whom the family of Louthe was proud. From a similar reason, or as a mark of

REMINISCENCES OF JOHN LOUTHE. 3

[Louthe=Henawd?]

[Louthe=Somayne?]

[Louthe.]

In Sautrey Church 9 Augusti 1613.

Upon a monument in the south side of the chancell:

. . . .
. . . .
. Mense Aprilis, Anno Domini MCCCCiiij. et
Maria uxor ejus, quor' animab' propiciet' deus. Amen.

[Moyne.]

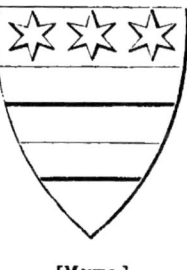
[Moyne.]

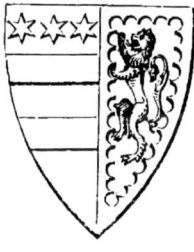
[Moyne=Somayne?]

---

feudal respéct, they were accompanied by those of the earl of Oxford, upon whom the family were doubtless dependent at Castle Hedingham. The coat of Louthe or Lowth is blazoned thus: Sable, a wolf salient argent and in dexter chief a crescent of the second. The first impalement appears to have been intended for Stukeley, the wife of Edmund Louthe (p. 4): it was properly Argent, on a fess sable three mullets of the field (as on the monument, p. 6). The fourth coat seems to partake of the like error, in having two bars instead of a fess. The fifth impalement is the same as that impaled on the monument of Moyne below: with a bordure nebulée instead of engrailed it is assigned by Glover to

Thomas Louthe became possessed of the manor of Kettlebers in Cretingham, Suffolk, either from his wife or his mother the heiress of Mulso.[a] He died on the 26th Oct. 1533, having survived his son Edmund and grandson Lionel, whereupon Margaret his great-granddaughter, being then of the age of four years and more, was by inquisition found to be his heir.

Edmund Louthe had died in 1522, of wounds received in an affray with two of his neighbours, the circumstances of which are related at length in the following pages[b] by his son John, who represents the occurrence as a shameful and deliberate murder. Its perpetrators were tenants of the abbey of Sawtrey, and the son plainly asserts that this atrocity was instigated by the monks. He adds that the widow, who was Edith daughter of John Stukeley, lord of Stukeley near Huntingdon, sued an appeal of murder, but that, through ecclesiastical influence, her suit was unavailing, her late husband being regarded as a heretic.

Lionel Louthe, the son of Edmund, died in 1532[c] (the year before his grandfather,) having married Elizabeth, eldest daughter of sir Thomas Blenerhasset of Prenze in Suffolk; who was remarried to Francis Clopton esquire of Melford park in the same county.[d]

Margaret Lowth, the heiress, carried the representation of the family into that of Cornwallis. Sir John Cornwallis, of Brome in Suffolk, the lineal ancestor of the earls and marquesses Cornwallis, and who died steward of the

---

[a] In the note from the Inquisition on his death, (Inq. 26 Hen. VIII.) "Pro terris in Sawtre, Bealmes man', [et] Stilton," given in the Visitation 1613, p. 11, his wife is named Thomasine. John Loude (in his Reminiscences hereafter) states that she was Anne, daughter of sir Edmund Mulso. A pencil note in MS. Coll. Arm. Vincent 125, f. 40, makes Anne, daughter and coheir of Thomas Mulso of Newton, the mother of Thomas Louthe. Mr. A. Page, in his "Supplement to the Suffolk Traveller," 1844, 8vo. p. 91, states that the heiress of Mulso was Anne, only daughter of William Mulso the son of Thomas. Mr. Davy's Suffolk Collections do not clear these discrepancies, but the following notes in them show that the manor of Kettlebers descended from Thomas Mulso to Thomas Lowth:—

"Rentale manerii de Kessingland, fact. ibidem 16 Edw. IV. Imprimis, heredes Thomæ Mulsoe armigeri tenent manerium de Kettlebers, et alia terr. et ten. in Cretingham et Ashfield, et reddunt per ann. de libero redd. lij^s. vj^d.

(At another date.) "De Thoma Lowth pro manerio voc. Ketylburgh haule, lij^s. vj^d." (MS. Addit. 19,096, f. 180.)

[b] See pp. 35—39.

[c] Monument at Cretingham, described hereafter.

[d] Compare pedigree of Blenerhasset in Harvey's Visitation of Suffolk, 1561, and Davy's Suffolk Collections, MS. Addit. 19,118, f. 353.

household to prince Edward (afterwards Edward the Sixth) in 1544, by his will, made a few days before his decease, left "To my [third] son Richard my ward Margaret Lowthe, which I bought of my lord of Norfolk, to marry her himself if they both will be so contented, but if not that he should have the wardship and marriage of her, with all advantages and profits." The lady is described in the Cornwallis pedigree as Margaret, daughter and heir of Lionel Lowth, of Sawtrey-Beaumys in the county of Huntingdon, esquire. She was married [a] to Richard Cornwallis esquire, and had issue six children, of whom the eldest was John, and the second sir Thomas Cornwallis, groom-porter [b] to Queen Elizabeth and King James, knighted in 1603, to whom there is a remarkable monument, with his effigy, in the church of Porchester in Hampshire.

Richard Cornwallis esquire had resided at Okenhill hall, and was buried at Shotley, in Suffolk.[c] His widow resided at Badingham, and having reached an advanced age, she died on the 4th Sept. 1603, and was buried at Cretingham. A few years before she had erected in the church of that place, where her family had inherited the manor of Kettlebers, a grand monument to the heraldic glories of her race, and nominally to her father, who had died sixty-four years before. It is thus described by Mr. Davy: [d]

"Against the north wall of the chancel a large mural monument of stone, painted, and under the arch thereof, adorned with Attic pilasters, the figure of a man in armour, with his head bare, a ruff about his neck, kneeling to the front on a cushion, his hands joined and erect, his helmet and sword lying by his side. On the architrave above is the following inscription:

> Hunc tumulum charo vult Margarita parenti
> De Sawtry antiqua Louthorum stirpe creato.
> Cui pater Edmundus, Thomas avus, hic Leonellus,
> Hæc heres ex asse fuit, conjunxq. Richardi
> Cornwaleys, parili pietate et stemmate claro.
> Hoc viduata viro, quem sexta prole beavit,

---

[a] John Blenerhasset, of Barsham in Suffolk, esquire, brother to Elizabeth the wife of Lionel Louth, married Elizabeth daughter of sir John Cornwallis; and there were several other alliances between the two families.

[b] The office of groom-porter remained long in the Cornwallis family: the uncles of sir Thomas, Edward and Francis, having been successively groom-porters to queen Elizabeth.

[c] The date of his death does not occur, but it was more than forty years before that of his wife, as is stated in her epitaph.

Nunc annosa suis memoranda nepotibus offert,
Jure sepulturæ cineres venerata paternos."

On the pediment above, a large shield of five coats, three and two: 1. Louth, Sa. a wolf salient arg.; 2. Mulso, Erm. on a bend sa. three goat's heads erased arg. armed or; 3. Moyne, Arg. two bars sa., in chief three mullets of the second; 4. Milverton,[a] Arg. on a cross az. five garbs or; 5. Louth. Crest, on a knight's helmet and torse a demi-man full-faced, clothed sa., his right hand elevated, his left across his breast. On the dexter side of the arch a shield, quarterly: 1 and 4. Louth; 2. Moyne; 3. [Beaumeys]; impaling Mulso. Beneath this shield is written "Tho. Lovth—and Mulso." On the sinister side, another shield of five coats, as the large one above; impaling Stukeley, Arg. on a fess sa. three mullets of the field. Below this is written, "Ed. Louth—Stewcley." On the base of the monument: "Leonellus obiit A° D'ni MDXXXII. Margarita posuit MDXCVI." And in the middle of this inscription, Louth of five coats as before, impaling Blenerhayset, Gules, a chevron between three dolphins embowed sa., on the chevron a trefoil argent within an annulet or. Beneath this shield is written: "Leo. Louth—Blen'hayset."

The heiress's own monument stands in the same church, at the south-east angle of the chancel, facing westwards, inlaid with English marble, and inscribed on the cornice: In memoriam Margaritæ relictæ Richardi Cornwaleis armigeri hoc posuit Johannes filius.

On a black tablet these verses:

Shotleia busta viri, sed conjugis ossa sacellum
　Hoc tenet: unanimes corpore, morte duo.
Parturiit, fovit geniali fœdere sola
　Tergeminam prolem; junxit, adauxit opes.
Namq. lares coluit viduas labentibus octo
　Lustris, et nono mortua viva jacet.
Et tu nate tuæ priscos venerate Penateis
　Matris, qua vivis, vivere morte jubes.
　　Obiit 4° die Septemb. 1603°.

On the summit of the monument, Cornwallis of nine coats: 1. Cornwallis, 2. Buckton, 3. Braham, 4. Tye, 5. Tyrrell, 6. Samford, 7. Butler, 8. Mepersall,

---

[a] This coat was not Milverton, but Beaumeys, as borne by the ancient family which gave its name to one of the manors of Sawtrey. (Visitation of Huntingdonshire, 1613, p. 16.) The Louths appear to have assumed the quarterings of Moyne and Beaumeys, and the crest of Moyne, whether by any right of blood may be doubted: but see some further remarks on this point in the Appendix.

9. Cornwallis; impaling Louth of five coats, 1. and 5. Louth, 2. Mulso, 3. Moyne, 4. [Beaumeys]. Crests of Louth and Cornwallis, but both broken. On the upper frieze, between festoons of fruit, are two shields, Cornwallis of six coats, impaling Blenerhasset; and the like impaling Molineux of nine coats; on the lower frieze four shields, Hearing, Bacon, Dade, and Futter, each impaling Cornwallis quarterly of six (as more fully blazoned by Mr. Davy in his descriptions).

By a deed of 34 Eliz. 16th Jan. Margaret Cornwallis of Badingham, widow, late wife of Richard Cornwallis esquire deceased, with John Cornwallis her eldest son, &c., recites a settlement on John 23 Dec. 30th Eliz. of the manor of Sawtrye in Huntingdonshire,—to the use of Margaret for life; to John for life; to such wife as John may leave him surviving during her life; to Philip son of said John, and his heirs male; to Thomas son of said John, in tail male; to Francis, &c.; to the heirs male of John; to Thomas son of Margaret, and his heirs male; to the heirs of Margaret in fec.[a]

The manor of Kettlebers in Cretingham descended in the family of Cornwallis until the close of the seventeenth century, when Mary Cornwallis, the heiress of this branch, having married John Rabett gent. he held his first court in the year 1701. The Rev. Reginald Rabett was lord of the manor in 1810, and in that family is still vested the representation of the family of Louth at Cretingham.

We return to the member of the family whose Reminiscences have led us into these genealogical researches.

JOHN LOUTHE, the writer of the following pages, was the youngest son of Edmund Louthe, and born in the summer of 1519. He tells us that on the day when his father received his mortal wound he was a child of three years old, and carried in his father's arms. The circumstances of his father's fate appear to have imbued him with a thorough detestation of monks and priests, and yet eventually he was himself ordained and amply beneficed.

He received his education in the colleges of William of Wykeham at Winchester and Oxford, to the former of which he was admitted at the age of fourteen,[b] and had for his fellow-student and friend John Philpot, afterwards archdeacon of Winchester, and a distinguished Protestant martyr, of whom he relates various anecdotes. And at Winchester he received his first impressions of Protestantism from a perusal of Frith's "Disputacion of Purgatory."

---

[a] MS. Addit. 19,096, f. 180.

[b] "1534. Johannes Lowthe de Sawtre, xiiij annorum in festo Nat. (*sc.* Sancti Johannis Baptistæ.) Linc. Dioc. *In margine,* recessit Oxon." Register of Admissions to Winchester College.

8   NARRATIVES OF THE REFORMATION.

He became a fellow of New college on the 24th July, 1540, and so continued until 1543; and was admitted to the degree of bachelor of laws.[a]

Having been taken into the service of sir Richard Southwell, a privy councillor, (master of the ordnance, and one of the executors of Henry VIII.) he accompanied the eldest son of that gentleman to Bene't college, Cambridge, where his name occurs as "mr. Lowth" in fellows' commons in the year 1545,[b] and afterwards to Lincoln's-inn, in which latter quarter he describes himself as narrowly escaping from detection and consequent imprisonment as a heretic.

After the accession of Elizabeth, Louthe received several ecclesiastical preferments. On the 20th of April, 1560, he was installed prebendary of Leicester St. Margaret's in the cathedral church of Lincoln[c]; on the 22nd July, 1561, prebendary of Gaia Minor in the church of Lichfield.[d] In 1562 he became chancellor of Gloucester, which office he retained until 1570. In the same year (1562) he was proctor of the church of Gloucester at the convocation, but did not appear when the votes were taken on the changes in the articles and common prayer.[e] In 1565 he was collated by Thomas Young archbishop of York to the archdeaconry of Nottingham[f]; and on the 7th October, 1567, he

---

[a] See note [c] below.

[b] Masters, History of Corpus Christi or Bene't College, 1749, 4to. p. 342. A biographical notice of Louthe is there given, derived entirely from Strype, whose sole authority was Louthe's own narrative, which is now before us. Strype, however, fell into more than one misapprehension. He stated (Memorials, vol. i. p. 368,) 1. That "he was a member of Bene't College, and after removed thence to the inns of court;" but Louthe does not tell us that he was himself either a member of Bene't college or of Lincoln's-inn, but merely that he taught mr. Southwell at both places. 2. Strype states that his pupil was "afterwards sir Richard Southwell, a privy counsillor," &c. but it will be found that Louthe distinctly describes his pupil as the son of sir Richard. Strype erroneously makes him tutor both to father and son. Though unnoticed by Anthony à Wood, Louthe certainly went from Winchester to New college, Oxford, and completed his own education at that university. Misled by Strype, Masters has further (at p. 373) claimed sir Richard Southwell as a member of his college, and given a memoir of him accordingly.

[c] His name is printed as "John Londe, LL.B." in Le Neve's Fasti Ecclesiæ Anglicanæ, edit. Hardy, 1854, ii. 169. The next prebendary mentioned was installed 1581.

[d] "John Lounde, Lanne, or Lownde," Hardy's Le Neve, i. 609. The next prebendary collated 1578.

[e] Strype, Annals, i. 339.

[f] Willis, Cathedrals, i. 107. He was installed on the 30th June, 1565.

was instituted to the rectory of Gotham, which he held until his death. On the 2nd March, 1568-9, he was instituted to the vicarage of St. Mary's in Nottingham, which he resigned in 1572. In 1570 he became prebendary of Dyndre in the church of Wells.[a] On the 7th August, 1574, he was instituted to the rectory of Hawton near Newark, which he resigned in October 1589.

In the year 1572 he contributed to the work of a physician, who resided near Nottingham,[b] and wrote in praise of the medical waters of Bath and Buxton, the following commendatory lines:—

Johannis Ludi Archidiaconi Nottinghamiensis Τετραδικαστίχον *in laudem et usum Thermarum nostrarum.*

> Balnea sunt variis calefacta salubria morbis,
> Ad multosque usus ως πολυχρηστα valent.
> Non externa valent curare pathemata tantum,
> Ast interna etiam tollere posse scio.
> Si bene quis novit thermis cautissimus uti,
> Proderit ille sibi: sin male, damna ferent.
> Ni prius evacues, pletorica corpora lædunt,
> Nec minus et succis corpora facta malis.
> Gens sua quæque solet plenis extollere buccis,
> Anglica sed cunctis sunt meliora duo.
> Altera rex Bladud nobis, comes alt'ra [c] Salopæ
> Exornata dedit sumptibus ipse suis.
> Tot bona (lector) habes magno tibi parta labore,
> Præter sudorem nil tuns Author habet.

The archdeacon of Nottingham died in the year 1590, having shortly before made his will, in which he mentions his son John Louthe, then in his minority: the son of Mary Louthe alias Babington his wife. To that son he left his house at Keyworth in Nottinghamshire, in which he then resided; and for want of heirs of the said John the house was entailed to the heirs male of the testator's daughter Thomasine the wife of mr. Zachary Babington of Lichfield; and, such failing, to the heirs male of Humfrey Louthe of Sutton in Ashfield, cō. Nottingham, gentleman,—to the heirs male of William Louthe of Maldon in Essex, gentleman,—to those of Robert Louthe of the Queen's majesty's

---

[a] Le Neve's Fasti Eccl. Angl. (edit. Hardy,) i. 193.

[b] "The Bathes of Bathes Ayde: compendiously compiled by John Jones, Phisition, anno Salutis 1572, at Asple hall besydes Nottingam."

[c] *i.e.* Buxton. This alludes to the second part of doctor Jones's work, which sets

court,—to those of Peter Louthe late of Nottingham; so that there were several junior branches of the family, though the main stock in Huntingdonshire had terminated in a female heir. The archdeacon's widow was to occupy the house during his son's minority; but in the case of her re-marriage she was to vacate it in favour of her brother mr. Francis Babington clerk, who was made one of the supervisors of the will, together with the archdeacon of Nottingham for the time being, Henry Pierpont esquire, Launcelot Rolston gentleman, mr. Richard Symney, mr. John Parker, and mr. Humfrey Louthe the testator's cousin; the widow being executrix. He desires his body to be buried in the north side of the choir of St. Mary's at Nottingham, and a small monument of brass to be nailed upon a stone in the wall to his memory; but no such memorial is mentioned by the historians of Nottingham as having existed in recent times. He also contemplates that funeral sermons might be preached by his " scholars and friends," which seems to intimate that he continued a schoolmaster after he was well preferred in the church.

WILL OF JOHN LOUTHE, ARCHDEACON OF NOTTINGHAM.
(From the Original in the Registry at York.)

In the name of God, Amen. The xxixth daye of July, anno Domini 1590, I John Louthe, archdeacon of the archdeaconrye of Not', whole of bodie and mynde, thanked be God, doe make this my last will and testament in maner and forme followinge.

First, I give and bequethe my soule into the handes of Allmightie God my heavenly Father, who hath from the begininge of the world ordayned his sonne Jesus Chryst to be a Saviour and Redeemer to me and to all other sinners that beleve to be saved by the deathe and passion of Chryst, in whom only I hope and surely trust in my harte to be redeemed from all my sinnes and by non other meanes.

And as touchinge the disposinge of my transitorie goodes I doe give and bequeth to my daughter Thomazine Babington the wyffe of mr. Zacharie Babington of Litchfeld the some of xx^{li} poundes of good and lawfull money of England, to be payd her for her chyldes parte, besydes those thinges which she and her husband mr. Zacharie Babington have allreadie taken and receaved at my handes to their owne use: which some of xx^{li} poundes my mynde and will is shalbe payd to her at two severall dayes of payment next after my decease, viz. the one hallf therof within three monethes next after my decease, and the other half to be payd her within foure monethes next after that.

Item I doe give to my sonne John Louthe the sonne of Marye Louthe alias Babington my wyffe my mansion house with all other houses and buildinges therunto belonginge, scituate, lyinge, and beinge in Kayworthe within the countie of Nottingham, wherin I nowe dwell, with all and singuler the appurtnances appertayninge unto yt, and all other landes, pastures, medowes, feedinges, commons, royalties, and comodities whatsoever which in anie wyse appertayne unto the same house and landes; to have and to hold the same house with all landes and commodities appertayninge to yt as aforesayd to the sayd John Louthe my sonne the sonne of the sayd Marye duringe his naturall lyffe, and after his decease to the heyres of his bodie lawfully begotten for ever, provyded notwithstandinge that duringe the minoritie of the sayd John Louthe my sonne I give and bequeth unto the said Mary Louth my wyffe (so longe as she keepeth her self widowe) the use, occupyinge, and possessinge of the sayd house and landes, with all and singuler the appurtenances aforesayd; and by this my last will and testament doe ordayne and appoynte that she shall and may peaceably and quyetly without anie maner of lett, interruption, or contradiccion of anie person or persons whatsoever, have, hold, use, occupie, possesse and enjoye to her owne proper use and uses all that my sayd mansion house and landes with all and singuler their appurtnances as aforesayd, so that yearly, and from yeare to yeare duringe the minoritie aforesayd, she doe well and trulye paye, satisfye, and content, or cause to be payd, satisfyed, and contented, unto the sayd John Louthe my sonne for and towardes his mayntenaunce and bringinge up in good learninge ten poundes of good and lawfull Englishe money at the feastes of the Agnunciacion of Marie and St. Michaell th'archangell by equall porc'ons : and allso so that duringe her sayd widowheade and the sayd minoritie she doe mayntayne and uphold the sayd mansione house with all other the buyldinges thereunto appertayninge in good and sufficient reparacions : and yf it fortune that Marye my sayd wyffe doe marrye duringe the minoritie of my sayd sonne, then my last will and mynde is that from and after the daye of her sayd marriage she shall have nothinge to doe with my sayd house and landes, neyther that she shall occupie, possesse, or enjoye anie parte or parcell therof, but that forthwith she shall leave and departe from the same : and from and after the daye of her sayd marriage, by this my last will and testament I doe ordayne and appoynte that my brother in lawe mr. Francis Babington shall duringe the minoritie of my sayd sonne peaceably and quyetly occupye and enjoye my sayd mansion house and landes in suche maner and sorte and not otherwayes as my sayd wyffe shold have donne yf she had kepte her self widowe. And for want of heyres of the bodie of the sayd John Louthe my sonne lawfully by him to be begotten I doe give the same house and landes with all and singuler the commodities and appurtnances appertayninge unto yt as aforesayd to the heyres males of my daughter Thomazine Babington lawfully begotten of her bodie for ever. And for wante of suche

I doe give the same house and landes with all and singuler the commodities and appurtnances appertayninge unto yt as aforesayd to the heyres males of Humfrey Louthe of Sutton in Ashfield in the countie of Nott. gent. lawfully begotten of his bodie for ever. And for wante of suche heyres males of his bodie lawfully begotten I doe give the same house, landes, and commodities with th'appurtnances as aforesayd to the heyres males of William Louthe of Maldon in Essex gent. lawfully begotten of his bodie for ever. And for wante of suche heyres males of his bodie lawfully begotten I doe give the same house and landes and commodities pertayninge to yt as aforesayd to the heyres males of Robert Louthe of the queenes ma^{ties} courte lawfully begotten for ever. And for wante of suche heyres males of the same Robert Louthe to the heyres males of the bodie of Peter Louthe late of Nottingham lawfully begotten for ever. And for wante of suche heyres males of the bodie of the sayd Peter Louthe to remayne to the crowne of England for ever.

The residewe of all my worldly goodes not herin given nor bequeathed I doe give and bequethe the same wholly and fully to Marye Louthe my sayd wyffe and to John Louthe my sayd sonne equally to be devyded betwyxt them imediatly after that my funerals are fully discharged, my debtes clearly payd, and legacies sett outt: after whiche devision equally made my last will and mynde is that all that whole part and porcion which shall fall out to be due and belonginge unto my sayd sonne John Louthe shalbe delyvered into the bandes of my sayd brother in lawe Frances Babington by him to be used and letten forthe for the benefyte, commoditie, and good mayntenaunce in learninge of my sayd sonne, so that the sayd Frances Babington doe with one or two sufficient suerties enter into sufficient bonde unto Marie my sayd wyffe to repaye all that sayd parte and porcion unto the sayd John Louthe my sonne at his full age of xxi^{tie} yeares or when otherwyse he shall lawfully demaunde the same: and in the meane tyme duringe his sayd minoritie, to paye unto my sayd sonne yearly for and towardes his sayd mayntenaunce in good learninge all the increase and proffitt that shall redounde by his sayd parte and porcion. And for the bodie of my sayd sonne duringe his minoritie I make Mary my wyffe and Frances Babington my sayd brother in lawe tutors and gardians.

(jur.)

And of this my last will and testament I make Marye my sayd wyffe my full and sole executrix, revokinge herby all former wills and testamentes. And I doe ordayne and make the supervysors herof my good brothers in Chryst the archdeacons of Nottingham my successors for the tyme beinge, the right worshipfull mr. Henry Perpoynte esquyar, Lancelot Rolston gent., mr. Richard Symney, mr. John Parker, mr. Frances Babington my welbeloved brother, and mr. Humfrey Louthe my cosine. And my mynde and will is that my executrix doe bestowe xx s. in gloves and bestowe them uppon my supervisors, viz., to everye one accordinge to his callinge and degree, to see to the full-fillinge of my will, and the educac'on of my sonne in true religion in the universities and the innes of the courte, untill he come to the age of xxiiii^{ue} yeares as I have sett downe in my whyte written booke.

And as for my bodye I commaunde my executrix and will my supervysors to see yt buryed in the north side in the quyer in St. Maries in Nottingham without anie pompe or solemnitie, savinge only a sermon to be made to teache the people to dye well: and a small monument of brasse to be made with my name, to be nayled uppon a stonne in the wall. I leave it to the discrec'on and devoc'on of my executrix what sermons shalbe made by my scollars and frendes, and what money shalbe delt to the poore.

In witnesse wherof unto this my last will and testament I the sayd John Louthe have subscrybed my hande the day, moneth, and yeare first above written.

Further I the sayd John Louthe the testator, concerninge the bestowinge of John Louthe my sonne in marriage, I referre it to mr. Henry Perpoynte esquyer, Frances Babington clarke my brother, and Launcelot Rolston gent., or to two of them. In witnesse whereof hereunto I have putt my hande and seall the daye and yeare above sayd.   JOHN LOUTHE, Archd. Nott.

  These being witnesses,
       (jur.)   (jur.)   (jur.)
  FRANCES BABINGTON, RICHARD SYMNEY, WILLIAM BARKER.

And further my will is, and by this my last will and testament I doe ordayne and appoynte, that yf yt shall please God to take awaye the lyffe of my sayd sonne John Louthe duringe his minoritie, that then Mary my sayd wyffe shall duringe her naturall lyffe hold, occupie, possesse, and enjoye (notwithstandinge her marriage yf hereafter she shall marrye) all that my house and landes aforesayd with all and singuler the appurtnances whatsoever as aforesayd to her the sayd Marye and her assygnes, yeldinge and payinge therefore yearly duringe her sayd lyffe unto William Babington sonne of Zachary Babington of Litchfeld aforesayd fyve poundes of good and lawfull Englishe money at the feastes of the Agnunciacion of Marye and St. Michaell th'archangell by equall porcions. In witnesse wherof hereunto allso I have subscrybed my name the daye and yeare aforesayd.

                                     JOHN LOUTHE, Arch. Nott.

  Witnesses herof,
       (jur.)   (jur.)   (jur.)
  FRANCES BABINGTON, RICHARD SYMNEY, WILLIAM BARKER.

14   NARRATIVES OF THE REFORMATION.

The death of the archdeacon shortly after the making of his will is shown by its being proved at York on the 12th September following its date.

What became of his son John has not been ascertained. His son-in-law Zachary Babington, M.A., was chancellor of the diocese of Lichfield in 1581, was made prebendary of Curford in that church Feb. 19, 1583-4, and installed precentor July 10, 1589. He afterwards proceeded doctor of laws at Oxford in 1599.[a]

The ensuing anecdotes, which exist in Louthe's own handwriting among the papers of Foxe the martyrologist, directed on their back "To Mr. John Foxe, p'chere, at mr. Jo. Dayes, printere," are dated in the year 1579. Very small portions of them were published by Foxe,[b] but various others were worked up by Strype in different places of his Memorials and Annals, and Life of Cranmer. They were disregarded[c] by the editors of the last edition of the Actes and Monuments.

The writer wished his name to be kept secret, and it was evidently on that account that he somewhat disguised it by writing *Loude* instead of Louthe, for in the MS. he continually wrote *Louthe* habitually, and altered it to *Loude*. Foxe effectually, though apparently by accident, fulfilled that object by printing the name *Lond*. In the Catalogue of the Harleian Manuscripts it is perverted into *Lodon*.

---

[a] Wood's Fasti Oxon. His successor as precentor was appointed in 1608, and his successor as chancellor in 1613. The epitaph of his grandson Zachary Babington esquire, at Whittington near Lichfield, is printed in Shaw's Staffordshire, i. 378.

[b] See pp. 19, 20.

[c] Except in the following brief notice, wherein the writer's name is mistaken, and a Lansdowne MS. is quoted instead of the original in the Harleian collection: "A little before this he received one from Mr. John Lond, containing several new materials for his Martyrology, and insisting more especially on the miserable end of divers Romish priests, as of Dr. Wyllyams, the priest of St. Margaret's Eastchepe, &c. Lansdowne MS. 982, fol. 103." Life of John Foxe, by the Rev. George Townsend, M.A. p. 208.

John Loude to John Foxe.

[MS. Harl. 425, f. 134.]

Salutem in Christo Jhesu.

The love that I beare to the churche of Chryste constraynythe me to gyve yow thankes for the happy and dayly paynes yow take in settynge forthe the worthy actes of those late martyres of Chryste in Englande. That worke servythe to the glory of Chryste, the comforte of his members lyvyng, and godly memory of them which are departed; to the overthrow of Antichryste and eternall shame of all antichrysteanes; and I doghte not but that booke wyll brynge to repentance the rable of the reste bloody butcheres yet lyvynge, so many at lest as are not gyvyne up into a reprochfull mynde, who have shutt up theyre eyes that thei may not see, &c. Of these sorte are they that cry dayly, " Lyes, lyes! more lies founde in the booke of Actes and Monumentes of Martyres!" Wherwith yow owght not to be discowraged (as I truste yow are not), but rather encowraged to go forwarde in the same. *Tu solus hanc Spartam nactus es, hanc adorna.* Rejoyce that yow are lyke to them same martyres that so were rayled apon, yea lyke to Jeremy, crying: *Cur fecisti me virum rixæ? hominem objurgiorum!* When ye reade of these Romyshe raylynges, ye may have greate joye and cawse to thanke God that in this poynte ye are resembled to his owne sonne the lorde Jhesus Chryste. The dyvyles cryed against hym; but they most rored when thei sawe thei muste come forth of the man, and lose theyre kyngdome and power. Therfore wryght styll, cease not, seyng the booke dothe so muche good in Chrystes churche, yt wyll doe more good after your dethe then lyff. The memory of mr. John Philpott,[a] ons my compaygnion in Wynthone,[b] Oxforde, and London, wyll never dye. The same may be sayd of the other sanctes and martyres, and *god a mercy*[c] to yow, and your booke. God wyll not forgett your labores and paynes, that hathe cawsed his sainetes, his servantes, and

---

[a] Archdeacon of Winchester: of whom Loude gives some anecdotes hereafter.

his enymies to be in perpetuall memory. Yt ys he that gyvyth yow the wytt, the lernyng, the wyll, the philopony, and infrangyble diligens. Els your helthe wolde be a lett, these peynes wold weary yow, these tawntes wold dismay yow, wych dayly come forthe of those lyyng lypps that crye, " Lyes, lyes ; so many lynes so many lies!" Yet they perceave not that are of that religyone, how that the father of lies and murder hathe devysed by ther helpe to deface the heavenly doctryne of our Savioure Jhesus Chryste, by whome comythe all trewth and grace, beynge hymselfe the lyght to lyghten the gentyles, and to be the glory of hys people Israel. You are weak and to weake of yourself to doo this noble acte; but he hathe enabled yow therto, that sayd to Pawle, *Virtus mea in infirmitate perficitur.*

Admitte that a Lovanyone luske,[a] lyinge longe in wayght with so many felows, hath fownd in yowr great volume some smalle unthroths (untruths), muste he therfor cry owt lyke a dyvylle agaynst the whole booke, for a letter, a syllable, a man's name, a towne, or suche tryfle ? *In multis peccavimus omnes.* The poettes can suffer theyr good Homere sometyme to slomber and sleepe, and the papistes theyr

[a] "A *luske*, lowt, lurden, a lubberly sloven," &c. Cotgrave. See also Nares and Halliwell. The "Lovanyone luske" intended by Louthe was probably Alanus Copus, who was a real person (see Wood's Athenæ Oxonienses, edit. Bliss, i. 455,) but under whose name the more celebrated Nicholas Harpsfield (archdeacon of Canterbury, and bishop elect of Winchester,) published his Dialogi sex contra Summi Pontificatus, Monasticæ Vitæ, Sanctorum, sacrarum Imaginum Oppugnatores et Pseudo-Martyres. Antverpiæ, 1566. The sixth dialogue was especially directed against Foxe's work, and Foxe himself answered it at considerable length in the matter of sir John Oldcastle lord Cobham. To the charge of having uttered " lies " he thus earnestly replied : "This *Alanus Copus Anglus* contendeth and chafeth against my former edition, to prove me in my historie to be a lyer, forger, impudent, a misreporter of truth, a depraver of stories, a seducer of the world, and what els not ? whose virulent woordes and contumelious termes, how well they become his popish person, I knowe not. Certes, for my part, I never deserved this at his hands wittingly, that I do know. Maister Cope is a man whom yet I never saw, and lesse offended, nor ever heard of hym before. * * * * * And therefore seriously to say unto you (M. Cope) in this matter, where you charge my History of Actes and Monuments so cruelly, to be full of untruthes, false lies, impudent forgeries, depravations, fraudulent corruptions, and feyned fables ; briefly and in one word to answere you, not as the Lacones answered to the letters of their

erthly God the Pope; they can full smothly solve in horryble sores of lyffe, doctrine, relygione, and conscience. An historiographer ys excusable, not when he maketh a lye, but when he of an other's informatione setteth down an untrothe. Then wee and the papistes must neades alow the commun rule: *Sit fides penes aucthorem: imo sit culpa penes eundum.* In some thynges that yow wryght, I can shew that yow have not putt in wrytyng very muche that wolde dawnte the adversares, honor God, comforte his churche, and sett owt the mighty power of God. As here folowing I wyll doo yow understand.

Now to yow pestilent papistes: I myght more justely falle owt with my brother John Foxe then yow, I (aye), for that [he] hathe not wrytten these thynges so necessary as ys declared. But he hathe one answere for us bothe: " The fawlte was not in me, but in the informatione gyven, or not gyven; truly gyven, or not truly gyven." But this I say, yf mr. Foxe wer as swhyfte a scrybe as Esras, yet he shoulde not be able to wryght all your abhominable lyffes and doctrines, yowr cruell tormentyng and manaclyng of Chrystes saynctes in this lyff, and (lyke divyles) ye labore so muche as any fynde of hell can do to bereave them, by yowr doctrine, of lyff everlastyng. Then what lye can he or any man wryght of yow, but yt shalbe fownde trew, ether in your detestable crueltee, fylthy sodomy, or divyllyshe doctrine: he as muche offendythe that thus termythe yow, as he that should call yowr father the divill knave, by whose suggesyons yow fullfylle the measure of your fathers in all manner of crueltee and butchery of godly men. Theyr blood with Abel's cry owt for vengans agaynst yow. Yowr forfathers could not murder all God's chyldren, for some escaped theyr handes, and some were not

adversarie, with *si*, but with *ò si*, Would God (M. Cope) that in all the whole booke of Actes and Monuments, from the beginning to the latter end of the same, were never a true storie, but that all were false, all were lies, and all were fables! Would God the crueltie of your catholikes had suffred all them to live of whose death ye say now that I do lie. Although I deny not but that in that booke of Actes and Monuments, containing such diversitie of matter, some thing might overscape me, yet have I bestowed my poore then borne as yet to fulfyll the number of their bretheren by martyrdome; but those that to yow were left by them, how butcherly have yow slayne! Ye are the chyldren of your murdryng fathers, havyng the same hate that they to Gode [and] godlynes, the same tyranny, all laws caste behynde yow, the same doctrine, the same syar the devyll, and therfor the same murderyng hartes as perteynyth to suche a race, to make havoke (O cruell wolves!) of Chrystes flocke. God forgive yow; God open yowr eyes; God, thorow repentance, make yow meeke Pawles, wych have ben so ragyng Sawles, thretnyng blasphemously wrath and slawghter to innocent lambes of Chrystes flocke!

Now, mr. Foxe, thoghe your booke ys paste the prynte, yet I wyll sett downe truly here (God ys wytnes) what I have creably herd of some of the martyres more then yowr booke reportyth, in the wych I beleeve I shall nether make lye, nor tell lye. The aucthores therof ar so lawfull, I myght saye authentycke. Of whom I may say with the poett: *Quorum pars magna fuere.* I know not whyther ye may be occasyoned to use any of these additionall historyes wych I have sent yow, as a taste of many more I have wrytten, *a Martyrio Jo. Frythi.* I pray yow encreace yowr booke, for I hope it wyll be adbrydged,[a] and also enlarged, when yow shalbe gon to Chryste.

Nam tuns hic genium fertur habere liber.

Oportet imperatorem stantem et militem Christi pugnantem mori. Cogita quæ dico, inquit S^{tus} Paulus.

The examynatyone of a blynde boy called the blynde boy of Gloucester[b] afore doctor Wylliams the judge. And of the myserable ende of the same judge.

Thys boy called blynde Tome was browght afore the sayd doctor

---

[a] This anticipation, which has since been so repeatedly fulfilled, was accomplished shortly after Louthe wrote. The first Abridgement of Foxe's work, by Timothe Bright doctor of phisicke, was printed at London, 1589, in 4to.

[b] This blind boy had already figured in Foxe's narrative of the last days of bishop Hooper. When the bishop was brought to Gloucester on the 8th of February, 1555-6, the day

Wyllyams the chawncelor,[a] and John Barkere alias Taylore the register,[b] in the consistory by the south dore in the nether ende of the churche. The offycers in whose custody the boy remeyned, by commandment of the chawncelor, presented the poore boy at the barre before the judge. Then doctor Wyllyams examined hym apon sondry articles magistrall and usuall emonge the tormentors at that tyme, as ye may fynd folio (*blank*) in mr. Foxe.[c] And namely he urged the article of Transubstantiatyone.

Wyllyams. Doest yow not beleeve that after the wordes of consecratione of the preeste that ther remaynyth the veery body of Chryste? *Tome.* No, that I doo not. *Wyllyams.* Then yow arte an heretyke, and shalte be burnte. Who tawght thee thys heresy? *Tome.* Yow, mr. Chawncelor. *W.* Where, I pray thee? *Tome.* When in yonder place (poynting with his hande and lokyng[d] as it were towerde the pulpytt, standynge apon the north syde of the

---

before his suffering at the stake: "The same day, in the after noone, a blinde boy, after long intercession made to the guard, obtained licence to be brought unto master Hooper's speech. The same boy not long afore had suffered imprisonment at Gloucester for confessing the truth. Master Hooper, after he had examined him of his faith, and the cause of his imprisonment, beheld him stedfastly, and (the water appearing in his eyes) said unto him: Ah, poore boy! God hath taken from thee thine outward sight, for what consideration he best knoweth: but he hath given thee another sight much more precious, for he hath indued thy soule with the eye of knowledge and faith. God give thee grace continually to pray unto him that thou lose not that sight, for then shouldest thou be blind both in body and soule." (Folio edition 1641, iii. 153). Subsequently, at p. 702 of the same volume, we read that the blind boy's name was Thomas Drowrie, and that he was finally burned at Gloucester, about the fifth of May 1556, together with Thomas Croker a bricklayer. Foxe has on that occasion introduced the conversation given in the text, "Ex testimo. Io. Lond." as our author's name is there misprinted.

[a] See p. 20.

[b] "John Tayler, alias Barker, occurs soon after the foundation of the bishopric, and August the 31st, 1569." (Rudder, Hist. of Gloucestershire, p. 170.) In 1552, the sum of forty marks was settled to be paid yearly to John Tayler, alias Baker, (*sic*) gent. for keeping the register of the bishop of Gloucester. Strype's Memorials, ii. 357.

[c] — "such usuall articles as are accustomed in such cases, and are sundry times mentioned in this book." Foxe, *ubi supra*.

[d] Above the word "loking" is written "turning," and so Foxe has printed.

churche). *W.* When dyd I so teache thee? *Tome.* When yow preched there (namyng the day) a sermone to all men as well as to me, apon the sacrament. Yow sayd the sacrament was to be receaved spiritually by fayth, and not carnally and really as the papistes have hertofore tawght. *W.* Then do as I have done, and yow shalt lyve as I do, and escape burnynge. *Tome.* Thoghe yow can so easly dyspense with yowr selfe, and mocke with God, the world, and yowr conscyence, I wyll not so doo. *Wyllyams.* Then God have mercy apon thee, for I wyll reade thy condemnatory sentense. *Tome.* Godes wyll be fulfylled!

Here the register stoode up and sayd to the chawncelor, Fye for shame, man! Wyll ye reade the sentense, and condemne yowr selfe? Away, away! and substitute another to gyve sentense and judgement. *Wyllyams.* Mr. registere, I wyll obbey the lawe, and gyve sentense me selfe acordynge to myn offyce. And so he redd the sentense with an unhappy tonnge, and more unhappy conscience.

Ex testimonio John Taylore alias Barker, Registrarij Glouc',
olim ex cenobio Oxon. quod vocatur Omnium Sanctorum.

The strawnge and hasty [a] dethe of the same doctor Wyllyams.[b]

When God, of hys inestimable mercy havyng pytye of us, and pardonyng owr synnes for hys sonnes sake Chryste Jhesus, hadd now taken from us that blooddy prynces and sent us thys jewell of joye the quenes majestie that now raygnyth (and long myght she

[a] The word "hasty" is altered into "fearful" by Foxe, who (edition 1641, iii. 962) appended this anecdote to his series recounting "God's punishment upon persecutors, and contemners of the Gospel." He does not there give the authority of John Loude, nor of Loude's informant the dean of Gloucester.

[b] John Williams, LL.D. He had been first appointed chancellor of Gloucester jointly with Richard Brown, LL.B. 28 Nov. 1541. "This Williams, in king Henry's reign, appears very zealous in the execution of the six articles. In the next reign he was a sudden convert to protestantism, and he began queen Mary's with depriving several clergymen of their livings for marriage. In 1555 he condemned Henry Hicks, a carpenter or joiner in this city, to carry a faggot in Berkeley church and in this cathedral. He was some time

raygne!) over us, and that the commissyoners for restitutione of religione were commyng towarde Gloucester, and the same day doctor Wyllyams the chawncelor dyned with W. Jenynges[a] the deane of Gloucester, who with all his men were booted and ready at one of the clocke to set forwarde towerd Chyppyng Norton, abowte xv. myles from Gloucester, to meete the commissyoners, wych wer at Chyppyng Norton, and sayd to hym, Chawncelor, are not thy boots on? *Chawnc.* Whye should I putt them one? To go with me (quoth the Deane) to meete these commyssioners.[b] *Chawnc.* I wyll nether meete them nor see them. *Deane.* Thow muste needes see them, for now it ys paste twelfe, and they wylbe here afore three of the clocke, and therfor, yf thow be wyse, onne with thy bootes and lett us go togyther, and all shalbe well. *Chawnc.* Go yowr wayes, mr. deane; I wyll never see them.

As I seyd, W. Jenynges the deane satt forwarde with hys company towarde the commissyoners; and by and by commyth one upon

incumbent of the Holy Trinity in Gloucester, of Rockhampton, Beverstone, Painswick, Siddingtou St. Mary, Coln St. Dennis, and Walford, and a prebendary of Gloucester." After dr. Williams's death, his office was performed by the vicar-general of the province of Canterbury, during the vacancy of the see, after which John Louth, the writer of these pages, succeeded to it. Rudder, History of Gloucestershire, p. 163.

[a] William Jennings, B.D. chaplain to the king, became in 1541 the first dean of Gloucester, having been previously a monk of St. Peter's and prior of St. Oswald's in that city. He must have been a person very accommodating to the changes of the times, as he held the deanery until his death in 1565, when his body was buried before the door of the choir. See his other preferments and epitaph in Willis's Cathedrals, ii. 729, and Rudder's History of Gloucestershire, p. 161. Bishop Hooper's dedication of his Annotations on the Thirteenth Chapter to the Romans, commences "To my very loving and dear-beloved fellow-labourers in the word of God, and brethren in Christ, William Jenins dean of the cathedral church in Gloucester, John Williams doctor of the law and chancellor, and to the rest of all the church appointed there," &c. Hooper's Works, printed for the Parker Society, ii. 95.

[b] This commission for visiting the dioceses of Salisbury, Bristol, Exeter, Bath and Wells, and Gloucester, was dated July 19, 1559, and addressed to William earl of Pembroke, John Jewel, S.Th.P., Henry Parry, licentiate in laws, and William Lovelace, lawyer. Strype's Annals, i. 167. Sir John Cheyne was apparently substituted for the earl of Pembroke, as shown by one of their reports: see the life of Jewel prefixed to his Works printed for the Parker Society, pp. xiv. xv.

horsebacke to the deane, saying, "Mr. chawncelor lyethe at the mercy of God, and ys speechlesse." At that worde the deane with his company prycked forwarde to the commissyoners and told them the whole matter and communicacion betwene them two as above; and they sente one of theyr men, with the beste woordes they cowlde devise, to comforte hym, with many promises. But to be shorte, albeyt the commissyoners were nowe nearer Gloucester then the deane and his company thoght, makyng veary greate haste, especyally after they hadd receaved these newes, yett dr. Wyllyams, thoghe false of religione, yet trew of his promyse, kepte his ungracions covenante with the deane, for he was dedd er they came to the cyty, and so never sawe them in dede.

Hoc mihi narravit dictus decanus Glouc. cum ego Jo:
Loude apud eum una cum multis aliis ceneremus.

Hys woman or howsekeper (for suche wold bee with owt wyves, but not with owt women) told hur fryndes many tymes, that hur master kylled hym selfe with eatyng of rew. *Jo.* Λουδε. A lerned man may hereby gathere that the doctore havyng an evyll conscience, and no good opinione of the commissyoners' curtesy, poysoned hymself, *more Romano*, but, as it semeth by conjecture, receavyng suche a chearefull message by poste from the commissyoners, wold have recovered hym selfe by medicyne, to late taken; for nuttes, rew, and fygges, ys a good antidotary preservative agaynst poysone, being taken in tyme. Otherwyse, acordyng to the verse,

——————— sero medicina paratur
Cum mala per longas invaluere moras.

The Commissyoners were these: mr. Jewell,[a] mr. Alley,[b] mr. Parray,[c] mr. Lovelase,[d] mr. Dalabare,[e] &c.

[a] John Jewel, afterwards bishop of Salisbury 1559.
[b] William Alley, bishop of Exeter 1560.
[c] Henry Parry, afterwards an exile at Frankfort. Zurich Letters, iii. 763.
[d] William Lovelace, serjeant at law 1567. In 1572 he was recommended by Lord Burghley to be steward of archbishop Parker's liberties. Correspondence of Parker, Works, (Parker Society,) p. 405. See also the Index to Strype's Works.
[e] Anthony Dalaber, of St. Alban's hall, Oxford, brother to the parson of Stalbridge in

The tragicall lyff and ende of a ryght Catholyke preeste at London.

Ther ys a lytle paryshe (I thynke called St. Margaret^a) in the ende of Estcheape, in the wych served a curate of as good religione as lyvyng, for bothe were sterke nowght, as any man by that wych folowyth may judge, *si homo ex fructibus*. To be shorte, and as clenly as I can devise in suche bawdy men's matters. A commandement was gyven that all curattes (what so ever) should not be at sermones nor servyce longer than ix. of the clocke, that then the curattes with the paryshes myght come to Poles crosse and heare the prechers. To this sayd this good curatt, " I wyll (quod he) make an ende of service at the proscribed hower gladly, seing I muste needes so doo. But so longe as any of these heretykes preche at the Crosse as nowe adayes thei do, I wyll never here them, for I wyll not come there. I will rather hange." He was not so well occupied, as ye may conjecture, by the proces of the matter. This curatte tooke an howse-ende or a chamber in the paryshe wheare he served. Yt chawnced the rente to be behynde. The rentegatherer was angry, and axed wheare he was. " Belyke (sayd the neyghbores) he ys gonne by Erythe bote into Kente, to some good wyves labore, as he usythe every munday or sonday at night to doo." The rent-gatherer takyng these wordes for a jeste, sayd in a great fume, " Telle hym, and understand yow also his neyghbores, that yf the rente be not payd me at suche a tyme, &c. I wyll breake apon the chamber dore and distrayne." The day and tyme came, and the rente-gatherer was there with a smyth and brake apon the dore. At

Dorsetshire. He was the author of a long and very remarkable narrative respecting the persecutions of those who entertained the new doctrines in Oxford, inserted by Foxe in his Actes and Monuments (commencing at vol. v. p. 421 of Townsend and Cattley's edition), respecting which see Dr. S. R. Maitland's Essays on subjects connected with the Reformation in England, 1849. 8vo. pp. 13 et seq., and the Rev. J. A. Fronde's History of England, 1856, ii. pp. 45 et seq.

^a Possibly St. Martin Orgar: for there seems to have been no church there dedicated to St. Margaret.

the entryng thei fownd an horryble stynche; when the people drew neare they saw a woman, all moste kneelyng in a cheare, hanged in a roope; but approchyng neare, thei perceaved that it was a man smothely shaven and pared to the harde lether, maggottes crawlyng owt of his mouthe, eyes, and eares. The paryshners sayd it was there curatte. The crowner's queste came to fynde the cawse of his dethe. The jury wold not abyde the stynche, but hadd rather lese theyre fynes and amercyments then theyre lives. So the crowner was enforced to brynge a wrytt called a *decem tales de circumstantibus*, and by virtew of that wrytt toke among other one mr. W. Warren to be of the jewry, whose syster ys yet alyve, maryed to mr. Burton chawndeler in Estchepe. She and other awncyent men of the paryshe can declare his name and all other particuler circumstaunces, and avarre it trewe to theyre faces that shall denye it. I wyll sturre no longer in theyr downge that ar of the pope's wyveles clergye, lest they cry owt "Lyes! lyes!" agaynst me, as they lately dyd against mr. Foxe for tellyng the truthe. Only this I crave on them, that thei wold skanne with this history the saying of Willielmus Westmonasteriensis, and specially Polydore Virgil *De Invent. Rerum*, lib. 5, c. 4, concernyng the chastitie of theis cleane-fyngred gentlemen of the pope's clergy. Thys mr. W. Warren one of thys jury sayd that he [the curate] customably wente in Kente apon sonday at nyght, *et nocte profitebatur artem obstetricandi inter homines non sui sexus.* [a]

[a] That a man should practise the art of midwifery appears to have been, in the eyes of John Louthe, a crime of heinous magnitude, perhaps scarcely increased by the circumstance of his being a priest. The late Dr. Samuel Merriman, who was as conversant with the literature as with the practice of his profession, in a letter signed Obstetricus in the Gentleman's Magazine for Jan. 1830, has traced the history of the terms Midwife, Man-Midwife, Accoucheur, &c. showing the several objections that have been made to the second, and various substitutes that have been proposed. He says that "the earliest date at which I have found the word Man-midwife is 1637, when it was employed in the preface of 'The Expert Midwife.'" Midwife he regards as a contraction of *modir-wife*, the old English word *modir* having been used both for the mother and the womb. It may be presumed that midwifery was little if at all practised by men in England before the year 1637. The first book published in English on the subject was "The Byrth of Mankynde; newlye

Thes histores ar to be preserved in memory of man, to the conversione of many yet lyvynge and lykyng Egipte and Babilone ; as the arses of the Philystines wer made of sylver by Godes commande,[a] and reserved to the perpetuall shame of that idolatrous natyone.

Ex testimonio W. Warren unius juratorum dictorum.

Of an aunciente protestante called mr. John Petite.

This John Petite was one of the fyrste that with mr. Fryth, Bylney, and Tyndall cowght a swheetnes in Godes worde. He was xxt[i] yeares burgesse for the cyty of London, and free of the Grocers, eloquente and welspoken, exactly sene in hystores, songe, and the Laten tongue.[b] King Henry 8. wolde axe in the parlamente tyme, in hys waighty affayres, yf Petite wer of his syde; for ons, when the kyng required to have all those somes of mony to be gyven hym by acte of parlamente whych afore he hadd borowed of certeyn persons, John Petite stode agaynste the byll, sayinge " I can not in my conscience agree and consent that this bylle should passe, for I know not my neighbores estate. They perhaps borowed it to lend the

translated oute of Laten into Englysshe, 1540," 4to. This was originally written by a German, Röslin, or, as he classically styled himself, Eucharius Rhodion. The first edition, which contains some of the earliest copper-plate engravings published in England, is dedicated to queue Katheryne by her physician dr. Richard Jonas: the subsequent editions, of which there are many, bear the name of the translator, dr. Thomas Raynold. See an account of this work, by T. J. Pettigrew, esq. F.R.S. and F.S.A. in the Medical Portrait Gallery, vol. i. (memoir of Sir C. M. Clarke, Bart.) The original MS. copy presen ed to queen Katharine is in the possession of Mr. Pettigrew, and was exhibited by him to the Society of Antiquaries.

[a] This alludes to chapter vi. of the first book of Samuel, where the offerings in question are in our translation termed " golden emerods." Such offerings representing all kinds of diseases and deformities are still customary in India, and are usually made of silver. See an interesting note on the subject in Knight's Pictorial Bible.

[b] Notwithstanding the high character given by Louthe to John Petit, and his important position for twenty years, as one of the four citizens representing London in Parliament, I have failed to find any other memorial of him. The city historians are silent regarding him, and so is Mr. Heath in his History of the Grocers' Company, and even his name as a member of parliament does not appear on the lists, from their being imperfect in the reign

kyng. But I know myn owne estate, and therefor I freely and frankly gyve the kyng that I lente hym." This burges was sore suspected of the lord chawncelor and the prelacy of this realme, that he was a fawtore of the relegione that they called newe, and also a bearer with them in pryntyng of theyr bookes. Therfore mr. More [a] commyth apon a certeyne tyme to hys howse at Liones kay,[b] then called Petites kay, and knokkyng at the doore, mrs. Petite came towerd the dore and seinge that it was the lord chawncelor she whypped in haste to hur husbonde, beinge in his closett at his prayers, saing, " Come, come, husbonde, my lorde chawncelor ys at the dore, and wold speake with yow." At the same worde the lorde chawncelor was in the closett at hur backe. To whom mr. Petite spake with greate curtesy, thankyng hym that it wold please his lordship to visitt hym in his owne poore howse; but, becawse he wold not drynke, he attended apon hym to the dore, and, ready to take hys leave, axed hym yf his lordship wold command hym any service " No (quod the chawncelor), ye say ye have none of these newe bookes?" " Your lordship sawe (sayd he) my bookes and my closett " " Yet (quod the chawncelor), ye muste go with mr. lieutenante. Take hym to yow," quod the chawncelor to the lyeutenante. Then he was layd in a doungeone apon a padd of strawe, in close prison; his wyffe might not come unto hym nor brynge hym any bedd. After longe sute and dayly teares of his wyff Lucy Petite, she obteyned license to send hym in a bedd, and that he myght be broght to his aunswere, wheare they hadd gotten a lytle old preest, that should say he hadd Tyndale's testamente in Englyshe, and dyd helpe hym and suche other to publyshe theyre heretycall bookes in Englyshe, as thei termed them. But

[a] The illustrious sir Thomas More, who, notwithstanding his great intelligence and love of learning, was not only immoveably attached to the ancient faith, but very zealous as a persecutor of those who entertained the new doctrines. See Mr. Froude's remarks on his illegal practice of detaining untried " hereticks " in prison, History of England, 1856, ii. 75.

[b] " Next to (Billingsgate) is Sommer's key, which likewise tooke that name of one Sommer dwelling there, as did Lion key of one Lion owner thereof, and since of the signe of the Lion." Stowe's Survay.

now at laste when mr. Petite hadd caght hys dethe by so nawghty harbor of the lord chawncelor, he was called openly, and the preeste that should have accused hym, axed mr. Petite forgyvenes, saying, " Mr. Petite, I never saw yow afore this tyme; how should I then be able to accuse you?" And so he was suffered to go whome, but he dyed immediatly aftere apone the same yll harborowe. He thoght his payne came over his cheste lyke a barre of yron.

Here is to be remembred a strange thynge or two. When John Frythe[a] was in the Tower, he came to Petites kay in the nyght, notwithstanding the straight watche and warde, by commandment, &c. At whose fyrst commyng mr. Petite was in dowght whether it was mr. Frythe or a visione: no lesse dowghting, nor otherwyse, then the Apostles, when Rode the mayde broght tydynges that Peter was gott owt of prison.[b] But mr. Frythe shewed hym that yt was God that wroght hym that liberty in the harte of his keper one Philippes, who, apon the cautyone of his owne worde and promyse, lett hym go at liberty in the nyght to consulte with godly men. The same underkeper suffred mr. Petite, being imprisoned under mr. Bylney,[c] by removyng a borde, to dyne and suppe to gyther, and to cheere one and othere in the Lorde, with suche symple fare as papistes' charitee wold alowe them. The trothe ys, when [the] lorde chawncelor came to serche his closett, ther laye undernethe mr. Petite's deske a new testamente in Englyshe and an other in Laten above, yet the chawncelor saw it not, by what meanes God knoweth, and I leave it to every godly man's judgemente.

Thys mr. Petite wold neades be buryed in the churche yarde, and the preested [d] preestes powred sope ashes upon hys grave, affirmyng

---

[a] John Frith, having denied the real presence, was burned in Smithfield, July 4, 1533. See Index to the Parker Society's works, p. 335. His " Disputacion of Purgatory " is noticed hereafter.

[b] Acts, xii 31.

[c] Thomas Bilney, who suffered in Smithfield, March 10, 1531. See Froude's History of England, 1856, ii. 84. To him Latimer owed his conversion.

[d] Sic in MS.

that God wold not suffer grasse to grow upon suche an heretyckes grave, and many of the Balaamytes came to see and testyfie the same.

In fyne, mr. Petite, albe yt he had great ryches by his fyrste wyff (being his mistress and a widow) and specyally by his seconde wyff Lucy Wattes, dawghter and heyre unto the kyng's grocer mr. Wattes, yet he dyed not ryche; for ij cawses, the one for that the lord chawncelor made hym pay the debte of one for whose aparance mr. Petite stoode bownd in lawe. The party was sycke of a tympany, therfor mr. Petite was enforced to bryng hym in a carte to London an hundryth myles by estimacion, wherof he dyed; but the chawncelor, of a popyshe charyte, wold neades lett the pryncypall go, and take it apon the suertee, J. P.

An other cawse was thys: mr. Petite gave muche to the poore, and specyally to poore prechers, suche as then wer on this syde the say and beyonde the say; and in his debte booke these desperatte debtes he entred thus,—"*lente unto Chryste;*" and so commanded his exequutors to demande non of those debtes. Hys wyll therfor amounted not above the valew of viij^{xx} for his ij dawghters unmaryed, Audrey and Blanche Petite, over and besydes those desperatt debtes and his land in Shoredyche and Waltamestowe. One W. Bolles, the laste husbond of Lucy Petite, hathe the land in Shorledych, yet alyve, and receaved vij^{xx} lib. of sir Jeffray Gates,[a] a debtor of Petite's, and so muche goodes besyde as he therwith was able to by the receavorshipp of Chester, Derby, Nottyngham, and Lincoln. Lytle of it came to mr. Petite's chyldren.

Teste ipsius uxore Lucia Petite.

---

[a] Sir Geoffrey Gates was in 1523 a captain of the army sent into France under the duke of Suffolk. (State Papers, vi. 170.) He died in 1526, leaving as his son and heir sir John Gates, afterwards vice-chamberlain and captain of the guard to king Edward VI., who was beheaded with the duke of Northumberland in 1553. (Morants Essex, ii. 146.)

How dangerous a thyng it ys to communicate with papistes in ther service, may appere by this history following.

Mr. Wylliam Forde,[a] some tyme scholer and after ushere of Wykam colleadge besyde Wynchester, beinge at length with muche adoo broght from the popyshe doctrine (*assiduo jurgio et contentione Jo. a Luda*) became at laste a greate enemye to papisme in Oxforde, being there felowe and civilian as mr. John Philpott was in Wykam colleadge; and afterwardes being ushere under mr. John Whight,[b] scholmaster.

Ther was many golden images in Wykam's colleage by Wynton. The churche dore was directly over agaynste the usher's chamber. Mr. Forde tyed a longe coorde to the images, lynkyng them all in one coorde, and, being in his chamber after midnight, he plucked the cordes ende, and at one pulle all the golden godes came downe with *heyho Rombelo*.[c] Yt wakened all men with the rushe. They wer amased at the terryble noyse and also disamayd at the greevous sight. The corde beinge plucked harde and cutt with a twytche, lay at the

[a] "1534. Willielmus Forde, de Brightwell, xiij ann. in festo Mich. præteriti. *In margine*, Hypodidascalus Wynton: Rector de Newberye." Register of Admissions to Winchester College.

[b] John White, head schoolmaster of Winchester college 1534, warden of Winchester 1541, bishop of Lincoln 1554, and of Winchester 1556; deprived 1559; died 1559-60. See Index to the works of the Parker Society, p. 786; also Machyn's Diary, Index; The Chronicle of Queen Jane and Queen Mary, p. 174; and Collectanea Topog. et Geneal. vii. 213. His first entrance at Winchester is thus recorded: "1521. Johannes Whyte de Farnham, xj an. in festo Nat. D'ni præterito—Sutherye. *In margine*, Inform. Wynton. Custos Wynton." (Register of Admissions.) On his examination in bishop Gardiner's cause, in 1551, he took credit for having instilled into his scholars the doctrine of the royal supremacy, declaring "that about twelve years ago, or thereabouts, as he doth remember, this deponent (then being schoolmaster of the college of Winton) did, by commandment of the bishop of Winchester, make certain verses extolling the King's supremacy, and against the usurped power of the Bishop of Rome; which said verses this deponent caused his scholars to learn, and to practise them in making of verses to the like argument; the said bishop encouraging this deponent so to do." (Foxe, first edit. ii. 845.)

[c] The burden of a song. It occurs—*rumbylowe*—so early as 1314, attached to a rhyme made by the Scots on the battle of Bannockburn, which is introduced by Fabyan

church doore. At laste they felle to serchyng, but mr. Forde, moste suspected, was fownde in his bedd; yet he hadd a dogges lyff among them, mr. Whight the scholemaster, the felows of the howse, and the scholers, crying owt and raylyng at hym by supportacyone of their master. Lewde men lay in waight for mr. Forde many tymes, and one nyght going into the towne he muste neades come whome to the collydge by the towne walles, the gattes of Trinitee colleadg be(ing) shutt. This was espyed, he was watched, and when he came to a blynd darke corner by Kynges gate, they layd one hym with staves; he clapped hys gowne coler, furred with foxe furre, rownd abowte his head and necke; they layd on hym some strookes, but by Godes providence the moste parte, in the great derkenes, dyd lyght apon the grownd; so they ranne away, and lefte mr. Forde for dede; but he tumbled and roled hym selfe to the gate, for thei hadd made hym paste goinge; and then he cryed for helpe, and people came to take hym up, and bare hym to his lodgyng.

Now to the purpose. Mr. Forde, in queue Maries dismole days, was in mr. Rychard Whalleis howse at Welbecke;[a] he was commanded to go with his master to sir George Perpountes knyght,[b]

[a] The abbey of Welbeck (now the residence of the duke of Portland) was granted to Richard Whalley in 30 Hen. VIII. Richard Whalley esquire, of Sibthorpe and Screveton in the county of Nottingham, was steward to Edward duke of Somerset, and receiver-general of the county of York. See two letters of his, and other notices of him, in Tytler's "Edward VI. and Queen Mary." He was involved in his master's trouble (see The Literary Remains of King Edward VI. pp. 241, 303, 355, 423), and deprived of his office, but retained much of his wealth, and founded a family long resident in Nottinghamshire. "The Grounds of Artes, by Robert Record, doctor of physicke," first edit. 1549, is dedicated "to the Ryghte Worshypfull mayster Rycharde Whalley Esquyre." He died Nov. 23, 1583, aged 84; and there is an engraving of his monument, with his effigy, in Thoroton's History of that county, p. 130. One of his grandsons, Walter Whalley, S.T.B. was resident at Cherry Orton in Huntingdonshire in 1613, and entered his pedigree in Nich. Charles's visitation book,—printed for the Camden Society, 1849, p. 35.

[b] Sir George Pierrepont, ancestor of the earls Manvers, and the extinct dukes of Kingston, was the son of sir William Pierrepont by his second wife, daughter of sir Richard Empson, chancellor of the exchequer. He purchased, 32 Hen. VIII. some manors that had belonged to the abbeys of Welbeck and Newstead. He was knighted at the

dwellyng at Wodhowse a myle of. There he herde chawntynge, syngyng, and torche-berynge in day-light at masse. Apon this he fell in a myslyking of hym self. The dyvyll tempted hym continually, specyally in the nyght, as many knew. At laste G. Petite, the sonne of mr. John Petite, told these news to John Loude, how his old frynd and scholer was tempted of Sathan to kylle hym selfe apon a smale occasyon, as some thoght. Then John Loude, from Adenborow [a] in Nottinghamshere, wrote a comfortable letter by G. Petite to mr. Forde, at readynge of whych letter he greatly rejoced, and toke spirituall comforte; ofte tymes kyssyng the letter, *et gratias agens Deo et ejus servo J. L.* And so at laste being well recomforted, he was made person of Newbery by the meanes of mr. Forteskew [b] some tyme his scholer in humanitee, rather then folower in religione, and, with continuall paynes in techyng the grammer schole ther and prechyng, he chawnged this lyff for a better in great feablenes of body more then of sowle and mynde.

Yet one Rychard Wever of Brystole felle into lyke temptacyone for hearyng masse, and receavyng a great space muche consolatyone by the great and tedious travayle of one precher now neadles to be named, yet at laste, when he should go whom,c he ranne to the infamous mylles of Brystolle, and cowght a chylde of vij yeares age in his armes, and so lepped in to the water and wer bothe drowned.

Tower Feb. 22, 1547-8, previously to the coronation of Edward VI., and died March 21, 1564. "The Newes owte of Heaven both pleasaunt and joyfull," written by Thomas Becon at Alsop in the Dale in the Peak of Derbyshire, were dedicated as a new-year's gift "to the right worshipful master George Pierpount," to whom the author acknowledged himself to be greatly bound. (Becon's Works, printed for the Parker Society, i. 37, 44.) The passage in the text seems to show that he afterwards sympathised with the opponents of Becon. Yet his son Henry was evidently a friend of Louthe, being appointed one of the supervisors of his will. (See p. 12.)

a Now Attenborough. Louthe may have had the living: but Thoroton, the historian of Nottinghamshire, gives no lists of incumbents.

b Perhaps sir Adrian Fortescue, whose widow Anne, daughter of sir William Read, was remarried to sir Thomas Parry. In 1554 Thomas Parry esquire, and his wife dame Anne Fortescue, resided in the college of Wallingford. In 1585 she was buried at Welford, six

It is not to be conceled that this poore miser, tempted nyghtely, and almoste choked of the fynd, for none other cause then is rehersed, fownd a longe tyme unspeakable comforte of the saying of saint Paule,[a] "Chryste came into this world to save synners, of the wych I am the greatest;" pretendyng a great reverence and love to the prechere, and ever recyvyng the sayd sentense; but being broght to the servyce at the colleag a^o 4 *Elizab.* he was cleane altered, and that love turned in to a servile feare and terror of the prechere, seekynge occasyones to steale from behynde hym, but beinge of hym espyed, he wolde be marvelously abashed, and as it wer tremble for feare, thoghe of the prechere he hadd all the fayrest and plesant wordes that he cowld devyse.

By this doble history, wych is well known to many, all men I truste may lerne that the masse was never devised with owt the dyvylle, seing the heeryng of masse hathe so divyllyshe effect in those that yelde unto it.

Hæc qui scripsit ecce coram Deo vera esse novit.

Of mr. Quynby of Oxforde.

After the apprehensyone of John Frythe [b] many were detected [c] in Oxforde, as this mr. Quynby,[d] Talbot,[e] John Man,[f] all of the New colleadge; and Bartholomew Traheron,[g] an olde disciple.

[a] 1 Tim. 2.   [b] In 1533.

[c] This was a customary term, and one which may be frequently found in the pages of Foxe, signifying impeached or informed against.

[d] I have not ascertained the christian name of this Quinby, but he was probably a relative of Anthony Quinby, bachelor of law, whose memory has been preserved in the following epitaph placed "under the proportion of a man on a brass plate," in the east cloister of New College chapel.

> En nuda Antonii Quinby lapis iste, Briani
>   Wottoni hic positus sumptibus, ossa tegit.
> Hic duo (viventes sic junxit amor) sua jungi
>   Post mortem optabant corpora corporibus.
> Ast aliter Dominus decrerat: namque Brianus
>   Londini, Oxonie conditur Antonius.

(For Notes [e] [f] [g] see next page.)

John Man recanted, whom mr. Traheron called the stonny ground, on whom the good seedes of God's worde tooke no rowte. Talbote

> Primum in lege gradum pariter suscepit uterque,
> Cultor uterque Dei, doctus uterque fuit.
> Det Deus in celis animus jungatur uterque,
> Disjunctum quamvis corpus utrumque jacet.
> Obiit Antonius xxix die Maii MDLIX.
> Brianus vero xiv calend. Feb. MDLX.

Wood's Colleges and Halls of Oxford (edit. Gutch), 1786, vol. iii. p. 212; where it is added that Quinby's friend Brian Wotton was buried in the churchyard of St. Alban's, London, his father Edward lying in that church. The following are the entries of the admissions of the two friends at Winchester in the same year:

"1547. Antonius Quinbye de Fernham, Winton. dioc. xiij an. in f° Paschæ præt.

"—— Brianus Wotton de parochia S'ci Albani, London. dioc. xiij an. in f° Simonis et Judæ præterito." (Register of Winchester College.)

Among the witnesses examined in the proceedings against bishop Gardiner in 1551, was "Robert Quinby of Farnham clothmaker, where he was born, of the age of 27 or thereabouts:" see Foxe, Actes and Monuments, first edit. ii. 841.

e This was Robert Talbot, one of our earliest English antiquaries, who wrote a commentary on the Itinerary of Antoninus. Wood tells us that he became fellow of New college (after he had served two years of probation), an. 1523, and left it five years after, being expelled for heresy. That he afterwards "sterte back" in his faith, as Loude tells, appears to be confirmed by the provisions of his will. See the memoir of him in Athenæ Oxon. (ed. Bliss) i. 263. His name is not to be found in the register of Winchester college.

f John Man is said to have been born at Lacock in Wiltshire, but the entry of his admission at Winchester states that he came from Winterbourne Stoke, which is in the same county, but more than twenty miles from Lacock. It is as follows: "A.D. 1523. Johannes Manne de Wynterbourne Stoke xj an. in f° Assump. præt." He was elected from Winchester to New college 1529, proctor of the university 1540. He also was expelled New college for heresy, but in 1547 was made principal of White hall, and in 1562 warden of Merton college. In 1565 he became dean of Gloucester. He died in 1568. See memoir of him in Athenæ Oxon. (edit. Bliss) i. 366. He had a contemporary at Winchester of the same name and nearly the same age, admitted "A.D. 1527. Johannes Manne de Wrytyll, xij an. in f° Omn. Sc'r'm præt. *In margine*, Rector de Horwood."

g Bartholomew Traheron was either of Exeter college or Hart hall. He became library-keeper to king Edward the Sixth, and was made dean of Chichester 1551. See the memoir of him in Athenæ Oxon. (edit. Bliss) i. 323, and various incidents of his

also sterte backe lyke Deimcy[a] (He serves the lord Wriothysley, teachyng his chyldren), and were never the lesse expulsed by the warden, doctor John London.[b] Quynbe was imprisonned veary strayghtely in the steeple of the New colleadg, and dyed halfe sterved with colde and lacke of foode. He desyred his fryndes that came to see hym that he myght receave the Lordes supper in both formes; but it wold not be graunted. He was axed of his fryndes what he wold eate; he sayd his stomache was gonne from all meate excepte it wer a warden pye.[c] "Ye shall have it," quod they. "I wolde have but two wardens (quod he) baked: I meane, to be playne (sayde he), owr warden of Oxforde and owr warden of Wynchester, London and More;[d] for suche a warden pie might do me and Christes churche good; wheare as other wardens from the tree

[a] This name is very obscure in the MS. The next passage is written in the margin. It apparently relates to Talbot.

[b] John London, D C.L. is a person whose name frequently appears in connection with the visitation and suppression of the monasteries, for which purpose he was a visitor appointed by Henry VIII. (See Letters on that subject edited for the Camden Society by Mr. T. Wright.) His entry at Winchester is thus recorded: "A.D. 1497. Johannes London de Hammolden, filius tenentis Oxon. xj an. in festo Nat. D'ni præt.—Berks. *In margine*, Custos Oxon." (Register of Admissions to Winchester College.) He was elected warden of New college in 1526, and remained so until 1542. He was also a canon of Windsor, dean of Osney, and of Wallingford: for his other preferments see Wood, Colleges and Halls (edit. Guteh), iii. 188, and Fasti Oxon. edit. Bliss, i. 47. He died in 1543 in the Fleet prison, to which he had been committed on a charge of perjury.

[c] It is perhaps too well known to require remark that the warden was a species of baking pear, said to have derived its name from the Cistercian abbey of Warden in Bedfordshire.

[d] "A.D. 1492. Edwardus More, de Havant, filius tenentis Winton. xiij an. in festo Nat. D'ni præt. *In margine*, Infor. Wynton. Custos Wynton." (Register of Admissions to Winchester College) In explanation of the designation "filius tenentis," which but rarely occurs in the register, the Rev. W. H. Gunner remarks, that the tenants of the college property had by the statutes a right to consideration in the appointment to scholarships, and in the very early indentures of election they are bracketed as persons residing *in locis ubi bona collegii vigent*. Among those who supplicated for the degree of B.D. at Oxford in 1518, but no one was admitted, was "Edw. More of New college, who was admitted the eighth warden of Wykeham's college near Winchester 29 Oct. 1526, and dying 1541, was buried in the choir of the chappel there." (Wood's Fasti Oxon. edit. Bliss, i. 47.)

can doo me no good at all." Thus jestyng at their tyranny, thorow the cherfulnes of a saffe conscience, he turned his face to the walle in the sayd belfry; and so after his prayers sleapte swheetly in the Lorde.

But to what open shame doctor London was afterwardes putt, with open penance with two smockes on his shoulders, for mrs. Thykked and mrs. Jennynges, the mother and the daughter, and how he was taken with one of them by Henry Plankney in his gallery, being his syster's sonne—as it was then knowen to a number in Oxforde and elsewheare, so I thynk that some yet lyvynge hathe it in remembrans, as well as the penner of this history. J. L.

Of the shameful murderyng of one mr. Edmund Loude of Sawtrey, by the monkes and preestes of Sawtrey Abbey, aboute a° 13 H. 8, A° D° 1522. A° 5 post Lutheri predicationem.

This Edmund Loude, the sonne and heyre of mr. Thomas Loude of Hynnyngam castle,[a] Cretyngam,[b] and Sawtry, a myle from Sawtre abbey, descended of noble parentage: for his mother, Anne Loude, was the dawghter and heyre of sir Edmund Molso; hys grandmother Kateryn Dudley, maryed to Lionell Loude; his great-grandmother was Mary of Henawd, maryed to Rogere Loude, and cossen to Lyonell erle of Ulstere and duke of Clarense. He was an enymy to the wanton mounkes of the abbey, and to two lewd persons of Sawtrey,[c] for they hawnted moste shamfully the wyves of mr. Thomas Loude hys tenantes in the towne. At the wyche mr. Loude the father, and Edmund the sonne, specyally founde fawte with thys rule of the monkes and preestes, and some tyme when the howses by them were watched, and the monkes with theyr

[a] Apparently Castle Hedingham in Essex: see note in p. 3.

[b] Cretingham, in Suffolk: see p. 4.

[c] Sawtrey had two churches, dedicated to All Saints and Saint Andrew respectively, otherwise called Sawtrey Moygne and Sawtrey Beaumys, and consequently two parsons, or rectors. The monks were Cistercians, and their house a cell of that of Warden in Bedfordshire. At the survey in 26 Hen. VIII. William Aungeli was abbot, and the clear

tenantes' wyves, the mounkes wolde beate downe the walles, and slypp away to the abbey. So that some tyme ther was hott skyrmyshes emonge tham. Harken, ye Catholykes, to the catholyk lyff of yowr bretherne! At one tyme they cawsed the peace to be taken of mr. Edmund Loude, and for breakyng of yt gotte hym in Cambrydge castle; unto hym resortyd one Rychard Wyne, an abbey lubberde of Ramsey and Sawtrey. He was an atturney, who sayd unto mr. Loude, then the kyng's prisoner, " A! Loude, hadd it not ben better for yow to have lyved quietly at Sawtrey, and hunt and hawke at yowr pleasure, then here to remeyne a prisoner agaynste yowr wylle?" " No (sayd mr. Loude), I am here but for strykyng a lecherous knave, and I cownte it better to be here for so small a cawse then to be sett in the stockes, as thou werte, for stealyng sylver spones at Ramsey abbey;" and with that reached Wyne a blow with his fyste, and dashed out all hys for-teeth, by wych blow he lysped as longe as he lyved. Thys blow was declared to the chaste clergymen in the country, and by them to the myghty clergy at the courte, and by them in the moste greevous manner to the kynge: thynkyng thys hadd ben ynoughe to have rydd hym owt of thyr way at Sawtrey. But see the goodnes of God, and the clemency of the prynce! The kyng lawghed hertely at the peltyng [a] lawyer's deformitee, and thoght it a condigne rewarde for suche a sawey felow, saying, " Do yow thynke yt was wel donne of hym to upbrayde owr prisoner, beyng imprisoned by hys meanes? He was served well ynough. I perceave Loude ys a talle [b] jentylman: wee do pardon hym of his fawlte and imprisonment." So Edmund Loude cume whom agayne after he hadd ben ther awhyle, makyng mery continually with mr. Benet Molso and divers other gentylmen studentes in the universitee, who being of kynne to hym came dayly to make mery with hym.

[a] " A very common epithet with our old writers to signify paltry or contemptible." Glossary by Archdeacon Nares, who gives examples from Shakspere's Lear and Richard II., Beaumont and Fletcher, Ascham, &c.

[b] This was a term implying not merely tall, but one of good personage and manly bearing.

In shorte tyme the mounkes and preestes of Sawtrey lyke swhyne revolted to theyr dyrty podles, and former stynkyng lyff. And Edmund bearyng hym self bolde of the kynges late saying, and of hys fryndes in the courte by raysone of hys blood, warned and thretened them beatyng, yf they wolde not forbeare their resorte to hys father's tenantes and hys. And see the chawnce! One of these persons, the person of St. Andrew's, hadd ben at Walsyngham, who was a notable horemaster, and commyng home he kyssed many wyves, and amongs them Kateryn Loude, dawghter to Edmund Loude, openly in the churche yerde of Allhalows, for then it was thoght an holynes, commyng from thens, to kysse maydes and women; and the leacherous Catholyk hadd opinione that mr. Edmund Loude wolde not be offended at his doynges. But it came no soner to mr. Loude hys eares, but he, after hys woute, toke hys molspade[a] in hys hand, and by chawnce quyckly mette with the preeste. The good persone lykyng not hys lookes, downe upon hys knees, of with hys cappe, prayinge hym not to bett hym, for he was within holy orders. "O thou bawdy knave, (sayd mr. Loude,) darest yow kysse my dawghter? Wylt yow not leave thys wemen's cumpanye?" And seing hys new brode shaven crowne, he toke up a cow cusen or cow turde with his spade, and clapped it upon his crowne; addyng to his ill deede worse wordes: "Yow, (sayde he,) all the sorte of yow, wyll er it be longe be gladd to hyde yowr shaven pates, rather then they shoulde be seene."

Besydes thys, the sayde Edmund Loude conceaved suche an hate agaynst that religione and that holy preeste, that he came into the churche and plucked the felowe from the altare as he was abowte to make his God.

Shortely after, the cleane-fyngered clergy havyng encouragement ynoughe bothe above in the courte and in the country, they contrived how he should be made away. This Edmund Loude used to

---

[a] This word is not in the glossaries: it was either a mould-spade, or one used in digging for moles.

walke a quarter of a myle to a greate pasture he hadd called Wood-fylde close (vjC acres within an heage) assigned hym for his wyves joynture, Edyth the dawghter of John Stuecly lord of Stuecly ny Huntyngdon; and he hadd with hym in his armes John Loude ᵃ hys yowngeste sonne, of the age of iij yeares and more. Sodenly rushed owt behynd the hedge and bushes Skelton the father, and Skelton the sonne, tenantes to the abbatt, well weapened. Mr. Loude knew thei came to dispatche hym, and they sayd no lesse. " Yet, (sayde he.) do no harme to my lytle boy." With that they fearsely layd at hym, and he at them. At laste comythe the good catholyke preste in hys surplysse, with holy water, and the cunstable herde of thys tragycall murder prepensed, and thoght to shew hym self not to laches in doing his dewty, and came to them, fyndyng mr. Loude nothyng hurte, but he hadd catholycally basted the catholykes men, so that they preyed peace of hym. And he to take breth was contented to hold hys hand. The cunstable commanded the peace in the kinges name to be kepte: they all agreed to obbey; so that mr. Loude wold delyver his forreste bylle to the cunstable, wich he was lothe to do, but for the cunstable's fayre promyses. They gave place to mr. Loude to go afore them, and the cunstable nexte. There when he was apon the style to go over, Skelton the father cawght hym by the armes, and Skelton the sonne strooke hym apon the hedd, and so he felle of the style; the clobbe was gotten in Monkes wodd, half a myle from Sawtrey. So the preeste came to sone with his holy water, for mr. Loude was alyve at hys commynge, yet he was caryed whom,ᵇ and was speechlesse, for the fylme called the *pia mater* was peryshed with the blow. Yet he lyved about vij dayes after, and makyng all thynges straight the world, forgave all hys enymies, and was layd up in a swheete reste, under the alter of God, lookyng for the joyfull resurrectyone. Hys wyff sued an appeale of murder, but many delays wer made, and nothyng done, for

---

ᵃ The writer of this narrative.
ᵇ *i. e.* home.

hur husband was taken for an heretycke, the clargy was mighty; but see the vengens of God: Skelton with his sonne rune away; the father was hanged, and the sonne drowned: the preestes coulde never gett the pardon of the good kyng.

Vindica sanguinem nostrum de iis qui, &c.[a]

More of mrs. Anne Askewgh.[b]

Thys good gentlewoman Anne Askewgh,[c] syster to the ryght worshipfull sir Francys Askewgh[d] and mrs. Dysney of Norton Dys-

[a] Probably alluding to Revelations, vi. 10.

[b] That is, more than Foxe had already published. The history of the religious persecutions of Anne Askew was written by herself, and, shortly after her cruel execution, was first printed at Marburg, in the county of Hesse, 12mo. 1547, with a long running commentary by John Bale, afterwards bishop of Ossory. This has been reprinted entire, in Bale's Select Works, for the Parker Society, 1849. Without Bale's " elucydacyon," but with some other additions, the narrative was introduced by Foxe into his Actes and Monuments; and from that source it has been retailed in an endless variety of forms. Anne Askew is certainly one of the most interesting personages commemorated in Foxe's pages, and, in addition, her story has the charm of autobiography. It has been related with care in the Rev. Christopher Anderson's Annals of the English Bible, 1845, vol. ii. pp. 190—200 : and is still more fully developed in the Rev. James Anderson's Ladies of the Reformation, 1855, pp. 136—179. But by none of her biographers, even including the last, is due prominence given to her connection with the Protestant party at court, and her influence with queen Katharine Parr, which, if we may credit the commentary upon Foxe's narrative written by Robert Parsons the Jesuit (and which will be found in the Appendix), was very considerable.

[c] Anne Askew was a daughter of sir William Askew, or Ayscough, of South Kelsey in Lincolnshire, and was married at an early age to a gentleman named Kyme, resident in the same county, from whom she separated in consequence of ill-usage, and came to London, apparently to prosecute her cause in chancery. Her mind, however, was more occupied with the great business of religion, and her Protestant zeal raised her public as well as private enemies : who, finding her equally unyielding in spiritual as in temporal matters, crushed without mercy a woman whom they could not intimidate. She had dropped her married name, and the identity of her unworthy husband is uncertain : but on this point see the Appendix.

[d] Sir Francis Ayscough was sheriff of Lincolnshire in 1544. Another brother, Edward, was servant to archbishop Cranmer, and became one of the gentlemen pensioners. See the note on the Gentlemen Pensioners in the Appendix.

ney ᵃ in Lincolneshere, was lodged before hur imprisonement at an howse over-agaynste the Temple. And one great papiste of Wykam colleadge,ᵇ then called Wadloe, a coursytore of the Chawncery, hott in his religione, and thynkyng not well of hir lyffe, gott hymselfe lodged harde by hur at the nexte howse, for what purpose I neade not open to the wyse reader; but the conclusyon was that, wheare he came to speake evyll of hur, he gave her the prayse to mr. Lyonell Trockmorton ᶜ for the devouteste and godliest woman that ever he knew, "for (sayd he) at mydnyght she begynneth to pray, and cessyth not in many howers after, when I and others applye owr sleape or do worse." ᵈ

Hur fyrste examinacion in the Tower.ᵉ

My lorde mayre, sir M. Bowes,ᶠ syttyng with the cownsell, as

ᵃ Jane Ayscough was married first to sir George St. Paul of Snarford, co. Lincoln, and secondly to Richard Disney esquire, of Norton Disney in the same county, who died in 1578. See pedigree of Disney in Hutchins's History of Dorsetshire, second edit. iv. 390.

ᵇ By this name it must be presumed that Louthe meant the college of Winchester, as before in p. 29.

ᶜ Strype, Eccles. Memorials, vol. i. p. 387, has incorrectly styled him *sir* Lionel. He was Lionel Throckmorton, gentleman, of Flixton, in South Elmham, Suffolk, a nephew of the author (see note in the Appendix).

ᵈ Misprinted by Strype, "appyed our sleep, or to work." Eccles. Memorials, i. 387.

ᵉ This examination was not in the Tower, but when Anne Askew, having first been examined by an inquest at Saddlers' hall, was denounced to the civil authority in order to be committed to prison: "Then they had me unto my lord maior, and he examined me as they had before, and I answered him directly in all things as I answered the quest before. Besides this, my lord maior layd one thing to my charge, which was never spoken of me, but of them; and that was, *Whether a mouse, eating the host, received God or no?* This question did I never aske, but in deede they asked it of me, whereunto I made them no answer, but smiled." This is the foundation of the story which Louthe has *improved* as in the text. Anne Askew was committed by the lord mayor to the Counter, and whilst there was visited by a priest, who followed up the argument on the mouse: "Fourthly he asked, if the host should fall, and a beaste did eate it, whether the beast did receive God or no? I answered, 'Seeing you have taken the paines to ask the question, I desire you also to assoile it yourselfe, for I will not doe it, because I perceive you come to tempt me.' And he said it was against the order of schooles that he which asked the question should answere it. I told him I was but a woman, and knew not the course of schooles." In the text,

(For Note ᶠ see next page.)

moste meetest for his wysdome, and seeing hur standyng apon lyff and dethe, " I pray yow, (quod he,) my lordes, gyve me leave to talke with this woman." Leave was granted. *Lord Maiore.* Thou folyshe woman, sayest thow that the prestes can not make the body of Chryste? *A. Askowghe.* I say so, my lorde, for I have redd that God mayd man; but that man can make God I never yet redd, nor I suppose ever shall red yt. *L. Maiore.* No? yow folyshe woman: after the wordes of consecratione, ys it not the Lordes body? *A. Askowghe.* No, it ys bot consecrated bredd, or sacramentall bredd. *L. Maior.* What, yf a mowse eate yt after the consecratione, what shalbecome of the mowse? What sayeste thow, thow folyshe woman? *A. Askowghe.* What shall become of hur say yow, my lorde? *L. Maior.* I say that that mowse is damned. *A. Askew.* Alacke, poore mowse! By this tyme the lordes had ynowghe of my lorde maiores divinitie, and perceavyng that some cowld not keape in theyr lawghyng, proceeded to the butchery and slawter that they entended afore thei came thither.

I being alyve must neades confesse of hur now departed to the Lorde, that the day afore her exequutione, and the same day also, she hadd an angel's countenance, and a smylyng face; for I was with Lassells, sir G. Blagge,[a] and the other, and with me iij. of the

Louthe tells his story in ridicule of the lord mayor's divinity, without adverting to the circumstance that Foxe had already published the particulars more accurately. The question whether the sacrament eaten of a mouse was the very and real body of Christ was, however, gravely entertained by various learned doctors, and variously argued. Bishop Gardiner maintained that "a mouse cannot devour God," though, on the other hand, " Christ's body may as well dwell in a mouse as in Judas." (Detection of the Devil's Sophistry, pp. 16, 21.) See other opinions stated in Bale's Select Works, p. 154. It was this question that brought sir George Blagge into trouble, as related in the next page.

[f] Sir Martin Bowes, goldsmith. See a note respecting him in Machyn's Diary, at p. 335: to which it may be added that a copy of his portrait is at Gibside, co. Durham, the seat of the earl of Strathmore. it is described by Mr. Surtees, History of Durham, ii. 254, who remarks in a note, "He was not immediately of the house of Streatlam, but a descendant of Bowes of York." The Goldsmiths' Company still possess a handsome cup presented to them by sir Martin Bowes: it is engraved in H. Shaw's " Decorative Arts."

Throkmorton's,[a] syr Nicholas being one [b] and mr. Kellum the other,[c] by the same token that one unknown to me sayd, "Ye ar all

the King's privy chamber, who being falsely accused by syr Hugh Caverley, knighte, and master Littleton, was sent for by Wrisley lord chancellour the sonday before Anne Askew suffered, and the next day was carried to Newgate, and from thence to Guildhall, where he was condemned the same day, and appoynted to be burned the wensday folowing. The words which his accusers had laid unto him were these: *What if a mouse should eat the bread? then, by my consent, they should hang up the mouse.* Wheras in dede these words he never spake, as to hys lives ende he protested. But the truth, as he sayd, was this, that they craftely to undermine him, walking with him in Paul's church after a sermon of doctour Crome, asked if he were at the sermon, and he said yea. ' I heard say (saith master Littleton) that he sayd in his sermon that the masse profiteth neither for the quick nor for the dead.' ' No? (saide master Blage) wherefore then? belike for a gentleman when he rideth a-hunting, to kepe his horse from stumbling.' And so they departing, immediately after he was apprehended (as is shewed) and condemned to be burned. When this was heard among them of the pryvye chamber, the king hearing them whispering together, whych he could never abide, commaunded them to tell hym the matter. Where upon the matter being opened, and sute made to the king, especially by the good erle of Bedford, then lord privie seal, the king being sore offended with their doings, that they would come so nere him, and even into his privie chamber, without hys knowledge, sent for Wrisley, commaunding him eftsoones to draw out hys pardon himself, and so was he set at libertye ; who, comming after to the king's presence, ' Ah, my pig! ' sayth the king to him (for so he was wont to call him). ' Yea (sayd he), if your majestie had not bene better to me then your bishops were, your pig had bene rosted ere this time.' " Foxe, it appears, was told that he had committed an error in naming " master George Blag to be one of the privie chamber ; " which he excuses by noting "that although he were not admitted as one of the privie chamber, yet hys ordinary resort thether, and to the kynges presence there, was such as, although he were not one of them, yet was he so commonly taken." (Edit. 1576, p. 2007.) Sir George Blagge was examined in the proceedings against bishop Gardiner in 1550, and was then thirty-eight years of age. See his memoir in Athenæ Cantabrigienses, 1858, i. 104.

[a] So the MS. though only two are named. The third was probably Lionel, (already mentioned in p. 40,) a cousin of the other two.

[b] Sir Nicholas Throckmorton, fourth son of sir George Throckmorton, of Coughton, co. Warwick, by Katharine daughter of Nicholas lord Vaux of Harrowden. He was aged thirty-five in 1550, "and one of the King's privy chamber," when examined in the proceedings against bishop Gardiner. (Foxe, edit. 1563, 807.) He had a memorable escape from a trial for treason in the reign of Mary (see Chronicle of Queen Jane and Queen Mary, p. 75.), and afterwards became one of the most distinguished men of his age. See Wotton's Baronetage, 1741, ii. 358.

[c] " The fifth son of sir George (Throckmorton) was Kenelme." Ibid. p. 359.

marked that come to them; take heede to your lyffes." And mr. Lassels,[a] a gentleman of a ryght worshipfull howse of Gatforde in Nottynghamshere ny Wursoppe, mownted up in to the wyndow of the litle parloure by Newgate, and there satt, and by hym syr Georg. Mr. Lassels was mery and cherefull in the Lorde, commyng from the hearyng of sentense of his condemnatione, and sayd these words: " My lorde byshoppe wold have me confesse the Romane churche to be the Catholycke churche, but that I can not, for yt ys not trew."

When the hower of derkenes came, and theyr exequutione,[b] &c. mrs. A. Askow was so racked [c] that she could not stand, but the

[a] Anne Askew had three fellow-sufferers, who are described by Foxe as " one Nicholas Belenian, priest, of Shropshire, John Adams a taylor, and John Lacels gentleman of the court and household of king Henry." Foxe prints a letter of Lascelles, " written out of prison," being an exposition of his faith: it is signed " John Lacels, servaunt late to the king, and now I trust to serve the Everlasting King with the testimony of my bloud in Smithfield;" and a letter of Anne Askew (also printed by Foxe) is addressed to him. He was either a younger son of Ralph Lascelles of Sturton, co. Notts. esq. by a daughter of Topcliffe, or else a younger son of Richard (son of Ralph) by Dorothy, daughter of sir Bryan Sandford: both which Johns died s. p. Bryan Lascelles esquire was of Sturton and Gateford in 1575. (Vincent's Notts. 117, Coll. Arm. f. 181.) The martyr was not improbably the same John Lascelles who appears in the proceedings against queen Katharine Howard, and whose sister Mary was one of the principal witnesses against that queen. This was bishop Burnet's opinion, who says: " it is likely he was the same person that had discovered queen Katharine Howard's incontinency, for which all the popish party, to be sure, bore him no good will." (History of the Reformation.) He is described as " a gentylman of Furnyvalles inne," in the Grey Friars' Chronicle; where the name of " Hemmysley a prest, wyche was an Observand frere of Richemond," is given instead of Belenian; whilst Stowe and bishop Godwin call the priest Nicholas Otterden, and the tailor Adlam instead of Adams.

[b] This passage has been misunderstood by Southey in his History of the Church, in both editions, for he states that " The execution was delayed *till darkness closed*, that it might appear the more dreadful." As Mr. Anderson has remarked (Ladies of the Reformation, p. 174), Louthe's allusion is evidently to the words of Christ to his enemies, " This is your hour and the power of darkness." It was a summer's day, Foxe states about the month of June; but Bale, Stowe, and Grey Friars' Chronicle fix it to the 16th of July.

[c] *i.e.* had been so painfully racked, a few days previously. After her condemnation, Anne Askew was taken one afternoon to the Tower, and subjected to the rack, in the hope that she might be forced to name some ladies or gentlewomen about the court

dounge carte was holden up betwene ij sarjantes, perhaptes syttyng there in a cheare,[a] and after the sermone ended, they putt fyar to the reedes; the cowncell lookyng one, and leanyng in a wyndow by the spytle,[b] and emonge them syr Rychard Southwell,[c] the master of the wryghtor herof. And afore God, at the fyrst puttyng-to of the fyar theyre felle a lytle dewe, or a few pleasante droppes apon us that stode by, and a pleasant crackyng from heaven. God knoweth whyther I may truly terme it a thounder cracke, as the people dyd in the gospell,[d] or angell, or rather Godes owne voyce.[e]

because I lay still, and did not cry, my lord chancellor [Wriothesley] and master Rich tooke pains to rack me in their own hands, till I was nigh dead." In this tragic scene, Louthe's ridiculous story of the lord mayor and the mouse has evidently not its proper place: but it was the only time that Anne Askew was in the Tower. Some writers have cast discredit upon the fact that Anne Askew was racked at all, apparently forgetting that it rests upon her own authority. The reader will find in the Appendix the remarks of Mr. Jardine and Dr. Lingard, with some evidence which they neglected to consider.

[a] Foxe states, "shee was brought into Smithfield in a chaire, because she could not goe on her feet, by meanes of her great torments." It is difficult to ascertain the precise purport of Louthe's account, which is exactly as above printed.

[b] The hospital of St. Bartholomew. One of the most curious cuts in Foxe's work (edit. 1563, p. 678) represents "The description of Smythfielde, with the order and maner of certayne of the Counsell, sytting there at the burnyng of Anne Askewe and Lacels with the others." The populace are kept from the area by a ring-fence, within which stands the pulpit from whence an admonitory sermon was delivered by doctor Nicholas Shaxton. The back-ground exhibits the hospital buildings and church of St. Bartholomew.

[c] See p. 8.   [d] John xii. 29.

[e] "Credibly am I informed by divers Dutch merchants which were then present, that in the time of their sufferings the sky, abhorring so wicked an act, suddenly altered colour, and the clouds from above gave a thunder-clap, not all unlike to that is written Psalm lxxvi. The elements both declared therein the high displeasure of God for so tyrannous a murder of innocents, and also expressly signified His mighty hand present to the comfort of them which trusted in him, besides the most wonderful mutation which will, within short space, thereupon follow. And like as the centurion, with those that were with him, for the tokens showed at Christ's death, confessed him to be the Son of God, Matt. xxvii. so did a great number at the burning of these martyrs, upon the sight of this open experiment, affirm them to be His faithful members. Full many a Christian heart has risen, and will rise, from the pope to Christ, through the occasion of their burning in the fire." *Bale*, who continues his discourse upon the thunderings at much further length.

But thys I well know, that I could not, for feare of damnatione, stand by and say nothyng agaynste theyre cruelte; therfor I with a lowde voyce, lookyng to the cownsell, sayd, "I axe advenganse of yow all that thus dothe burne Chrystes member." I hardly escaped a cartar's blow at that same worde, and forthwith departed to mr. Southwel's howse by Charterhowse, wheare was mr. W. Moryshe,[a] gentylman ushere fyrst to mr. Pace,[b] and afterwarde to kyng Henry viij., and there kepte in pryson with syr Rychard Southwell knyght, by commandement of the lorde Rych and others, who wold fayne have hadd hym bornte, for his lordshyppe of Chyppyn Onger. And to hym I declared what I herde and saw in Smyth fyld; and nyghtly, thoghe he wer but symply lodged, and I lay nyghtly in my sylke bedd and good lodgyng in a parloure by mr. Rychard Southwell my pupyll,[c] yet I used to leave myn owne

[a] "William Morice of Chipping Ongar, in the county of Essex, esquire, and Ralph Morice, brother unto the said William," are mentioned in the narrative of Latimer's communication with James Bainham (afterwards burnt) in the dungeon of Newgate, printed by Strype, Memorials, vol. iii. p. [236]. William Morice was the son of James Morice, a gentleman attached to the household of the lady Margaret countess of Richmond, and employed by her in the building of her colleges in Cambridge. William Morice escaped a fatal termination to his imprisonment by the death of Henry VIII. In the first parliament of queen Mary was passed " an acte for the repeale of a statute made for the uniting of the parishe churches of Ongar and Grenestede, in the countie of Essexe," which statute in the preamble of the act of Mary is stated to have been made " by the sinister labour and procurement of one Wyllyam Morys esquier, your Grace's late servaunt deceased, some time patrone of the parish churche of Ongar aforesayd, and one of the burgesses of the parliament holden at Westminster," 2 Edw. VI. " inordinately seking his private lucre and profitt." (Statutes of the Realm, iv. 234.) Ralph Morice his brother was secretary to archbishop Cranmer, and a full account of him is given by Strype, Memorials of Cranmer, p. 425. In the Ecclesiastical Memorials, i. 386, Strype inadvertently makes William the father of Ralph.

[b] Richard Pace, some time Latin secretary to Henry VIII, dean of St. Paul's 1519, and also dean of Exeter and Salisbury. He died at his vicarage of Stepney in 1532. See a memoir of him in Wood's Athenæ Oxon. edit. Bliss, i. 64, and see the index to State Papers, 1852, vol. xi. p. 615.

[c] Afterwards Richard Southwell esquire, of Horsham St. Faith's in Norfolk, whose marriages and issue will be found in Lodge's Peerage of Ireland, (edit. Archdall,) 1789, vi. 6 : but no other particulars of his history are there stated. According to sir Henry

lodgyng and go and lye with hym, conferryng with hym of hys answeres wych he hadd to make in religione afore the cownsell. For this thyng I was vehemently suspected, and also for that mr. Allyngton confessed to the benchers of Lincoln Inne that I hadd lessoned with hym abowte the sacrament, and, namely, towchyng the sense of *hoc est corpus meum.* And when mr. Foster,[a] mr. Roper,[b] and mr. Gryffyn,[c] benchores, came to lay me up upon suspicione, they came fyrste to have mr. Southwel's good wyll, whose sonne I tawght the Latyng tonnge, the laws civyll and temporall. Mr. Southwell sayd that he knew no suche thynge by me, but that I was a quiett man in hys howse and hadd well served hys turne, &c., " but doo yow (quoth he,) as yow thynke good." So I escaped.

Ther was one mr. Webbe, an olde preeste, who beyng veary neare[d] syr Rychard Southwell, used to speake veary well of me, when hys master wold say, " He wyll make my boye lyke hymselfe, to(o) good a Latinyste and to(o) greate an heretycke." In dede mr. Rychard Southwell was some tyme of good religione, so long as he was my pupyll in Benett colleage, and in the innes of the courte.

Now towching the commendacion of Wadlo and the blessed ende of thys woman, and thys heavenly noyse, I can say no more, butt leave every man to hys owne judgement. Meethoght yt semed rather that the angels in heaven rejoysed to receave theyre sowles unto blysse, whose bodies then popyshe tormentors caste into fyar, as

---

Spelman, who relates the scandals of the Southwell family in his History of Sacrilege, all sir Richard's children but the youngest daughter were really illegitimate, having been born of his second wife Mary (Darcy) whilst his first wife Thomasine (Darcy) was living.

[a] William Foster, reader at Lincoln's inn 35 Hen. VIII. and again 6 Edw. VI. Dugdale's Origines Juridiciales, p. 253.

[b] Perhaps William Roper, some time clerk of the King's Bench, son of John Roper attorney-general, and son-in-law of the great sir Thomas More.

[c] Edward Gryffyn, reader at Lincoln's inn 29 Hen. VIII. and again 36 Hen. VIII. made " generall atturney of all courtes of recordes within England," 30 Sept. 1553, and who continued attorney-general during the whole of the reign of Mary.

[d] *i.e.* in his confidence.

not worthy to lyve any longer emonge suche helhowndes. God send me no worse ende (O, ye bloodthyrsty papystes!) then yow procured for these holy persons! I thynke ye wyll say Amen, and Amen say I.

More of mr. John Philpott.

He being the sonne of syr Peeter Philpott [a] knyght, ny Wynton, was putt to Wykam colleadge,[b] wheare he profyted in lernyng so well, that he leyd a wager of xx[d] with John Harpsfylde [c] that he would make ijC verses in one nyght, and not make above iij. faultes in them. Mr. Thomas Tuchyner,[d] our scholmaster nexte afore mr. Whyght, was judge, and adjugged the xx[d] to mr. Philpott.

[a] Sir Peter Philpot was seated at Compton near Winchester. He was the son and heir of sir John Philpot of that place, sheriff of Hampshire in 16 Hen. VII., and K.B. at the marriage of prince Arthur in 1501, by Alice, daughter of William lord Stourton. Sir Peter is also styled a knight of the Bath, but it does not appear when he was so made. He was esquire when he served sheriff of Hampshire in 16 Hen. VIII., and knight when he again served in 27 Hen. VIII. In 1539 he was summoned to attend the reception of the lady Anna of Cleves: see the Chronicle of Calais, p. 177. He married Agnes, eldest daughter and co-heir of Thomas Troys of Hampshire esquire, by whom he had issue, three sons,—Henry of Barton, ob. s. p.; "John the martyr;" and Thomas, ancestor of those of Thruxton and Compton; and two daughters, married respectively to Egerton and Boydell, both of Cheshire. (MS. of Philipot the Herald in Coll. Arm.) The name of the daughter resident in the neighbourhood of Winchester does not appear.

[b] "A.D. 1526. Johannes Phylpott de Cumpton, x. an. in fest. Nat. D'ni præt. *In margine*, Archidiaconus Wynton." Register of Admissions to Winchester college.

[c] John Harpsfield, afterwards archdeacon of London (1554), brother to Nicholas, archdeacon of Canterbury. "1528. Johannes Harpysfyld de London, xij. an. in festo Pentecost. præt. *In margine*, Archid. London. Theo. Prof." (Register of the Admissions to Winchester college.) He was a fellow of Winchester from 1534 to 1561. See biographical notices of him in Wood's Athenæ Oxon. (edit. Bliss) i. 439; the Index to Machyn's Diary; and The Examination and Writings of John Philpot, (Parker Society,) p. xxx.

[d] There were two masters of this name, John and Richard, the latter of whom was succeeded by John White in 1534. Louthe is therefore in error as to his christian name —

"1526. Jo. Tychener informator incipit docere.

"1531. Richardus Twychene informator incipit docere." (College Register.)

Both John and Richard came from Oakingham, and they were probably brothers:—

Wheane Stephen Wynton[a] bare ever yll wylle agaynste this godly gentylman, and forbadd hym prechyng often tymes, and he coulde not in hys consciance hyde his talante under so good a prynce,[b] and in so popyshe a diocesse, at laste he [the bishop] sent for certeyn justices who came to his howse, named Wolsey,[c] and there callyng mr. Philpott " Roge," &c., " My lorde, (sayd he,) doo yow kepe a privy sessyons in yowr owne howse for me? and calle me roge, whose father is a knyght and may dispende a 1000 lib. within one myle of yowr nose? He that can dispende x lib. by the yeare, as I can, I thank God, ys no vacabond, &c. *Wynchester.* Canste thow dispende x lib. by yeare? *Philpott.* Axe Henry Frances, yowr syster's sonne. *Henry Frances* (kneelyng downe). I pray yow, my lorde, be good lorde unto mr. Philpott, for he ys to me a good landlorde. *Wynchester.* What rente doste thow pay hym? (*Frances.*) I pay him x lib. by yeare. At thys worde Stephen Wynthon was aferde and ashamed, for makyng so lowde a lye apon a gentleman, and a lerned gentylman. So the kyng Edward 6. harde of thys by the helpe of mr. Sternolde.[d]

Gentle reader, yow muste remember that Stephen Wynton preferred thys Henry Frances to the baylywyk of the Clynke,[e] that ys, he made hym capteyne of the stews and all the whoores therto

---

"1515. Johannes Towchener de Okynggame, fil. ten. Oxon. xiij an. in festo Omn. Scrm. præt. *In margine,* Informator Wynton. post Rector de Colyngbourne."

" 1518. Ric'us Twychener de Okyngame; xiij annorum in festo Sc'i Laurencii præteriti. *In margine,* Informator Wynton. post duxit uxorem."

John was admitted fellow of New college July 18, 1521, and Richard April 12, 1524.

[a] Bishop Stephen Gardiner.   [b] King Edward the Sixth.

[c] Wolvesey palace, near Winchester college.

[d] Thomas Sternhold, groom of the robes to Henry VIII. and Edward VI. ; better known as one of the translators of the Psalms into English metre. See notices of him in the Parker Society's volume of Select Poetry, p. xlvi., and in the memoir of King Edward VI. prefixed to his Literary Remains (printed for the Roxburghe Club), pp. lv. lvi.

[e] " The next is the Clinke, a gaol or prison for the trespassers in those partes; namely, in old time, for such as should brawle, frey, or break the peace on the said Bank, or in the brothel-houses, they were by the inhabitants thereabout apprehended and committed to this gaol, where they were straitly imprisoned." (Stowe's Survay.) See several passages

belongyng.[a] And in dede he proved an excellent cutter and ruffyne. Lerne, lerne, yow Chrysteanes, by thys unchrysteane prelate, verteusly to provyde for yowr yowthe.

Of Cooke the register [of Winchester], a persequutor of mr. Philpott, and Godes venjance apon Cooke.

Thys Cooke,[b] what with polyng and shavyng both laytee and clergy in Wynthon diocesse, came to greate welthe. And as those offycers having ons thyr offyce by patente can do, he flattered apon Stephen Gardyner to gett, and fawned as faste apon doctor Poynett[c] hys successor to holde it styll. And under them bothe he was ennymye to mr. Philpott,—for religione under Stephen, for a yearly pensyone under mr. Poynett, wyche he sayd the archdeacon was to pay to the byshoppe. Thys matter bredd the good gentylman trobles intollerable, and great slaunder in that diocesse to them bothe; whyle so good a byshopp at the settyng on of so ranke a knave coulde fynde in hys harte to persequute hys brother, for lernyng and lyff more meete for the byshoprych then the archdeaconry. Well, to defalcate unnecessary talke, thys Cooke hadd maryed a lady, and so roode with more men then the lerned archdeacon; and, to please the bishopp, he forstalled the way betweane Wynchester and mr.

from old writers relative to the Clink in Cunningham's Hand-book of London, 1849. The bishop of Winchester's palace itself frequently went by the name of the Clink.

[a] "Thou that giv'st whores indulgences to sin!"
The duke of Gloucester to cardinal Beaufort bishop of Winchester, in Shakspere's Henry VI. Part I. act i. sc. 3. The privileges of the stews were finally abolished in March 1546.

[b] John Cooke, registrar of the diocese of Winchester. See his examination relative to bishop Gardiner in Foxe, first edit. p. 860, but it gives no particulars of him. Whether he is to be identified with one who entered Winchester college in 1539 is doubtful: "1539. Johannes Cooke de Droxford (?) xij. ann. in festo Septem dormientium [27 July] præt. Winton. dioc." (Register of Admissions.)

[c] John Ponet, translated from Rochester to Winchester 1551, deprived 1553; well known as an ardent Reformer. See Index to Parker Society's Works, p. 615; also

Philpott's syster, who dwelt iij. myles from the cyty, and there lying lyke a theeff in waight for hym, sett hys men apon hym and sore beate hym; for mr. Philpott hadd as lusty a courage to defend hymself as in disputacyone agaynste popyshe prelattes to impugne theyr doctrine. He being thus beatten, hurte, and wounded, thoghe a lytle afore the chawnge, yet remedy he could none have, for the byshopp and his register were agaynst the archdeacon. The lyke at thys day ys practised of our prelates under owr noble quene Elizabethe.[a]

To conclude, marke the ende of the bishoppe, wych I lyste not to reherse, and the open shame that thys ragyng register was putt to. When mr. Robert Horne[b] was now byshoppe of Wynchester, and sett forwarde pure religione, wych hys register abhorred, and wold gyve no heare to hys accustomed flatterers (whych he more myslyked), he sett certeyn yowng boyes of the grammar schoole to rayse an unsavery slawnder of the byshopp, viz. that they, being in a tree, should see the byshoppe committe advoutrey under the same tree, or suche an other unlykely tale they tolde. The register hadd thys ofte in hys mouthe. At laste the byshopp, lyke a wyse man, hearyng of it, broght it to the quenes virteous and moste honorable cownsell. There Cooke in that hyghe court was dressed lyke a schoolyone or one of the blacke garde,[c] not muche unlyke suche an one yf any man that knew hym lyste to describe hym. Now he was compelled to shew the authors of this slawnder, Cooke hadd none other then boyes for the authores, besyde that the tyme, place, and persone were so unlykly. To close up the matter in fewe, thys schoolyon of the pope's blacke garde was adjudged by the

[a] Is this a reflection of archdeacon Louthe upon his diocesan archbishop Sandys?

[b] Robert Horne, consecrated Feb. 16, 1561, died June 1, 1580.

[c] The scullions and inferior officers of the royal household, when following queen Elizabeth's train in her Progresses, were by the common people jocularly termed the *black guard*; to which various allusions occur in old writers. See Nares's Glossary, *sub voce*, the Parker Society's Index, Nichols's Progresses of King James I. vol. ii. p. 402, &c. In all appearance, the term of reproach which has become so common in modern times, dates its origin from this popular jest.

awarde of those noble cownsellors to stande at Poles crosse, and to declare and preche there hys owne shame; but with owt blushyng, for hys syde panche and Croydon complexyone^a wolde not suffer hym to blushe, more then the black dogge of Bungay.[b]

I saw the good man make many and great fryndes, with often and longe watchyng at my lorde of Leycester's chamber dore, with a myghty powche hangyng by hys myghty Bonnar pawnche.[c] But my lorde wolde not so muche as looke upon hym, nor heare hym speake. Yt muche rejoysed me, remembryng at that tyme what I hadd herde of mr. Philpott, &c. My sayde lord dyd lyke hym self, and I truste it may provoke all other of lyke nobilitee to shew lyke cowntenance to suche Cookes. Marke, good reader, that God wyll not always leave the wronges unpunyshed that Catholykes doo to his saynctes.

$\alpha\upsilon\tau\sigma\varsigma\ \epsilon\phi\alpha.$

[a] *i.e.* as black as the faces of the colliers or charcoal-burners at Croydon, the great market from which the metropolis was then supplied with fuel for cooking.

[b] The "black dog of Bungay" dates from the year 1577, only two years before Louthe was writing. "This Black Dog, or the Divel in such a likenesse (God he knoweth who worketh all!) running all along down the church with great swiftnesse and incredible haste, among the people, in a visible fourm and shape passed between two persons, as they were kneeling upon their knees, and occupied in prayer as it seems, wrung the necks of them bothe in one instant clene backwards, insomuch that even at a moment where they kneeled they strangely dyed," &c. See a contemporary pamphlet entitled "A Straunge and Terrible Wunder wrought very late in the Parish Church of Bongay, a town of no great distance from the citie of Norwich, namely the fourth of this August in ye yeare of our Lord 1577, in a great tempest of violent raine, lightning and thunder, the like whereof hath been seldome seene. With the appeerance of an horrible shaped thing, sensibly perceived of the people then and there assembled. Drawen into a plain method according to the written copye by Abraham Fleming." The tract has a rude woodcut in the title-page of a black dog with large claws. The greater part of it is reprinted in the Rev. Mr. Suckling's Collections for Suffolk: and the parish register records the names of two men who were "slayne in the tempest in the belfry in the tyme of prayer upon the Lord's day ye iiijth day of August." See also Notes and Queries, Second Series, vol. iv. p. 314.

[c] An allusion to the person of bishop Bonner, so often caricatured in the cuts of the Actes and Monuments of Foxe.

The fyrste occasyone of the cardynal's overthrowe, by good queue Anne.[a]

Ther was a yownge fayre gentlewoman wayghtyng apon the countes of Pembroke, the lady Anne Boleyne. Ther was also in servyce of the same noble countese one mr. George Zouche,[b] father to syr John Zouche. This yowng jentleman was a sutor in way of maryage to the sayde yowng gentlewoman called mrs. Gensforde;[c] and amonge other lovetyckes,[d] mr. Zowche plucked from hur a booke in Englyshe called Tyndale's Obedience.[e] At the same tyme

[a] Queen Anne Boleyne, and cardinal Wolsey.

[b] See hereafter, p. 57.

[c] George Wyatt, who wrote the life of queen Anne Boleyne which Mr. Singer has appended to his edition of Cavendish's Life of Wolsey 1825, was indebted for his information chiefly to two ladies—" one that first attended on her both before and after she was queen, with whose house and mine there was then kindred and strict alliance." This was mistress Anne Gainsford, who became the wife of George Zouche esquire, of Codnor in Derbyshire, mentioned in the text. She was one of the daughters of sir John Gainsford of Crowhurst in Surrey, who died in 1543, (and who like his royal master had six wives,) by his second wife Anne, daughter of Richard Haut, widow of Peyton ; and her sisters of the whole blood were, Mary married to sir William Courtenay, Katharine married to sir William Finch, and Rose married first to George Puttenham and secondly to William Sackville of Blechingley. (Pedigree of Gainsford, in History of Surrey, by Manning and Bray, iii. 174.) Wyatt (besides the anecdote which ensues) tells the following on the authority of Nan Gainsford : " There was conveyed to her (Anne Boleyne) a book pretending old prophecies, wherein was represented the figure of some personages, with the letter H upon one, A upon another, and K upon the third, which an expounder thereupon took upon him to interpret by the king and his wives, and to her pronouncing certain destruction if she married the king. This book coming into her chamber, she opened, and finding the contents, called to her maid of whom we have spoken before, who also bore her name, Come hither Nan, (said she,) see here a book of prophecy ; this he saith is the king, this the queen, and this is myself with my head off. The maid answered, If I thought it true, though he were an emperor, I would not myself marry him with that condition. Yes, Nan, (replied the lady,) I think the book a bauble, yet for the hope I have that the realm may be happy by my issue, I am resolved to have him whatsoever might become of me."

[d] So the MS. qu. Love-tricks ? It is so read by Strype, Memorials, i. 112.

[e] The Obedience of a Christian Man, by William Tyndale, first published in 1528—" a bold performance, in which the author vindicates the diffusion of the Scriptures in the mother tongue, unfolds the duties of men in their different relations and conditions of life,

the cardinall hadd gyven commandmente to the prelattes, but specially to doctore Samsone deane of the kynges chappell, [a] that they shoulde vigilantely gyve eye to all men for suche bookes, that they came not abroode, specyally to the kynges knowleadge [b]; but it felle

exposes the false power claimed by the pope, and condemns the doctrines of penance, confession, satisfactions, absolutions, miracles, tho worshipping of saints, and other popish dogmas." (Ladies of the Reformation, by the Rev. James Anderson, 1855, p. 75.) In 1528, remarks Mr. Offor the biographer of Tyndale, was published the most valuable of his compositions, The Obedience of a Christian Man. Mr. Offor has a copy of the first edition, in small 4to. published May 1528, once the property of the princess afterwards queen Elizabeth. It has her autograph beautifully written, but with all the pomp worthy of a Tudor, *Elizabeth, doughter of England and France.* "This book," adds Mr. Offor, " probably assisted to fix her principles in favour of the Reformation." (Memoir of William Tyndale by George Offor, prefixed to the reprint of Tyndale's New Testament, 1836.) The Obedience of a Christian Man is reprinted in the first volume of Tyndale's Works, edited for the Parker Society, by the Rev. Henry Walter, B.D., F.R.S.

[a] Richard Sampson, afterwards bishop of Chichester 1536, and of Lichfield and Coventry 1543; died 1554. See Athenæ Cantabrigienses, 1858, i. 119.

[b] George Wyatt, in his life of Anne Boleyne, gives another and somewhat different relation of this anecdote. After remarking that her society was advantageous to the king, inasmuch as "her mind brought him forth the rich treasures of love of piety, love of truth, love of learning," in proof of that assertion he proceeds,—" that of her time (that is, during the three years that she was queen) it is found by good observation that no one suffered for religion, which is the more worthy to be noted for that it could not so be said of any time of the queens after married to the king. And amongst other proofs of her love to religion to be found in others, this here of me is to be added:—That shortly after her marriage, divers learned and christianly disposed persons resorting to her, presented her with sundry books of those controversies that then began to be questioned touching religion, and specially of the authority of the pope and his clergy, and of their doings against kings and states. And amongst others, there happened one of these, which, as her manner was, she having read, she had also noted with her nail as of matter worthy the king's knowledge. The book lying in her window, her maid (of whom hath been spoken) took it up, and as she was reading it, came to speak with her one then suitor to her, that after married her; and as they talked he took the book of her, and she withal, called to attend on the queen, forgot it in his hand, and she not returning in some long space, he walked forth with it in his hand, thinking it had been hers. There encountered him soon after a gentleman of the cardinal's of his acquaintance, and after salutation, perceiving the book, requested to see it, and finding what it was, partly by the title, partly by some what he read in it, he borrowed it and showed it to the cardinal. Thereupon the suitor was sent for to the cardinal, and examined of the book, and how he came

apon the wycked man's hede that he moste feared; for mr. Zowche was so ravyshed with the spryght of God, speakynge now aswell in the harte of the reader as fyrste in harte of the maker of the booke, that he was never well but when he was reedyng of that booke. Mrs. Gaynsforde wepte becawse she could not get the booke of her wower George Zouche, and as he was named so was he a zowche, a swheete

by it, and had like to have come into trouble about it, but that it having been found to have pertained to one of the queen's chamber, the cardinal thought better to defer the matter till he had broken it to the king first, in which meantime the suitor delivered the lady what had fallen out, and she also to the queen, who, for her wisdom knowing now what might grow thereupon, without delay went and imparted the matter to the king, and shewed him of the points that she had noted with her finger. And she was but newly come from the king, but the cardinal came in with the book in his hands to make complaint of certain points in it that he knew the king would not like of, and withal to take occasion with him against those that countenanced such books in general, and especially women, and, as might be thought, with mind to go further against the queen more directly if he had perceived the king agreeable to his meaning. But the king, that somewhat afore distasted the cardinal, as we have showed, finding the notes the queen had made, all turned the more to his ruin, which was also furthered on all sides." Upon this version of the story the following remarks have been made: "Wyatt represents the cardinal as bringing the book to the king to point out what he thought Henry would dislike, and to complain of those who countenanced such books. But this is obviously not irreconcileable with the account given in Foxe's (Louthe's) MS.; nor is the king's continued hostility to Tyndale incompatible with his being pleased for a time with a powerfully written book, pressed upon his notice by the lady Anne; nor yet with his clearly perceiving that the author had justly rebuked the inroads made upon the authority of princes by an usurping priesthood." (Doctrinal Treatises by Tyndale, edited for the Parker Society, by the Rev. Henry Walter, B.D., F.R.S., vol. i. p. 130.) The Rev. Christopher Anderson observes: "This incident therefore must in substance have occurred, although Foxe (*i. e.* Louthe) goes on to build far too much upon it. The words, in Henry's mouth, were probably nothing more than a compliment to the lady; or, at best, a transient feeling, similar to one of old, in the mind of king Herod towards John the Baptist. But be this as it might, Campeggio was off to Italy, and the sun of royal favour had set upon Wolsey for ever." (Annals of the English Bible, i. 220). Dr. D'Aubigné, in his History of the Reformation in England, book xx. chapter x. has availed himself of both versions of the story, and extended its detail to considerable length, interweaving various extracts from Tyndale's book, and throwing the whole into a dramatic narrative. It is also related in like manner in the Rev. James Anderson's "Ladies of the Reformation," 1855, where, at p. 76, is a well-designed sketch by J. Godwin, of Zouch snatching the book from the hands of mistress Gainsford.

well-favored gentylman in dede.[a]   And he was as ready to weepe to delyver the booke.

In lyke manner was I in Wykam's colleadg, when mr. Thomas Hardyng[b] delyvered me John Frythes Purgatory[c] to reade for two dayes; but I begged it and craved it for xxiij. dayes; by thys I lerned how lothe mr. Zouche was to delyver the cowntes' booke.

But see the happe, yea the providence of God: mr. Zowche standyng in the chappell afore doctor Sampson, ever reedyng apon thys

---

[a] In the absence of any other example of the word *zowche* in the sense apparently given by Louthe, the reader is offered the following extracts from Florio's Italian Dictionary, entitled "Queen Anna's New World of Words," 1611.

Zócco, a log, a block, a stocke, a stump.

Zúcca, any kind of gourd or pompion.

Zucchéro, any kind of sugar.

Zúgo, a gull or ninny; also a darling, a wanton, a minion.

The first was certainly a word adopted into the English language, and by the family of Zouch itself, for the stump of a tree or, branching vert, surmounted by a white falcon, was the principal device on the standard of John Zowche of Codnor, temp. Henry VIII. (Excerpta Historica, p. 315: see also John son and heir of the lord Zowche, p. 323.) But John Louthe's sense appears to resemble rather one of the other words.

[b] The following record of Harding's admission to Winchester college shows that he was born at Bickington in Devonshire about four years later than, from Anthony à Wood's account, is generally stated: "1528. Thomas Hardijng de Bekyngton xij. ann. in festo Annunc. præt. *In margine*, Canonicus, Thesaurarius Sarum. Theol. Professor." As a member of New college he graduated at Oxford, B.A. 1537, M.A. 1541, B.D. 1552, D.D. 1554, was made professor of Hebrew 1542, treasurer of Salisbury July 17, 1555, and deprived in 1 Elizabeth. After having been chaplain in the household of that great patron of the Protestants the duke of Suffolk, Harding returned to the church of Rome, and is remembered by the letter which the lady Jane addressed to him on his apostasy. He was also celebrated for his controversy with bishop Jewel, occasioned by the latter's "Apology for the Church of England": see Lowndes's Bibliographer's Manual. Harding died at Louvaine in 1572. See the memoir of him in Wood's Athenæ Oxon. (edit. Bliss,) i. 402, and Walcott's William of Wykeham and his Colleges, 1852, p. 397.

[c] "A Disputacion of Purgatory made by Jhon Frith," published at first without date, but it is supposed in 1532, the year during part of which Anne Boleyne was countess of Pembroke. The works of Tyndale, Frith, and dr. Robert Barnes, were edited by Foxe in 1573. There is a modern edition of the works of Tyndale and Frith by Thomas Russell, A.M. in 1831, 3 vols. 8vo.

booke, the deane never havyng hys eye of the booke, called the gentylman to hym, and snatched the booke owt of hys handes, axed his name, whose man he was, [and] delyvered it over d^{no} *Cardinali*. The countes axythe Gaynsforde for the booke. Gaynsforde on hur knees, &c. tolde all the circumstances. Shee was not sory, nor angry with either of them two, perceavyng therby that the yowng gentylman was coght with God's spryght (as mr. Harding sayde to me for cawse above rehersed). " Well, (sayd shee,) yt shalbe the deerest booke that ever the deane or cardynall tooke away." The noble woman goeth to the kynge; apon her knees she desyrythe the kynges helpe for hur booke. Apon the kynges token[a] the booke was restored. Now, bryngyng the booke to the kyng, she besowght his grace moste tenderly to reade the booke. The kyng redd and delyghted in the booke, " for, (saythe he,) thys booke ys for me and all kynges to reade." In lytle tyme the good kyng and faythfull servant of God, by the helpe of thys vertuous lady by meanes as yow here, hadd hys eyes opened to see the truthe, to serche the truthe, to avance God's religione and glory, to abhorre the pope's doctryne, hys lies, hys pompe and pryde, to delyver his subjectes owt of the Egyptione derkenes, the Babilonian bondage that the pope hadd browght hym and his subjectes unto. And so contempnyng the threttes of all the world, the power of pryncis, rebellyones of his subjectes at whome, and ragyng of so many and myghty potentates abroode, sett forwarde a

---

[a] When the king or other person in authority required a verbal command to be obeyed, he sent a "token," usually a signet ring, or one he was well known to wear. Of this custom two examples are supplied in the following passage of the history of John Frith. " The day before the day appointed for his execution, my lord of Canterbury (Warham) sent one of his gentlemen and one of his porters whose name was Perlebeame, a Welchman borne, to fetch John Frith from the Tower unto Croidon. This gentleman had both my lord's letters and *the King's ring* unto my lord Fitzwilliams, constable of the Tower, then lying in Canon rowe at Westminster in extreme anguish and paine of the strangullion, for the delivery of the prisoner. Master Fitzwilliams, more passionate than patient, understanding for what purpose my lord's gentleman was come, banned and cursed Frith and all other heretikes, saying, *Take this my ring* unto the lieutenant of the Tower, and receive your man your heretike with you, and I am glad that I am rid of him."

reformacione in religione, begynynge with the tryple-cornet a hedde fyrste, and so came downe to the members, bishoppes, abbettes, pryors, and suche lyke. Marke but the lyght occasyone of this reformatione, and the effectuall sequell, and ye muste neades say: That wych God hathe shaped muste neades be wroght.

Abissus multa juditia tua, Domine.

[The death of mr. Zouch, of Codnor castle in Derbyshire.]

Thys noble jentleman, lynially descended from the lord Gray of Codner castle,[b] hadd hys dayes cutt of and hys vertuous lyff shortened by the Maryane persequutione, for offycyall Woodcocke of Derbyshire sent owt proces for mr. Sowche, notwithstandyng hys age, imbeciletee, and worshyppe. So that he was (to save lyffe) compelled to flee to hys lordshyppe of Benefylde,[c] takyng Sandfordes howse, wych hadd to strayght roome for hys familye, wherby he colde not have hys accustomed order of dyett that he hadd at Codnere, wych was once a weeke (by my cownsell as he sayde) to swheate standyng by the fyer syde, wyth warme sheetes holden at

[a] The writer probably intended an equivocal expression, triple-crowned or triple-horned. Strype, Memorials, i. 113, has read it "triple-crowned."

[b] Codnor castle, in the parish of Heanor, nine miles from Derby, came to sir John Zouch, a younger son of William lord Zouch of Haringworth, in or about 1526, on the death of his wife's nephew Henry last lord Grey of Codnor. George Zouch esquire, who married Anne Gainsford, and is the subject of Louthe's anecdotes, was the son and heir of sir John. The Codnor estate was sold by sir John Zouch and John Zouch esquire his heir apparent in 1634. (Lysons, Derbyshire, p. 181.) In Wolley's Derbyshire collections is a record of the court of Exchequer, Mich. term 24 Hen. VIII. relating to the tenure of the manors of Hoo, Halstowe, and Aylesford, in Kent; Benningfield, co. Northampton; Codnor, co. Derby; and Weston-hay, co. Bedford, belonging to George Zouch esquire. (MS. Addit. Brit. Mus. 6698, art. 16.) Margaret Zouch, sister to George, was married to sir Robert Sheffield, and was mother of Edmund first lord Sheffield of Butterwick: see Topographer and Genealogist, 1846, i. 264.

[c] Benefield, near Oundle in Northamptonshire, also derived from the family of Grey to Zouch, sold by sir John Zouch temp. Eliz. to sir William Hatton. (Bridges's Northamptonshire, ii. 397.) Mr. Sandford was probably the tenant.

hys backe. And this was to hym in stede of a stowffe [a] called *Laconicum*. Therfor the good gentylman was enforsed to returne whom, for he fell sycke, and iij. of his chyldren, and many of his servantes; yet he hadd but xl. persones there; and in the way he dyed, or immedyatly at his commyng whom (home), I am uncerteyne. Wee parted at Ketlebee by Melton Moubrey, with suche cheere as those dysmole dayes required.

A lytle before hys goinge from Benefylde, I fyndyng there one Cooke, chapleyn in Lincolnes inne (*Edwardo regnante*), hyred now to say masse, knowing hym a lytle afore a detestore of the masse, I tolde hym my mynde veary hotely, beinge in my spryght coarcted, as Pawle was so to doo before many. Cooke hadd on hys syde a great man, as syr John Zowch knowyth; yet this good mr. George Zowch toke my parte, castyng no parells nor daunger, yt was to me a great comforte, but sayd that great man [b] yet lyvyng, Yow, Augustyne Bar.,[c] and suche other wyll make hym lose lyff and lyvynges

---

[a] *i.e.* a stove. Laconicum *sc.* balneum, a sudorific bath, a sweating-room. Cicero Attic. 4, 10, 2. Riddle's Latin-English Lexicon.

[b] May not this great man have been sir William Cecill, afterwards lord Burghley? whose timidity and temporizing in the reign of Mary form such a blemish in his illustrious career.

[c] Over this abbreviated name Strype has in the manuscript written "Barnes", but it is probable that the person intended was Augustine Bernhere, a Swiss who attached himself as a personal attendant on bishop Latimer, and was the editor of some of his works. "This Augustine (says Foxe) being a Dutchman, was Latimer's servant and a faithfull minister in the time of king Edward, and in queen Maries time a diligent attendant upon the Lord's prisoners." Side-note to Bradford's last letter to Bernher, which concludes thus, "The keeper telleth me, that it is death for any to speak with me, but yet I trust that I shall speak with you." See a note upon him in Bradford's Writings, (Parker Society,) vol. ii. p. 186: and see also the General Index to Strype's Works. Foxe, when describing a secret congregation of Protestants which was maintained in London throughout Mary's reign, says "they had divers ministers, first master Scamler, [afterwards bishop of Peterborough and Norwich,] then Thomas Foule, after him master Rough, then master Augustine Bernher, and last master Bentham," afterwards bishop of Lichfield and Coventry. Bernhere eventually became rector of Southam in Gloucestershire. By several of the letters of John Careles he is shown to have married Elizabeth, the sister of that martyr. "Note, that both these (Bernhere and his wife) departed in quiet peace, the one 1565, the other 1568." Side-note by Foxe.

all. In dede hys zeale and love to God's worde mayde hym lose no lesse.

Teste Jo. Loude.

Thus muche I thought expedient to intimate unto yow, mr. Foxe, havyng acquayntans with yow in Oxforde,[a] in Monjoy howse,[b] and Stepney.[c] The matter ys trew; as yow thynke good, ye may buylde ther one.

In an hystoriographer ys required asmuche as the ordinary othe requyryth of the exequutor of a testamente. " Ye shall swhear that as for your owne actes thys ys a trew testamente, and as for others' factes ye beleeve yt ys trew." That ys to say, in few, a cronicler settythe downe what he hath *aut ex propria scientia, hic fides postulatur; aut ex alieno auditu*, ther credulitce excusyth; wheryn yf some thynges be not trew yet the Lovaniall L. [d] may not ryghtly terme yt a lye, for it ys but an untrothe tolde, not made, of the penner. And so muche saith the Evangelyste,[e] Sieut nobis tradiderunt qui ab initio fuerunt ipsi ministri, et viderunt, &c. But John, speakyng *ex sua ipsius notitia*, wrytithe more confidently, viz. Quod vidimus, audivimus, prospeximus, which may be an answer to them for us bothe. Meum nomen celatum cupio, opto siquidem omnibus ignotus, mihi et Christo notus mori. Perge servire Christo ejusque ecclesiæ.

Tuus J. L. 1579.

The last sheet is directed on its back,
  To m^r Joh'n Foxe p'chere,
   At m^r Jo. Dayes printere.

---

[a] Foxe was admitted of Brazenose college in 1532, elected fellow of Magdalen in 1543, and expelled his fellowship for heresy in 1545.

[b] Probably the house of lord Mountjoy in London.

Perhaps in the mansion of the lord privy seal Cromwell.

[d] See before, p. 16.

[e] Luc. i. [2.]

II.

THE IMPRISONMENT OF JOHN DAVIS,
A BOY OF WORCESTER,
WRITTEN BY HIMSELF IN AFTER LIFE.

(MS. Harl. 425, f. 69.)

In the preceding paper, archdeacon Louthe has related the sufferings endured, for conscience sake, by a blind boy of Gloucester. The present is the history of the persecutions, for alleged heresy, of an offender of the same period of life, in the city of Worcester. John Davis was a lad of good parentage, a pupil in the grammar school, and likely to be the heir to his uncle Thomas Johnson, an apothecary: but the jealousy of Alice Johnson, his aunt, together with his early predilection for reading the new testament in his mother tongue, and his presumption in composing a ballad on the "shaven crowns," prematurely raised him a host of enemies. After a long and painful imprisonment, he would have incurred like the boy at Gloucester the last cruel penalty of cremation, under the merciless act of the Six Articles, had not the death of king Henry delivered him from his perilous position, together with so many more of the destined victims of the priesthood.

Foxe made use of this narrative, but condensed it into much shorter compass. His abridgment will be found in his edition of 1596, at p. 1879. No subsequent notice has been hitherto taken of the manuscript.

It was written whilst doctor Nicholas Bullingham was bishop of Lincoln, that is, within the period 1560—1570 (see p. 65); and it appears to have proceeded from the pen of John Davis himself, as Foxe says, when mentioning the trial with a candle, " yet *(as the party himselfe to me assureth)* felt no burning thereof." At the close Foxe adds of Davis,—" who is yet alive, and a profitable minister this day in the Church of England: blessed be the Lord, *qui facit mirabilia solus.*"

The yere of our Lorde 1546, and in the last yere of kinge Henrye the eight, in the citie of Worcester, was there a childe caled John Davis, of the age of twelve yeres and under, who dwelled with one mr. Johnson a pothicary, his ownckle, with whome allso dwelled

JOHN DAVIS, A BOY OF WORCESTER. 61

one Peter Goffe, prentice, whiche in the tyme of the vi. Articles woulde reade the testament in Inglish, and such godlye bookes as he then coulde gett. His mistris manye tymes hering hym so reade would moste sharplie revile him, for she was then and is still to this daye an obstinate papist. At length she disclosed the same to one of her secte and affinite, a jolye stowte champion, indewed with more riches then wisdome or godlie zeale; and thus consulting together theye invented, with their adherents the canons of the cathederall churche, with the chauncelour that tyme being, whose name was Johnson,[a] chauncelor to docter Heath then bishopp of Woorcetour, to intrap and snare the sayde Peter, yf theye might by anye meanes heare hym or see hym with having anye testament or other godly booke; but he, perceyving their purpose, kept him sellf owt of their danger; notwithstanding, to urge hym, this worthie wise man Thomas Parton would reade openlie in the streat, sytting at his dore or ells lening at his shopp window, that all men passing by might hear, a booke [b] named *The hunting of the hare with curres and bandoges*, a trym tragedie dowbtles, and more estemed with the pope's champions then the bible or booke of the Lorde. But when he perceived he coulde not apprehend the saide Peter to hurte hym, he woulde sometyme thretin hym that, yf he caught him reding suche bookes as he harde saye he did reade by the confession of his mistres, that he would make him twine or untwine; but his threatninges prevailed him not, for he was sircomspecte, and kept him owt of their bloody fingers.

[a] Robert Johnson.

[b] This book or pamphlet has not been traced, but it seems to have been a parody or reply to doctor William Turner's *Hunting of the Romish Fox*, published in 1543, under the pseudonym of William Wraughton : the popularity of which appears not only from Turner's subsequent publications of *The Rescuyng of the Romish Fox*, 1545; *The huntyng of the Romyshe Wolfe* (after 1553); and *The hunting of the Fox and Wolfe, because they did make havoc of the sheep of Jesus Christ* (see Athenæ Oxon. edit. Bliss, i. 363, and the memoir of Turner in Hodgson's Northumberland, II. ii. 456); but also from bishop Bale's *Yet a course of the Romish Foxe*, 1543, published under the name of Johan Harrison (see Herbert's Ames, iii. 1554).

Notwithstanding, their thirst coulde not be quenched withowt blood; by meane whereof they shortly invented a newe interprise, and, bycawes the spite that Alice Johnson bare to John Davis her husband's next kinsman, to whome shee supposed the saide Thomas Johnson her housband woulde leave some porcion of his goodes, having no child as it was like, for God had made her barren, and he had no other kinsman (as he would often saye) in all the wourld, whiche increased the more the deadly hate of his wyf; for she never loved him, bicawes her housband so tendered him, and that appered at the death of the sayd Thomas Johnson, for she cawsed her housband to revoke that hee did give him by will, either being past memorye or ells specheles,—a good note of her love.

But shortlie after these papestes attempted to bringe their longeloked purpose to passe, by one Alice wife to Nicholas Organmaker alias Brooke, and Oliver their sonne, that the said Oliver should fawne freendshipp of the saide John Davis, as thowghe hee weare verye desirous and joyfull of his company; manye tymes saieng, " I woulde wee had some good Inglish bookes to reade; for my mother cannot abide this pilde pristes nor their popish service; but had I good bookes I coulde please her well to reade everye night." Then said John Davis, "I will bringe a booke with me;" and so he did bringe a testament, and reade unto them. Then they requested him to leve the booke behinde hym; but he said the booke was not his, neyther could he so doe. Then thei requested him to tell them what abuses weare in the Churche, and howe hee did like the vj. Articles; and he breeflie toulde them what he thowght; " but I cannot now tarye (saide hee) least I be shent." Then thei sayd, " Bicawes ye shoulde avoyd blame for comyng hether, wright your mynde." But hee sayd, " I have no suche leisour, nor place; yet would I gladly do yt to doe you good; but to-morow I shall to Peryewood feeldes to gather eyebright[a] to still, and yf Oliver and you will gather for me, I will wright all my mynde." And they agreed so to doe.

[a] Eyebright does not appear to be noticed in doctor William Turner's Herball. In that by John Gerarde, chapter 216 treats "OF EYE-BRIGHT. *Euphrasia*, or Eyebright, is a small

And on the morow every one of them, according to ther promyse made, mett in the fieldes, and the sayd John Davis did wright his hoole mynde uppon the Sixe Articles, and made them allso a ballet caled, *Come downe, for all your shaven crowne.*

But at lengthe this longe-hiddin conspiracie burst owte, for incontinent this woman within one half howre she browght this wrighting to the sayd Parton; and the sayd Thomas Parton disclozed the same to the chauncelour and regester and other pristes; which laide their heads together, and towlde them howe they might bringe their pourpose to pass; and cawsed the sayd Thomas Johnson his ownckle to be their instrument to trye whether yt were his hand or no; and he, under the coulour of friendshipp, came to the sayd childe saieng, " I have kept the at the gramer skoole a great while, and am minded to have you to keepe the shopp, for your aunte is not in quiet with Peter bicawes of his bookes, wherefore I must putt hym awaye; but before I soe doe let me see how you can wright." So he tooke penn and paper, and wrote these verses folowing—

Of all treasur cunning is the flower.
Loke uppon Diogenes whiche was both wyse and sad,
To obtayne this treasur Cunninge what labour that he had.

---

low herbe not above two handfuls high, full of branches, covered with little blackish leaves, dented or snipt about the edges like a saw: the flowers are small and white, sprinkled and powderd on the inner side, with yellow and purple specks mixed therewith. The root is small and hairie. This plant grows in dry medows, in green and grassie wayes and pastures standing against the sunne. Eye-bright beginnith to floure in August and continueth unto September, and must be gathered while it flowreth for physick's use. . It is very much commended for the eyes. Being taken it selfe alone, or any way else, it preserves the sight, and being feeble and lost it restores the same." Then several prescriptions are given, concluding thus : " Three parts of the powder of eye-bright and one part of maces mixed therewith, taketh away all hurts from the eyes, comforteth the memorie, and cleareth the sight, if halfe a spoonfull be taken every morning fasting with a cup of white wine." (Gerarde's Herball, 1633, p. 663.) Drayton describes the gathering of eyebright:

" And in some open place, that to the sun doth lye,
He fumitorie gets, and eyebright for the eye."—Polyolbion, Song 13.

And Milton alludes to it under its more learned name—
—— " Then purg'd with *euphrasy* and rue

So hee (the uncle) toke this wrighting, and went to these papists. But whether he (John Davis) knewe,[a] but the first newes that he harde was earlye in the morning his ownkle bid him make cleane the stable in the Leche street,[b] and hee asked leve to gather herbes, but hee sayd, "Naye, there are inowghe to still this two daies of yesterdaies gathering; wherefore get you to the stable." And he obeyed hym, knowing his faete was browght to light, and that no good was ment to him, but trouble. But he no sooner entered the stable but the boye Oliver cam after hym saieng, "John Davis, I praye you reade this same wrighting once or twice over, that I maye learne to reade it to my mother perfectlie." But he, perceiving his Judas-like trick, sayde, "Get the hence! I must doe my busynes." But he was so importune in requesting that he could not bee ridd of him. Then stept he into a litle howse, and there he spied Thomas Parton and his ownckle Johnson standing under a wall harkening, thinking to have taken them reding the foresayd wrighting; but when he perceyved their trechery, "Have thie mother and thou dealt thus Judasly with me? Take this for thie paynes;" and lent him two or thre blowes with a brome; and he cryed. Then came theye in running, saying, "What is the matter?" Then sayd Oliver, "Mr. Johnson, I woulde have had your boye to have reade this wrighting whiche he made yesterday, and hee woulde not." Then sayd Parton, "What wrighting is that? let me see." But Parton knew yt right well; but sayd so for a cullor. Then did theye force John Davis to reade the same before them. Then sayde Parton, "Neighbour Johnson, yee have well bestowed your money to bring upp suche an herytique, so yonge as hee is." Then sayd Johnson, "I loked for joye of him, having no childe of myn owne, nor kinsman that I knowe; but nowe he shall have as he hathe deserved." And so Parton laide handes on him; and his ownckle

[a] A syncopised phrase signifying that a person more than suspected what he did not positively know.

[b] "So called from its having for many ages been the only accessible approach to the cemetery of the cathedral, by which the dead were brought thither for interment." Green's History of Worcester, 1796, 4to. ii. 4.

bownde his armes behinde hym, and browght hym to the towle-shopp,ᵃ in the citie of Worcetour, mr. Dooding and mr. Richard Dedicote being bayliffes ᵇ till the next Mighellmas after.

Then was he commaunded to the freeman's prison; at whiche tyme one Richard Howbrough, brother-in-law to Richard Bullingham, which Bullingham ᶜ is brother to the reverend father in God Nicholas bishopp of Linkcolne,ᵈ being keper of the prison, cam abowght nyne of the clock as the custum was to see their prisoners saffe, and sayd merely, " Thou hoorson, how wilt thow doe? they will burne the." And he sayd, " They can do no more than God will suffer them." " Tush! (sayde he) prove by the candle ᵉ how thou canst abide the fire." And he did soo, sayeing, " I am not affraide of the fire." And so he helde his finger a good space, the other holding the candle, not willing to hurt him; till at length with admyracion he sayde,

ᵃ This was evidently the town-hall or head-quarters of the municipal government, apparently deriving its name from being the office for collecting toll. The more ordinary term for such places in olden times was *toll-booth*, and sometimes, the *tolsey*.

ᵇ William Dodington and Richard Dabitote, bailiffs in 1545, according to the list given in Nash's History of Worcestershire, vol. ii. Appx. p. cxii. But the name of the former was doubtless Dodding, as it is given ibid. under 1543, when he was lower bailiff: and there was a Thomas Dodding bailiff in 1558, 1562, and 1564. The other, whose name was probably Dabitote (after the ancient Worcestershire family of d'Abitot), was senior bailiff in 1547. A Humphrey Debitote occurs bailiff in 1518 and 1521.

ᶜ Richard Bullingham was lower bailiff of Worcester in 1561, and upper bailiff in 1563. A Thomas Bullingham had filled those offices in 1528 and 1530.

ᵈ Nicholas Bullingham was born in Worcester; educated at Oxford; was consecrated bishop of Lincoln 1559, and translated to the see of his native city in 1570. He died in 1576, and was buried in the cathedral, where his monument remains, with a demi-effigy, as described in Green's History of Worcester, i. 154, and engraved in Dr. Thomas's Survey, 1737, 4to. p. 41. See a memoir of bishop Nicholas Bullingham in Wood's Athenæ Oxon. edit. Bliss, ii. 813. There was also a John Bullingham, bishop of Gloucester 1581—1596, and previously prebendary of Worcester, whose memoir is ibid. col. 862.

ᵉ This test was not unusual. One of Foxe's cuts represents Bilney burning off the forefinger of his right hand, on the day before his submission to the fire at Norwich. Another exhibits bishop Bonner burning with a candle the hand of Thomas Tomkins, whose body soon after was burned in Smithfield. In a third, Edmund Tyrrell, of Colchester, is burning in like manner the hand of one Rose Allin; and in the same place bishop Bonner is stated to have forcibly closed the hand of a third person upon a live coal.

CAMD. SOC. K

"Felest thow not the heate?" and he sayde, "No;" but he woulde skarse beleve him till he had loked, and sawe he was not so muche as skorched. So he locked the dores, sayeing, "God night."

Shortly after there came another prisoner unto the same prisone, for what cawes he knewe not; but it fortuned, the prisone being half timbred or rather better, some of the clay of the wall was falen; so that this prisoner sayd to the keeper, "This heritique boye hath broken the wall to steall owte;" by meanes wherof he was put in an inner prison caled the peep-hole, but yet without irons, untill Mighelmas; till one Robert Yowle [a] was chosen lowe-baylef, a joly Catholik, whiche quicklie bestowed his charite uppon him, laieng on a payer of bolts that he coulde not lifte up his small legs, but lening on a staff slipp them forward uppon the grownde, the beneffete whereof is an extreame colde in his anckles to this daye, whiche he shall cary to his grave. Moreover he was fayne to lye on the colde grownd, in those boltes, having not so muche as a lock of strawe nor clothe to cover him withall, but two shippeskins. Furthermore, one Feerefilde, a waker,[b] coming nightlie throwgh the guilde-hall to go to the prive, as he sayd, woulde come and call this child at the hold, whether of his owne mynde or sett on by some other papest he knewe not, but these weare his woordes, "Whie doste thow not recant? thow wilt be feared one tyme or other, as I have, by robing the devill, which

---

[a] Richard Gowle in Nash's list (Hist. of Worc. Appx. p. cxii), but no doubt in error, for under the name of Robert Youle he occurs as higher bailiff two years later, for 1548; and again in 1552 and 1559.

[b] It must not be supposed that this was a watchman, or a particularly wakeful gentleman, who took nightly walks instead of lying in bed; but the writer means the occupation which is commonly written *walker*, that is, a fuller, or dresser and finisher of cloth. Worcester was at this period a great clothing town. Leland says, "The wealth of the towne of Worcester standeth most part by drapering, and no towne in England, at this present tyme, maketh so many clothes yearly as this towne doth." (Itin.) In 1590 queen Elizabeth, "at the humble petition of our wellbeloved of the misteryes or faculties of weavers, walkers, and clothiers of our cittie of Worcester," granted them a charter of incorporation, of which Rowland Berkeley, citizen and weaver, was nominated the first master, and two weavers and two walkers the first wardens: see it printed in Green's History of the city, vol. ii. Appendix, No. xvi.

is like a raged colte, whiche hath ledd me abowght this hall all night or now, and at length lawgh me to skorne, and sayd *howgh hoo.*"[a]

Others would come and say, " Thow shalt be burned, thow heretique, this weke," and " that weke," " this daye " and " to-morow." Furthermore nether mother nor none of his kinn that durst come at him.

At length, to ease his payne, theye put into the same prison to him, to beare him company bicawes he was alone, one attaynted of treason, caled William Taylour, being a mad-man and owt of his wittes; who in his frontique fittes would many tymes profer to thrust him in with a knyf whiche the sayd madman had to cutt his meate withall.

Moreover, there came two pristes, canons of the cathedcrall churche, the one called Jolyf,[b] the other mr. Yewer.[c] To them was browght his wrighting against the Six Articles, and his ballet called *Come downe*, which after they harde yt reade, and had resoned with him, they burst owte in a pelting chaf, sayeing, " Hathe disclosed the in tyme, being such a ranck heritique at this age; but God hath cut the of, else hadest thow bene the notablest herytique in all christindome." Thus in a great fury, threatning fier and fagot, and that shortly, they departed. Whether thei ware sent to [d] the bishopp or no he knewe not, but shortly after mr. Johnson the chauncelor sate in the guildhall uppon the said John, and there were browght in his accusers and were sworne; and 24 men were sworne and went on his quest, and fownd him gilty; but he never cam before the chauncelor. This did he to make all things in a redines against the comyng of the judges, that there might be no delay, but spedye execution; for the whiche cawes sake he was sent to the common jayle,[a] and there did lye amonge theves and murtherers; but God prevented their poorpos, and toke awaye kinge Henrye the eight owt of the troblesom woorlde. Yet notwithstanding he was araigned, being holden upp in a man's armes at the barr; the judges being Portman[b] and Marven,[c] which when they perceived that they coulde not burne him, woulde have had him presently whipped.

Then stept upp John Bourne then esquire,[d] and sayd, "And please you, my Lordes, he hathe bene sore inowghe whipped allredy." Thus had he no farther troble; saving he laye in pryson a weke after. Many woulde have had him awaye from the barr, and especially a priste; but the sayd John Bourne toke him whome (home), and the gentlewoman his wyf did anoynte his legges her owne selfe with oyntment, which leges were styf and numbde by reson of the irons, for he laye in prison from the 14. of August till within 7 daies of Ester. And the said mr. Bourne travailed to bringe him to beleve in the sacrament, sayeing it was Christes verye flesh and blood in fourme of bread; for, yf Christ sayd he should have given us his bodye rawe in fleshe and blood, we shoulde have abhorde yt. But at lengthe sayd his wyf, "Let us put awaye this herytique, least he mare my sonne Anthony."

Moreover, in the dayes of queene Marye he was accused by six protestantes; and so constrayned to depart the contry, traveling painfully unknown to any; and solde his patrimony, which God had sent him by his parentes, to releve him in that tyme of necessite; to the which provident God be all honour and glory for ever!

Muche more myght be spoken of his last troble but for breveties sake.

[a] This was in the Foregate, at Worcester: his former prison at the toll-shop or guildhall.
[b] Sir William Portman, a judge of the King's bench 1547, afterwards chief justice.
[c] Sir Edward Mervyn, a judge of the King's bench 1541.
[d] Afterwards sir John Bourne, secretary of state: who will figure more conspicuously in Underhill's Autobiography hereafter. He resided at Battenhall near Worcester.

III.

MARTYRDOM OF EDWARD HORNE
AT NEWENT IN 1558.
[MS. Harl. 425, fol. 121.]

THE following paper was written in correction of a statement which thus appears in Foxe's first edition, 1563, fol. +1546:

" Jhon Horne. And a woman. Martyrs. September 25. (1556.)

" Nowe not long after the death of the said youngman at Bristow, in the same manner wer ii. mo godly martirs consumed by fire at Wutton underhedge in Glocestershier, whose names are above specified, which died very gloriously in a constant fayth, to the terror of the wicked, and comforte of the godly. So graciously dyd the Lorde worke in them, that death unto them was lyfe, and lyfe with a blotted conscience was death."

If the corrections now given proceeded from sound information, Foxe was wrong not only in the christian name of Horne, but in the year of his death; which appears to have been 1558 instead of 1556. The 25th September, 1558, would have been rather less than "eight weeks" before queen Mary's death, on the 17th of November.

Who mr. John Deighton, the writer, was we do not know: but Strype (Eccles. Memorials, iii. 463) supposes him to have been "a worthy minister in those parts."

WHERAS in the last edition of mr. Fox his famous works caled *the booke of Martyrs*, as likewise in all the former editions, there is mention made of one John Horne and a woman that suffered martyrdome for the testimony of their faith at Wotton-under-Edge in Gloucestershere, let it be knowne that the matter is mistaken through the default of those that made the certificate for mr. Fox out of the registers of Gloucester or Worcester; for it cannot be proved that any such person or woman suffered at Wotton aforesaide. But it is true that one Edward Horne suffered martyrdome at Newente in the said diocesse, and was burnt there in a place caled the Court Orchard nere the churchyard; and his wife was condemned with him, but she recanted and refused to suffer with him. I have bine at the place and spake with one or ij of the same parish that did se him there burnt, and do testifie that at his death he sunge the 146. psalme, untill that his lipps were burnt away, and then they sawe his tonge move untill he fell downe in the fier. They of the parish do say they knowe the ij persons that made the fier to burne him, and they weare ij glovers or fell-mongers, whose names I have in my note-booke. He was executed about viij weekes before queene Mary died.

The sonne of this martyr is now livinge in the same parish, and caled Christopher Horne, an honest poore man, beinge about 78 or 79 yeres, and borne in queene Maries tyme, about a quarter of a yere before his father suffered. His mother, that promised to suffer with hir husband and recanted after she was condemned, was after married to one Whocke of the parish of Teynton, within a myle or 2 of Newent, where her first husband was borne; *et hoc ex relatione ejusdem Christopheri Horne,*

By me JOHN DEIGHTON.

I wish for the reverence I beare to the memory of Mr. Fox, whose person and place of dwelling I knew, and the honor and love I beare to his works, that this smale error, which is none of his, weare amended.

IV.

AUTOBIOGRAPHICAL NARRATIVE OF THOMAS HANCOCK,
MINISTER OF POOLE.

[MS. Harl. 425, fol. 124.]

This narrative is preserved among the papers communicated to Foxe, but he made no use of it. Strype has given some extracts in his Ecclesiastical Memorials, vol. ii. book i. chapter 9; vol. iii. chapters 7 and 66; and others in his Memorials of Cranmer, book ii. chapters 7 and 26.
Thomas Hancock took the degree of bachelor of arts at Oxford in 1532. (Wood's Fasti Oxon. edit. Bliss, i. 51.) He was afterwards one of the exiles at Geneva. The present narrative is imperfect; and his history after his return to England in Elizabeth's reign has not been recovered.

The laste yeare of the regne of king Henry the 8th, I, Thomas Hancock, master of artes and curate of Amporte,[a] *dioces. Wintonie,* was suspended *a celebratione divinorum* by doctor Raynold,[b] who yet levith, than comissary under doctor Steward, who was than chanseller to bisshop Gardner, they leying too my charge the breache of the Six Articles, by cawse I tawghte owtt of 9 *cap. Hebreorum* thatt owre Savior Christ entered once into the holy place, by whych he optayned unto siners everlasting redemption; that he once suffered; and that his body was once offered to take away the sinnes off many people; and thatt one only oblation suffised for the sinnes of the hole wordle.

[a] Amport, 4½ miles from Andover, Hants.
[b] Robert Reynolds, LL.D , prebendary of Lincoln 1555, Winchester 1558, died 1595.

The first yere of the regne of king Edward 6., I, the sayde Thomas, having licence of bisshop Cranmore, preched at Christchurche Twinham, *in comit. Sowthe.*, where I was borne, mr. Smythe vicar of Christchurche and bachyller of divinite being present; where I, taking my place owt of the 16. S^t. John, v. 8, *Spiritus sanctus arguet mundum de peccato, de justitia, quia vado ad Patrem,* &c. Heyre dothe owr Savior Christ saye that he goeth to the Father, and that we shalle se him no more. The prist being than at mas, I declared wnto the people that that the prist dothe holde over his head they dyd see with their bodily eyes, but our Savior Christ dothe heyre say plainly that we shal se him no more; than yow that doo kuele unto hytt, pray unto hyt, and honor hytt as God, doo make an idol of hytt, and yowre selves doo commyte moste horrible idolatry. Wherat the sayde vicar mr. Smythe, sytting in hys chayre in the face of the pulpett, spake thes wordes: "Mr. Hancocke, yow have done well untyll nowe, and nowe have you played an yll kowse parte, whych whan she hathe geven a good messe of mylke overthroweth all wyth her fote; and soo all ys lost;" and wyth thes wordes he gote hym owtt of the churche.

The first yere all soo of kyng Edward I all soo preched in St. Thomas churche att Salisbury, doctor Oking [a] chawnselar too bishop Kapeu and doctor Steward [b] chawnselar too bishop Gardner being present, with divers others of the clergy and laytye. My place [c] being *Omnis plantatio quam non plantavit Pater meus cœlestis eradicabitur.* By the whych place I inveyed agaynst the superstitius cæremonies, as holy brode, holywater, images, coopes, vestments, &c.

---

[a] Robert Oking, D.C.L. at Cambridge 1534, chancellor first of Bangor and afterwards of Sarum, archdeacon of Salisbury 1547: see Athenæ Cantabrigienses, i. 197. He was presented to the rectory of Collingbourne Ducis, co. Wilts, by Edward earl of Hertford, in 1545, and held it until 1554. (Hoare's South Wiltshire.)

[b] Edmund Steward, D.C.L. at Cambridge 1541; chancellor first of Norwich and afterwards of Winchester; dean of Winchester 1553-4; died 1559: see Athenæ Cantabrig. i. 265.

[c] Matt. xv. 13.

and att the laste agaynst the idoll of the alter, proving hytt to be an idoll, and no God, by the first of St. John's gospel,[a] *Deum nemo unquam,* &c., with other places of the olde testament; " but that the prist holdeth over hys heade yow doo se, you knele before hytt, yow honor hytt and make a idoll of hytt, and yow yowr selves are moste horrible idolaters:" whereatt the docters and sartayne of the clargie wentt owtt of the church, I chargynge them thatt they were nott of God, by cawse they refused too heyre the word of God. The sermon being ended, the mayore, mr. Thomas Chaffen,[b] came unto me, layinge too my charge a proclamacion, in the whyche was commandement geven thatt we shulde geve no necname wntoo the sacrament,[c] as *rownd Robin,* or *Jack in the box;* wertoo I awnswered thatt hytt was noo sacrament, but an idoll, as they doo wse hytt.

[a] John i. 18.

[b] Thomas Chafyn was mayor of Salisbury in 1547 and Christopher Chafyn in 1550. In 1557 mr. Thomas Chafyn the younger is mentioned; and in 1565 Thomas Chafyn was one of the gentry of Salisbury with goods valued at 180*l.*, being the second person in the town in point of wealth. History of Salisbury (Hoare's South Wiltshire), pp. 274, 696, 812.

[c] " Also this same time (Jan. 1547-8) was moche spekyng agayne the sacrament of the auter, that some callyd it *Jacke of the Boxe,* with divers other shamfulle names; and there was made a proclamacyon agayne shoche (such) sayers, and it (yet) bothe the prechers and others spake agayne it, and so contynewyd." (Chronicle of the Grey Friars of London, p. 55.) An original copy of this proclamation is preserved in the collection of the Society of Antiquaries. It is dated the 27th Dec. 1547, and was made in pursuance of " a good and godly acte and estatute (made in the recent session of parlement) against those who doeth contempne, despise, or with unsemely and ungodly woordes deprave and revyle the holy sacramente of the body and blood of our Lorde, commonly called *the sacrament of the Aultar.*" The statute is 1 Edw. VI. cap. 1. Statutes of the Realm, 1819, iv. 2.

Bishop Coverdale, in the preface to his translation of Calvin's Treatise on the Last Supper, has this passage : " I will speak no more as concerning their fond inventions about the ministration of this most blessed sacrament, lest I should be thereby an offence or stumbling-block to the weak brothers, whose consciences are not yet fully satisfied as concerning the true belief of this holy mystery : I mean, lest I should give them occasion to do as certain fond talkers have of late days done, and at this present day do invent and apply to this most holy sacrament names of despite and reproach, as to call it *Jack in the box* and *Round Robin,* and such other not only fond but blasphemous names." (Coverdale's Works, Parker Soc. p. 426.) In the last examination of bishop Ridley, before the queen's commissioners, Sept. 30, 1555, referring to a sermon which he had delivered at Paul's cross, (the precise date of which does not appear,) he said, " You shall understande there

74   NARRATIVES OF THE REFORMATION.

Att thatt tyme was one Huntte and Richard Whyghtt [a] commytted to the gayle for such cawse by doctor Geffery,[b] who was chawnsler too byshop Capon,[c] and soo wolde the maior all soo have committed me too the gayle, had nott six honest men ben bownde for me thatt I sholde awnser att the next syses.

Whan I came to the sises, syr Michel (Richard) Lister [d] being lord chefe justice, wylled me too have sertayne to be bownde for me that I shold nott goo before the king in his procedings. I makyng not haste too gett me sewarties, my lord chefe justice called upon me very earnestly that I shold get sum too be bownde for me. The bisshop sitting att the bench, I requested him thatt, forasmuch as my troble was for the worde of God, that he and hys chaplyn, on(e)

were at Paules, and divers other places, fixed railing billes against the sacrament, terming it *Jacke of the Boxe*, the *Sacrament of the Halter*, *Round Robin*, with like unsemely termes; for the whiche causes I, to rebuke the unreverend behaviour of certaine evil-disposed persones, preached as reverently of that matter as I might." (Foxe, edit. 1576, p. 1650.)

[a] Foxe, under the year 1558, gives at considerable length "The story and condemnation of John Hunt and Richard White, ready to be burnt, but by the death of Q. Mary escaped the fire." In a side-note Foxe remarks, "Rich. White, now vicar of Malbrough in Wilshire:"—See an additional note in the Appendix.

[b] William Geffrey, or Jeffrey, D.C.L. 1540, sometime principal of St. Edward's hall and afterwards of Bradgate hall, Oxford, archdeacon of Northampton 1549, chancellor of Salisbury 1552-3; died 1558. "Not long before the death of queen Mary dyed doctor Capon, bishop of Salisbury. About the which tyme also followed the unprepared death of doctour Geffrey, chancellour of Salisbury, who in the midst of his buildings, sodainly being taken by the mighty hand of God, yelded his lyfe, which hadde so little pittye of other men's lyves before. Concerning whose crueltye partly mention is made before [in the case of Hunt and White]. As touching moreover this foresayde chancellour, here it is to be noted, that he departing upon a Saterday, the next day before the same he hadde appoynted to call before him 90 persons, and not so fewe, to examine them by inquisition, had not the goodnes of the Lord, and his tender providence, thus prevented him with death, providing for his poore servauntes in tyme."—Foxe, "God's punishment upon Persecutors."

[c] John Capon, alias Salcot, who having been successively abbat of St. Benet Hulme, and of Hyde by Winchester, was made bishop of Bangor 1533, and of Salisbury 1539. He died 1557. See his memoirs in Athenæ Cantabrigienses, i. 171.

[d] The lord chief justice of the common pleas was sir Richard (not sir Michael) Lyster. See in the Winchester volume of the Archæological Institute, 1846, a memoir by Sir Frederick Madden on sir Richard Lyster's monument and effigy in St. Michael's church, Southampton, which had been attributed to lord chancellor Wriothesley. Sir Richard's son and heir was sir Michael Lyster; he died in August 1561, before his father. See

master Reve,ᵃ wolde be bownde for me. My lorde chefe justice rebuked me by cawse I chose my sewartis ᵇ owt of the benche, saying thatt yf he wolde be my sewertye he wold nott take hym. Soo I stode styll, nott sekyng any to be bownde for me; werat my lord was nott very well pleased, and sayde unto me, " Why seke you nott summe too be bownde for yow?" I awnseryd that I knew nott too whome too speake.

There was present a wollen-draper, on Hary Dymoke, who asked my lord what the band was, who awnswered on hundred powndes. He sayde agayne, that a hundred of them wold be bownd in an hundred pownde for me; another sayde that a thowsand of them wold be bownd in 1000 pownde for me; wherat my lorde rebuked me, saying: " Se what an wpproare yow make among the people." I sayd wnto him: " I pray yow, my lord, lay no such thyng to my charge; I stand before yow, and store nott; hytt ys God that moveth ther harttes thus too speak; I prayse his name for hytt." Than dyd my lorde agayne enter talke wyth th'above named Hary Dymoke; and asked hym whether ten of (them) wold be bownd in an cˡⁱ., for yf an hundereth shold be bownde in an hundred pounde, the names then wold occupy more inke and papyr than the obligation. Hary Dymoke aunsered that I had no rewle of my selfe in that place,ᶜ and thatt they thowghtt thatt I wold breake the band, whych yf I sholld, hytt wold greve them too forfytt x li. apece, but in thatt qwarell to forfet xx s.ᵈ apece hytt wold never greve them. So was the first

---

Machyn's Diary, p. 8, where, by a like confusion as here, the son is called sir Richard. In addition to Sir F. Madden's pedigree it may be remarked that the first wife of the lord chief justice was Jane, daughter of Ralph Sherley of Wiston, in Sussex, and widow of sir John Dawtrey, of Moorhouse in Petworth. (Stemmata Shirleiana, 4to. 1841, p. 145.) Also that the wife of his grandson, the daughter of lord chancellor Wriothesley, was married *first* to William Shelley of Michelgrove: see Machyn's Diary, p. 273.

ᵃ *i. e.* probably, the bailiff of the bishop, (who might also be his chaplain.) who " for a long series of years took precedency of the mayors of the city." History of Salisbury, (Hoare's Wiltshire,) p. 698: where a list of bailiffs is given, but it does not name the officer at this period. ᵇ Sureties.

ᶜ Strype here inserts " *i. e.* the pulpit." The meaning seems to be that Hancock held no benefice or other authorised place or appointment in Salisbury.

ᵈ Misprinted " xx pound " by Strype, Ecclesiastical Memorials, ii. 73.

band discharged, and my lorde bownd x. of them in x li. and my self was bownd in 90 li.

Thys done, I ryd from Salesbury unto my lorde off Somersett hys grace, who lay at thatt (tyme) at Syan. I reqwested hys grace thatt I mowghtt have hys letter for the discharge of them thatt were bownde for me: he cawsed my lord treasurer hys honor that now ys, whoo than was master of the reqwestes,[a] to wryt to my lorde chefe justice for the discharge of the band; wych letter, whylst I was wyth my lorde att Hampton [b] too deliver, the bell rong too the sermon. My lorde asked me whether I mynded too preach? I awnsered yea. My lorde sayd unto me that Hampton was a haven towne, and that yf I shold teache such doctrine as I tawght at Sarum the towne wold be divided, and soo sholde hytt be a way or a gapp for the enemy to enter in, and therfor he commawnded me that I shold nott preache ther. I awnswered thatt I wold not take thatt for a forbiddyng, butt that forsomuch as the people resorted too the church att the ringyng of the bell too heyre the worde of God, they shold nott returne whome (home) agayne voyd of God's word. My lorde sayde agayne unto me thatt I shold not preache, and thatt ther was on in the Tower (meanyng bysshopp Gardnar) that he wold beleve before 400 such as I was. I awnsered hym thatt he spake those words betwyxt him and me, but, yf I had record of them, he wold nott speake them. Soo my lorde sent for the mayor and hys bretherne. Mr. maior asked me whether I wolde be content that an other shold supply the rome for me? I awnsered yea; and thatt I was as wylling too heyre the word as to preach my self. Soo dyd mr. maior send too on mr. Gryffeth, who dyd preache; and my lorde being present, he chalenged him that he, being chefe justice of the law[c], dyd suffer the images in the churche, the idoll hangyng in a string over the alter, candlestikes and tapers on them wppon the alter, and the people honoring the idoll, contrary too the law; wyth much other good doctrine. I praysed God for hytt. And thus

---

[a] William Cecill (afterwards lord Burghley).   [b] *i. e.* Southampton.
[c] Misprinted "land" in Strype, Eccles. Memorials, ii. 73.

were my frends of Sarum thatt were bownde for me discharged there band.

Thys troble being overcum, an other foloweth; for, after thys, I was called the same yeare, whych was the first yeare of kyng Edward, to be the minister of God's word at the town of Pole, *in comit.* Dorset, whych town was at the time welthy, for they enbraced God's word, they were in favors with the rewlars and governors of the realme, they were the first thatt in thatt parte of England were called Protestantes; they dyd love one an other; and every one glad of the company of the others; and soo God powred his blessing plentifully wpon them; but now, I ham sory too sett my pen too wryte hytt, they have becum pooer, they have no love to God's word, they lacke the favor and frendshop of the godly rewlars and governors to defend them; they fall from there profession; they hate one another, one can not abyd the company of the other, but they are divided emongst them sellves; butt, O Lord God, heavenly Father! which workest all things for the best unto thine elect and chosen, and arte a God of mercy and long suffering, suffer nott that towne of Poole, yf hytt be thy good wyll, too cum to dessolation; butt, mercifull God, who haste the hartes of all men in thine bandes, and dost turne them whom thow wylltt turne, geve them hartes to repent, and powre thy blessings uppon them thatt they may embrace thy word, thatt they may be nott only heyrers butt obedientt folowers and doers of the same, thatt they may love one another, and soo powre uppon them thy blessings, thatt they may cum nott to a worse butt to a better state, for thy dear son Christ Jhesu's sake, our only mediator and advocate!

I being the minister of God's worde in that towne of Poole, preching the word uppon sume sunday in the mouthe of Juli, inveyed agaynst idolatry and covetousnes, taking my place owtt of the 6th of Timothy, *Deus immortalis est, et lucem habitat inaccessibilem, quem nemo hominum vidit sed nec videre potest.* The bryghtnes of the Godhed ys such thatt hytt passeth the bryghtnes of the sun, of aungells, and all creatures; soo thatt hytt cannott be seen with owr bodyly eyes, for noo man hath seen God at any tyme and leveth. The prist at thatt time being att mas, yf hytt be soo thatt noo man hath sene God, nor can se God with thes bodyly eyes, than thatt whych the prist liffteth over his head ys nott God, for yow doo se hitt with yowr bodyly eyes; yf hytt be nott God, yow may nott honor hytt as God, nether for God. Whereatt olde Thomas Whyghtt,[a] a greate rych marchantt, and a ringleader of the papistes, rose owtt off hys seate, and wentt owtt of the church, saying, "Come from hym, good people; he came from the divell, and teacheth wnto yow divlish doctrine." John Notherel,[b] alias John Spicer, folowed him, saying, " Hitt shal be God whan thow shalt be but a knave."

The same yeare, in the day of All Saynctes, as they call hytt, after thatt I came from expownding sum place of the scriptures, at evening prayer, the above named Thomas Whyghtt, John Notherel, and William Haviland[c] came too the prist, commawnding him that he shold say dirige for all solls: I commawnding hym the contrary, they sayd they wold make me too saye dirige; I awnswered, nott whyle they leved. Than dyd they all as hytt wer with on mowth call me knav and my wyff strompett, som of them threatning me thatt they wold make me draw my gutts after me. The maior, being an honest good man, Morgan Reade[d] by name, thrust me into the qwier, and pulled the qwyer dorse fast too, commanding them to kepe the king's peace: but they spared nott to call the maior knave; the maior had much worke too stopp thys horly burly, untyll he had gotten the chef of them owtt of the churche.

Soo was I driven agayne too be a senter too my lord of Somersett hys grace, who wylled me too resorte to mr. Cicel than master of

[a] The name of Thomas Whyte occurs in the list of mayors of Poole in 1504, 1510, 1511, 1517, 1531, 1538, in 1545 Thomas Whyte senior, and in 1551 Thomas Whyte junior. The family were afterwards seated at Fittleford, in the parish of Stourminster Newton: see a pedigree in Hutchins's Dorsetshire (second edit.) iv. 183.

[b] John Northerell was mayor of Poole in 1540, 1547, and 1552.

[c] William Havyland was mayor of Poole in 1523, 1533, and 1544. Others of the family occur from 1494 to 1537.

[d] Morgan Rede was mayor of Poole in 1548.

requestes, but now lord treasurar of England. I had all soo an other letter for my qwyetnes in preaching of God's word in the towne of Poole. From that time I continewed in Poole untyll the death of good king Edward, in whose dayes, before the last apprehension of the dewke of Somersett, ther (was) on Woodcock's wyffe [a] thatt reported thatt ther was a voyce folowing her, whych sownded always in her years, thatt he whom the king dyd best trust sholld deceyve him, and worcke trayson agaynst him. Thys she reported long tyme, wntyll sir Wylliam Barkley [b] sent her too London too the cownsel. She was not long ther, butt came whome agayne with her purse full of mony, and after her comyng whome she was more bwsy in thatt talke than before; soo that she came too a market towne 4 mylls from Poole, called Wymborne, wher she reported thatt the voyce continewed folowing her as before. Ther were ij marchantes of Poole thatt hard her, and toke a note of her wordes, and came too my howsse and cownselled me too sertyfy my lord of Somersett of hytt. Soo I came too my lord too Syan and sartyfied my lord of the words, declaring untoe my lord thatt "he whom the kyng did best trust wold deceyve him and worke trayson" we dyd nott know, but thatt all the king's loving subjects dyd thinke thatt hys grace was most worthy to be best trusted, and thatt hys grace hath ben in troble, and thatt all the kyng's loving subjects dyd pray for his grace to th'Almighty too preserv his grace, thatt he may never cum in the like troble agayne.

My lord dyd aske of me whether I had any note of the wordes or noo. I awnsered I had, butt nott too present unto hys grace, by cawse I had a remembrance for bokes and other thyngs thatt I had too by.[c] My lord liked wel of hytt; and folding the paper, wett hytt with hys spettyll, and soo tore owtte my rememberance and gave hytt me, speaking thes wordes, "A syrra, thys ys strange, thatt thos things sholld cum before the cownsell, and I nott heyre of

[a] Misprinted *Woocock* by Strype, Memorials of Cranmer, p. 264.
[b] This was sir William Berkeley of Beverstone Castle in Gloucestershire, who married lady Margaret Poulet, daughter of the first marquess of Winchester. [c] *i.e.* to buy.

hytt. I ham of the cownsel all soo." He asked me, "Butt before whom of the cownsel thinke yow?" I answered "I know nott sartayne, my lord; but as I suppose." He sayde, "Before whom suppose you?" I awnsered, "Before my lord treasurer; by cawse sir William Barkley, who sent her upp with ij of his servantes, maryed my lord treasurer's dawghter." My lorde sayde, "Hytt ys like too be soo." Thys was the last time that I saw or spake with my lord of Somersett, being iij wekes before hys last apprehension.

Att his fyrst apprehension the reportt was thatt the duke of Somersett (whatt time he was fett owtt of Wynsor castell), having king Edward the 6th by the hand, shold say: "Hytt ys nott I thatt they shote att; thys ys the marke thatt they shote att:" meaning the king;[a] whych by the seqwel proved too trew; for thatt good, godly, and verteuus king leved nott long after the deathe of thatt good dewke.

After the deathe of kyng Edward the 6th, qwene Jane, who was vertuous and godly, was proclaymed kwene (butt agaynst her wyll, as the reporte was). She rayned nott above 8 or 9 dayse, butt qwene Marye was proclaymed qwene, in whose time the churche of Christ dyd florishe and was tryed by the deathe of many vertuous, lerned, and godly martyrs of Christ Jhesu. Qwene Mary was proclaymed qwene by my lord Wylliams[b] in Oxford, St. James's

---

[a] "Item, you declared and published untruly as well to the King's majestie, and other the young lords attendant upon his majesties person, and to the King's subjects at divers and sundry times and places, that the said lords at London minded to destroy the King; and you required the King never to forget it, but to revenge it, and likewise required the said young lords to put the King in remembrance therof; to the intent to make sedition and discord betweene the King's majesty and his lords." This is the 26th article charged upon the duke of Somerset, as printed in Stowe's Chronicle. The protector had, in his distress and embarrassment, no doubt indiscreetly made some such appeal, in order to obtain support, as on the King's behalf.

[b] Sir John Williams was master of the jewel-house and treasurer of the court of augmentations in the reign of Edward VI. Having taken an active part in the establishment of the authority of queen Mary, he was destined to higher honours. He became chamberlain to king Philip, and was created lord Williams of Thame in 1554. Having been appointed lord president of Wales, he died in that office in 1559. See Machyn's Diary, Index.

daye,[a] whoo, after she was proclaymed, dyd sett forth a proclama-cion,[b] which came too my handes, whych dyd declare what religion she dyd profes in her yowthe, thatt she dyd continew in the same, and thatt she mynded too end her lyf in the same religion; wylling all her loving subjects too embrace the same. Thys proclamation dyd soo encorage the papistes thatt they, forgetting ther dewty and obedience to God, and too declare there obedience wntoo there qwene, wold have the mas and other superstitius ceremonies in post haste; butt I toke uppon me too reade the proclamation wntoo them, and too declare the meaning of hytt; thatt, whereas in the proclamacion she wylled all her loving subjectes too enbrace the same religion, they owghtt to enbrace the same in her being there princes, thatt ys nott too rebell agaynst her, being there princes, but too lett her alone with her religion. This satisfied nott the papistes; but they wolde nedes have ther masking mas, and soo dyd olde Thomas Whyght, John Notherel, and others, bwylde upp an alter in the churche, and had procured a fytt chaplin, a French prest, on syr Brysse,[c] too say there masse; butt there altar was pulled downe, and syr Brysse was fayne too hyde hys headd, and the papistes too bwlde them an alter in ollde master Whyght's howse, John Craddock hys man being clarcke to ring the bell, and

[a] The 25th of July. From the letters printed in the Chronicle of Queen Jane and Queen Mary, pp. 9-12, it might be supposed that the proclamation took place at Oxford on an earlier day.

[b] Dated the xviij August, and printed at length by Foxe.

[c] Named "sir Brysse Tayller" in the list of rectors or curates of Poole in Hutchins's Dorsetshire (second edit.) ii. 21. He was settled in the town at least eight years before, as in an inventory of church jewels and ornaments made Nov. 30, 1545, "in presens of Thomas Whyt the eldyr then beyng mayr, Richard Havyland, Wylyam Havyland, and Thomas Gylleford then beyng one of the churche wardens," occurs "i chales parsell gyllt that sir Tailar syrvyth withall." (History of Poole, by John Sydenham, 1839, 8vo. p. 310.) Poole was in the parish of Canford. Leland says: "Pole is no town of auncient occupying in marchandise, but rather of old tyme a poore fisshar village, and a hamelet or membre to the paroche church. It is *in hominum memoria* much encreasid with fair buildings and use of marchaundise." But he afterwards adds, "There is a fair chirche in Pole."

too help the prist too mas, untyll he was threatned that yf he dyd use too putt hys hand owtt of the wyndow too ring the bell, that a hand-goon sholde make hym too smartt, thatt he sholld nott pull in his hand agayne with ease.

Soo had the papistes there mas in mr. Whytte's howse, and the Christians the gospel preched openly in the churche.

The papistes all soo resorted too the churche too heyre the word of God, nott for any love they had too the word, butt too take the preachar in a trypp, for divers articles they tooke owtt of my doctrine, of the which they accused me before the cownsell, att the tyme of the first parliament; emongst the whych one of them was thatt in my doctrine I tawghtt them thatt God had plaged thys realme most justly for owr sinns with thre notable plages, the which withowtt spedy repentance wtter destruction wold folowe.

The first plage was a warning too England, which was the posting swet, that posted from towne to towne, throwghe England, and was named *stope gallant*,[a] for hytt spared none, for ther were dawncyng in the cowrte at 9 a'clocke thatt were deadd or aleven a'clocke. In the same swett also at Cambredge died too worthy impes, the dewke of Swffok hys son Charells, and hys brother.[b]

The second plage was a threatning to England, whan God toke from us our wyse, verteuus, and godly king Edward the sixth.

The thyrde was to be robbed and spoyled of the jewel and treasure of God's holy word; the whych utter destruction shold folow wythowtt spedy repentance; for had nott owr godly, wyse, lerned, and marcyfull qwene Elizabeth stond in the gappe of Goddes wrathe, and bene the instrumentt of God too restore the everlasting

---

[a] Another instance of this name being given to the sweating-sickness has been mentioned in the notes to Machyn's Diary. It is in the register of Uffculme, co. Devon, " the hote sickness, or *stup-gallant*." In the register of Loughborough in Leicestershire it is termed "the swat called *New acquaintance,* alias *Stoup knave and know thy Master*."

[b] See note in Machyn's Diary, p. 318; and see the Literary Remains of King Edward VI., p. 330. Their deaths were at the bishop of Lincoln's palace at Buckden, whither they had been removed from Cambridge.

word of God wntoo us, we had been bandslaves unto the prowde vicius Spanyard.

O eternall omnipotentt and moste mercyfull God, who dyddest by thy mercyfull providence preserve our moste gracious qwene Elizabeth in the dangerus dayse of the rayne of her maiesties most unnaturall syster qwene Mary, to this end, thatt thow, a moste mercyfull God, woldest by her majestye sett forthe thy glory, in restoring wntoo us agayne the jewel and treaswre of thy moste sacredd and holy worde, we beseche the, O Lorde, make ws thankfull; preserve her majesty, thatt, yf hytt be thy blessed wyll, we may long time enjoye thys gret treaswre and jewell of thy most holy worde, thatt her grace may, by thy myghty powre, soo protect and defend thys her realme from the rewle and governmentt of strange nacions, thatt we may never be spoyled agayne of the same, and thatt hyt may please the of thy mercyfull goodnes so to rewle and govern ws thatt are her subjects with thy grace, thatt we may be diligentt heyrers of thy word, and obedientt folowers of the same, so thatt for owre wnthankfullnes we provoke nott thy wrathe (as in the dayse of good king Edward) too take from ws soo most godly, pitiful, and peaceable a princes, butt thatt she may a long time rewle and govern both thes her realmes of Ingland and Earland, too the vtter confusion of the papistes her enemise, and too the greate comforte of thy chyldren her loving subjects. Grant thys for thy dear son Christ Jesu's sake!

An other article thatt much offended, for the whych I was exempted owtt of the first general pardon thatt qwene Marye grawnted, was thatt I rebuking ther idolatrous desyre too have there supersticious ceremonyse and ther idolish mas, and too putt downe the gloryowse gospel of Christ Jesus, dyd in my doctrine aske them, how thys mowght be donne, and how they wold bring hytt to passe, having the law of the realme and the glorious gospel of Jesus Christ agaynst them, and God being agaynst them, in whom they had ther trust. I sayde, " Yowr trust ys in fleshe; so yow forsake the blessing of God and heape wppon yow hys curse: Jeremi 17. sings: *Maledictus homo qui confidit in homine, et ponit carnem brachium suum, &c.* What fleshe ys thatt you trust unto, Stephen Gardnar's the bysshop of Winchester? He hath ben a Sawle; God make him a Pawle! He hathe ben a persequutor; God make hymme a faythfull preacher!"

Thes wordes so much offended, thatt I was nott thowghtt worthy to enjoye the qwene's pardon; whereuppon I was cownselled by master Wylliam Thomas, the clarcke of the cownsel,[a] for savegard of my lyfe, too flee; and so came I to Roane in Normandy, wheare I dyd continew the space of ij years, and halfe a yeare I spent at Parys and Orlyance. After thatt, heryng of a Englishe congregation att the citie of Geneva, I resorted thyther wyth my wyfe, and on of my chylldren,[b] wheare I continewed thre yere and sumwhatt more. In the which citie, I prayse God, I dyd se my lord God moste pewrly and trewly honored, and syn moste straytly punnisshed: soo hytt may be well called a holy citie, a citie of God; the Lorde powre hys blessings wppon hytt, and continew hys favore toward hytt, defending hytt agaynst there[c] enimyes!

After the deathe of qwene Mary, in the happy beginning of the regne of our sofferayne lady qwene Elyzabeth . . . . (*unfinished.*)

---

[a] William Thomas, made clerk of the council April 19, 1550. (King Edward's Journal.) He wrote various historical papers for the instruction of king Edward, some of which are introduced in Strype's works; and an edition of his writings was published in 1774, 8vo., with notes by Abraham D'Aubant, esq. Of his unhappy end in the reign of Mary, see both Machyn's Diary and the Chronicle of Queen Jane and Queen Mary.

[b] In the *Livre des Anglois*, preserved in the archives of the city of Geneva, among those received into the church in Nov. 1556, or shortly after, occur the names of "Thomas Hancock, his wife, and Gedion his sonne." On the 7th of April in the following year occurs the baptism "Sarah, the daughter of Thomas Hancock, Anthony Gilby being the godfather."—which Anthony Gilby was afterwards vicar of Ashby-de-la-Zouche. Livre des Anglois à Genève, edited by John Southerden Burn, 1831, 8vo. pp. 9, 14.

[c] *i. e.* their. Strype has substituted "his."

V.

THE DEFENCE OF THOMAS THACKHAM, MINISTER,
IN HIS CONDUCT TOWARDS JULINS PALMER.

JOSCELINE or Julins[a] Palmer suffered at the stake at Newbury on the 16th July, 1556; and the particulars of his case are related by Foxe at considerable length. He was a native of Coventry, where his father " had sometime been maior, and occupied merchandise, albeit he was an upholster by his mysterie." His education had been received at the school of Magdalen college, Oxford, under master Harley, afterwards bishop of Hereford; and, after attaining to a fellowship at Magdalen, he was in 1550 admitted to the office of reader in logic in that college. So strong at that period were his views in favour of the Romish faith, that he was expelled the college before the death of king Edward, and became a teacher of children in the house of sir Francis Knollys. After Mary's accession he was restored to his fellowship; but his sentiments then underwent a change which led to further troubles. This is attributed in great measure to his horror in witnessing the merciless treatment of Ridley and Latimer at Oxford, when a sympathy in their sufferings led to an examination of the principles and the faith which sustained them. Thereupon Palmer finally quitted his fellowship, and purchased the appointment, originally granted by letters patent to Leonard Coxe, of the mastership of the grammar-school at Reading; but there he did not stay long: for on his study being searched, there were found in it "certain godly books and writings, amongst the which was his replication to Morwine's verses touching Winchester's epitaph, and other arguments both in Latin and English, written by him against the Popish proceedings, and specially against their unnaturall and brutish tyrannie executed towards the martyrs of God."

At this time Palmer came in contact with Thomas Thackham, the writer of the following paper. Thackham succeeded as master of Reading school, by

---

[a] Not *Julius*, as it came to be printed in the later editions of Foxe; but *Julins*, which appears to have been the colloquial pronunciation of Josceline. The error has made its way into Wood's Athenæ Oxonienses, edit. Bliss, ii. 842, and Fasti, i. 125, 232. In an epitaph in Ripon cathedral (1651) we read of " D. Julins Hering Evangelii dispensatoris valde fidelis."

purchase, as he states: but from other accounts it would seem that Palmer did not consider his own retirement to be final, and during a visit which he incautiously made to the town, his arrest was facilitated, as was thought, by Thackham's means.[a] This charge of treachery, as related in the first edition of Foxe's Actes and Monuments, Thackham denied with great asseveration, but it appears that he was only partially credited. Foxe removed Thackham's name from the story of Julins Palmer in part, but only in part, and inserted the following explanation:—

"Here by the way, gentle reader, I have by a little digression to geve thee to understand, concernyng one Thomas Thackham, for that the said Thomas Thackham, in the storie of this Julins Palmer, was noted and named, in our former booke, to be a doer and a worker against the said blessed martyr: he therefore beyng not a little agreved, made his reply agayne in writyng, for purgation and defence of hymselfe against the false information of his slanderer. Albeit for his confutation in writyng I passe not much upon, eyther what he hath written or can write. Onely the thing that mooveth me most is this: for that the sayd Thomas Thackham not long since, commyng to me hymselfe, hath so attested and deposed against the information, with such swearing and deep adjuration, takyng the name of the Lorde God to witnesse, and appealyng to his judgment to the utter perdition of his soule if it were not false which by information was reported of hym, and hee faultlesse in this matter: to which beyng so, I could not otherwyse refuse, but to give credit to his othe, and upon the same to alter and correct so much as pertaineth to the diffamation (as he calleth it,) of his name, referring the truth of the matter to his owne conscience, and the judgements of the Lord God, to whom eyther he standeth if it be true, or falleth if it be false."

The fact was that Foxe's informants still insisted that their version of the story was the true one. Together with Thackham's statement now printed,

---

[a] Thackham's "slanderer" in his reply charged him that Palmer was at last apprehended at Reading "by your procurement, because he was earnest upon you for money, or elles to make a re-entrye into the Schoole accordyng to covenauntes: for he had tolde his frendes by mouth at his last beyng at Oxford, whiche was the second day of Juyn before he suffered (as apered by his owne handwrityng yet to be shewed) that if he durst he would remove Thackham from the Schole, because he performed not covenauntes with him, and payd him not his money accordyng to promes. And because he was busye with Thackham for the same, he sayd that he and others threatened him yet agayne very sore, to exhibite his owne handwrityng against him, except he would geve over his full interest in the Schoole, and departe quyetly without any further molestyng of Thackham. And then he sayde they helde his nose to the gryndstone" (f. 37 b.)

itself somewhat diffuse, is preserved a rejoinder which occupies no less than sixty-four folio pages, and is still incomplete. Of this a portion only can be here given, by way of specimen of its style and contents; but where subsequently any counter-statement of importance occurs, it shall be placed at the foot of the page, beneath the statement made by Thackham.

It appears most probable that the party from whom Foxe received the narrative of Julins Palmer,—called by Thackham "the slanderer," and in the reply "the gatherers" (in the plural number), were, principally, Thomas Purye, afterwards a preacher at Beverstone in Gloucestershire, and John Moyer, also a minister, formerly of Reading, and a fellow-sufferer there with John Bolton.[a] The former addressed the following letter to Foxe on the subject:

(MS. Harl. 416, f. 100.)

Right reverend and beloved in the Lord. I have receved your letters, together with Thackam's answer; which I perceave you have well perused, and do understand his craftye and ungodly dealing therin, that I may not say fond and foolish. For he doth not denye the substance of the storye, but only seeketh to take advantage by some circumstancys of the tyme and place, wherin yt may be ther was an oversight, for lacke of perfect instructions or good remembrance at the begynning. He confesseth that he delyvered a letter of Palmer's own hand to the maior of Readinge, which was the occasyon of his imprisonment and death: onlye he excuseth him selffe by transferring the cryme *a seipso in martirem*. Briefly his whole end and purpose is to geve the world to understand, that the martir was gyltie as well of incontinencye, as also of wylfull casting away of hymselfe. O impudent man! The wyse and godly reader may easylye smell his stinkinge hart. He careth not though he out face the godlye martir, and the whole volume of martirs, to save (as he thinketh) his owne honestye and good name. Howbeyt I doubt not but God wyll confownd him to his utter shame, and reveal his cloked hypocrysie, to the defence of his blessed martir, and the whole storye. Though many off them be dead that gave instructyons in tymes past, and now could have borne witnesse, yet, thankes be to God, there want not alyve that can and wyll testifye the trueth herein to his confusyon. No dylygence shall be spared in the matter, as shortly I trust you shall understand. In the meane while Thackam nede not be importunate for an answer. He reporteth him selffe to the whole towne of Readinge, therfore he must geve us some space. The God of trueth defend yow, and all other that mayntayne his trueth from the

---

[a] See hereafter, p. 96.

venemous poyson of lyers! *Vale in Christo, qui ecclesiæ suæ te diu servet incolumem.* From Beverston in Gloc'shere, Maij vj^{to.}

Yours in the Lord, THOMAS PURYE, minister.*

Directed, To the right reverend in God, Mr. Jhon Foxe, preacher of the ghospell in London, be thes dd. at Mr. Daies the printer, dwellyng over Aldersgate beneth S. Martens.

For "help in stopping the malicious and envious mouth of Thomas Thackam," Purye applied to John Moyer, minister at Corsley in Wiltshire, already mentioned. Moyer's answer, dated "from Corsley this 18 of May," and addressed to "master Perry, preacher at Beverstone," was inserted by Foxe in his *addıtamenta* (see an extract in p. 96.)

In Strype's Memorials, vol. iii. Appendix lix, will be found a paper entitled "Informations gathered at Reading, 1571," from which in great measure was drawn up—probably by Purye, the elaborate reply now in the MS. Harl. 425. The latter commences in the following manner:

(MS. Harl. 425, f. 33.)

To the Title [of Thackham's statement].

The story was not brought to mr. Foxe, nor written against Thomas Thackham by the name of minister; but against one Thomas Thackham. And as it was delyvered to mr. Foxe by one alone, so was it gathered and instructions geven by dyverse of good credite, whiche also earnestly favoured the Ghospell. And so litle breache of charitie was then betwene them and you, that if they all, or any one of them, had knowen you or understood where you dwelt, and had learned that you are a minister and now repentaunt and sound in religion, they could well have spared your name untouched; and so voyde of malice they are knowen to be, that they are enemyes to no man lyvyng, and have bene ever desyrous to lyve peaceably with all men, *Salva religionis et consciencie integritate;* neither maye it be proved that they are

---

* His name as rector of Beverstone occurs in Atkyns's Gloucestershire, 1712, p. 275, misprinted Bury; corrected to "Purey" in Bigland's History, p. 177. In Bigland, p. 178, is the epitaph of "Catherine Purye, wife of Thomas Purye, Minister of the Word in this place," who died 1 Dec. 1604, æt. 67 (*sic*); and in Rudder's Gloucestershire, p. 284, are six Latin verses inscribed on the chancel wall at Beverstone, headed "A° 1604. Ætat. 69, Epicedium Katherinæ Pury."

sclanderous in this poynte. And it is well knowen that none of theim ever reyled sclander upon any man lyvyng, nor ever delighted in that vice, but allwayes detested and abhorred it utterly. And of that whiche they have written of you, they were not the devysers but the reporters, and reported it not of malice towardes you, whome they never sawe nor knewe, but of love towardes the truthe, and for conscyence sake, as they had heard and learned, accordyng to the scripture whiche sayth, Proverb 21. *A true man boldely speaketh as he hathe heard.* And that the worst of theim is utterly voyde of all soche faultes as you here charge theim withall, as good profes wilbe brought as ever you shall bryng to clere your awneselfe from those vices that here in the entrye of your book you burthen theim with.

The first Section.

"Gentle reader" you saye, &c. In dede you repete this woord so oft and manifold tymes in your short aunswere, that it maye be thought (consyderyng the weakenes of your cause) you supposed it very nedefull for you to crave favour, to flatter the reader, and to trye rather his gentlenes then his justice. And here it standeth you in lytle steade to insinuate youre selfe to youre "gentle reader," with the rehersall of your good dedes, as did the proude boastyng pharisey: for many wicked men have bene knowen to have interteyned godly men; and the ungodly have often interteyned the godly by Goddes appoyntment, who bathe compelled his enemys sometyme to deale frendly with his frendes. And God graunt that it be not proved that you wrought your good dedes then with as good devocion as did that pharisey in the Ghospell.

It were hard to know who this preacher was, and at what time he signefyed this thing unto you, so darkly, that you had leasour to bethink yourselfe of all these good dedes: Was he not rather playne with you, and did not you make him as unready an answere as you aunswered one at Cicester, that charged you therwith? at what tyme you so faltered and faynted, and had so litle to saye for youreselfe, that the partie was bothe sory and ashamed on youre behalf to heare it. But now that you have taken heart of grace, and after good conference with certeyn that favour your cause, and beare now ij faces in one whood, as you have heretofore done, have well bethought yourselfe and serched out howe they be affected, you have faced rather then fasshoned out an aunswere, God wote full weake and worthy of your doynges.

And to begyn withall, you that with soche aucthoritie and so imperious as if the catt had lycked you cleane, reprehended others for lyeng, when they tolde you the truthe: coulde not yourselfe absteyne from one lye at the first dashe, even in the narracion of your beneficiall good dedes touchyng John

Bolton, where you tell a long tale how he was delyvered by youre meanes at the maior's handes, and that you were bounde for his appearance, &c. The story of Bolton and dyverse in Readyng do testefye that he was set at libertie and discharged without bondes, and that by sir Praunces Inglefielde of his owne mocion, and not by the maiour through your meanes and frendship. Moreover I heare saye that mr. Bowyer [a] was then maior, and not mr. Edmondes, and thus one of your good dedes is cut of by the waye. As concernyng that good lady Vane, there is no doubt but if she were now lyvyng she woulde declare many thinges that should sound smally to your prayse, as dyverse at this daye do knowe by the reporte that she gave you many tymes in their heryng. Further, lyke as you would seme to conceave a good opinion of Palmer and of mr. Foxe, even when you insinuate and declare the contrary, so here, although you prayse Bolton, to have bene taken for a rank heretike (as you terme it) and of good religion, yet you would that men should take him to be skant an honest man, in purposyng never to save you harmeles from your bande, leavyng you to paye the forfeyt, whiche I beleve was woorth as many pence as there be shelynges in a grote. Youre benefits were not registred in the booke, as you saye, some smaller were, because belyke they were so small that they passed awaye invisible, and could not be felt, sene, nor understand.

After the vauntes of your good dedes, rehersed to purchase the reader's good will, whome so often you crye upon, callyng hym "gentle reader," and after you had (beyng *conscius propriæ iniquitatis*,) sought for the story of your awne mocion, fearyng least somewhat that laye hid would come to light : you connyngly saye, that you were put in mynde of others to searche for the story, and founde matters farre otherwise then you loked for, or coulde suspect. Then, least by sayeng nothing you should seme to yelde yourselfe guyltie, you endevour to make somewhat of nothing, chargyng yourselfe with more then you are charged with in the storye. And, least you should seme to saye to litle, you take upon you to saye moche more then enough, and more then standeth with truthe.

The story nameth suche popishe enemys as Palmer had in Readyng, or thereaboute, " the viperous generacion;" it calleth theim in generall ypocrites and dissemblers, but whether you were to be counted among theim allwaye, or whether he had none other enemys there but you and those men that conveighed the writynges out of his study or not, the storye sayth nothyng. But you, that knowe best belyke to whome the sayd termes ought to be applyed,

---

[a] Robert Bowyer was mayor of Reading in 1553, the first of queen Mary, and again in 1558 and 1570, and one of the burgesses to parliament in 2 Mary.

dare to affirme, that the slaunderer meaneth you and calleth you a breaker up of Palmer's studye, and a thefe. Yet he meaneth you not: neyther maye it be gathered by the wordes of the storye that he meant you: wherfor, here is another lye, for you are called neither studye-breaker, nor thefe. But nowe, seyng you will have all referred unto you, take it to you hardelye, for you knowe best whether you be best worthy of it or no.

Also, whereas you will nedes be one of theim that brake up his studye and stole out his wrytynges, be lyke you knowe somewhat, or elles you would not so applye it to yourselfe. But because you hope that now by the meanes of their deathe that would have confessed the truthe, you should skape free, you charge the gatherers of the story with more than you are burthened withall. For where sayth the storye that you stole theim oute, or consented to the stealyng? It sayth, that soche men as you had suborned to beare wytnes against him, did it, and yet whether they altogether, or the more parte of them, the storye doth not playnly and precisely defyne, but speaketh in the plurell nombre thus, that there were iij false witnesses by you suborned, whiche men or witnesses had robbed his study. And after it foloweth well, that you and they bothe, you by accusyng, and they by witnessyng, burdened him with dyverse crymes there rehersed. This playne meanyng and wordes of the text, beyng a grammarian, you coulde not chose but see and understand; yet you saye that you are called thefe, which wordes your boylyng conscience (as it may be supposed), knowyng youre selfe gwyltie, or at the least accessory to it, caused you to utter by the meanes of some humane infirmitie, ether to advoyde all suspicion, knowyng that soche as were hable to advouche it to your face be dead, and hopyng to face out soche as yet lyvyng will testefy that they heard it, or hopyng that you are not espyed at all, and that no man dare saye ought against you. Or elles God, which is a just opener of secretes, forced you to wrest the wordes into this sence, that men maye gather that, if no man elles maye be founde to testefye this truthe agaynst you, yet you yourselfe should minister occasion of suspicion agaynst your selfe. Moreover, by these your wordes, you bryng a certeyn man in mynde, and cause him to call to remembraunce that Palmer himselfe had tolde him, that by one Thackham's procurement certeyn writynges that conteyned matter of greate daungier were conveyed out of his study, whiche partie will be foorthcommyng to depose the same at all calles. The Lorde mende your heart with repentaunce! that you maye rather chose a litle shame in this worlde, then everlastyng shame in the worlde to come, for God will reveale *abscondita tenebrarum*. Verely if you had stand in awe of Goddes just judgementes, beyng this stryken as it semeth with the remorse of your awne conscience, you would have left this joly shewe of bravery, and secretly to God alone cryed *peccavi*, besechyng him to cease the rygour of his wrath by this gracious warnyng, least a worse chaunce befall you hereafter. But now in these your procedynges, and by your wordes, you geve men a taste what maner of man you have bene, and what you yet seme to be. And who would not mervell that you, beyng now a minister and a preacher, should thus rashly and without all regard or discrecion of persons, either threaten mr. Foxe with suytes of lawe (for you saye, you were counsayled to trye the lawe with him; and I here saye also that you threatened mr. Foxe to have out an action of the cace against him), either with soche odyous and sclanderous titles to upbrayd the reporters of this storye, without all regard of offence, causyng the woorde of God to be evell spoken of among the wicked, and the papistes to triumph when they shall heare of soche dissencion among theim that indifferently professe the Ghospell; wherby the truthe of the doctryne, that bothe parties maye nowe professe, were lyke to be slaundered by theim whome you call the sclaunderer, and the aucthorite therof elevated and debased by you, and therewith (asmoche as lyeth in you) the whole storye of Marters discredited, whiche thing you forget not, but consyder full well, where you saye that the sclaunderer bathe herein more sclaundered the volume wherin it is written then you of whome it is written. And this you would gladly have knowen and brought to passe, as may be gathered by the gredy desyer that you have to publishe your childyshe aunswere, full of falsehoode and stomack and contrarietie, as playnly apereth in the same.

Mr. Foxe is not so childyshe a man, and so lighte of credite, to suffer himselfe to be abused, as you saye, and woulde the worlde should thinke (though you cloke and dissemble it) and to geve eare to soche a mannes reporte as you make the sclaunderer to be. Soche is your charitie, that to justefy yourselfe, you care not what nor whome you deface, God, his worde, the truthe, the indicter, the prynter, the reporters, the story and all. It woulde better have becommed you (if you were in dede the man that you desyer to be coumpted) to have sought laufull and just meanes to make it apere, that Palmer and you contynued lovyng and faithfull frendes to the ende; and so, after you had informed mr. Foxe of the same, to have desyred him, either to clere youre name in some other edicion, as he clereth certeyn men in this later edicion of a great slander that they were charged withall in the former volume, even in this story of Palmer: or at the least to omytte your name, as he hathe omytted moche in this later edicion, that by oversight eskaped him in the first. But now it semeth that you have bene provoked and egged forward, by some craftie and envyous papistes; or elles God of purpose woulde have you to utter your awne shame and rebuke in your awne hand writyng: *sed nunc, ne nimis extra callem,* I will touche a worde or two more, and so make an ende of this section."

This will suffice to show the spirit and style of the Reply: other portions will be found in the notes, and at the close of this article.

[MS. Harl. 425, No. 15, f. 18.]

An answere to a slaunder untruely reported by mr. Foxe, in a certen boke intytuled the seconde volume off the ecclesiasticall historye, conteynynge the Actes and Monumentes off Martyres, whiche was broughte unto hym, and, as it maye be supposed, by some uncharytable and malycyous slaunderer, agaynste Thomas Thackham mynister, wherby yt maye well appere unto the gentle reader bothe how much the wryter of that historye hathe bene abused, and howe wrongfullye the sayd Thomas Thackham hathe bene slaundered.

Gentle reader, after that I was secretly advertysed by a godlye precher that I was in the Boke of Marters, I began to call myselfe to an accompte wheather yt were for persecutinge any godlye persone in the trublesome tyme of quene Marye, other for helpinge and delyveringe any that was in daunger. After longe debatinge with mysellffe for whether off theyse twoe causes I was cronycled, at the laste, I take God to wytnes, by the verye testymony off my conscyence (which is a faythfull register off thoughts and workes) I fownde myselffe innocent from the blode of all men, and from evyll dealinge towardes any lyvinge creature.

Than I began to thynke that some frende off good wyll had enformed mr. Foxe, howe that in the tyme off persecutyone I kepte secretlye the ladye Vane,[a] which for her zeale, vertew, relygyone,

[a] Styled by Foxe " the good lady Vane," when he prints a letter of John Bradford, resolving certain questions which she demanded. " This lady Vane was a speciall nourse and a greate supporter, to her power, of the godlie Saints which were imprisoned in queue Maries time. Unto whom divers letters I have both of maister Philpot, Careles, Traherne, Thomas Rose, and of other moe ; wherein they render unto her most gratefull thankes

godly lyffe, and bountyfulnes towardes the poare bretharne, deserved as greate comendacyone as any one man or woman lyvinge at that tyme, which sayed ladye Vane was with me xxj^{ti}. wekes;[a] for whose cause, imedyatlye affter her departinge, at the commandment

for her exceeding goodnes extended towarde them, with their singular commendation and testimonie also of her christian zeale towardes God's afflicted prisoners, and to the veritie of his Gospell. Shee departed of late at Holburne, anno 1568 ; whose ende was more like a sleepe then any death: so quietly and meekly shee deceased and departed hence in the Lord." Foxe, edit. 1576, p. 1559. Again, "Unto whom (lady Anne Knevet, of Wimondham, near Norwich,) not unworthiely may be compared the ladie Elizabeth Vane, who likewise being a great harborer and supporter of the afflicted martyrs and confessors of Christ, was in great hassardes and daungers of the enemies, and yet notwithstanding, thorough the mercifull providence of the Lorde, remained still untouched." Ibid. p. 1965.

A large number of the letters mentioned by Foxe were published by him both in "The Letters of the Martyrs, 1554," 4to. (reprinted in 1837), and in the Actes and Monuments. Among them is one letter of lady Elizabeth Vane's own writing, addressed to Philpot: it is signed F. E., probably meaning E(lizabeth) F(ane). It appears that Philpot had requested a scarf to wear at the stake. " Because (writes the lady) you desire to show yourself a worthy soldier, if need so require, I will supply your request of the scarf ye wrote of, that ye may present my handywork before your Captain, that I be not forgotten in the odours of incense which our beloved Christ offereth for his own : to whom I bequeath both our souls and bodies." That this act on the part of Philpot was not singular is shewn by the following passage : "Some *for triumph* would put on their scarfes, some their wedding garments, going to the fire; others kissed the stake, some embraced the fagots," &c. Foxe, edit. 1610, p. 873.

No personal particulars of the lady Vane are to be collected from her correspondence or from the ecclesiastical historians,—except the date of her death, as above stated by Foxe. She has been supposed (Index to the Works of the Parker Society) to have been the widow of sir Ralph Vane, who was hung in 1551-2, as one of the principal adherents of the duke of Somerset: and such may be accepted as the truth, though her name does not appear in the pedigree of the family of Fane or Vane. Sir Ralph died without issue, when, though his principal estate of Penshurst was forfeited, and granted to the Sidneys, his more ancient family property of Hadlow in Kent went to a cousin, Henry Fane, who was compromised in Wyat's conspiracy, and narrowly escaped with his life, but lived to become the lineal ancestor of the dukes of Cleveland. (See Hasted's Kent, i. 411, note k, ii. 315.) The following entry, confirmatory of Foxe's statement respecting the lady's decease, is from the register of burials at St. Andrew's Holborn : " 1568. The 11th of June. The lady Elizabeth Vane." A book of the lady Elizabeth's Psalms and Proverbs was published by Robert Crowley : see additional note in the Appendix.

[a] " As touching the friendship showed unto the lady Vane, and his zeal therein

off syr Francis Inglefylde,[a] one off the quenes majesties prevye counsell, my studye was broken up and my bokes taken awaye by one Clement Burdette, parsone off Inglefylde,[b] and I kept fyrste in close prysone at Inglefylde ten dayes and after sent prysoner to Readinge, wear I was kepte at one mr. Aldewurthes howse, then beinge mayore,[c] whear nethar my wyfe neather any other myghte speake

uttered, truth it is that he received her into his house for money for a small space, in the which time they two did not well agree, for that she could not suffer his wickedness of words and gestures unreproved, but that his wife many times, being of more honesty, made the matter well again ; but, to be short, such was his friendship in the end towards that good lady, being out of his house, that she feared no man more for her life than him. And I being her man, she gave me great charge always to beware of him." Letter of John Moyer to Thomas Purye, printed by Foxe. Among the "Informations gathered at Reading, in 1571," we read—" Item. Jhon Galant sayth, that the ladye Vane, talking with hym, called Thackham ' dissemblynge hypocrite ;' and told hym how he deceaved poore people, with that which she dyd skymme off, and would not geve to her dog."

[a] Sir Francis Inglefield, son of sir Thomas Inglefield a judge of the common pleas, was one of queen Mary's household before her accession to the throne, and suffered imprisonment with sir Robert Rochester and sir Edward Waldegrave in defence of the religion therein maintained. He was rewarded after her accession with the office of master of the court of wards and liveries, and a seat in the privy council. He was member of parliament for Berkshire throughout that reign. Retaining his devoted attachment to the church of Rome, he afterwards went abroad, was indicted for treason and outlawed in 6 Eliz., and attainted by Parliament in 28 Eliz. He died at Valladolid about the year 1592. The family of baronets, who enjoyed that title from 1612 until the death of the distinguished antiquary sir Henry Charles Englefield in 1822, were descended from his brother. See further of him in Wotton's English Baronetage, 1741, vol. i. p. 258.

[b] Clement Burdett was the second son of Thomas Burdett esquire, of Bramcote, co. Warwick, by Mary daughter of sir Robert Throckmorton, of Coughton in the same county. (Wotton's Baronetage, 1741, vol. i. p. 333.) He was cousin-german to sir Francis Englefield, whose mother was Elizabeth daughter of sir Robert Throckmorton. (Ibid. p. 258.) Foxe, in his story of John Bolton, speaks of sir Francis Englefield with his bloody *brother* the parson of Englefield. Burdett was official to the bishop of Salisbury, and at Palmer's examination held a long altercation with him on the doctrine of transubstantiation, which is detailed in Foxe.

[c] Thomas Aldworth, mayor in 1557, as before in 1551, and afterwards in 1571. He was also one of the burgesses for Reading in the last parliament of Philip and Mary, and the first of Elizabeth. During his mayoralty in 1557 he received king Edward the Sixth in the town, as described in Man's History of Reading, 4to. 1816, p. 22.

with me, as mr. Vatchell[a] off Colee and many in Readinge at this daye can testyfie.

And yff uppon this accasyone I was not named thear, I supposed that one John Bolton,[b] somtyme off Readinge, had informed mr. Foxe how frendlye I delte with hym when all the frendes he had durste not helpe hym; which Bolton (as it was supposed) feyned hymselfe mad, in wych his madnes he rayled upon quene Marye, and therefore was apprehendyd and cruelly tormented in the prysone at the towne off Readinge, wyche Bolton at the lenght becam sober and off a bettar mynde, whose beinge their I with others muche pytyed, and the more because he semed off a good relygyone;

[a] Thomas Vachell, one of the burgesses for Reading in five parliaments, 30, 32, 36 Hen. VIII., 1 Mary, and 2 and 3 Philip and Mary. He occurs as "master Fachel of Reading," one of the commissioners for the trial of Marbeck and others at Windsor in 1543. A remark he made is said by Foxe to have been the cause of Marbeck's being cast; and, as he was the lowest of all the bench, he gave judgment on that occasion. He was made surveyor of the demesne of the dissolved abbey of Reading in 31 Hen. VIII, and his descendants were baronets: see Coates's Reading, pp. 78, 125.

[b] John Bolton's story, which was written by himself, is printed by Foxe under the year 1554; and a commentary upon it, pointing out several misstatements, is given in Strype's Memorials, vol. iii. Appendix, No. LVIII. This is signed, "By me, John Moyer," and dated "At Wotton, this 18th of March, anno D'ni 1564:" which Moyer (already mentioned in p. 88) had been the real author of the libel for which Bolton was prosecuted, and a fellow-sufferer with him. The same writer in his letter to master Purye, comments thus upon Thackham's statement in the text: "As touching his frendship towards John Bolton in prison, I am sure he never found any, as they that used to visit him can somewhat say; except you count this friendship that, he (Bolton) being bereft of his senses, Thackham brought him to yield unto the papists, and as a right member of them became his surety that he should be obedient unto them. And he (Bolton) being burdened in conscience therewith, fled away unto Geneva; in the which flying Thackham had nothing said unto him, which showeth that he was their instrument. And this [was his] friendship to John Bolton." But this is partly contradicted in the "Informations gathered at Reading anno 1571," in which it is stated that, "Bolton, of whom Thackham speaketh, was set at lybertie by sir Praunces Inglefield, without any suerties, as appeareth in the storye of Bolton. Also Jhon Ryder of Readinge capper and Wyll'm Dyblye weaver do beare witness therunto. And of this Bolton hymselfe, dwelling in Longe lane by Smythfield in London, can tell more. He ys a sylke weaver."

whearfore I traveled with one mr. Edmunds, then mayor there,[a] and besowghte hym, synste all he had spoken paste hym in the tyme off his madnes, that he wolde stand his good master, and take some charytable waye for his delyverance. After a longe suete hee graunted his delyverance, upon condycyone that he wolde put in two suartyes besydes hymselffe, which wolde be bownde in v li. apece that he shold appeare the nexte sessyons; but when by reasone off the tyme his verye frendes durste not become suertyes for suche a treator and ranke an heretyke as Bolton was then thoughte to be, then I desyred mr. mayor to take me alone with Bolton, which he gentlye graunted, and bownde us in v li. a pece for Bolton's appearaunce the nexte sessions, and thus was this myscrable captyve set at lybertye and departed; but purposinge, as yt proved after, never to save me harmelesse, for when the sessyons was he lefte me to paye the forfyte; and because I fynde smaller benefytes bestowide upon good men and women at such tymes regestred in that volume, I thoughte that this mighte have bene the cause why mr. Foxe sholde made some mentione off me.

But after I had gotten the volume and had reade in the hystorye off one Julins Palmer, wheare my name was, I founde an other matter. One had tolde an other manner off tale to mr. Foxe for me, farre otherwyse than I loked for, eather coulde suspecte; but wheras this pryvie accuser and malycious slaunderer calleth me dyssemlinge hipocryte, false brother, a suborner off false wytnesses, a breaker up off Palmer's studye, a theffe, a blodye acusar, bestowinge upon me more off his liberalytie then off my desartes, with dyvarsse other names, as in that he causeth mr. Foxe to laye to my charge yt will bettar appeare, my purpose ys not, gentle reader, to matche hym with lyke skolding termes; but by answearinge trulye for mysellfe (as yt shall be well tryed) to prove howe falselye he bathe belyed me, and howe muche he hathe abused mr. Foxe, the

[a] William Edmunds, mayor of Reading in 1550, and previously in 1540; burgess for the town in the parliament of 14 Hen. VIII.

wryter off the hystorye. But now to come to my answer. This he begynethe.

(Second Section.) *The Slaunderer.*

" Afterwardes, as Palmer went alone musinge and ponderinge off matters, yt came into his heade to leave his appoynted jorneye, and to returne closelye to Readinge, trustinge by the helpe off frendes to receave his quarter's stypend, and convey his stuffe to the custodye off some trustye bodye."

Thackham.

Duringe the tyme that Palmer kepte the frescole in Readinge, he was payed his stipende by the auditer every halfe yeare, and dyd never receave yt quartarly, as it is well knowne; thearefore the cause off his returne to Readinge coulde not be in hope to receve his quarter's stypende. Besydes this, Palmer was not put from the scole, but dyd willingly resigne the pattent unto me for suche monye as we dyd agree uppon; which monye he recevyd off me before I had the patent,[a] as I can prove and have to shewe. Thearfore be no meanes can yt be true that this slaunderer hathe sayed, that Palmer came to Readinge trustinge by some frendshipe to receave his quarter's stipind. He sayethe his intent was also to convey his stuffe to the custodye off some trustye bodye. When Palmer yeldid the scole to me, he condycyoned that I shoulde place hym with some honeste gentilman wheare he myghte teche childeren, and lyve to his conscience; wyche I performed, for I placed hym at Horsyngtone with one mr. Raffe Lee,[b] whose sone and heyre he taughte; wheare he was setled, and all that he had; from the which his master, he came to Readinge off very purpose to see his hosties,

[a] This was denied: "where it apereth that within five dayes before his swete sufferyng for the testimony of Christes truthe, he apoynted a faithfull frende of his, then a felow of Magdalen college, to be his laufull deputye or attorney to receave for him and to his use a certeyne some of money at the bandes of Thomas Thackham skoolmaster at Readyng." (Reply, f. 38.)

[b] See a note in a subsequent page.

with whome he had bourded befor, and to delyver to one mr. Edmundes a letter which he wrote at his master's howyse, as yt is well knowne. Concernynge his stuffe, which he sayethe here that Palmer wold convey to some trustye bodye, yt is to be provyd that when Palmer went to his master he lefte not one penyeworthe behynd hym. As for beddinge he had nevar non. His apparell was no more then he daylye ware. He had nevar above fyve or syxe bokes, which he toke to hym to Horsyngtone, wheare he dwelte, and was well placed; but by this slaunderer's informatione yt should appeare that Palmer was dryven to forsake his scole, and that he was at his wyttes ende, not knowinge what to doe, that he was unprovyded for, that he fled from Readinge and durste not tarye to take up his wagis, that he reacevyd the same quarterly, that he left when he fledd his stuffe behynde hym in daunger to be loste; wheroff thear is not one worde true, so that when this slaunderer had proposed to present mr. Foxe with this infamatione agaynste me, he knewe that yt shoulde be nedefull for hym to frame suche an entraunce as myghte brynge with yt some shewe off that sholde followe, whear, as a connynge poet, he feynethe that Palmer went alone musynge and pondred off manye matters, had purposed to jorneye one waye and then closly returned an other waye, tellethe whether he came and feynethe too causes off his thyther resorte, wych was to obtayne his quarter's wages, and to convey his stuffe from his hostyce howse unto some trustye bodye; whearoff thear is nothinge true. But, gentle reader, even as the begynninge ys, suche mydell and ende doythe he make, as yt shall playnly appere.

(Third Section.) *The Slaunderer.*

" To Readinge he comythe, and takethe up his lodgynge at the Cardinalles hatte, desyringe his hosties instantlye to assygne hym a close chamber, whear he myghte be alone from all resorte of companye."

Thackham.

Durynge the tyme that Palmer dwelte with mr. Lee he neaver came to anye other hosties but to the cokes howse wheare he bourded when he was scolemaster theare; to the wyche howse he came from Horsyngtone, and thear dyned the same daye that he was taken and brought before the commyssyoners; and yff it can be provyd that ever he came to the Cardinall hatte in Readinge,[a] and called for a closse chamber,[b] as this slaunderer hathe heare feyned and informed master Foxe, I am content to suffar suche punishment as shalbe due for a moste wycked offender, to the triall whearof I put myselffe to the worshipfull of the towne of Readinge and others wyche knowe the matter, as the good-man Gatley, mr. Edmundes, [and] those that dwell in the Cardinall hatte.

(Fourth Section.)   *The Slaunderer.*

" He came not so closly but that this viperouse generatione had knowledge thearof; whearfore withowte delaye they layde thear heades togeather, and consulted what waye they myghte moste easely proceade agaynste hym to brynge thear olde cankred malyce to passe; and so yt was consydered, that one mr. Hampton, wych then bore twoe faces in one hoode, and under the pretence and coler of a brother played the parte off a dyssemblynge hypocrite, shoulde resorte to hym, and under the pretence off frendshipe shoulde feel and fyshe owte the cause off his returne to Readinge."

[a] " That mr. Palmer was fet from the Cardinal hatt in the night tyme, contrary to Thackham's assertion, the goodwyffe of the Cardynall hatt, with her sonne in law Harrye Singleton, and Stephen Netherclief ostler of the howse then and yet, do beare witnesse. The tyme was, to theyr judgment, betwene x and xj of the clocke at night, or thereabowt." Informations gathered in Reading, 1571.

[b] " And whether Palmer called for a close chamber or not, yt ys confessed by them of the howse that he was lodged in the closyst chambre in the howse, to wyt, in the chambre beyond the hall, and that there he was fetched owt. Also Stephen Netherclief the ostler saith that he called for a close chambre. The goodwyfe of the Cardynall hatt saith she was in a merveilous feare when they did fetch hym, and therfore belyke there were more than one seargeant." (Ibid.) It is probable that at this period the *ostler* of an inn was one who had the direction of internal arrangements, and not merely of those of the stables.

Thackham.

This slaunderer callethe us a " viperouse generatione," and sayethe that I wyth other, that is, Cope, Downer, and one Gatelye, made one Hampton an instrument, by whose practyse we soner myghte brynge ower myschevous purpose to passe. Let this be examined within the towne of Readinge, and yff it can be provid that evar Palmer came closley to the Cardynall hatte there, that evar I and my confederates knewe off his beyng thear, that we dyd ever consulte to betraye hym, as this slaunderer reportethe, that one Hampton became a instrument to compasse anye villanye agaynste Palmer, that Hamptone dyd ever talke with Palmer there, and dyd seke to fyshe owte the cause off his returne to Readinge, I submitte myselffe to be punished as a murtherer. I saye farther to the gentle reader, let yt be provid that I ever spake with Hampton in Readinge or in any other place, or that ever I was acqueynted with this Hamptone, or was ever in his companye to my knowledge,[a] I crave to be punished to the example off all wycked offendoures and shamlyse hipocrites. I assuar the gentle reader that it grevethe me more that he hathe so muche abused the wryter of the hystorye to whome he gave this informatione, then that he hathe so slaundered me, because he hath herein more slaundered the volume whearin yt is wryten, then me off whome it is wrytten. Thear was neaver information geven as I thynke by any man, were his malyce neaver so greate, but that some sentence and portione off

---

[a] In the Reply at this point is the following passage, which I quote for the sake of the remarkable notice of a *Flanders lock* which the simile presents: " Also, though you and youre confederates knewe not of his (Hampton) beyng there, yet either you alone, or you with some other, or youre confederates alone or with some other, knewe it. You allwayes seke to myngle thynges together when they should be severed, or to dissever them when they should be joyned together, to the entent you maye the better blynde the simplicitie of the matter, lyke unto the men that use to make soche Flaundyers lockes as be opened by order of certayne letters, who use to myngle other letters with those that serve to the purpose, to blynde and hynder them that seke to fynde out the true placyng of the letters wherby the lockes are opened." (f. 9.)

it was true; but from the begynninge off his information to the ende yt shall neaver be provyd that one sentence off this slaunderer's reporte is trew, for the triall whearoff I put myselff to be tried by the inhabitantes off the towne of Readinge.

(Fifth Section.) *The Slaunderer.*

" Palmer, as he was a man symple and withoute all wrynckles off cloked colusyone, opened to hym his whole intent; but Hamptone earnestlye persuadid hym to the contrarye, declaringe what daungear myghte ensue yff this were attempted. Agaynste this counsell Palmer [replied] very muche, and as they waxed hotte in talke Hamptone flongea waye in a furye, and sayed as he had fysshed so should he fowle for hym."

Thackham.

Yff thou remember, gentle reader, what I sayed before, I nede not use many wordes to dysprove that wych the slaunderer bathe here reported; whearfore to this I brefflye answere, I knowe not wheather Hampton wear acqueynted with Palmer at Oxforde or not, but yt shal be neaver provyd that they mette at the Cardinall hatte and talked togeather, as this malyciouse slaunderer hathe informed mr. Foxe; yet, yff his tale be well marked, he handlethe cunninglye, fyrste in declarynge howe symple Palmer was, and withowte all cloked colusyone, and how Palmer and Hampton debated the matter and waxed hotte in thear talke, and howe Hampton departed in a furye, saynge that he shoulde fyshe as hee had fouled. Maye not this beweche, nay, daftly persuade the reader off this hystorye that it is very likelye to be all treue, or at the leastwyse that some parte off yt is treu? and yet I assuar the gentle reader, let this his informatione be examyned in the towne of Readinge, and yff ever yt be provyd that Palmer and Hampton ever met at the Cardynall hate thear, or had any suche talke, let me be punished to the example off all others.

(Sixth Section.)   *The Slaunderer.*

" Palmer, not suspectinge suche prepensed and dyvised myscheffe, as by this crouked and pestyferouse generatione was nowe in bruinge agaynste hym, called for his supper and went quyetlie to bed; but quietlye he coulde not rest there, for furthwith the offycers and thear retynue came russhynge in with lanterns and bylls, and required hym in the kynge and quenes name to make ready hymsellff, and quyetlye to departe wyth them."

Thackham.

There was never godly man so shamefully used or handled as the wryter of this historye by this wicked slaunderer. He sayth that Palmer called for his supper, and he was apprehended betwene twelve and one of the clocke in the afternone; he sayeth he went quietly to bedde at the Cardinall hatt, and he laye the night before he was apprehended eightene miles off at Horsyngton in his master's house, from whense he came to his hostys' house by tenne of the clocke in the forenone, and was commytted that day to prison before thre of the clocke in the afternone; he sayth that the offycers with their retynue cam russhing in apon hym with lanternes and bylles, and, as yt ys to be proved, one sergent only, whose name I knowe not, was sent by mr. Edmundes to his hosties howse to fetche Palmer to hym; of whose comynge when Palmer had warnyng, he gott hym prevelye by a backe dore into his hostys' gardeyn, whom the offycer espyed runnynge into the gardeyne, which offycer thruste oppen the wyckett and made after Palmer, and caught hym upon the toppe of a wall leaping into another man's backesyde. And thus hath this slaunderer lyed to mr. Foxe in saying that Palmer was taken at the Cardynall hatte, and he was taken in his hostyes' garden; in saying that yt was after supper, and yt was ymmedyatly after dynner; in saying that he was in bedde, and he was upon the toppe of a walle; in saying that many russhed in apon hym with lanterns and bylles, and one only sargent, which I thynke be yett lyvyng,[a] fett him with owte any weapon. God graunte that never godly writer mete with many suche informers as [b] this ys! Gentle reader, I submitte myself to the whole town of Reading to be tryed wheare this was done.

(Seventh Section.) *The Slaunderer.*

" So the selly younge man, perceyving that he was thus Judaslye betrayed, withoute oppenyng his lippes was ledde away as a lambe to the slawghter, and commytted to warde; whome the keeper, as a ravening wolfe greedy of his prey, brought down into a vyle stynkkyng and blynde dungeon prepared for theves and murtherers, and there he kept hym hangynge by the legges and fete in a payre of stockes so highe that [well near [c]] no parte of his bodye towched the grounde. In this prisone he remayned x dayes."

Thackham.

This slaunderer here sayeth that Palmer was ledde from the Cardinall hatte to the prison; but he lyeth every worde; the sergent, takyng hym as he was lepping over the walle, brought hym to mr. Edmondes, which went with Palmer straighte-waye to the vysyters, which as yt happened satte the same daye at the Bare,[d] in a parler on the lefte hande as ye enter in, which ys at this daye to be proved; whome after the visiters had examyned, and founde hym nothing conformable to them, they sent ymedyatly for one Welche the keper of the towne gayle, which when he was come they delyvered Palmer

---

[a] " Yet, when all is done, you buyld all your bravery herein upon the credyte of one poor catchepolle." (Reply, f. 11.) I quote this merely to show that the terms *serjeant* and *catchpole* were synonymous. In modern times our serjeants of police are officers in command of inferior constables; in the sixteenth century the serjeants were the men under the orders of a commanding *constable*. See in Underhill's narrative hereafter, Newman the ironmonger serving as constable of the night watch at Newgate. The chief of the whole force was sometimes styled the *headborough*.   [b] *In MS.* and.

[c] These words are supplied from the printed text of Foxe.

[d] " The Golden Bear inn, a very old building, now a dwelling-house." Coates, *History of Reading,* 1802, p. 332.

to hym, wylling that he shulde be kept in close prison, and that no man might speake with hym; at what tyme I was present myself, as I wyll after more at large declare. And concernyng his hanging by the legges so highe that no parte of whitte[a] of his boddy might towche the grounde, this slaunderer doth belye the jayler; for so sone as he hadde broughte Palmer to the jayle, which ys no depe dungeon to speke of, he shutte the nether dore and the upper dore, which being shitte no bodye might come at hym. The same evenyng the keper, whose name was Welche, came to me, and moche lamented Palmer's troble, and sayde that he, as he was moche bounde to hym for teaching his sonne when he was scole-master, so would he nowe be gladde to shewe hym all the favour he mighte; "but, (sayeth he,) Mr. Thackham, you harde what charge I hadde to kepe hym so close that no boddye shulde come at hym; he walketh in the prison, butt I have shutte the upper dore." I sayde unto hym, "Albeit I knowe that ye be nott of his religion, yet syns he haith by your owne confession done you pleasure, I pray you shewe hym all the favour that you may;" which he promysed to do. And when he parted from me he sayd that he had no money; then I delyvered the keper iij^s. to geve him; not that I owed hym anye,[b] but trusting he shulde have byn delyvered, and have payde me agayne. And after that I sente hym at thre sundrey tymes iij^s. at a tyme, wherof he never payde me any penye, butt at the stake he requested his keper, which of a weaver became a sumner, and after dwelte in Salysbury, to desyer me to forgive hym the xij^s. which I lente hym in the prison. And I assuer the, gentle reader, that this keper whome this slaunderer calleth "ravenyng wolfe, gredye of his praye," was to Palmer a very frende, and shewed hym all the frendeshippe that he

---

[a] *Sic MS. qu?* or whit.

[b] In the Reply, this and nearly every other statement of Thackham is discredited, and combated to the uttermost, and from point to point. As already stated, the special pleading, whether one side or the other was right, is not worth the space it would occupy. But many phrases and expressions are remarkable. And here the writer says, "but in dede this is another *Banbury glose* to make your cause probable." (f. 12 b.)

colde during the tyme of his abode there; and therefore moche ys this slaunderer to be blamed for so raylyng at hym, and if the keper be deade I dought not butt his honest neighbours will repete the same.

(Eighth Section.) *The Slaunderer.*

The firste examinacion and accusacion of Palmer.

" After this he was brought before the maior, and there, by the procuerment of a false brother, one Thomas Thackham, not mr. Thackham of Durresley in Glocestershere, butt another of the same name yett alyve and no kyn to hym, which had obteyned the prefermente of the free scole for hym and his assignes, he had dyversse and enormiouse crymes layde to his charge."

Thackham.

Gentle reader, this slaunderer ys no chaungeling, for as he lyed in the begynnyng, soe he nowe lyeth in the myddle, and wyll doe unto th' ende. Suerlye, except he had of verye purpose abused the wryter of this historye, and of the [like] shameles spight slaundred me, he colde never have had the mynde to have forged so false a reporte, nether the face to have brought hym suche an untrothe. He sayeth that by my procuerment he was broughte owte of the prison, where he hanged by the heles, before mr. mayer; but I assure the, gentle reader, that after he was fyrste examyned at the Beare in Reading, before the commyssioners, and by them sent to the prison, as ys affore sayde, as farre forth as I knowe, Gode I take to wytnes, he neaver came owte of prison untyll he was sent for to Newberye before the same commyssioners, nether dyd the maior ever see hym after that he had presented Palmer to the commyssioners at the Beare in Reading as ys afforesayde; and for my parte I take Gode to wytnes after that daye I never sawe hym, butt sent to hym as ys afforesayde, and therefore nether dyd I procner this godlye younge man to come before the mayer, nether dyd the maior ever after that day talke

---

ᵃ Foxe altered this to " the procuerment of certain false brethren (the Lord knoweth what they were), who had been conversant with Palmer, and robbed his study."

with Palmer, as I harde, for other commyssioners appoynted for the same purpose had that matter in hande. He calleth me "false brother." Because his tonge ys no slaunder, and that all he hath sayde shall torne to his owne shame, I am nott angrye with hym. Gode make us bothe trewe brotherne! I waye not his colorycke termes; he speaketh lyke hymself.

He sayeth "one Thomas Thackham, not mr. Thackham of Durresleye in Glocestershere." Trulye mr. Thaokham ys moche bounde to this slaunderer, whatsoever Thomas Thackham ys. As lyttle as this rayler estemeth me, and wolde have other esteme of me, I was nether cobbler nor taylor before I was made a mynyster;[a] but of that degree of scole as mr. Thackham. But I tell the, gentle reader, if one of us twayne muste be the worker of this villaynous acte agaynste Palmer, as this slaunderer semeth to inferre, I assure the yt muste nedes be mr. Thackham of Durresley, for ytt ys nott I, as yt shal be well proved; butt yf nether he nor I dyd ytt, what shulde move this slaunderer to name ether of us? He sayeth I had obteyned the preferment of the free scoole for me and myne assigns. Yt is well knowen in the towne of Reading that I nether hadde nether ever sued for any other pattent [b] then that which one Coxe badde graunted

[a] " In deede, as the gatherers of this story, when they wrote it, had not heard that you were a minister, nor of what religion you were: so they knew full well that mr. Thackham of Dursley was bothe a learned devyne, a phisicion, and a godly preacher, and that he hathe a brother of the same name, not unlyke unto himselfe; and therefore in conscience they thought it their partes (seyng cache of theim is called Thomas) to exempt theim from the name of this quarell that perteyned nothing to theim. And yet is mr. Thackham of Dursley nothing the more beholdyng to theim for doyng this their duetye. Where in disdayne that you are not called 'mr.' you seme to signefy that you are of some degree of Schoole: trulye, although you be so, it forceth not moche. Yet verely some do suppose that you are of greater degree of schole than a cobler or a taylor, of whome you speake so contempteously and disdeynfully, as if no cobler nor taylor in England were worthy of the name of a master. Agayne, I doubt not but some shal be found that have bene taylors and coblers, and are at this present as worthy ministers as you." (Reply, fol. 15.) The writer (f. 26) admits his knowledge that Thackham (his opponent) was also "a phisician."

[b] The letters patent were granted to Leonard Coxe in 1541, with a yearly pension of 10 li.: the same sum having been assigned to the school, out of the crown rents of the town,

unto hym and to his assignes by kynge Henry,[a] which Coxsys tyme came to Bylson,[b] then to me, after to the vicar of Saynt Gyles,[c] then to Palmer, after to me agayn by Palmer's owne offer, as yt shall afterwards appere; and when Coxe dyed, to whom yt was fyrste graunted, then was that patent of no longer force.

After whose death the towne of Reading obteyned all the quenes landes there in fee-farme, and hadde the placing of the scole-master, with alowaunce to paye hym, and have at this day; and if I had sued for a newe patent in my owne name, as I neaver dyd, what coulde this have hurte Palmer? seeing he had resygned the scole to me longe before, and had receyved his money for the pattent, as I am well able to prove.

He sayeth that when I hadde broughte Palmer before the maior I layed dyverse and enormiouse crymes to his charge. Yt shall never be proved that I and Palmer came before the maior; yt shall never be provyd that I ever layed any thinge to Palmer's charge. He was an honest vertuouse younge man, and I never kuewe any hurte by hym, neather shall ytt be proved that I dyd at any time laye oughte to his charge, as this slaunderer sayeth I dyd.

(Ninth Section.) *The Slaunderer.*

" For this Thackham, takyng upon hym the offyce of an accuser, hadde suborned iij. false wytnesses, to wytte Coxe, Gately, and Downer, which men under the name of brethern hade bene conversant with him and robbed his studye, as ys afforesayd. These burdeyned hym with treason, sedicion, surmysed murther, and adultery."

[a] Leonard Cockes, or Coxe, author of The art or craft of Rhetoryke, 1532, and other works. (See memoirs of him in Coates's History of Reading, 1802, pp. 322-327; and Athenæ Cantabrigienses, 1858.)

[b] Leonard Bilson, of Merton college, Oxford, M.A. 1546. He was uncle of dr. Thomas Bilson, bishop of Winchester. (See Coates's Reading, p. 327.)

[c] John More was presented to the vicarage of St. Giles's by sir Francis Englefield, and instituted Nov. 14, 1540. He appears to have held it to 1561. (Coates's History of Reading, p. 350.)

Thackham.

Coxe ys dedde,[a] which lyving was never acquaynted with Palmer which was of that honestye and goode nature, and so lyved in the fere of Gode, well knowen to be an honeste professor of his worde, that by my [b] meanes in any respecte he wolde have byn proved a false witnes for any rewarde, which yf he were lyving wolde answer this to the shame of the slaunderer. Downer ys also dedde, which lyving was alwaye Palmer's frende and never soughte to hurte hym, as the towne of Reading woll wytnes. Gately I thynke yett lyvyth, which to the shame of this slaunderer wyll both testefye that I never procured hym to be a false wytnes agaynst Palmer, and also that he

[a] In the "Informations gathered at Reading, 1571," it is remarked that "Thackham speaketh of one Coxe in his answer; and the story meaneth another called William Coxe, the cooke which was Palmer's hoste." This charge of presumed duplicity is thus enlarged upon in the Reply. "Now, as before you playde the sophister, blyndyng the truth sometyme with the difference and otherwhile with the confusion of tyme, place, and order of thinges, so here also you endevour to cast a myst before our eyes *ex differencia personarum*, convertyng your talke from that Coxe whiche is meant and touched in the storye, and applying it to another verye honest man of the same name, not meant nor spoken of, and now dead. Belyke you were so moche ashamed of your olde frende William Coxe, that is to(o) well knowen, and also by you confessed, to have bene a great doer against Palmer, that you thought best to bewtefie the deformitie of him with the honestye of a very godly man of the same name, and it is a worlde to se what peynes you take with many wordes to commend a verie good man, knowen to have bene so godly that he litle neded your prayses. But you would not have wrested the sence of the storye to this Coxe, nor praysed him so moche, savyng that you thought that the worthynes of his name would purchase great credite to your lyes and tales, and for every childe that knoweth you and William Coxe the cooke, that was Palmer's hoste, knoweth, that you could not do this by errour and ignorance, but of a set purpose to helpe up your market. And because you be very lothe to have your frende Coxe yet lyving to be knowen, or youre alone legerdemayn and craftie conveyaunce to be sene, whensoever you speake of William Coxe, or of any thing that concerneth him (as you do often), you never call him by his name, but sometyme he is the cooke, sometyme the woman's housband, sometyme Palmer's hoste, sometyme his hostesse' housband; but his name you dissemble still, lyke a craftie crowder expert in these feates, not by wit and arte, but by often practice and long contynuaunce. You walk naked in a net, and thinke you go invysible, and yet you are afrayd of the light. The Lorde stryke your olde hearte with repentaunce before he pluck you awaye!" (fol. 16 b.)

[b] *So in MS. qu?* no.

never robbed his studye. Gentle reader, whatsoever this slaunderer haith here malyciously reported, yt shall neaver be proved that I, Coxe, Gatelye, or Downer [a] dyd come before the maior with Palmer, or ever layed any thinge to his charge, or ever came into his studye; yett doth this slaunderer call us theves, and sayeth we robbed his studye.

Yt shall also be proved that when Palmer was apprehended he had no studye nor chamber in Reading, for he then dwelled, as I sayde before, with mr. Raff Lee, at Horssyngton, in Buckinghamshire, eighte miles from Reading; from whence he came that daye by tenne of the clocke in the forenoone; at the which Horssington his bokes and rayment was, wheare he taughte scole; so that we colde nott robbe his studdye butt we muste goe to Horssington, for at Reading he hadde nether chamber, studdye, bokes, apparell, scrippe, nor scrowle. Except the dyvell hadde dyrected his penne, he colde not have presented mr. Foxe with so manye lyes in so fewe wordes, but he muste sometymes have hytt apon some truthe.

This slaunderer sayeth that I, with false wytnesses as I badde, charged Palmer before the mayer with treason, sedition, surmysed murder [b] and adultry. Yf I, with my [three [c]] false wytnesses Coxe, Gately, and Downer, dyd ever bringe Palmer before the mayer and burdeyn hym with suche crymes, yt ys to be thoughte that eyther the mayer's wyff, which I thinke ys yett alyve, or some of his brethern, or some of the offycers, or some of the towne, can wytnes with this slaunderer that this ys trewe; butt nott one lyving in that towne wyll testefie that we ever so behaved ourselves towardes Palmer, or that I ever came before the maior with Palmer. I take Gode to wytnes that I ever was perswaded that Palmer was free from treason, sedition, murder, and adultry; and that I have here sayed

---

[a] "For Downer, I have heard no evil of him. For Gately, and Radley, now vicar of St. Lawrence [John Radley, instituted Nov. 29, 1565, resigned 1574,], and Bowyer a tanner, they three left no means unpractised to catch and persecute the members of Christ, as I myself can well prove." (Letter of John Moyer to master Purye.) Gateley was the man who, being the constable (see p. 117), really searched Palmer's study: which was in the school-house. (Informations, &c.)

[b] matter *in MS*.   [c] *Blank in MS*.

I dought nott butt the inhabytaunce of Reading wyll affyrme to be trewe.

(Tenth Section.) *The Slaunderer.*

" To whome Palmer answered that yf suche horrable and heynous crymes might be proved agaynst hym, he wolde pacyently submytt hymselfe to all kynde of tormentes that colde be devysed; ' butt, O ye cruell bloodsuckers! (sayeth he,) ye folowe the olde practyses of your progenytores, the wolvyshe generacion of pharyses and papists; butt be ye well assured that Godes eye allreadye seeth your subtyl devyses and craftye packyng, and woll not suffer this owtragiouse furye of your venemouse townges and fyrye hartes to eschape unponysshed!' All this whyle no mencion was made of heresye or heretycall wrytting."

Thackham.

Here the slaunderer bringeth in Palmer answering for himself and raylyng at me and my procured false wytnesses; but lett the holle towne of Reading be examyned, and yt[a] shall never be proved that we ever broughte hym before the maior,[b] and that we thus charged

---

[a] *MS.* yet.

[b] " In the begynnyng of this section, you seke to dasyll our eyes in the clere daye, even as the fishe called a cuttell, to shift himselfe in the clere water that he maye not be sene, casteth foorth a certeyn black substance to darken the water, so you here, to hide the truthe from mennes eyes, cast foorth wordes to darken the true sence of the storie, and to leade awaye the reader's mynde to another meanyng ; for where as the storye sayth that by your procurement, when he was brought before the maior, dyverse crymes were layde to his charge, (whiche thing might have bene done without company, betwene the maior and and Palmer alone, or elles in the presence of fewe besydes,) yet you woulde the reader should thinke that the maior sate formally *pro tribunali;* that Palmer, together with Thackham, Gateley, Coxe, and Downer were solemply brought foorth ; that the playntif and defendant, with the witnesses, accordyng to forme of lawe, were openly called in the face of the courte ; that the accuser pronounced openly against him; that the witnesses were formally charged, and did in open audience depose and testefye against him; that Palmer was openly convicted, the maior pronouncyng sentence against him in publique assembly. But the story importeth no soche thing; and the worlde knoweth that in those

hym, and that he thus answered for hymself and rayled on us. There ys of this, gentle reader, not one worde trewe: lett the people there be judge.

(Eleventh Section.)   *The Slaunderer.*

" The greatest proves agaynst hym were these: First, that Palmer said the quene's sworde was nott putt in her hande to execute tyrrannye, and kyll and murther the trewe subjectes.[a]

2. That her sworde was to(o) blunte towardes the papistes, but towardes the trewe Christyans yt was to(o) sharpe.

3. That certayn servantes of sir Frauences Knowles and other [resorting to his lectures [b]] fell owte amonge themselfes, and were lyke to have commytted murther, and therefore he was suer [c] of sedition and prevyer [d] of unlawfull assemblies.

4. That his hostys had wrytten a letter unto hym, which they had [intercepted [b]], wherin she required hym to returne to Reading, and sent her commendacions by that token that the knyffe laye hydde under the beame; wherbye theye gaythered that she hadd conspyred with hym to murther hur husband.

5. That they founde hym alone with his hostyes by the fyer-syde [in the hall [b]], the dore being shutte to them."

Thackham.

This shamelesse slaunderer bringeth in fyve artycles which I, Coxe, Gately, and Downer dyd laye to Palmer's charge before the mayer, and maketh me the ringe-leadere in promoting the same to the maior; wherefore of necessyte I muste answer them.

dayes fewe thinges were done formallye and justly, and that the martirs were hardly suffered at that tyme to plead for theimselves openly, but that most thinges touchyng theim that professed the Gospel were handeled in *hucker mucker* against all order of lawes, reason, and conscience, &c." (Reply, f. 19.) In an earlier passage the writer had expressed himself in the same way: "Many thinges were handeled in those dayes in *hucker muck*er, and with moche percialitie."

[a] servantes of God *in Foxe*.   [b] Foxe.   [c] a sower.   [d] a procurer *in Foxe*.

1. To the firste I answer that I take Gode to wytnes I never harde Palmer saye any suche wordes as in the firste artycle this slaunderer sayeth that I with others dyd laye to his charge, neather can ytt be proved that we ever broughte hym before the maior to charge hym therewith.

2. To the seconde article I answer in lyke manner.

3. To the thirde artycle I answer that I neather kuewe of any suche dissention, neather dyd I laye any suche matter to his charge; and further I saye that I never harde of yt, much lesse colde I laye suche a matter to his charge, except I wolde have done then by Palmer as this slaunderer doth by me, off malyce devyse agaynst Palmer that which I never kuewe, muche lesse had byne able to prove, which wolde have fallen owte to my greate shame.

4. To the fowrth I answer that when this letter was intercepted I was at Salysberye, and knewe nothing of yt untyll my returne, which was fyve dayes after; and when I went to bedde my wyff tolde me what had happenyd to Palmer syns my departure; howe the cokes wyff, which was his hostys, had caused a letter to be wrytten, and sent to Palmer, and howe the same letter was taken by the waye upon Cawsome brygge,[a] and broughte to the maior; and howe that Palmer came from mr. Lee's the next day folowing, nott knowing of anye such matter, for whome the mayer sent ymmedyatly, and after examinacion had at the sute of the husbande, Palmer was sent to the cage. All this was done, and Palmer was returned agayn to mr. Lee's, before I came home, as I shal be well able to prove; of which his troble I knewe no more then the childe newe borne, I take Gode to witnes, yet doth this slaunderer make me the chief hearin. Also I doughte nott, gentle reader, nay I am suer that yt ys yett to be proved, who wrotte the letter, whoe carryed the letter, who dyd entercepte the letter, and that I herein shalbe clered, though this slaunderer layeth all to my charge; but trewthe yt ys that Palmer's hostys' husbande shewed me the letter a weke after,

[a] Caversham bridge.

declaryng what his wyff and Palmer ment to doe, to whome I answered that in conscience I dyd verelye beleve that Palmer neaver ment any suche vyllayny towardes hym; to the tryall of which I commytt myself to the whole towne of Reading.

5. To the fyfte, I answer that yt might be that they were founde sytting alone by the fyer, and the dore shutte to them; butt I dyd never see them sytt alone together and the dore shutte, neather dyd I ever present any suche thinge to the mayer; neather dyd I heare that any other man dyd signifie so moche to the mayer at any tyme, I take Gode to recorde. And by that which I have sayde before yt may easely appere, gentle reader, how falsely this slaunderer belyeth me in that which foloweth.

(Twelfth Section.)   *The Slaunderer.*

"When this evydence was geven uppe, the mayer dysmyssed them, and went to dyner, commanding Palmer to the cage,[a] to make hym an open spectacle of ignominie to the eyes of the worlde; and Thackham, the better to cover[b] his owne shame, caused ytt to be bruted that he was soe punished for his evyll lyff and wyckednes allreadye proved agaynst hym."

Thackham.

Here this slaunderer bringeth me in for the chieff worker agaynst Palmer, and telleth howe to cover my shame I conveyed the matter after that I with others whome I procured had layed all these artycles to Palmer's charge; and this too, reader, may seme a lykely tale; butt lett yt be proved that I was there, or as I sayde before knewe of Palmer's troble, or was there when he was sent to the cage, and I wyll be gyltye of all that this slaunderer haith and shall

---

[a] "The cage then stood over the entrance into the churchyard belonging to St. Lawrence's parish, and now forms part of mr. John Blandy's house: it was rented of the parish by the corporation, at the yearly rent of twelve-pence." (Note in Man's History of Reading, 4to. 1816, p. 198.)

[b] colorr *in MS.*

herafter laye to my charge; and wheras he sayeth that I, Coxe, Gately, and Downer procured Palmer this troble, he belyeth us all; for Palmer came before the mayer and was from thence sent to the cage at the onelye suete of the coke, his hostyes husband, which layed to Palmer's charge that he with his wyff had agreed to kylle hym, and thus moche I harde after my returne by the coke hymself when he shewed me the letter. But marke, I beseche you, gentle reader, howe this shameles lyer haith forgotten hymself. He sayde before that Palmer was fett from the Cardinall hatte owte of his bedde in the night by offycers, and had to the dungeon, and so forth, as ys afforesayde; and nowe ys Palmer fett owte of prison, broughte before the maior, accused by me and others, and from thence sent to the cage; and true yt ys that when his ostys sent the letter, Palmer was at mr. Lee's, eightene miles of; which Palmer returned from thence to Reading very shortelye after, knowing nothinge of the letter that was intercepted, which shulde have come to hym; and ymmedyatly upon his returne he was sent for by the mayer at the sute of the coke, and so commytted to the cage, and went nott from the prison to the cage as this slaunderer falselye reportyth. Yt was long after before he was commytted to the prison, and that was done by the commyssioners, and not by the mayer, as yt ys well knowen; for after he came owte of the cage he went to his master agayne; and yf the well-meanyng wryter of this historye knewe howe moche this malliciouse slaunderer had abused hym he wolde beware of suche a fellowe all the dayes of his lyff. As I sayde before I saye agayne, I take Gode to wytnes I kuewe no more of his commyng before the mayer nor of his being in the cage then the childe that was borne the same nighte, and yett this slaunderer ys nott ashamed to make me the cheeffe instruement and doer herin.

(Thirteenth Section.) *The Slaunderer.*

" In the afternone Palmer came to his answer, and dyd so mightelye and clerlye deface their evydence, and so defende his owne innocencye, provyng also that the sayde letters were by themselfes forged, that the mayer hymself was moche ashamed that he had borne with them, so that he soughte meanes he might conveye hym awaye prevelye."

Thackham.

What tyme of the day Palmer was ffett owte of the cage, howe he clered hymself,[a] and whether the mayer were ashamed of his doinges or nott, I cannot tell, for as yt shal be proved I was nott at home. I knewe nothing neather of his fornones examynacion, neather of his afternones examynacion. Gatelye, whome he here slaundereth, the mayer's wyff, with others there yet lyving, can declare the trothe; butt I dare affyrme, that yf the mayer were lyving, he wolde soe answer this slaunderer which sayeth he was ashamed of his doinges, that this slaunderer wolde be ahsamed of his sayinges.

(Fourteenth Section.) *The Slaunderer.*

"But now to the bloodye adversaries. When they sawe the matter frame so evill favouredly, and fearinge least if he shold escape privily, ther doinges wold tend no lesse to ther shame and daunger then to the maior's dishonesty also, they devised a new pollicye to bringe to passe ther longe hidden and festred malice against him, which was their [b] extreme refuge; for wheras before they were partly ashamed to accuse him of heresye, seeinge they had bene counted earnest brethren themselves, and partly afraid bycause they had broken up his studye, and committed theft, yet now, lest ther iniquitie shold have bene reveled to the worlde, they

---

[a] "Albeit you knowe not (as you saye) how Palmer clered himselfe, and be also certeyn that he clered not himselfe, as the storye reporteth, yet I woulde you should right well understand that the God of truthe hathe made it knowen to the godly: yea, heaven, earth, and hell shall, to his everlastyng comfort, and to the confusion of his enemyes, and all blooddye papistes, perceave and knowe, that, by the assistance of Goddes holye spirite the Comforter, he mightely and clerely confounded his enemyes and defended his owne innocency against them." (Reply, f. 21 b.)

[b] *MS.* this.

put both feare and shame aside, and beganne to refricate and rippe up the olde soare, the skarr wherof had bene but superficially cured, as ye have hard, and so, to coloure ther former practises, chardged him with [the] writinges that they had stollen owt of his studye."

Thackham.

Now this sclaunderer, well armed with railinge tearmes, leapinge from lye to lye, from falshoode to falshoode, as though he were never to be reproved, goeth on still after his accustomed maner, and saith that Thackham, with the other bloody adversaries and theves, to avoide the shame and daunger that was like to insue, and to kepe the maior from dishonesty, beganne a new practise to bringe an olde grudge to passe, saith we brake up his studye, and fetched owt writinges, wherwith we charged him before the maior. Yt shall never be proved, gentle reader, that we brake up his studye, or ever were in his studye, or toke one paper from thence, or that we ever brought him before the maior, or laid any suche matter against him; and seeinge this sclaunderer calleth us theves, it standeth us upon that be lyvinge to cleare it, or els ther is no time past but that we may resceive a felon's rewarde, which is to be hanged; and if I ever was in his studye, or can tell whether he had a studye or not, I desire to have a shamefull deathe; and I doubt not but Gately is as well able to cleare him selfe of this robberye.[a] Let it be proved that I ever complayned of Palmer to the maior, or ever came with Palmer before the maior when he was examyned, and I will be giltye of all that this sclaunderer hath laid to my chardge.[b]

[a] " Where you doubt not but Gatelye is well hable to clere him selfe of this great robbery, you are the bolder so to saye, because he was at the tyme constable [see note in p. 110] and might do it by good authorite. Notwithstandyng, good men maye be bolde to call him thefe for his laboure, seyng that before God it was playne robbery ; and in the judgment of the Godly learned, that thinge maye well be sayd stollen, whiche is by fraude, sleight, or violence taken from a just man, even by an officer." (Reply, f. 23.)

[b] " The worst that ye could then do was to accuse him wrongfully, and to laye that

Trewe it is that one only letter was the cause of all Palmer's troble that he had before the visiters, and so consequently of his deathe, which letter at the earnest request of Palmer I carried to the maior; which letter Palmer wrot in Buckinghamshire, and brought with him to Readinge the same day that the visiters sate at the Beare; to the writinge wherof if I had bene priveye (as I was not) I had bene hanged, as the maior and the comissioners tolde me afterwards; of the which letter, I assure the, gentle reader, that Coxe, Gately, and Downer never knewe, which they never towched nor sawe, nether any creature lyvinge but Palmer, I and the maior, of the which letter I will speake more hereafter.

(Fifteenth Section.) *The Sclaunderer.*

"Thus Palmer was once againe called owt of prisone to appeare before the maior and Burdet[a] the officiall and two other justices, to render an accompt of his faithe before them, to answere to sutche informacions as were laid against him; and when they had gathered of his owne mouthe sufficient matter to trappe him, they devysed a certificat or bill of instructions against him, to be directed to doctour Geffery,[b] who had determyned to hold his visitation the next Tuesday at Newbury, which was the xth of July;[c] and thus were these false witnesses and bloodye accusers wyncked at, and the innocent delyvered to the lyon to be devoured. When it was concluded that Palmer shold be sent over to Newbury, the said letters testimoniall were conveied over togither with him."

---

thing to his charge, whiche if he woulde have renounced and forsaken, he might have lyved in earth more prosperously than ever you could, or have done, by often chaungyng your typpet and turnyng your coate." (Reply, f. 23 b.)

[a] Clement Burdett, rector of Englefield, before noticed.
[b] See before, p. 74.
[c] xvith *in Foxe, edit.* 1576, *p.* 1843.

Thackham.

Whether Palmer were called againe .owt of prisone after he was comitted thither by the commissioners which sate at the Beare as aforsaid, I can not tell; but to my knowledge he was never brought owt of Welche his prisone before he was sent for by the comissioners to Newbury, and if he were brought forth of the prison to be examined before the maior and others as he saith here he was, I take God to wytnes it was not by my procurement and my confederates the innocent Palmer was delyvered to the lyon to be devoured, and that we bloodye accusers were wyncked at. The sclaunderer shall well knowe that I will not be wincked at; but loke what may be proved against me I will have the ponishement with all extremitie, and thus end to answer so shameles a sclaunderer. And albeit, gentle reader, that whosoever shall reade this that my adversary hath caused the godly writer of this history to put in writinge, and by printinge the same to publishe it to the worlde against me, Coxe, Gately and Downer, bloodye accusers and false witnesses against Palmer, as he tearmeth us, consideringe how boldly he reporteth us, with what reasons he perswadeth it, with what order he telleth it, with how haynous offences and felonous actes he chardgeth us, with how spitefull and railinge wordes he useth us, what uncharitable and odious names he giveth us, might easely be perswaded that he hath not lyed every sentence from the begynnyge.

But, gentle reader, marke well my offer. If this sclaunderer shall ever be able to prove that of all he hath informed against me, and hath procured mr. Foxe to publishe abroade, one sentence be trewe, I beseche the counsell that I may have suche ponishement that all other wycked hipocrites may beware by me. If I were not cleare, and yet wold be so bolde to take upon me to reprove that which mr. Foxe, a godly preacher, by his informacion hath published, as it were to deface him, and his so famouse a worke, I were worthy to be handled to the example of all others. But to deface mr. Foxe was never my purpose, blessed be God for him! I reverence him as a most excellent jewell of this our age, and accompt of him as of a principall piller of relligion. But a worshipfull knight of our contry, sir Robert Lane,[a] and one mr. Yelverton[b] a counsailor of the lawe and recorder of Northampton, wher I dwell, ofte times tolde me, and divers of my friendes sent me worde, that they marvailed that I wold neither confesse my faulte, neither answere it if I were innocent. Some gave me counsell to have an action of the case against mr. Foxe for sclaunderinge me; some said that mr. Foxe was not in faulte, but that I shold answere the sclaunderer, wherunto I agreed.

I assure the, gentle reader, if I had in queue Maries time persecuted Palmer, and xx[ti] more besides him, I wold be as ready now to confesse it in open audience, as ever Paule[c] was to confesse what a tyraunt he had bene, or as ever this sclaunderer was willinge to lay it to my chardge; for it were nothinge to my shame so to do, but to the glory of God, to my singuler comforte, and rejoysinge of all my frindes; but the matter standinge as it dothe, and that not one sentence is to be proved trewe that this sclaunderer hath informed, whether it were better for me to be evill thought of, and hold my peace, or els by some meanes to defend myne innocencye, be thou judge, gentle reader.

Here hast thou, gentle reader, myne answere to this sclaunderer, which he shall never be able to disprove. Nowe will I telle the howe Palmer behavyd himself in Readynge, howe he lefte his schole, whither he departyd thence, and by what meanes he came to his trouble.

Palmer had the schole when he came to Readynge of one sir John

---

[a] Of Horton, co. Northampton: see a note in Machyn's Diary, p. 394.

[b] Afterwards sir Christopher Yelverton, serjeant at law 1599, judge of the queen's bench 1602, died 1607: ancestor of the earls of Sussex. See an account of him in Collins's Peerage, 1779, iv. 338.

[c] "In deede S. Paul (whose example for a shewe to mocke an ape withall you bryng in) was never a tyrant, but a persecutor we reade he had bene : yet when he persecuted, he never bare ij. faces in one whoode, as you did in quene Maries tyme, and God graunt you be voyde of it now!" (Reply, f. 26.)

More, vycar of Saynete Giles,[a] in quene Maries tyme, which he taught diligently, behavyd himself honestly, came to the churche many sondaies and holidayes with his schollars, and satte in Sayncte Johnes chappell, [and] lyved so quyetly among them, that I dare swere he had not one enemy in the towne. This Palmer taught a sonne of one John Rydgies, the quenes servaunte and one of the stable;[b] which boye, ether for his negligence in learnyng, ether for some shrewd turne, he bette in the schole. Rydgies, thincking that he had gyven his sonne more correction then he deservid, in a great rage came into the schole, and boxed Palmer about the eares, and so departed. Palmer taking this grevously, that he had so muche misused him, toke a pitche-forke of his hostyes, and laye iij. or iiij. daies in wayte for Rydgies in the Vasterne,[c] beneath one John Ryder's garden,[d] to have done him some displeasure, as he wente to a close that Rydgies had toward Causam bridge, but could at no tyme mete with him. After that he had thus watched Ridges,

[a] See p. 108.

[b] At the dissolution of monastic houses king Henry determined to maintain the abbey of Reading as a royal palace; and, though it was not often occupied in that capacity, yet we find king Edward VI. lodged there, as " the Kinges Place," on his visit to the town in 1552, and king Philip and queen Mary in 1554. Camden says, " The monastery, wherein king Henry the First was interred, has been converted into a royal seat; adjoining to which stands a fair stable stored with noble horses of the king's." It was on account of this royal stable that mr. Ridges, the officer mentioned in the text, had his residence at Reading. The abbey was still regarded as royal property in 1650, when it was surveyed as parcel of the late possessions of king Charles: see Coates's Reading, p. 267.

[c] To the north of the town, at the back of Friars' street, in the map given in Coates's History of Reading, will be found fields called, The home Vastern, The little Vastern, and The farther Vasterns. There is now a short street called Vasterne street. Fasterne great park near Wotton Basset was subject to right of common for the inhabitants of that town, (see the Topographer and Genealogist, vol. iii. 1858, p. 22,) and perhaps the derivation of the name is from waste or common land, in the Latin *vastum*. Otherwise, they might be old inclosures in which cattle were kept *fast*.

[d] " Master Rider of Reding, a faithfull favourer of Goddes gospell," as Foxe terms him, who sent his servant to Palmer the night before his departure to Newbury, " with a bowed groat in token of his good harte towarde hym," offering to provide him with any necessaries that he lacked. He has been mentioned before in p. 96, note [b], as " John Ryder of Reading capper."

CAMD. SOC. R

he told me howe he had done, and what he had purposed. I told him that Ridgies was to(o) good for him, willing him not to seke to be revengyd of him, but to tell the maior and the masters of the towne. " No, (sayd Palmer,) for by that meanes I shall never prevaile, for he can make moe frendes then I."

One fortnight after, Palmer came to me and said, that he would geve up his schole, yf he might have reasonably for the patent, which hunge but apon the liffe of one olde man called Coxe.[a] I told Palmer that synce quene Marie came to the crowne, I was put from my vicaridge there, and was constrayned to labour sore for my lyvynge. For, as it is well knowne, I went every weke foure-score myles save foure, on foote, to bye yearne, and sell it agayne at Reading, of which tedyouse journeys and paynefull travayle I waxed werye. Wherfore I sayd that yf in time to come he were disposed to leave the schole, so that I could gette the good wyll of the towne to kepe it agayne, I would geve him with reason for the patent. Palmer said that he was content that I should have it before an other yf he did yelde it up; and so we partyd for that tyme.

A moneth after, he came to me againe, and said that he was come to be as good as his promysse, which was to graunte me his good wyll to have the schole before any man. I thanckyd him, and demaundyd of him what he would requyre for the patent. He sayd I should do iij thinges for him: the one was that I should geve him fourty shillinges in his purse; the other was, that I should geve him foure poundes to bye him apparell, or els be suerty for as muche apparell as came to foure poundes; the third was, that I should provyde him some place, where he might teach a gentleman's children, and lyve to his conscyence. I aunsweryd him agayne, that I must requyre lykwyse iij thinges at his handes; first that I might procure the good willes of the worshipfull of the towne, to become the schole-master agayne; secondarily, that I might have a tyme to procure such a place for him, where he might lyve safely, quyetly, and to his conscyence; thirdly, that he would take xl[s] in hande, and

---

[a] Leonard Coxe: see before, p. 108. The patent granted to Coxe will be found in the Appendix.

the residue at ij convenyent tymes, and therwith bye that he lackyd himself; which Palmer grauntyd with good wyll.

Then rode I first to Horsynton in Buckinghamshire to one master Raffe Lee,[a] which had one sonne, whom I had taught before; and tolde him that, yf he would have a scholmaster with him, to teache his sonne Edward Dunne Lee,[b] I could provyde him of an honest, quyet, sober, and learnyd young man; wherof master Lee was glad, and requestyd me so to doe, and he would compound with him for such a stypend as he should reasonably requyre. I returned to Reading and told Palmer what I had done, and howe I had sped; wherwith Palmer was content. Then we appoynted a day to repayre to the gentleman, and to bargayne for his stypende, and so we did; whome master Lee and his wyffe lyked very well.

Then after we were returnyd unto Readinge agayne, I wente to master Edmundes,[c] mr. Edward Butler,[d] master Thomas Turner,[e] [and] master Aldworth,[f] my very frendes, declaryng to them that

[a] Horsington is Horsenden in Buckinghamshire. The manor, with that of Saunderton, belonged to the family of Donne, but appears to have been temporarily held by Ralph Lee esquire. He presented to the rectory of Horsenden in 1554, and to that of Saunderton in 1572. In the latter year he received a grant of arms, being then styled of Saunderton. In that year also his wife Frances, daughter of Thomas Joanes, was buried in the Savoy church, London, Somerset herald attending. Ralph was the son of Thomas Lee, elder brother of Francis the grandfather of sir Thomas Lee who married the heiress of Hampden of Hartwell. His name, with that of his son and heir Edward, the pupil of Julins Palmer, occurs in the Lee pedigree. (Compare Lipscombe's Buckinghamshire, vol. i. p. 163, vol. ii. p. 334, vol. iii. pp. 626, 628.)

[b] This occurrence of two *prænomina*, so unusual at the period, is very remarkable. It seems to imply a relationship between Ralph Lee and the Donnes. Was his wife a widow of one of the Donne family?

[c] See before, p. 97.

[d] Edward Butler was mayor of Reading in 1554, 1559, 1575, and 1581; and a fifth time (perhaps at the close of the mayoralty of a mayor dying when in office), according to his epitaph formerly in St. Lawrence's church: which will be found in Ashmole's Berkshire, and in Coates's Reading, p. 174. In Ashmole's time there existed brass-plates, now lost, representing master Butler in his gown, his wife, his three daughters and his grandchildren. He died July 7, 1584.

[e] Thomas Turner was mayor in 1556, 1560, and 1567.

[f] See before, p. 95.

Palmer would leave the schole, and dwell with a gentleman; and desyred them that I might have their good willes to teache yt agayne, for I was wery of playing the packe-man, and of my tedyous journeys to Salesbury wekely; which aunsweryd that they thought no lesse, and that I should have their good willes to kepe the schole agayne. This done, Palmer and I came bothe to master Edmundes, steward of Readinge,[a] to have our wrytinges made, where it was agreid that I should paye Palmer xl^s in hande, and enter into bondes, to paye him the other iiij^{li} at ij other tymes by evyn porcions, and yf the said sommes were not aunsweryd according to covenantes, that then it should be lawful for Palmer to resume his patent, and enjoye the same as in his former estate. It was also agreed apon, that master Edmundes should kepe the patent and resignation, and all other wrytinges, untill the laste xl^s were payd. And thus I entrid to kepe the schole, and Palmer went to master Lee's to dwell, and there contynewed. And after Palmer had receyved his last payment, master Edmundes delyvered me the patentes, resignation, and all other writinges.

But albeit Palmer was well, and where he might have lyved quyetlye, yet (as it is well knowne) he could not tarye x dayes from his hostyes, but often resortyd unto her, so that he grewe to be evill thought of, and her husband began to mystruste him, albeit I thincke he gave never any suche cause. But so often resortyd Palmer from Horsyngton to his hostyes, that her husband began to suspecte him. Then was a letter interceptyd, which she wrote to him; which being sene, her husband kepte. And at Palmer's next returne to Readinge, (as was tolde me,) by the cookes meanes his hostyes' husband, Palmer was brought before the maior, and com-

---

[a] Steward of the estates formerly belonging to Reading abbey, and now to the crown. (see before, p. 121.) In July 1552 the office of steward of the borough and lordship of Reading, and of the possessions of the late monastery, was granted to the marquess of Northampton. (MS. Reg. 18 C. XXIV. f. 244 b.) The same office was afterwards héld by the family of Knollys, who resided in the mansion formerly the abbey, and there entertained queen Elizabeth for some days in the year 1572.

mytted to the cage; at which tyme, whatsoever the slaunderer hath sayd of me, I was not at home, nether knowe I any thinge therof, untyll fyve daies after yt was done, God I take to recorde.

Then was Palmer brought fourth of the cage, and warned by the maior to come no more at his hostyce, and was let returne againe to Horsyngton, where he dwelled with master Lee. Whether his master kuewe of his trouble or not, I cannot tell.

Notwithstanding this punishment and warnyng geven him by the mayre to com no more to his hostis, Palmer came to his hostis agayne on Tuesdaye as I thinke about x. of the clocke in the forenone; and as I sat at dinner he sent his hostis' sister, a litle wentche, for me to come and speake with him. Be twelve of the clocke I came to him, and when I was come he sayde unto me, "Mr. Thackham, I thinke ye have harde howe I have bene used here of late by the meanes of my hoste, who as I thinke is perswaded that I resorte to his house for some yvell purpose. I have a letter here which I have written to mr. Edmundes, wherin I have declared how I have bene abused and wherin; and have therin so clered myselfe that, when he hath red yt, I dowbt not but he will thinke better of me then at this present he doth; which letter I beseche you to deliver for me unto him." I answered, "Mr. Palmer, I thinke yt better that ye deliver it yourselfe." "Nay, (sayd Palmer,) he so reviled me when I was here laste, that I knowe he cannot abyde me; but by your meanes, and at your requeste, he will receave my letter, and read yt. Herein you shall doe me a great pleasure." "Mr. Palmer, (sayd I,) yf the deliverye of your letter may stand you in stede, I will carrye yt unto the mayre, and further doe you what pleasure I can." So I toke the letter, beinge faste sealed, with the superscription to mr. Edmundes; and when I cam to master Edmundes he sate in his studye writinge an obligation; to whom I sayd that master Palmer had requested me to bringe a letter, besechynge him to read the same; wherein he should perceive howe innocent he was of all that his hoste or any other had layd to his charge. "Well," (sayd mr. Edmundes,) laye yt downe, and I will loke apon yt anone."

And so I departed. Within one halfe hower master Edmundes sent for me agayne. When I came he sayde, " Mr. Thackham, Palmer hath written here no suche matter as ye tolde me of, but doth rayle at the quene and her lawes. I am her majesties officer, and maye not conseale yt, nether will." " Sir, (sayd I,) yf he have overshote himselfe in any thinge, I beseche you take him not at the worste." " Well! (sayd mr. Edmundes,) goe your waye, I maye not conseale yt, neather will I." And as I was departinge out of his wickette, he whisteled (as his maner was) for one of his sargentes. I went home to my schole, wher I walked, marvelinge what wolde come of yt.

So sone as I was gone, the mayre, mr. Edmundes, commaunded the sergent to goe to the cookes howse, and call Palmer to him. When the sergent knocked at the cookes dore, his hostis' sister spied him, and told Palmer who was at the dore. Palmer, heringe that an officer was come for him, conveyed himselfe out of the kitchen dore into the bac-side, and so into his hostis' garden. The sergent at the dore sawe him goe that waye, and thruste open the dore and folowed him, and tooke him at the ende of [his] hostis' garden about to leape over a wale; and broughte him to the mayre.

Yt happened that the very same daye ther sat at the Beare in Reading doctor Jefferye,[a] the parsone of Inglefelde,[b] with diverse other commissioners. When the sergent was come with Palmer, the mayer commanded him to goe with him; whom Palmer folowed, not knowing (as I thinke) whether he would bringe him. The mayer went streyght-waye to the Bere, wher the commissioners were, in a parler apon the righte hande as ye come into the inne. When the mayer was come to the commissioners, he declared unto them how the man whom he brought had sent him a letter, wherin was contayned matter which he would not conseale, and so he delivered the letter to them; and then the commissioners willed him to sit downe at the table's ende which is nexte to the strete; and when the mayer was sett downe, they asked who broughte him

---

[a] See pp. 74, 118.   [b] Clement Burdett: see p. 95.

the letter. The mayre answered one mr. Thackham, ther scholmaster. "I praye you, mr. mayer, (sayth docter Jefforye,) let him be sent for." So the mayer commanded his sargent to goe for me. When the sargent came to me, I was walkinge in the schole. The sergent sayd that the commissioners commanded me to come to them. I went with him. When I came before them, doctor Jefferye (as I thinke), or some other of them, asked me whether I delivered the letter to the mayre or not.[a] I sayd that I did deliver the letter to him. They asked me whether Palmer and I did devise yt; and which of us wroughte it. I answered that yt ys to be thought that I would answere that I did neather write yt nor knowe of the writinge therof; "but, sir, (sayd I,) I will not answere the question, let this man (meaninge Palmer, which stode by me,) answere how it was." Palmer then immediatlye answered, "Sir, I wroughte yt, and I will stand to yt; and as for this man, he nether wroughte yt, nether knewe what was in yt, but delivered yt to mr. mayre at my requeste." Then sayd the parsone of

[a] "At the last, to make your tale credible, you saye that one, you knowe not who (yet no man knewe the commissioners better then you), asked you, whether you were prevy to the letter that you delyvered, whereunto you saye that Palmer as a man yet once agayne willyng to dye, though he ranne awaye first from the sergeant, or rather as an impudent man, not content to write raylyng matter against his prince and the lawes, but redely to advouche it, made quyck and spedy aunswere immediatly without any deliberacion or craving of pardon (as a desperate Dick desyrous to dye without cause), and boldly sayd, 'Sir, I wrote it, and will stand to it. As for mr. Thackham he knewe not what it was. *Quare si me queritis, sinite hunc abire.*' O trym tale! now mr. Thackham (*teste se ipso*) is clered, and Palmer become giltie of his awne deathe! But if Palmer did confesse it to be his letter and hand-writyng, why were you sent for and examyned aboute the writyng therof? shall we think that they did not first demaund of Palmer, whether he wrote the letter or no? no doubte they did; wherunto when he had aunswered that he wrote it not, then were you immediatly sent for; and to be playne with you, it shalbe proved by the witnes of honest and godly men, that Palmer himselfe, beyng in prison, did greatlye complayne to his frendes, that he was betrayed, that his hand was counterfeated, and that Thackham had forged a letter in his name, and brought it to light, to cause him to be examyned of his conscience. And therewithall you presented also, accordyng to your awne tale, other thinges of his awne hand writyng, howbeit greatlye against his will, and not at his request, as you write." (Reply, f. 32.)

Yenglefelde to me: "Master Thackham, I wishe that ye teache gramer and let divinitye alone."

By this tyme was Wellche, the keper of the prisone, com into the parlar, and I was bed depart; wher I lefte Palmer talking with them stoutly; but when I was agaynst one master Borne's dore a I loked backe, and sawe Palmer cominge with the keper of the prison; and after that daye I never sawe Palmer,b nether came he out of prison so farre as I knowe any more, before he was sent for to Newberye, wher he was areyned, condemned, and burned.

He that had Palmer to Newberye was a wever with a blacke beard, which became a sumner, and went after to dwell at Salsberye: whiche tolde my wife that Palmer, beinge at the stake, requested this sumner to have him commendid to master Thackham, and to pray him to forgeve hym the twelve shillinges that he owed him, which xij^s I lent him when he lay in prison; for in consideration that I had a benefite at his hand I thoughte yt my duetye the rather to helpe him in that extremyte.

Thus haste thou hard, gentle reader, howe I delte with Palmer; howe his troble begane, how he was used, and by what occationes: which yff you compare with that the rayler hath caused mr. Fox to wryte, you shalt not find one sentense trewe.

Finis.

From Northampton, the xxxth of January,
   the yeare off ower Salvation 1571.
      By me, THOMAS THACKHAM.

---

[a] John Bourn, mayor of Reading in 1546, 1547 and 1552; burgess in parliament for the town 6 Edw. VI. and 1 and 2 Philip and Mary.

[b] "Where you saye that after that daye you never sawe him, I saye agayn, the lesse grace was in you, and the greater token it is that you had dealt Judasly with him; for elles, seyng (as you saye) that you were Palmer's great frende, and that the keper was his speciall good frende and yours also, it maye be thought you were either wicked, or very colde and without godly zeale and charitie, that in all the space that he laye in that dongeon, you would neither visite him, nor finde meanes once to beholde him along, as Peter folowed Christ. But, alas! Judas also never sawe Christes face after he had betrayed him." (Reply, f. 32.)

In addition to the passages of the Reply which have already been given in the introduction and the notes, the following may be appended, as containing a summary of the several points in dispute. The severity and acrimony of the writer has been already manifested: and perhaps we may in charity conclude that to a great extent he wrote rather from zeal than knowledge, particularly as he admits that he had never had any personal acquaintance with Thackham:—

"Whether your aunswere be reproved or no, first reade this Replye, and understand of further profes that are to be brought foorth, and then at length God graunt that you maye speake and professe as your conscience dothe and shall leade you to do! And, if you compare your awne wordes indifferently with the story, you shall the better and the soner see your awne follye.

"The storye sayth that Palmer clered himselfe from all soche crymes as were objected against him. But you, to clere your awne selfe, doubt whether he clered himselfe or noe, at the least you saye that he did not so clere himselfe as the story reporteth. Belyke, because you are a phisician, you have some other purgacion for him in store, if you might have your awne foorth. The storye sayth that you and others presented certeyn letters against him, full sore against his will, that were written with his awne hand, whiche letters had bene by certeyn enemyes of his stollen out of his study, conteynyng soche matter against him, as wherby he was detected and first knowen to the magestrates to be a protestant: you denye it, and to make up your awne mouthe, you saye that he wrote the letters of purpose to have theim shewed, and that in dede you delyvered theim: but though they were daungerous, yet he besought you with earnest sute and request to be the instrument wherby he might procure his awne deathe. The storye sheweth honest causes of his last repayr to Readyng: you hardly (*sic*) to confute the same, affirmyng that he came purposely to see a woman for whome he had bene vehemently suspected, accused, ponysshed, and from whose company although he had bene by speciall commaundment forbydden by the maior, yet he coulde not kepe himself ten dayes together from comyng xviij myles to see her. The storye sayth, he was taken in an honest inne: you saye he was taken in a suspected house, from the whiche he could not absteyne or withholde himselfe. The storye sayth that the maior was ashamed that he had executed ponyshment unjustly upon him by the intimacion and sute of certeyn uncharitable men: you saye those men were godly, and that the maior was not ashamed, nor neded not to be ashamed, of his doynges. The story excuseth him of the adulterye that was blowen up upon him by the envyous papistes: but you seme to augment that wicked suspicion, and, as farre as you dare, you signefy that he was giltie. The story commendeth his simplicitie, patience, and long-animitie: you saye that he was a fighter, and coulde not suffer injurye, but refusyng the ayde of publique authoritie, he caught a pickforke in his hand, and ranne foorth lyke a madman, and wayted upon the high-wayes, sekyng private advengement of his enemy. The storye sayth, that righteousnes' sake was the cause of his deathe: you saye that a letter whiche you delyvered was the cause of his deathe. The story sayth he was betrayed by soche men as had bene his frendes: you saye it is not so, but he betrayed himself without any just cause, even when he might have lyved quyetly to his awne conscience. The story sayth he dyed a martir unto the Lorde; you saye in effect that he ended his life as a cast-awaye and wilfull destroyer of himselfe. To be short, the storie justefieth the martir: you, to justefie yourselfe, deface the martir. The storye seketh to clere him whome God hathe clensed, yea, whome God hathe justefied and glorefied: you seeke to defile the Lordes anoynted, shewyng yourselfe therein subject to the cursse of God, accordyng as it is written, *Plague theim, O Lorde, that defyle thy priesthood.*

"Thus let all the chosen faithfull of the Lorde both in Readyng and out of Readyng, to whose judgement herein I appeale, and by whome the storie maye stand or fall, let theim I saye now testefy and pronounce who deserveth the name and hathe playd the parte of a slaunderer, who is the lyer, who hathe rayled, &c." (f. 26-27.)

Again, "You hide yourselfe properly among the bushes, thinkyng that thing to be matter sufficient to discredite the whole, and to clere the dymnes of your owne cause. But if shall please God to geve you the grace once to heare his voyce, from among these thorncy thickettes, you shall tremble and quake, and beyng stroken with contricion, and remorse of conscience, you will crye *peccavi*. And thus I make an end, warnyng you yet once agayne, that if every thing in the story be not rehersed in soche order as it was done, or that the due course of tyme and place be not thoroughly observed, it is not greatly materiall, nor moche to be merveyled at, seyng that the gatherers of the storye were not present at the doynges, and the informers neither did nor coulde so exactly instruct theim of the tymes, orders, and places as they wisshed. For the dayes were soche that the godly whiche were hable more diligently to have observed circumstances, durst not be present (very few excepted). And the gatherers thought it not expedient to counsayll with the dull, doubtfull and dissemblyng papistes. As well as they were hable to do, they have done, and have not erred in the substaunce of the matter; if any defect be founde in certeyn circumstances the want therof shalbe supplyed (I hope) in the next Edicion." (f. 27 b.)

In the "Informations gathered at Reading, 1571," occur these paragraphs respecting Thackham's conduct in the reign of Mary:—

"Thackham protested in the pulpytt in the begynnynge of queen Marie reigne that he would seale his doctrine with his blud, and stand to it even unto deathe. Yet afterwards he shranke backe, and sayd that he would never be minister agayne."

But soon after he is stated to have contributed to the performance of the popish service:—

"Wylliam Dyblye wytnesseth that Thackam brought into the church leaves of olde popishe service, and that he with others dyd helpe to patche together the bookes, and to sing the fyrst Latin even-songe in the churche of St. Lawrence."

These charges receive some support from the records of the parish of St. Lawrence. In the churchwardens' book in 1553 is a memorandum of a desk left "in the hands of mr. Thackham, being vicar," and in 1554, "Rec^d of Thomas Thackham for his wifes seate vj^d." In 1559 (this is after Elizabeth's accession) the following entries occur in the parish accounts:—

"Item, paid to Thackham for iiii. salter bookes, vj^s.

"To Thackham, for one month's service, vj^s viij^d

"To mr. Thackham, for ij weeks service, v^s." (Ibid. pp. 224, 225.)

From these entries it appears probable that Thackham continued to officiate at St. Lawrence's throughout the reign of Mary.

There was a Thomas Thackham presented to the rectory of St. Mary at Wilton, by Henry earl of Pembroke in 1572, and to that of Hilpington, by Joan Longe, widow, in 1573. (Wiltshire Institutions, printed by Sir R. C. Hoare.)

There was a second Thomas Thackham master of Reading school in 1662: he was born in 1619, being the son of Thomas Thackham and Susanna Woodcock, who were married in 1617. See further of him in Coates's History of Reading, pp. 342, 343.

There was a Thomas Thackham married at St. Mary's Reading in 1697, and a Francis Thackham of Oakingham in 1722. (Ibid. p. 127.)

Note.—Among the errors in Strype's copy of Thackham's defence, is that of misreading the date at its close, (p. 128,) as 1572 instead of 1571. This error occurs in the Ecclesiastical Memorials, vol. iii. p. 356 and p. 362.

VI.

AUTOBIOGRAPHICAL ANECDOTES OF EDWARD UNDERHILL,

ONE OF THE BAND OF GENTLEMEN PENSIONERS.

THE partial publication of the following anecdotes has made Edward Underhill well known as an actor and relater of the events of his time. From the pages of Strype his name has passed into those of Miss Strickland and others of our popular historians, whilst in Mr. Ainsworth's romance of "The Tower of London" we see "the hot Gospeller"—as by his own testimony he was called, again presented to our acquaintance, and resuming his busy and zealous part.

The writer's grandfather, John Underhill, originally of Wolverhampton, acquired, in the year 1509, a lease for eighty years from sir Ralph Shirley, of the manor of Eatington, in Warwickshire, having married Agnes, daughter and heir of Thomas Porter, a former lessee of that manor in the reign of Henry VI. John left issue, 1. Edward, who in 1541 had a fresh lease of the manor of Eatington from the Shirleys, for the term of one hundred years, and whose posterity continued at that place[a]; 2. Thomas, of Honingham, in the same county.

Thomas Underhill, of Honingham, married Anne, daughter of Robert Winter, of Hudington, co. Worcester, and died before the 36th Hen. VIII., when the estate of Honingham was sold by his son Edward, the author of the ensuing autobiography.

Edward Underhill exchanged the life of a country gentleman for that of a soldier and courtier. In 1543 he served as a man-at-arms under sir Richard Crumwell, captain of the horsemen in the contingent sent to assist the emperor in the siege of Landreci, in Hainault; and in the following year, when king Henry went to Boulogne, sir Richard procured for Underhill a nomination among the men-at-arms who were embodied to attend upon his majesty's person, being a band of two hundred, attired in a uniform of red and yellow damask, with the bards of their horses and their plumes of feathers of the same colours.

At the revival of the band of Gentlemen Pensioners, in 1539, Edward Underhill was appointed one of its first members, and he continued to serve in it at the period of the ensuing anecdotes.

[a] The pedigree is printed in the Collectanea Topogr. et Genealogica, vol. vi p. 382.

In the year 1549 he a second time went to France on military service, accompanying the army of six thousand men sent under the command of the earl of Huntingdon, to check the French, who were then aiming at the recapture of Boulogne. On this expedition Underhill served as comptroller of the ordnance.

His subsequent history, except as connected with the religious persecution which forms the subject of the ensuing narrative, is merely that of domestic life. He had taken in marriage, in the year 1545, the daughter of a citizen of London, of an obscure and unknown family. It is difficult to ascertain the orthography of her maiden name; but according to the most credible account she appears to have been Joan, daughter of Thomas Perrynes.[a] She presented master Underhill with five sons and seven daughters[b], of whose births the following full particulars have been preserved:[c]

1. Anne, borne on St. John's day in Chrystmas 1548.
2. Chrystyan, borne the 16 of September 1548.
3. Elenor, borne the xth of November in A° 1549.
4. Rachaell, borne the 4 of February 1551.
5. Unyca, borne on Palmes Sonday (April 10) 1552.
6. Gylford, borne the xiij of July in A° 1553, and dyed yong. (This was the godson of Queen Jane, as related in the ensuing pages, and named after her husband the lord Guildford Dudley.)
7. Anne, borne the 4 of January 1554.
8. Edward, 2. son and now heyre, was borne the 10 of February 1555.
9. John, 3. son, died yong in A° 1556.
10. Prudence, borne in A° 1559, and dyed yonge.
11. Henry, 4. son, borne the 6th of September in A° 1561.

On " The xiiij of April (1562) was buried at St. Botulph without Aldgate, mistress Underhill, with a dozen of scucheons of arms; and there did preach for her—" one whose name is not recorded.[d]

In two pedigrees (Vincent 126, f. 25, and MS. Harl. 1167) Edward Underhill

---

[a] It is Perrynes in G.11 Coll. Arm., Perynes in H.12 Coll. Arm., Peromes in MS. Harl. 810; Perrins in MS. Harl. 1167; and Price in MSS. Harl. 1100 and 1563. In Dugdale's Warwickshire, edit. Thomas, p. 607, it is printed Percones. Underhill himself has written the name Speryne, hereafter, p. 153.

[b] Thomas's Dugdale's Warw. ut supra, on the authority of a pedigree shown to Cooke, Chester herald, at Warwick, July 16, 1564.

[c] MS. Harl. 810, f. 9.

[d] Machyn's Diary, p. 280. The arms of Underhill were, Argent, on a chevron between three trefoils slipped vert three bezants; quartering Porter, Sable, three bells argent, a canton ermine. "Thus by Clarencyeulx Harvy." (MS. Harl. 810, p. 9.) An old seal of the Underhill family now in the possession of Evelyn Philip Shirley, esq. M.P. of Eatington

is styled "of Bath Kington." This was not improbably Baggington near Coventry, to which neighbourhood he mentions his removal, in p. 171. The date of his death has not been ascertained.

The following anecdotes were written after the storm which fired the spire of St. Paul's cathedral in June 1561. Portions of them were introduced by Strype in his Memorials of Cranmer, book ii. chapter vii. and book iii. chapter xvii., and a further portion in his Ecclesiastical Memorials, vol. ii. book i. chapter vi. Foxe had not made any use of them; but he had published a previons communication from the writer, being an anecdote of king Edward's inquiries respecting "good Saint George," made at on the feast of the Garter in 1551, when Underhill and his fellow pensioners were waiting in the presence-chamber at Greenwich (see the Appendix).

(MS. Harl. 425, f. 85.)

Receaved of M. Vnderyll, hys examinations.

A NOTE off the examynacyon and impresonmentt off Edwarde Underehylle, sone and heyre off Thomas Underhylle, off Honyngham, in the countie off Warwycke, (gentleman, *altered to*) esquire, beynge off the bande off the pencyoners, for a ballett that he made agaynst the papistes, immediately after the proclamacyone of quene Mary att London, she beynge in Norfoulke.

The next daye after the quene was come unto the Tower,[a] the foresayde ballett[b] came unto the handes off secretary Borne,[c] who strayte wayes made inquiry for me the sayde Edwarde, who dwelled att the Lymehurst;[d] wiche he having intellygence off, sentt the shreffe

[a] The queen came to the Tower on the 3rd of August, 1553: see Machyn's Diary, p. 38.

[b] This ballad is perhaps not to be identified, even if a copy should chance to be in existence. It appears, however, from what passed before the council, that it was printed and published, and that the authority of Tyndale was asserted in it (see p. 140). Underhill afterwards mentions that he had written a ballad against dicers. One of his poetical productions will be found at the close of his anecdotes.

[c] Sir John Bourne, of whom Underhill gives some remarkable anecdotes hereafter.

[d] Limehouse was at this period a hamlet in the parish of Stepney. It was constituted a distinct parish by act of parliament in 1730. Its earlier name was Limehurst, as Underhill writes it, and as we are told by Stowe, in whose time "Radcliffe itself hath also been increased in building eastward (in place whereof I have known a large highway with fair elm trees on both sides,) that the same hath now taken hold of Lime-hurst, or Lime-host,

of Mydellsex,[a] with a company off bylles and gleves, who came unto my housse, I beynge in my bedde, and my wyffe newly leayde in chylde-bedde. The hygh constable, whose name is Thomas Ive, dwelled att the next house unto me the sayde Edwarde, whome the shreffe brought also with hym; he beynge my very ffrende, desyred the shreffe and his company to staye withowte ffor fryghtynge off my wyffe, beyng newly leyde; and he wolde goo feche me unto hym, who knokede att the doore saynge he must speke with me. I lyinge so nere that I myght here hym, called unto hym, wyllynge hym to come unto me, for thatt he was alwayes my verye frende and earnest in the Gospelle; who declared unto me that the shreffe, with a greate company with hym, weare sentt for me. Whereuppon I rose, made me redy, and came unto hym demaundynge what he wolde with me. "Sir, (sayde he,) I have commaundementt fromme the councelle to aprehende yow, and forthewith to brynge yow unto them." "Why, (sayde I,) it is now x off cloke in the nyght, ye cannott now cary me unto them." "No, syr, (sayde he,) you shall go with me to my house, to London, wheare yow shall have a bedde, and to-morrowe I wyll brynge yow unto them att the Tower." "In the name of God!"[b] (sayde I,) and so wentt with hym, requyryng hym yff I myght understande the cause. He sayde, he knew none "This nedede not then, (sayde I;) any one mesenger myght have feched me unto them;" suspectynge the cause to be, as it was indede, the ballett.

On the morrow, the shreffe, seynge me nothynge dismayde, thynkyng it to be sume lyght matter, wentt nott wyth me hymselfe, butt sent me unto the Tower wyth too of his men, waytynge upon me with two bylles, presoner-lyke, who brought me unto the councell chamber, beynge comaundyd to delyver me unto secretary Bourne.

Thus standynge waytynge at the councelle chamber doore, too or

---

[a] Sir William Garrard, afterwards lord mayor in 1555-6: see note in Machyn's Diary, p. 347.

[b] "In the name of God!" an extravagantly strong form of signifying assent.

thre off my fellowes the pencyoners, and my cosyn jarmene Gilbarte Wynter,[a] jentylman ussher unto the ladye Elizabethe, stoode talkynge with me. In the meanetyme commithe sir Edwarde Hastynges[b], newly made master off the horse to the quene, and seyng me standynge there presoner, frownynge earnestly uppon me, sayde, "Are yow cume? we wylle talke with yow or yow parte, I warrantt yow," and so went into the councell. With that my fellowes and kynsemane shranke away from me as men greately affrayde.

I dide then parseave the sayde syr Edwarde bare in remembraunce the contravcrsy thatt was bytwyxt hym and me in talke and questions off relegyone att Callis, when the ryght honorable the yerle off Huntyngetune[c] his brother wentt over generalle off vj. thowsande men, with whom I wentt the same tyme and was comtroler off the

[a] Underhill's mother, as already mentioned, was Anne, daughter of Robert Winter, who had an elder brother Gilbert, named in the pedigree of Winter, MS. Harl. 1566, f. 108 b.: but the Gilbert Winter of the text does not occur in that pedigree.

[b] Sir Edward Hastings was a younger brother to Francis earl of Huntingdon; knighted by the duke of Somerset in the Scotish campaign of 1547. He had been one of Underhill's comrades in the band of gentlemen pensioners (as hereafter mentioned, p. 144.) Having signalised his activity in promoting the accession of queen Mary, he was made her master of the horses in July 1553; a knight of the Garter 1555; lord chamberlain on the 25th Dec. 1557; and created lord Hastings of Loughborough on the 19th Jan. following. He died without issue in 1572. See copious memoirs of him in Nichols's History of Leicestershire, vol. iii. p. 577, together with an engraving of his figure in stained glass at Stoke Pogeis, co. Bucks, which is also given in Gough's Sepulchral Monuments.

[c] Francis second earl of Huntingdon 1544, K.G. 1549, died 1561. He married Katharine Pole, daughter and co-heir of Henry lord Montagu; and the royal blood (of Clarence) thus derived to his heir apparent Henry lord Hastings, attracting the ambitious regard of John Dudley duke of Northumberland, led that aspiring man to court his alliance. Lord Hastings was married to the lady Katharine Dudley at the same time as lord Guildford Dudley espoused the lady Jane Grey. This led to the temporary imprisonment of the earl of Huntingdon and his son at the accession of Mary, but the queen soon released them, probably from regard to sir Edward Hastings. The son's imprisonment was very short, for we are told that when the earl of Arundel brought the duke of Northumberland to the Tower on the 25th of July, he "discharged the lord Hastings, and had him away with him." The earl received two pardons, dated the 4th Nov. and 8th Dec. 1 Mary, and lord Hastings another. (Nichols's Leicestershire, iii. 580, 583.)

ordynaunce.ᵃ The earle beynge veseted with syknes when he came thether, for thatt I wentt over in his company, and could pley and synge to the lute, therwith to pass awaye the tyme on the nyghtes beynge lounge, for we wentt over in the Cristmas, wolde have me with hym in his chamber, and hadde also a greate delyght to heare his brother reasone with me in matters of relegione, who wolde be very hote when I dide overley hym with the textes off the screpture concernynge the naturalle presens of Crist in the sacramentt of the alter, and wolde sweare greate othes, specyally "by the Lord's foote," thatt after the words spokyne by the prist ther remayned no breade, but the naturalle body thatt Mary bare. "Naye, then it muste needes be so, (wolde I saye,) andᵇ yow prove it with souche othes." Whercatt the earle wolde lawghe hartely, sayinge, "Brother, geve hym over; Underhylle is to(o) goode for yow." Wherwith he wolde be very angrye. The greatest holde thatt he toke was off the thyrde off John, uppon those wordes, "And no mane assendithe upe to heavine butt he thatt came downe from heavene, thatt is to saye, the sone of mane wiche is in heaven." I drove hym from the vjth off John, and all other places thatt he coulde aleage; but frome this he wolde nott be removed, butt thatt those wordes proved his naturalle body to be in heaven and in the sacramentt also. I tolde hym he as grosely understode Cryst as Nicodemus dyde in the same place, off beynge borne anew; in my oppinnione any mane that is nott gevyne upe of God maye be satysfyde concernynge the naturalle presence in the supper of the Lorde, by the gospell off saynt John,

---

ᵃ Whilst Boulogne still remained in the possession of an English garrison, the French "placed the Rhinegrave, with divers regiments of Almains, lancequenets, and certain ensigns of French, to the number of four or five thousand, in the town of Morguison, midway between Bulloine and Calais, to impeach all intercourse between the two places. Wherupon the king of England caused all the strangers that had served the year [in England] against the rebels, to the number of 2,000, to be transported to Calais, and to them were added 3,000 English, under the command of Francis earl of Huntingdon and sir Edward Hastings his brother, to dislodge the French, or other wise to annoy them." (Hayward's Life and Reign of Edward VI.) The negociations shortly after ensued which ended in the surrender of Boulogne. ᵇ *i. e.* if.

redynge from the fyrst chapter unto the ende off the xvijth, with the witnes of the first of the Actes of the Apostles, off Crist's assencyone, and comynge agayne, yff ever he wilbe satisfyde, withowte the healpe of any doctors.

Undoutedly the aprehendynge off me was for this matter; butt the greate mercy off God so provided for me thatt mr. Hastynges was not att my examynacyone, for taryinge thus att the councelle chamber doore, doctor Coxks ᵃ was within, who came forthe, and was sent to the Marshalse; then came forthe the lorde Ferris,ᵇ and was committed to the Tower; thene it was dynnar tyme, and all weare commaunded to departe untylle after dynnar.

My too waytynge mene and I wente to ane alehowse to dynnar, and, loungynge to know my payne, I made hast to gett to the councelle chamber doore, that I myght be the fyrst. Immediatly as the(y) hadde dyned, secretarye Bourne came to the doore, lookynge as the wolffe dothe for a lambe, unto whome my too kepers delyvered me, standynge next unto the doore, for ther was moo behynde me. He toke me in gredely, and suhute to the doore; levynge me at the nether ende of the chamber, he went unto the councelle, showynge them off me, and then beckoned me to come neare. Then they begayne the table and sett them downe; the earle of Bedforde ᵈ sat as chefest uppermoste

---

ᵃ Richard Coxe, then dean of Westminster and afterwards bishop of Ely, who had been schoolmaster and almoner to the late king Edward. Underhill states hereafter that the 5th of August was the day when he was examined and committed to prison: and the accuracy of what he here relates with regard to doctor Coxe and lord Ferrers will be found confirmed in Machyn's Diary at p. 39: doctor Coxe was committed to the same lodgings n the prison of the Marshalsea which had been the same day vacated by bishop Bonner, as stated by Machyn, and also in a letter inserted in The Chronicle of Queen Jane and Queen Mary, p. 15.

ᵇ Walter Ferrers, first viscount Hereford, so created in 1549-50: but he still continued to be called "lord Ferrys," *i. e.* the lord Ferrers of Chartley, as here in the text; and by Machyn in The Chronicle of Queen Jane and Queen Mary, p. 26; and by Stowe on the same occasion. He had married the lady Mary Grey, great-aunt to the lady Jane. He was released from the Tower on the 6th of September, "with a great fine." (Machyn, p. 43.)

ᶜ John Russell, first earl of Bedford, who had been appointed lord privy seal by Henry VIII. in 1542, and continued in that office until his death, March 14, 1554-5.

uppon the benche; next unto hym the earle of Sussex ᵃ; next him syr Rycharde Southwelle ᵇ; on the syde nexte me sate the yearle of Arundell ᶜ; next hym the lorde Pagett ᵈ; by them stood syr John Gage, then constable of the Tower ᵉ; the earle of Bathe ᶠ; and mr. Masone ᵍ; att the bordes ende stoode sargant Morgane, ʰ that afterwardes died madde, and secretary Borne; the lorde Wentworthe ⁱ stood in the baye wyndoo, talkyng with one alle the whyle of my examynacyone, whome I knew nott.

ᵃ Thomas Ratcliffe, second earl of Sussex 1542—1556-7, K.G. 1554. He was captain of the band of gentlemen pensioners, as Underhill afterwards mentions. See note on him in Machyn's Diary, p. 355.

ᵇ Sir Richard Southwell, before mentioned in this volume by archdeacon Louthe, (p. 44,) had not been employed in the reign of Edward VI. but gave his zealous adherence to queen Mary. By letters patent dated 4 Dec. 1553, he received a yearly pension of 100*l.* for his services against the duke of Northumberland. (Rymer, xv. 355.)

ᶜ Henry Fitz-Alan, last earl of Arundel of his name 1543-1579, K.G. 1543. He was restored, on the accession of Mary, to his office of great master of the household, of which he had been deprived in favour of the duke of Northumberland.

ᵈ William lord Paget, also restored to favour and fortune by the accession of queen Mary, after he had been degraded from the order of the Garter in the reign of Edward VI. Queen Mary made him lord privy seal June 29, 1555-6.

ᵉ See note in Machyn's Diary, p. 349. He was constable of the Tower of London from 1540 until his death in 1556, and lord chamberlain from queen Mary's accession in 1553.

ᶠ John Bourchier, second earl of Bath 1539—1560.

ᵍ Sir John Mason, sometime secretary for the French tongue.

ʰ Richard Morgan, autumn reader at the Middle Temple and at Lincoln's Inn 1546, called to the degree of serjeant-at-law 1547. He was notorious as a zealous Romanist in the reign of Edward, and with sir Anthony Browne was sent to the Fleet on the 22nd March, 1550-1, " for hearing mass." (King Edward's Journal, p. 310.) He was made lord chief justice of the common pleas Sept. 5, 1553, and knighted on the morrow of the coronation of queen Mary, Oct. 2 following. His name is memorable in history as having presided at the condemnation of the lady Jane: and Holinshed and Foxe both relate that "Judge Morgan, that gave the sentence against hir, shortly after fell mad, and in hys raving cryed continuallye to have the ladie Jane taken away from him, and so ended his life." His funeral at St. Magnus London Bridge, on the 2nd June, 1556, will be found described in Machyn's Diary, p. 106.

ⁱ Thomas second lord Wentworth 1552.—1590. He was lord deputy of Calais at its loss in 1557: see his trial thereon in Machyn's Diary, p. 195.

Me lorde off Bedforde (beynge my very frende, for thatt my chaunce was to be att the recoverynge off his sone me lorde Russelle,[a] when he was caste into Temes agaynst the Lymehurst; whome I caryed to my howse and gott hym to bedde, who was in greate parelle off hys lyff, the wether beynge very colde;) wolde not seme to be famelyare with me, nor called me nott by my name, butt sayde, "Come hither, surray,[b] dydd nott yow sett forthe a ballett of late in printe?" I kneled downe, sayinge "Yesse, truly, my lorde; is thatt the cause I am called before your honors?" "Eae, mary,[c] (sayde secretary Bourne,) yow have one off them abowte yow, I am sure." "Naye, truly have I nott," sayde I. Then toke he one owt of his bosome, and reade it over distynkly, the councelle gevynge diligentt eare. When he badde endide, "I trust, me lordes, (sayd I,) I have not offendid the queen's majestic in this ballett, nor spokyne agaynst her title, but mayntayned it." "No have, syr, (sayde Morgane,) yesse I cane devide your ballett, and make a distynkcyon in it, and so prove att the leaste sedicyon in it." "Eae, syr, (sayde I,) yow mene off lawe wylle make off a matter whatt ye list." "Loo! (sayde syr Rycharde Southwelle,) howe he cane gyve a taunte. Yow mayntayne the quene's title, with the healpe off ane arantt herytyke, Tyndale." "Yow speake of papistes ther, syr, (sayd mr. Masone,) I praye yow, how defyne yow a papist?" I loked uppon hym, turnynge towardes hym, for he stoode on the syde of me, "Why, syr, (sayde I,) it is nott lounge syns you could defyne a papist better than I." With thatt some off them secretly smyled, as the lorde off Bedforde, Arundelle, Sussex, and Pagett. In greate haste syr John Gage toke the matter in hande. "Thow callest mene papist ther (sayd he). Who be they thatt thow jugest to be papistes?" I sayde, "Syr, I do name no mane; nor I come nott hether to accuse any, nor none I wylle accuse; butt your honors do knowe thatt in this

---

[a] Francis lord Russell: see p. 145 hereafter.   [b] Sirrah.
[c] marry, *i. e.* by Mary.

contraversy thatt hathe byn sume be called papistes and sume protestaynes." " Butt we mustt knowe whome thow jugest to be papistes, and thatt we commaunde thee uppon thyne alegens to declare." " Syr, (sayde I,) I thynke yff yow loke amonge the pristes in Poolles, ye shall fynde some old mumsymussis[a] ther." " Mumsymussis, knave, (sayde he,) mumsymussis? thou arte an herytike knave, by God's bloude!" " Ee, by mase![b] (sayes the earle of Baythe,) I warrantt hym ane heritike knave in dede." " I beseche your honores, (sayde I, spekynge to the lordes thatt satt att the table, for those other stode by and weare not then of the councelle,) be my goode lordes; I have offendid no lawes, and I have

[a] This was a term proverbially applied to those who were inveterate supporters of ancient errors, and satisfied in old usage did not care to inquire further. Tyndale, in his Practice of Prelates 1530, speaks of "mumpsimuses of divinity" among the doctors summoned to dispute upon the king's divorce from queen Katharine. Latimer introduces the term in two of his sermons: in that preached on the first Sunday in Advent 1552,—".when my neighbour is taught, and knoweth the truth, and will not believe it, but will abide in his old *mumpsimus*, then," &c., and in that preached on Sexagesima Sunday following,— " Some be so obstinate in their old *mumpsimus*, that they cannot abide the true doctrine of God." And king Henry himself, in his last speech to parliament, made in 1545, set forth the import of the term very plainly: "I see and heare dayly (he remarked) that you of the clergy preach one agaynst an other, teach one contrary to an other, inveigh one agaynst an other, without charity or discretion. Some be too stiff in their old *mumpsimus*, other be too busy and curious in their new *sumpsimus*. Thus all men almost be in variety and discord, and few or none do preach truely and sincerely the word of God, according as they ought to do." Upon which passage Foxe makes the following comment : " Princes which exhort to concord and charitie doe well, but princes which seeke out the causes of discord, and reforme the same, do much better. The Papist and Protestant, Heretick and Pharisee, the old *Mumpsimus* and the newe *Sumpsimus*, be terms of variance and dissention, and be (I graunt) *symtomata* of a sore wound in the common wealth," &c. The term may be traced up so early as 1517, when Richard Pace, in his treatise " De fructu qui ex doctrinâ percipitur," tells a story of an ignorant English priest who for thirty years together had read *mumpsimus* in his breviary instead of *sumpsimus*, and when a learned man told him of his blunder replied, " I'll not change my old *mumpsimus* for your new *sumpsimus !*" " Quidam indoctus sacrificus Anglus per annos triginta *mumpsimus* legere solitus est loco *sumpsimus*, et quum moneretur à docto ut errorem emendaret, respondit, Se nolle mutare suum antiquum *mumpsimus* ipsius novo *sumpsimus*." Paceus, De fructu qui ex doctrinâ percipitur liber. Basil, 1517, p. 80.

[b] " By the mass," an ordinary mode of asseveration with Roman Catholics.

sarved the quenes majesties father and her brother lounge tyme, and in ther sarvis have spentt and consumed parte off my lyvynge, never havynge as yett any prefermentt or recompence, and the rest off [my] felows lykewyse, to ower utter undoynges, unless the quenes hyghnes be goode unto us; and ffor my parte, I wentt nott forthe agaynst her majestie, notwithstandynge thatt I was commaundid, nor lyked those doynges." " Nò, butt with your wrytynges you wolde sett us together by the eares," saythe the yearle of Arundelle. "He bathe spentt hys levynge wantonly," saythe Bourne, "and now saythe he bathe spentt it in the kynges sarvis; wiche I am sory ffor. He is cume of a worshipefulle howse in Worsetershere." " It is untruly sayde off yow (sayde I,) thatt I have spentt my levyng wantonly, for I never consumed no parte theroff untylle I came into the kynges sarvis, whiche I do not repentt, nor douted off recompence, yff ether of my too masters hadde leved. I parseave yow Borne's sone of Worseter,[a] who was beholdon unto my uncle

---

[a] Sir John Bourne, probably as being known to be a stanch and zealous Romanist, was raised to sudden eminence on the accession of Mary. He was knighted on the morrow of her coronation, October 2, 1553; and licensed to keep forty retainers. He continued secretary through Mary's reign, and figures frequently in the pages of Foxe, who terms him " a chief stirer of persecutions." There is no pedigree of Bourne in the visitation of Worcestershire, and one in that for the county of Somerset, 1623, does not give the name of the father of sir John Bourne. Battenhall near Worcester, a manor and park, formerly the country residence of the priors of Worcester, was granted to sir John Bourne in 36 Henry VIII., and sold by his son Anthony in 13 Eliz. It appears from Nash's Worcestershire (ii. 201) that the name of sir John's wife, who has already occurred in p. 68 of the present volume, was Dorothy. In the reign of Elizabeth sir John Bourne, who was steward of the church of Worcester, entered into great disputes with the new Protestant bishop, Edwin Sandys, which led to various frays in Worcester, and eventually to sir John's imprisonment for six or seven weeks in the Marshalsea: of the particulars, full details will be found in the first volume of Strype's Annals. Sir John died in 1563, leaving his estates to his son Anthony (also mentioned in p. 68), and who was seated at Holt Castle, once the residence of the lords Beauchamp of Holt; but which, with most of his other estates, he sold to lord chancellor Bromley. Nash (ii. 311) terms him the " unfortunate son " of sir John. He figures in the frays with " the bishop's boys " above noticed. One of his daughters and coheirs was married to sir Herbert Croft. Gilbert Bourne, made bishop of Bath and Wells by queen Mary in 1554, (after having been a

Wynter,[a] and therfore yow have no cause to be my enemy; nor yow never knew me, nor I yow before now, wiche is to soone." " I have harde inough off yow," sayde he. " So have I off yow, (sayde I,) how that mr. Sheldone[b] drave you oute off Worsetershire for your behavyoure."

With thatt came syr Edward Hastynges from the quene in greate hast, saynge, " Me lordes, yow must sett all thynges aparte, and come forthwith to the quene." Then sayde the earle of Sussex, " Have this gentleman unto the Flete untyll we maye talke farther with him," although I was "knave" before off mr. Gage. " To the Flete? (sayde mr. Southewell,) have hym to the Marshalse." " Have the gentleman to Newgate, (saythe mr. Gage agayne;) call a couple of the garde here." " Ee, (saythe Borne,) and ther shalbe a letter sentt to the keper howe he shall use hym, for we have other maner off matters to hym then these." " So hadd ye nede, (sayde I,) or else I care nott for yow." " Delyver hym to mr. Garett the shreffe, (sayde he,) and bydde hym send hym to Newgate." "Me lorde," sayde I unto me lorde of Arundelle, for thatt he was nexte to me as they weare rysynge, "I trust yow wylle not se me thus used to be sende to Newgate; I am nother theffe nor trayter." " Ye are a noughtie

---

canon of Worcester from 1541,) was son of Philip, brother to sir John: he left his property to his brother Richard, from whom descended the Bournes of Wivelscombe in Somersetshire. Of him memoirs are given in Wood's Athenæ Oxonienses, and Cassan's Lives of the Bishops of Bath and Wells.

[a] Robert Winter of Wych, co. Worcester, by his second wife Katharine, daughter of sir George Throckmorton, had issue George, who married Jane daughter of sir William Ingleby of Ripley, co. York; which George Winter was apparently the uncle to whom Underhill alludes.

[b] The family of Sheldon had at this period spread into several branches, and it is difficult to identify the gentleman named in the text. See the pedigree of this ancient and long enduring house in Nash's Worcestershire, vol. i. p. 64. Most probably, however, the writer alludes to William Sheldon of Beoley esquire, who died at his house called Skilles in Warwickshire, 23 Dec. 1573, and was brought to Beoley and there buried; having married for his second wife Margaret daughter to sir Richard Brooke lord chief baron, widow of William Whorwood attorney-general to Henry VIII., which Margaret is buried at St. Thomas Apostle's London. (Visit. Worc. MS. Harl. 1352, f. 28.)

fellow, (sayde he;) you weare alwayes tutynge in the duke of Northumberlandes eare, thatt you weare." "I wolde he hadd gevyne better care unto me, (sayde I;) itt hadde nott byne with hym then as it is now.[a]" Mr. Hastynges[b] passynge by me, I thought goode to prove hym, although he thretnede before none (noon). " Syr, (sayde I,) I praye yow speake for me thatt I be nott sende unto Newgate, butt rather unto the Flete, wiche was first namede; I have nott offended; I am a jentylmane, as yow know, and one of your fellowes when you weare off thatt bande off the pencyonars." Very quyetly he sayde unto me, " I was nott att the talke, mr. Underehylle, and therfore I cane saye nothynge to it," butt I thynke he was welle content with the place I was apointed to. So went I forthe with my too fellowes of the garde, who weare gladd they hadde the leadynge off me, for they weare greate papistes. " Where is thatt knave the printer?" sayde mr. Gage. " I know nott," sayde I.

When we came to the Tower gate, wheroff syr John Abryges hadd the charge[c] and his brother mr. Thomas, with whome I was well aquaynted, butt nott with syr John; who, seynge they t(w)o off the garde leadynge me withowte ther halbartes, rebuked them, and stayde me whyle they wentt for ther halbartes. His brother sayde unto me, " I am sory yow shulde be ane offender, mr. Underhylle." " I am none, syr, (sayde I,) nor I went nott agaynste the queue." " I am glade of thatt," sayde he.

And so forthe we wentt at the gate, where was greate thronge off people to heare and se whatt presonars weare committed, and amoungst whome stoode my frende mr. Ive, the hygh constable, my next neyghboure. One off the garde wentt forthe att the weked before

[a] The duke was then a prisoner in the Tower, waiting his trial.

[b] Sir Edward Hastings.

[c] Sir John Brydges was made lieutenant of the Tower upon the accession of queen Mary, and she created him lord Chandos of Sudeley in April 1554. He was succeeded as lieutenant, in the following June, by his brother Thomas, who had previously assisted him in the duties of the office. (See the Chronicle of Queen Jane and Queen Mary, pp. 18, 53, 57, 76.)

me to take me by the arme, the other helde me by the other arme, fearynge be lyke I wolde have shifted frome them amongst the people. When my frende sawe me thus leade, who hadd wachede att the gate all the forenoone, he followed afarre off, as Peter dide Crist, to see what shulde become off me. Many also followed, sum thatt kuewe me, some to larne whatt I was, for thatt I was in a gowne of sattene.

Thus passed we thorow the stretes welle accompanyed unto mr. Garett the shereffe's howse in the stokes-markett. My frende mr. Ive tarryed at the gate. These t(w)o off the garde declared unto mr. shreffe thatt they weare commaunded by the councelle to delyver me unto hym, and he to sende me unto Newgate, saynge, " Syr, if it please yow we wyll carye hym thether." With thatt I stepped unto mr. shreffe, and, takynge hym a litle asyde, requested hym thatt, forasmoche as ther commissyon was butt to delyver me unto hym, and he to sende me unto Newgate, thatt he wolde sende me by his offycers, for the request was off mere malyce. " With a goode wylle," sayde mr. sherffe. " Masters, (sayde he,) you maye departe; I wyll sende my offycers with this jentyllmane anone, when they be come in." "We wylle se hym caryed, syr, (sayde they,) for ower discharge." Then the shreffe sayde sharpely unto them, " Whatt! do you thynke that I wyll nott do the councelles commaundementt? Yow are discharged by delyveryng off hym unto me." With thatt they departede. My frend mr. Ive, seynge them departe, and leave me behynde, was very gladde theroff, and taryed stylle att the gate to se farther.

All this talke in the shreffes halle dide me lorde Russelle,[a] sone and heyre to the earle off Bedford, heare and se, who was att

---

[a] Francis lord Russell, afterwards second earl of Bedford 1554—1585. At the end of July 1553 (says Machyn) " came to the Fleet the earle of Rutland and my lord Russell in hold." (Diary, p. 38.) Two of Bradford's letters are to lord Russell "being then in trouble for the veritye of God's gospell." He commends him as being highly privileged in being counted worthy to suffer for Christ's sake, and very strongly exhorts him to constancy and perseverance. (Letters of the Martyrs.) Two of Becon's works are

commaundement in the sherffe's howse, and his chamber joynynge unto the halle, wherinto he myght loke; who was very sory for me, for thatt I hadd byne familiare with hym in matters off relegyone, as welle on the other syd the seics, as at hoome. He sentt me on the morowe xx s., and every weke as moche wyle I was in Newgate.

When these too companyons off the garde weare goone, the shreffe sentt too off his offycers with me, who toke no billes with them, nor leadde me not, butt followed a prety waye behynde me, ffor as I sayde unto mr. shreffe, butt for order sake, and to save hym blameles, I wolde have gone unto Newgate myselffe att the counceles commaundementt, or his other.

When I came into the strete, my frende mr. Ive, seyng me have suche libertie, and souche distaunce betwyxt me and the offyceres, he stepped before them, and so went talkynge with me thorow Chepesyde; so thatt it was nott welle perseaved thatt I was aprehendide, butt by the greate company thatt followed.

The offyceres delyvered me unto the keper off Newgate as they were commaunded, who unloked a dore, and willed me to goo upe the steares into the halle. My frende Ive wente upe with me, where we founde 3 or 4 presonars thatt hadde the libertie off the howse. After a littelle talke with my frende, I requyred hym nott to lett my wyffe know thatt I was sende to Newgate, butt to the Counter,[a] untyll suche tyme thatt she weare nere her churcheynge, and thatt she sulde sende me my nyghte gowne, my bible, and my lute; and soe he departede.

dedicated,—" The Christian Knight " to lord Russell, and "The Monstrous Merchandize of the Romish Bishops " to Francis earl of Bedford. On the 3rd Dec. 1551, was held, at the house of sir Richard Morysin, a friendly conference concerning the sacrament between divers learned persons of the clergy and laity of both persuasions: among those present were the marquess of Northampton, the earl of Rutland, lord Russell, sir Anthony Cooke, sir William Cecill, and sir John Cheke. (Athenæ Cantabrigienses, i. 144.) These notices of lord Russell's religious sentiments are not included in Wiffen's Memoirs of the House of Russell.

[a] The Compter was the prison pertaining to the sheriffs of London, and at this period was

In a wyle after it was supper tyme. The borde was covered in the same halle. The keper, whose name was Alesaunder,[a] and his wyffe came to supper, and halffe a dosyn presonars thatt weare ther for feloneys; for I was the fyrst for relegyon thatt was sentt unto thatt presone, butt the cause why the keper knue nott. One off those presonars toke acquayntaunce off me, and sayde he was a sodyare under syr Rycharde Crumewell[b] in the jurney to

in Wood Street, whither it had been recently removed from Bread Street in the year 1555, for reasons stated at full in Stowe's Survay.

[a] Foxe relates that "Alexander the keeper of Newgate, a cruell enemye to those that lay there for religion, dyed very miserably, being so swollen that hee was more like a monster than a man, and so rotten within that no man could abide the smell of him. This cruell wretch, to hasten the poore lambs to the slaughter, would goe to Boner, Story, Cholmley and others, crying out, ' Rid my prison, rid my prison ; I am too much pestered with these heretikes.' The sonne of the said Alexander, called James, having left unto him by his father greate substance, within three yeares wasted all to nought, and when some marveled how hee spent those goods so fast, ' O, (said he,) evill gotten, evill spent ;' and shortly after, as he went in Newgate market, he fell downe suddenly, and there wretchedly died. John Peter, sonne-in-law to this Alexander, an horrible blasphemer of God, and no lesse cruell to the said prisoners, rotted away, and so most miserably dyed. Who commonly when he would affirme any thing, were it true or false, used to say, ' If it bee not true, I pray God I rot ere I dye ! ' Witnesse the printer herof [John Day], with divers other."

[b] Sir Richard Crumwell is stated to have been the son of one Morgan Williams, by a sister of Thomas Crumwell earl of Essex, lord privy seal and vicar-general of Henry VIII. This relationship has been doubted (see Gough's Memoirs of the Cromwell Family, 4to. 1785, p. 4): but a letter of his to the great man, in which he signs himself " Your lordshipps most bounden nephewe," will be found in Letters on the Suppression of the Monasteries, (printed for the Camden Society,) p. 146. During his uncle's supremacy there was a " great and triumphant jousting held at Westminster, commencing on May-day 1540, at which the six challengers were—sir John Dudley, sir Thomas Seymour, (both afterwards so distinguished in our political history,) sir Thomas Poynings, sir George Carew, Anthony Kingston and Richard Crumwell : who kept open household at Durham house in the Strand, and there feasted the king, queen, and court. On the second day Anthony Kingston and Richard Crumwell were made knights. On the third day sir Richard Crumwell overthrew master Palmer and his horse in the field, to the great honour of the challengers,"—probably the sir Thomas Palmer noticed in p. 158; and on the 5th May at the barriers sir Richard overthrew master Culpepper in the field. "The King gave to every of the said challengers, and their heirs for ever, in reward of their valiant activity, 100

Laundersey,[a] where he dide knowe me, whose sarvant I was at the same tyme; who the next yere followyng, when the famous kynge Henry viij[th] wentt unto Bollene, he putt me unto his majestie in the rome of a mane att armes, off the wiche bande ther was ij[c] off us uppon barded horsses, alle in one sute off readde and yalloo damaske, ower bardes off ower horses and plumes off fethers of the same colars, to attend uppon his majestic for the defense off his parsone.

After supper this goode fellow, whose name was Brysto, procured me to have a bedde in his chamber; who coulde pley well uppon a rebyke.[b] He was a talle mane, and afterwardes on off quene Maryes garde, and yett a protestayne, wich he kepte secrete, for eles he sayde he shulde nott have founde souche favour as he dide att the keper('s) handes and his wyff, for to souche as loved the gospelle they weare very cruell. "Welle, (sayd I,) I have sende

of St. John of Jerusalem." Stowe (in Survay). On this occasion the king is stated to have presented a ring from his finger to sir Richard Crumwell, in token of his approbation, saying, "Henceforth you shall be called my knight": and this incident is supposed to be commemorated in the Cromwell coat-armour—a lion rampant holding a ring. Sir Richard was in the same year made a gentleman of the privy chamber; and in that year also he was sheriff of the counties of Cambridge and Huntingdon; and he successively acquired the sites of nearly all the monastic houses in the latter county,—Hinchinbroke and Saltrey in 29 Hen. VIII., Ramsey in 31 Hen. VIII., St. Neot's and Huntingdon in 33 Hen. VIII. He converted the monastic buildings at Ramsey into a dwelling house; his son sir Henry and grandson sir Oliver (the latter the uncle of the protector) resided at Hinchinbroke.

[a] "In the month of July (1543) the king sent over sixe thousand men, under the leading of sir John Wallop, accompanyed with sir Thomas Seymour marshall, sir Robert Bowes treasurer, sir Richard Cromwell captaine of the horsemen, and sir George Carew his lieutenant. There was likewise sir Thomas Palmer, sir John Ransfoorth, sir John Seint John, and sir John Gascoigne knights, that were captaines of the footmen. They were appointed to joyne with the emperor's power, and so to make war into France." The town of Landreci in Hainault was beseiged, but the French king came to the rescue with a large army, and finally both parties separated without a battle. The particulars of this campaign will be found related in the introduction to the Life and Times of sir Peter Carew, recently edited by John Maclean, esq. F.S.A. 1857, 8vo. p. xxviii.

[b] A stringed instrument resembling a fiddle. 1530-1, March 11, "paied for a rebecke for great Guilliam, xxs." (Privy-purse Expenses of Henry VIII., p. 114.)

for my bible, and, by Godes grace, therin shalbe my dayly exersyse; I wylle nott hyde it frome them." " Syr, (sayde he,) I am poore; butt they will beare with you, for thatt they see your estate is to paye welle; and I wyll show you the nature and maner off them, for I have byne heare a goode wyle. They bothe do love musyke very welle; wherfore yow with your lute, and I to pley with yow on my rebyke, wylle please them greately; he lovethe to be mery, and to drynke wyne, and she also; yff yow wyll bestowe upon them every dynare and supper a quarte off wyne, and some musyke, yow shalbe ther whyte sone, and have alle ther favour thatt they cane show yow." And so it came to pase.

And now I thynke it goode a litle to dygrese frome my matter concernynge my impresonmentt and my delyveraunce; and to note the greate mercy off God showed unto his sarvantes in thatt greate parsecusyone in queue Mary's tyme; howe myghtelie and many wayes he presarved souche as dide feare hym, evyne as he presarved Danyelle, Jeremy, Paulle, and many in the olde tyme. Sume weare moved by his spirite to fle over the seyes; sume weare presarved stylle in Londone, thatt in all the tyme off parsecusyone never bowed ther knes unto Balle,[a] for ther was no souche place to shyft in in this realme as Londone, notwithstandynge ther greate spyalle and shearche; nor no better place to shifte the Easter tyme[b] in then queue Maryes courte, sarvynge in the rome thatt I dide, as shalbe showed hereafter. A greate noumber God dide strengthen constantly to stande to his worde, to gloryfye his name, wiche be praysede for ever and ever, worlde withoute ende! And sume he presarved for these dayes.

And now agayne to prosecute the matter of my trouble and wonderfull delyveraunce owt off thatt lothsume gayle off Newgate. When thatt I hadde byn ther abowte too wekes, thorow the evylle savers and greate unquyettnes off the logeynges, as also by occasyon

---

[a] Baal.

[b] At the season of Easter in particular it was expected that every person should be houselled, that is, partake of the sacrament of the mass.

150   NARRATIVES OF THE REFORMATION.

off drynkenge off a draught off strounge (malmesey *erased*) holloke[a] as I was goynge to bedde, wyche my chamber fellow wolde nedes have me to plege hym in, I was cast into an extreame burnynge ague, thatt I coulde take no reste, desirynge to chaunge my logenge, and so dide frome oon to another; butt noone I coulde abyde, ther was so mouche noyse off presonars, and evyll savours. The keper and his wyffe offered me his owne parler where he laye hymselffe, wyche was fforthist frome noyse, butt it was nere the kechyn, the savour wheroff I coulde nott abyde. Then dide she lay me in a chamber where she sayde never no presoner laye, wiche was her store-chamber, where she sayde all her plate and money laye, wyche was mouche.

So mouche frendshepe I founde att ther bandes, notwithstandynge thatt they weare spoken unto by dyvers papistes; and the Wood-moungeres of London,[b] withe whome I hadde a greate conflycte for presentynge them for false markynge off bylettes, they requyred the keper to show me no favour, and to laye yrones uppon me, de-clarynge thatt I was the greatist heretyke in London.

My very frende mr. Recorde,[c] doctor off phesyke, syngularly

[a] A kind of sweet wine, mentioned in Gascoigne's Delicate Diet. Lond. 1576. (Halliwell's Dictionary of Archaic Words.) Florio has " *Aigléuco vino*, sweet hollocke wine." Queen Anna's New World of Words, fol. 1611, p. 17.

[b] At this period the population of London was dependent for fuel chiefly on wood, and next on " coal," *i. e.* charcoal, made at Croydon and its neighbourhood, the supply of mineral or " sea " coal being very small. The woodmongers had their tricks of trade, and were subjected to frequent interference. Fabyan has recorded that in the winter of 1542-3 " a frost dured so longe, that many of the poore people cried out for lacke of woode and coales, that the maior went tó the woode-warfes, and solde to the poore people billet and faggot, by the peniworthe. Also this yere was an acte of parliament for wood and coal to kepe the full sise, after the Purification of our Ladie that shall be in the yere of our Lorde M.D.xliii. that no man shall bargaine, sell, bryng, or conveigh of any other size to be uttred or solde, upon paine of forfeiture." In 1561 we find " a woodmonger set in the pillory for false marking of billéts, with billets hanging about him." (Machyn's Diary, p. 267.) The Company of Woodmongers was not incorporated until 1605, but it had, like many others, existed as a voluntary association for long before.

[c] Robert Record, born at Tenby, co. Pembroke, in 1513, was elected fellow of Allsouls' college, Oxford, in 1531, and took the degree of M.D. at Cambridge in 1545. In 1549 he was comptroller of the mint at Bristol, and in 1551 was appointed surveyor-general of the mines and money in Ireland. His will was made in 1558, in the queen's bench

sene in alle the seven syencis,[a] and a greate devyne, visited me in the presone, and also after I was delyvered, to his greate parrelle yff it hadde byne knowne, who lounge tyme was att charges and payne with me gratis. By meanes whereoff and the provydence off God I reseaved my healthe.

My wyffe then was churched befoore her tyme to be a suter for my delyveraunce, who put upe a supplycacyone unto the councelle, declarynge my extreame syknes, and smalle cause to be committed unto so louthsome a gayle; requyrynge thatt I myght be delyvered, puttynge in sureties to be forthecumynge to aunswere farther when I shuld be called; wiche she obteyned by the healpe off mr. John Througemarton, beynge the master off the questes, and my cunetremane and kynesmane;[b] he, un-

prison, where he soon after died a prisoner for debt. His skill in various departments of science, and the efforts he had made to impart his knowledge to others, were worthy of a happier fate. See a catalogue of his numerous works in Athenæ Cantabrigienses, vol. i. p. 176.

[a] The Seven Sciences were accounted to be Grammar, Rhetoric, Logic, Arithmetic, Geometry, Music, and Astronomy; and these are personified, so late as 1645, in the engraved title-page of Howell's Familiar Letters. But when sir Thomas Gresham founded his college in London in 1575 he made a somewhat different selection, though still retaining the number of seven,—viz. Divinity, Astronomy, Music, Geometry, Law, Medicine, and Rhetoric. For these he founded the professorships which still subsist, thus providing a lecture for every day of the week. The idea probably originated with the assertion of Solomon, *Wisdom hath builded her house: she hath hewn out her Seven Pillars.* (Proverbs, ix. 1.) An interesting dissertation on the frequent and wide-spread adoption of a mystical signification of "The Number Seven" will be found in Household Words, May 24, 1856; and reprinted in "Lectures and Essays on various subjects, Historical, Topographical, and Artistic. By Wm. Sidney Gibson, Esq. M.A., &c. 1858." 8vo. p. 183.

[b] Younger brother to sir Nicholas (see p. 42): in conjunction with whom he sat in parliament for the borough of Old Sarum in 1 Mary. In his epitaph at Coughton he is described as "syr John Throkmorton knyght of Falronham [co. Worc.], the seventh sonne of syr George Throkmorton knyght of Coughton, sometime master of the requests unto queen Marie of happie memory, who in respect of his faythful service bestowed upon him the office of Justice of Chester, and of her counsayle of the marches of Wales, in whiche service he continued xxiij. yeares, and supplied within the same time the place of mr. Vice-President the space of iij. yeares." He was knighted by queen Elizabeth at Kenilworth in the first year of her reign, and died May 22, 1580. See further in Wotton's English Baronetage, 1741, ii. 359.

derstandynge who weare my enemyes, toke a tyme in ther absens, and obteyned a letter to the keper, subscrybed by the yearle of Bedforde, the yearle of Sussex, Wynchester,[a] Rochester,[b] and Walgrave,[c] to be delyvered, puttynge in suretye, accordynge to the requeste off my wyves supplycacyon; with whome Wynchester talked concernynge the crestenynge off her chylde att the churche att the Tower hylle, and the gossipes, wiche weare, the duke of Suffolke,[d] the yearle of Penbroke,[e] and the lady Jane then beynge quene, with the whiche he was moche offendide. My ladie Througemartone, wyfe unto syr Nycolas Througemartone,[f] was the

[a] Stephen Gardiner, bishop of Winchester.

[b] Sir Robert Rochester, comptroller of the household and chancellor of the duchy of Lancaster. He had served the lady Mary in the capacity of comptroller during her brother's reign, and in 1551 was committed to the Tower, together with the subject of the next note, and sir Francis Englefield, for resisting the order of the council which forbad the performance of mass in his mistress's family: see the Literary Remains of King Edward VI. pp. 336, 339, 348. He was one of the knights of the Bath at the coronation of queen Mary, and died on the 28th Nov. 1557, having been elected a knight of the Garter on the preceding saint George's day.

[c] Sir Edward Waldegrave (mentioned in the preceding note) was by queen Mary made master of her wardrobe and knighted on the morrow of her coronation, Oct. 2, 1553. His mother was Lora sister to sir Robert Rochester, on whose death in 1557 sir Edward succeeded as chancellor of the duchy of Lancaster. In 3 & 4 Philip and Mary he had been appointed a commissioner to inquire into heresies, &c., and false rumours, &c. against their majesties. After the death of his royal mistress he was in 1561 a second time committed to the Tower of London, and for the same reason,—" for hearing of mass, and keeping a priest in his house." On the 22nd April (writes Machyn) " were had to the Tower sir Edward Walgrave and my lady his wife, as good alms-folk as be in these days." The same writer records the unfortunate result: "The first day of September died the good and gentle knight sir Edward Walgrave, while in the Tower." His body was buried on the 3d by the high altar of St. Peter's in the Tower; and on the 8th his wife was released. (Machyn's Diary, pp. 256, 266.) Lady Waldegrave was Frances, daughter of sir Edward Neville: they were progenitors of the earls of Waldegrave, as will be seen in Collins's Peerage. [d] Henry Grey, duke of Suffolk, father of the lady Jane.

William Herbert, first earl of Pembroke, brother-in-law to queen Katharine Parr.

[f] Sir Nicholas Throckmorton has been already noticed at p. 42 of the present volume. His wife was Anne, daughter of Sir Nicholas Carew, K.G. and sister and heir to sir Francis Carew of Beddington in Surrey; by whom he had two sons and three daughters. (Wotton's English Baronetage, 1741, ii. 358.)

quenes debetie, who named my sone Gylfforde [a] after her husebande. Immediately after the crestenynge was done, queue Marye was proclamed in Chepesyde,[b] and when me ladie Througemarton came into the Tower, the clothe off estate was takone downe and all thynges defaced: a sodene chaunge! She wolde have goone forthe agayne, butt colde nott be suffered. Butt nowe agayne to the matter.

When my wyff badde obtayned the letter, joyfull she was, and brought her brother with her, John Speryne of Londone marchantt, a very frendly mane, and zelous in the Lorde, who was bounde with me before mr. Chedely justice off peace,[c] accordynge to the counceles lettres, who came into the presone unto me, for I was so syke and weake thatt I was constrayned to tary a wyle longer, and my wyffe with me daye and nyghte. Durynge alle the tyme off my sykness, I was constrayned to paye viij d. every meale, and as moche for my wyffe, and for every frende thatt came to se me, yff they weare alone with me att dyner or supper tyme, whether they came to the table or noo; and payde also xl s. for a ffyne ffor iernes, wyche they sayde they showede me greate favoure in, I shulde eles have payd iiij or v li.

Thus when they parseaved I dide nott amende, butt rather worse and worse, they thought it best to venter the matter, and provydede a horse-litter to cary me home to the Lyme hurst. I was so weake thatt I was not able to be ledde downe the steares; wherefore one thatt was sarvant to the jaler, who before tyme hade byne my mane, who was also very diligentt and frendely unto me, toke me in his armes and caryed me downe the steares to the horse-litter, wiche stoode redy att the presone doore, and went with me to my howse. Many people weare gathered to se my comynge forthe, who praysed

[a] See p. 133.

[b] On the 19th of July, 1553: see Chronicle of Queen Jane and Queen Mary, p. 11.

[c] Probably Robert Chidley, Autumn reader at the Inner Temple 21 Hen. VIII. and Lent reader 28 Hen. VIII., one of the four governors of that house 34 Hen. VIII., 3 & 4 Phil. and Mary, 1, 6, 8 Eliz., and its treasurer 34 Hen. VIII. He was called to the

God for my delyverance, beynge very sory to se my state, and the lamentacyone off my wyff and her frendes, who jugede I wolde nott leve untyll I came hoome. I was nott able to endure the goynge off the horse-litter; wherefore they weare fayne to goo very softely, and oftentymes to staye, att wiche tymes many of my aquayntaunces and ffrendes and others resortede to se me, so thatt it was too howres or we coulde pase frome Newgate unto Algate, and so within nyght before I coulde gett to my howse, wheare many off my neyghboures resorted to se me takone owte off the horse-litter, whoo lamentedde and prayde for me, thynkynge it nott possible for me to escape deathe, butt by the greate mercy of God. Thus I contyneued the space of viij or x dayes, withowte any lykelyhoode or hoope off amendementt.

I was sende to Newgate the vth daye off August, and was delyvered the vth daye off September.

The fyrste daye off October was quene Mary crowned, by wiche tyme I was able to walke upe and doune my chamber; and beynge very desyrous to se the quene pase thorow the cittie, gott uppe on horsebake, beynge scantt able to sett, gyrdide in a longe nyght-gowne with double kercheves aboute my heade, a greate hatt uppon them, my bearde dubed harde too; my face so leane and pale thatt I was the very image off deathe; wondred at off alle thatt dide beholde me, unknowne to any. My wyffe and neyghboures weare to-to sorry thatt I wolde nedes goo forthe, thynkynge I wolde nott returne alyve.

Thus wentt I forthe, havynge off ether syde off me a mane to staye me; and so wentt to the west ende off Polles, and ther placed myselfe amoungst others thatt satte on horsebake to se the quene pase by. Before her cumeynge I behelde Poles steple bearynge toppe and toppe-galantt lyke a ryalle sheppe with many flages and bannars, and a mane tryoumfynge and daunsynge in the toppe.[a]

---

[a] "Then was there one Peter a Dutchman stood on the weathercocke of Paules steeple, holding a streamer in his hand of five yards long, and waving thereof stood sometime on the one foote and shooke the other, and then kneeled on his knees, to the great marvaile of all people. Hee had made two scaffolds under him, one above the crosse, having

I sayde unto one thatt sate on horsebake by me, who hadde nott sene any corownacyone, " Att the coronasyone off kynge Edwarde I sawe Poles steple ly att ane anker,[a] and now she wearithe toppe and toppe-gallantt; surely the nexte wylbe shippewrake, or it be lounge;" whiche chauncethe sume tymes by tempestuous wyndes, sume tymes by lyghtnynges and fyre from the hevens. Butt I thowghte thatt it shulde rather periche with sume horible wynde then with lyghtnynge or thounderbolt;[b] butt souche are the

torches and streamers set on it, and one other over the bole of the crosse, likewise set with streamers and torches, which could not burne, the winde was so great. The said Peter had sixeteene pound thirteen shillinge and foure pence given him by the city for his costs and paines, and all his stuffe." (Stowe's Chronicle.) See another account of the same performances in the Chronicle of Queen Jane and Queen Mary, p. 30.

[a] —"and as hee (king Edward) passed on the north side of Paul's churchyard, a man of the nation of Arragossa [Arragon? or Saragossa? "an Argosie" *in Fabyan*,] came from the battlements of the steeple of Paules church upon a cable, being made fast to an anchor by the Deanes gate, lying on his breast, ayding himself neither with hand nor foote, but spreading them abroad, and after ascended to the midst of the cable, where he tumbled and played many pretty toyes, whereat the king and the nobles had good pastime." (Stowe's Chronicle.) Again, on king Philip's state passage through London in 1554 there was a similar exhibition : see Chronicle of Queen Jane and Queen Mary, p. 150.

[b] " On Wednesday the 4 of June 1561, betwene 4 and 5 of the clock in the after-noone, the steeple of Paules in London, being fired by lightning, brast forth (as it seemed to the beholders) two or three yards beneath the foote of the crosse, and from thence burnt downe the speere to the stone worke and bels, so terribly, that within the space of foure honres the same steeple, with the roofes of the church so much as was timber, or otherwise combustible, were consumed." (Stowe's Chronicle.) A contemporary pamphlet describing this calamity is reprinted in the eleventh volume of the Archæologia ; in the Appendix to Ellis's edition of Dugdale's History of St. Paul's ; and again in Poole's History of Ecclesiastical Architecture in England, 1848, 8vo. p. 406: in which it is stated that persons on the Thames saw lightning strike the spire. Heylyn, in his History of the Reformation, has favoured another story, that the accident was occasioned by the carelessness of a plumber ; but this is very properly corrected in a note of his recent editor the Rev. J. C. Robertson, edit. 1849, ii. 352. See also Machyn's Diary, p. 259, where it will be found that the spire of St. Martin's Ludgate was struck during the same storm. Heylyn also, one would hope with as little truth, though the passage in the text somewhat favours his view, asserts that " the Zuinglian Gospellers, or those of the Genevian party, rejoiced at this lamentable accident, affirming it for a just judgment of God upon an old idolatrous fabric, not thoroughly reformed and purged from its superstitions, and would

wonderfulle workes off God, whose gonnares wylnott mysse the marke thatt he dothe apoynte, be it never so little.

When the queue passed by, many behelde me, for they myght almost touche me, the rome was so narrow, marvelynge belyke that one in souche state wolde venter forthe. Many off my fellowes the pencyonars, and others, and dyvers off the councelle behelde me, and noone off theme all knewe me. I myght heare them saye one to another, "There is one lovithe the quene welle belyke, for he venterith greately to se her; he is very lyke never to se her more." Thus my men thatt stoode by me hard many of them saye, whose hearynge was quyker then myne. The quene herselfe when she past by behelde me. Thus mouche I thought goode to wryte, to show how God dothe presarve thatt semithe to mane impossyble, as many thatt daye dide juge off me.

Thus returned I hoome, and abowte to (two) monethes after I was able to walke to London ane easy pace; butt stylle with my kercheves and pale lene face. I muffeled me with a sarcenett, wiche the rude people in the strettes wolde murmure att, sayinge, "What is he? Dare he nott show his face?" I dyde repayre to my olde familiare acquayntaunce, as drapers, mercers, and others, and stoode talkynge with them and cheponed ther wares; and nott one off them thatt knew me. Then wolde I saye unto them, "Do you nott know me? loke better uppone me. Do you nott know my voyce?" For thatt was also altered. "Truly, (wolde they saye,) yow must pardone me; I cannott calle you to rememberaunce." Then wolde I declare my name unto them; whereatt they so marveled thatt they colde scarcely credite me, butt for the famelyare acquayntaunce thatt I putt them in rememberance off.

Thus passed I forthe the tyme att the Lyme hurst untyll crystmas

---

hatred unto all solemnity and decency in the service of God, performed more punctually in that church, for example's sake, than in any other of the kingdom." On the question whether the burning of Paul's church was to be regarded as a direct judgment of the Almighty, a controversy arose, originating with a sermon preached by dr. Pilkington, bishop of Durham, on the Sunday following the fire: this has been partially reprinted in Pilkington's Works, 1842, (Parker Society,) pp. 479—648.

was past, thatt I waxed somethynge strounge, and then I thought it best to shifte frome thence, for thatt I hadde there ferce enemys, specyally the vycker of Stepney,[a] abbot *qondame* off Tower hylle, whome I aprehendide in kynge Edwardes tyme, and caryed hym unto Croydone to Cranemer, bishope of Caunterbery; for thatt he distourbed the prechers in his churche, causynge the belles to be rounge when they weare att the sermone, and sume tymes begyne to synge in the quere before the sarmone weare halffe done, and sume tymes chalenge the precher in the pulpitt; for he was a strounge, stowte popyshe prelate, whome the godly mene off the paryshe weare wearye off; specyally my neyghboures of the Lyme hurst, as mr. Dryver, mr. Ive, mr. Poynter, mr. Marche, and others. Yet durst the(y) nott medelle with hym untylle it was my happe to cume dwelle amoungst them; and for thatt I was the kynges sarvantt I toke uppone me; and they wentt with me to the bishope to wittnes those thynges agaynst hym. Who was to fulle off lenite: a litle he rebuked hym, and badde hym doo no more soo. "Me lorde, (sayde I,) me thynkes yow are to jentylle unto so stowte a papiste." "Welle, (sayde he,) we have no lawe to ponyshe them by." "We have, me lorde, (sayde I;) yff I hadde your auctoryte I wolde be so bolde to unvycker hym, or mynnester sume sharpe ponyshementt unto hym and souch other. Yff ever it cume to ther turne, they wyll show yow no souch favoure." "Well, (sayde he,) yff God so provyde, we must abyde it." "Surely, (sayde I,) God wyll never cone yow thank for this, butt rather take the sworde from souche as wylle nott use it uppon his enemyes." And thus we departed.[b] The lyke favoure is showed now, and therfore the lyke plage wylle follow.

[a] Henry Moore made his profession as abbot of the monastery of St. Mary de Grace, near the Tower of London, on the 7th May, 1516. (MS. Harl. 6956, p. 74.) He was presented to the vicarage of Stepney by the executors of sir Richard Williams, *alias* Crumwell, the farmers of the rectory, on the 6th March, 1544; and the vacancy occasioned by his death was filled in November 1554. Newcourt's Repertorium Londinense, i. 740.

[b] "And this indeed was the constant behaviour of the archbishop towards papists, and such as were his enemies. For which he was now, and at other times, taxed by men of

158   NARRATIVES OF THE REFORMATION.

Ther was also another spitefull enemy att Stepeney, callede Banbery, a shifter, a dycer, a bore-hunter, lyke unto Dapers the dicer, Morgone of Salisbury courte, buskyne Palmer,[a] lustye Yownge,[b] Raffe Bagenalle,[c] Myles Partryge,[d] and souche others; with wiche cumepanyans I was conversantt a whyle, untylle I felle to redynge the scriptures, and folloynge the prechers. Then agaynst the wekednes off those mene, wiche I hade sene amounge them, I putt forth a ballett, utterynge the falcehood and knavery thatt I was made preve unto; for the wiche they so hated me thatt they reased falce slaunders and brutes off me, saynge thatt I was a spye ffor the duke off Northumberlande, and callynge me Hoper's champione, for a bylle thatt I sett upon Poles gate in defence off Hoper,[e] and another at Saynt Mangenus church, wheare he was to moche abused with raylynge billis cast into the pulpitt, and other wayes. Thus became I

to the Gospel, which he laboured to adorn, so was more likely to obtain the ends he desired than rigour and austerity." Strype (Memorials of Cranmer, p. 170.)

This feature in Cranmer's character was not unnoticed by his contemporaries, "So that on a time I do remember that dr. Hethe, late archbishop of York, partly mislıking this his over-much lenity by him used, said unto him, 'My lord, I now know how to win all things at your hand well enough.' 'How so?' quoth my lord. 'Marry,' saith dr. Hethe, 'I perceive that I must first attempt to do unto you some notable displeasure; and then by a little relenting obtain of you what I can desire.' Whereat my lord bit his lıp, as his manner was when he was moved, and said, *You say well; but yet you may be deceived.*" See Ralph Morice's character of Cranmer, in a subsequent page.

[a] The fame of these *roués* of the days of Henry VIII. is perpetuated only by the writer of the text, with some exceptions. "Busking Palmer," we learn from one of Stowe's Summaries (in which that nickname is mentioned), was the same person as sir Thomas Palmer, who was beheaded with the duke of Northumberland on the 22d August, 1553. See Machyn's Diary, p. 332, and the Life of Lord Grey of Wilton, p. 3. He had also the sobriquet of "long Palmer," as Foxe mentions when describing the persecutions in Calais in 1541.

[b] A person now unknown: Strype, Eccl. Memorials, iii. 204, has mixed up his name with the next, reading "lusty young Raulf Bagenal."

[c] Afterwards sir Ralph Bagenal: see a subsequent page of this volume.

[d] The name of sir Miles Partridge surpasses those of his fellows in the annals of gambling, as having played with king Henry for the heavy stake of the clock-tower of St. Paul's, which he won, and afterwards destroyed. He came to an untimely fate in 1551-2, when he was hung as one of the active partisans of the duke of Somerset : see Machyn, p. 15.

[e] John Hooper, bishop of Gloucester and Worcester.

odious unto most men, and many tymes in daunger off my lyffe amongst them, evyne in kynge Edwardes dayes; as also for aprehendynge one Allenc a falce prophecyer, who bruted thatt kynge Edwarde was deade, too yeres before it came to pas, who was a greate calker[a] for the same. Butt these jugelars and weked dicers weare stylle in favoure amoungst the magistrattes, and weare advauncede; who weare the soares [b] off sedissyone and the distroyers of the too dukes.[c] I praye God the lyke be not practesed by souche flatterers in these dayes, accordynge to the olde provearbe, *He thatt wylle in courte dwelle must corye favelle,* and

> He thatt wylle in courte abyde
> Must cory favelle bake and syde,[d]

for souche gett moste gayne. I was also callede "*the hoote gospellar,*" jestynge and mokynge me, saynge, " he is alle off the sprete." This

---

[a] *i. e.* calculator of nativities, &c. See hereafter, p. 173.   [b] sowers.

[c] *i. e.*, successively, Somerset and Northumberland.

[d] Underhill has here preserved to us an old metrical adage, which is not placed in any modern collection of proverbs, but which is very remarkable as showing the origin of our still familiar phrase *to curry favour,* which would else have remained in hopeless obscurity. Any one asked to say what he understood by " currying favour " would have answered, courting or procuring it (or, as Skinner did, *querir faveur*); but these would have been mere guesses, giving the general sense of the phrase, but not its derivation. To curry is to do the work of a currier, one who converts the skins of animals, *coria*, into leather (from the verb *corrado*); and next, in a secondary sense, the term is applied to the cleansing and dressing of the skins of living animals, which we now generally call grooming. This leads us to the meaning of " favelle;" it is one of the names formerly given to horses, descriptive of their colour, as Bayard, Blanchard, and Lyard were to brown, white, or grey. So, Fauvell was a bright yellowish colour, (diminutive of *fulvus,* tawny,) apparently the opposite of Sorell, which was dark. According to the chronicle of Robert of Brunne, one of Richard the First's horses was so called :
" Sithen at Japhet [Jaffa] was slayu *fauvelle* his stede,"
which in Richardson's Dictionary is misprinted *fanvell.* The operation of currying is grateful to a horse, and he is well pleased if he is thoroughly curried both on " back and side." In modern orthography therefore the old couplet runs—
> He that would in Court abide
> Must curry Fauvell back and side.

It is obvious then (as Mr. Douce remarks, in his Illustrations of Shakspeare, 1807, i. 474,)

was ther commone costome at ther tables to jeste and moke the prechers and earnest followers off the Gospelle, evene amoungst the majestrattes, or els in wantone and rybalde take (talk), wiche when the(y) fell into, one or other wolde loke thorow the borde, saynge, "Take heede thatt Underhylle be nott heare."

Att Stretforde on the Bowe,[a] I tooke the piks[b] off the alter, being of copper, storede with copper Godes, the curatt beynge presentt, and a popishe justes dwellynge in the towne, called justes Tawe.[c] There was commaundement it sholde nott hange in a strynge over the alter, and then they sett it uppon the alter. For this acte the justes' wyff with the women off the towne conspirede to have murthered me; wiche one off them gave me warnynge off, whose goode wylle to the Gospelle was unknowne unto the reste. Thus the Lorde presarved me frome them, and many other daungers moo; but specyally from helle fyer, butt thatt off his mercy he called me from the cumepany off the weked.

This Banbury aforesayde was the spy for Stepney parishe, as

that the phrase *to curry favell* was a metaphorical expression adopted from the stable. It occurs in the old story " How a merchande dyd hys wyfe betray," and in Chaucer, and also in a passage of Udal quoted by Mr. Richardson : Shakspere in his Henry IV. Part II. writes *curry* alone—" I would *curry* with master Shallow." The only place in which a proverbial distich resembling that in the text (but not exactly the same) has been found is Taverner's "Proverbes or Adagies gathered out of the Chiliades of Erasmus, 1569," 18mo. f. 44 : " He that will in court dwell must needes currie fabel ;" but Taverner was not aware of its origin, for he says, " Ye shal understand that *fabel* is an olde Englishe worde, and signified as much as *favour* doth now a dayes." This was not the fact : for *favel* is by Piers Plouhman used for deceit, from the French *favele*, fabula. Douce has noticed that the corruption from *favell* to *favour*, in the phrase " curry favell," occurs in Forrest's Isocrates, 1580 : to which we may now add an earlier example from the reply to Thomas Thackham, of which great part is printed in the present volume, and which was written about 1571 : " specially when you (beyng skolemaster there) coulde so connyngly dissemble and *currye favour* with the papistes." (MS. Harl. 425, f. 48.)

[a] This was an ancient chapel in the parish of Stepney, erected in the reign of Edward III., pursuant to a licence granted by bishop Baldock in 1311. It was made a parish church in the year 1719. [b] The pix.

[c] John Tawe was nominated Autumn reader at the Inner Temple 33 Hen. VIII. but did not read on account of the plague. He was Lent reader in 1 Edw. VI. and treasurer of the house 6 Edw. VI. and 1 Mary.

John a Vales, Bearde, and souche other weare for London[a]; who caused my frende and neyghboure mr. Ive to be sentt unto the Marshalsye, butt the Lorde shortlye delyvered hym; wherfore I thought it best to avoyd, bycause my nott cumeynge to the churche there shulde by hym be marked and presented. Then tooke I a litle howse in a secrete corner, att the nether endo off Woode-strete, wheare I myght better shifte the matter.

Sir Homffrey Ratclyffe[b] was the levetenauntt off the pencyonars, and alwayes favored the Gospelle, by whose meanes I hadd my wagis stylle payde me. When Wyatt was cume into Southwarke, the pencyonars weare commaunded to wache in armoure thatt nyght at the courte; whiche I hearynge off, thought it best in lyke suorte to be there, least by my absense I myght have sume quarelle piked unto me, or att the least be strekon owt off the boke for reseavynge any more wagis. After supper I putt one my armoure as the rest dide, for we weare apoynted to wache alle the nyght. So beyng alle armed, wee came uppe into the chamber off presense with ower pollaxes in ower handes, wherewith the ladies weare very fearefulle; sume lamentynge, cryinge, and wrynginge ther handes, sayde, " Alas, there is sume greate mischeffe towarde; we shalle alle be distroyde this nyght! Whatt a syght is this, to se the quenes chamber full off armed men; the lyke was never sene nor harde off." Then mr. Norres, who was a jentylleman ussher

[a] Foxe, in his chapter on God's punishment upon persecutors, states how " Dale the promoter was eaten into his body with lice, and so died, as is well known of many, and confessed also by his fellow John Avales, before credible witnesse." " Likewise the wretched end of Beard the promoter," which is not there further described; but it will be found related in the story of Thomas Mowntayne, hereafter printed.

[b] Sir Humphrey Radclyffe was the third son of Robert earl of Sussex by his second wife lady Margaret Stanley ; and brother to Henry earl of Sussex, the captain of the band of pensioners. (p. 139.) From his marriage with Isabella, daughter and heiress of Edmund Hervey esquire, he was seated at Elstow in Bedfordshire ; where, in the church, are their effigies, as described in the Gentleman's Magazine 1826, ii. 106. Sir Humphrey was installed at Windsor April 19, 1558, as proxy for William lord Grey of Wilton, then elected knight of the Garter. He died in 1566. He was the father of Edward the last earl of his family, who died in 1641.

CAMD. SOC.

of the utter chamber in kynge Henry the viij^{tes} tyme, and all kyng Edwardes tyme, alwayes a ranke papist, and therfore was now the cheffe ussher off queue Maryes prevy chamber,^a he was apoynted to calle the wache, to se yff any weare lakynge; unto whome Moore, the clarke off ower cheke, delyvered the boke off ower names, wiche he parused before he wolde calle them att the cumebarde^b, and when he came to my name, "Whatt! (sayd he,) whatt dothe he here?" "Syr, (sayde the clarke,) he is here redy to sarve as the rest be." "Naye, by God's body! (sayde he,) that herytyke shall not be called to wache heare. Geve me a pene." So he stroke my name owt off the boke. The clarke of the cheke sought me owte, and sayde unto me, "Mr. Underhylle, yow nede nott to wache, yow maye departe to your logenge." "Maye I? (sayde I,) I wolde be glade off thatt," thynkynge I hadde byne favored because I was nott recovered off my sykenes: butt I dyde not welle truste hym because he was also a papist. "Maye I depart in dede? (sayd I,) wylle yow be my discharge?" "I tell yow trew, (sayde he,) mr. Norres hathe strekon you owt off the boke, sayng these wordes, 'Thatt herytyke shalle nott wache here;' I telle you trwe what he sayde." "Mary, I thanke hym, (sayde I,) and yow also; yow could nott do me a greater plesure." "Naye, burdone nott me withalle, (sayde he,) it is nott my doynge." So departed I into

^a John Norris esquire. He and William Rainsford were the two gentlemen ushers who represented the dukes of Normandy and Guienne at the coronation of Edward VI. Though treated somewhat contemptuously by Underhill, he was a person of importance, and one of a family connected during many generations with the court, and allied to several families of the peerage: see the pedigree of Norris in Lipscombe's Buckinghamshire, vol. i. p. 233. He was elder brother to Henry Norris, beheaded in 1536 for the matter of Anne Boleyne: whose son was summoned to parliament by Elizabeth, and his grandson became earl of Berkshire. After the accession of Mary, sir Philip Hoby, who had held the office of usher of the Garter, or black rod, during the reign of Edward VI., resigned it for the purpose that it might be restored to the family of Norris, and by letters patent dated 1 May 1554, (which are printed in Rymer's Fœdera, xv. 386,) it was conferred on John Norres, one of the gentlemen ushers of the queen's privy chamber, and on William Norres, his son and heir apparent, or the survivor. John Norris died Oct. 21, 1564, having married Elizabeth, sister to Edmund lord Bray. ^b cupboard.

the halle, where ower men weare apoynted to wache. I toke my men with me, and a lynke, and wentt my wayes.

When I came to the courte gate, ther I mett with mr. Clement Througemartone,[a] and George Feris,[b] tindynge ther lynges to go to London. Mr. Througemartone was cume post frome Coventry, and hadde byne with the quene to declare unto her the takynge off the duke off Suffoke.[c] Mr. Feris was sentt from the councelle unto the lorde William Hawwarde,[d] who hadde the charge off the whache att London bryge. As we wentt, for thatt they weare bothe my frendes, and protestanes, I tolde them my goode happe, and maner off my discharge off the whache att the cowrte.

When we came to Ludegate it was past aleavene of the cloke. The gate was fast loked, and a greate wache within the gate off Londonars, but noone withowte; whereoff Henry Feckam hadde the charge under his father,[e] who belyke was goone to his father,

[a] Clement Throckmorton esquire, of Haseley in Warwickshire, was the third son of sir George Throckmorton of Coughton, by Katharine daughter of Nicholas lord Vaux: and married Katharine, daughter of sir Edward Neville, second son of the lord Abergavenny. (Wotton's English Baronetage, 1741, ii. 357.) In early life he served at Boulogne, and was cupbearer to queen Katharine Parr. He was M.P. for West Looe in 1571, and died in 1574. In 1555 mr. Clement Throckmorton charitably undertook to provide for the elder son of Thomas Hawkes when that martyr was sentenced to be burned at Coggeshall: see the letters of Hawkes to his wife and to master Clement Throckmorton printed by Foxe. His eldest son and heir Job was the supposed author of Martin Mar-Prelate; and was father of sir Clement Throckmorton, of Haseley, an eloquent speaker in the parliaments of the next century, in which he sat for the county of Warwick.

[b] George Ferrers, M.P. for Plymouth in 1542, a poet and an historian. For his biography see Wood's Athenæ Oxonienses, (by Bliss,) i. 443.; the notes to Machyn's Diary, p. 327; and those to the Chronicle of Queen Jane and Queen Mary, p. 188.

[c] Henry Grey, the father of the lady Jane. He was captured in his park of Astley near Coventry, and the particulars are given in Appendix VII. to the Chronicle of Queen Jane and Queen Mary.

[d] Brother to Thomas fourth duke of Norfolk; created lord Howard of Effingham 10 March 1553-4, lord chamberlain 1554, and lord admiral 1557; died 1573.

[e] Henry Peckham was the son of sir Edmund Peckham, who had been cofferer of the household to Henry VIII. and Edward VI. and was treasurer of the mint to Mary and Elizabeth. The son, in the year 1563, joined in the conspiracy of Henry Dudley, of

or to loke to the water syde. Mr. Througemartone knoked harde, and called unto them, saynge, " Here is iij or iiij jentyllemen cume from the courte thatt must cume in, and therfore opon the gate." " Who?" cothe one, " Whatt?" cothe another, and moche langehynge the(y) made. " Cane ye telle what ye doo, syrs?" sayd mr. Througemartone, declarynge his name, and that he hadd byne with the quene to showe her grace off the takynge off the duke off Suffoke, " and my logeynge is within, as I am sure sume off yow do know." " And," sayde Ferris, " I am Ferris, that was lorde off misrule with kynge Edwarde,[a] and am sentt from the councelle unto my lorde William, who hathe the charge off the bryge, as yow knowe, uppon weyghtie affayres; and therfore lett us in, or eles ye be nott the quenes fryndes." Stylle there was mouche laughynge amoungst them. Then sayd too or three off them, " We have nott the keyes, we are nott trusted with them; the keyes be caryed awaye for this nyght." " Whatt shall I do?" sayde mr. Througemartone, " I am wery and faynte, and I waxe nowe colde. I am nott aquaynted here abowte, nor no mane dare opone his doores in this daungerous tyme, nor I am nott able to goo bake agayne to the courte; I shall perishe this nyght." " Welle, (sayde I,) lett us goo to Newgate, I thynke I shalle gett in ther." " Tushe! (sayde he,) it is butt in vayne, we shalbe aunswered ther as we are here." " Welle, (sayde I,) and the worst falle, I can loge ye in Newgate; yow know whatt aquayntaunce I have ther, and the keper's doore is withowte the gate." " That weare a bad shifte, (sayde he,) I hadd almost as lyffe dye in the strettes; yett I wylle rather [than] wander agayne to the courte." " Welle, (sayde I,) lett us goo prove. I beleve the keper wyll healpe us in att the gate, or eles lett us in thorow his wardes, for he hathe a doore on the insyde also; yff alle

John Daniell, on the 8th of July in that year. (Stowe's Chronicle, and Machyn's Diary, p. 109.) He appears to have well deserved his fate, having behaved treacherously to his friends. He had sat in the late parliament for Chipping Wycombe.

[a] First at Christmas 1551-2, and again in 1552-3, as described with great delight by Machyn in his Diary, pp. 13, 28, 29: see also, for various particulars, Kempe's Loseley

this fayle I have a frend att the gate, Newmane the ierinmounger, in whose howse I have byne logede, where I dare warantt yow we shalle have logynge, or att the lest howse-rome and fyer." " Marye, this is wel sayde," saythe Ferris.

So to Newgate we wentt, where was a greate wache withowte the gate, wiche my frende Newmane hadde the charge off, for that he was the cunnestable. They marveled to se there torches cumeynge thatt tyme off the nyght. When we came to them, " Mr. Underhylle, (sayde Newmane,) whatt newes, thatt you walke so late?" " None butt goode, (sayd I;) we cume from the cowrte, and wolde have goone in att Ludgate, and cannott be lett in, wherfore I pray yow yff yow cannot helpe us in here, lett [us] have logynge with yow." " Mary, that ye shalle, (sayde he,) or go in att the gate, whether ye wille." " Godamercy, jentylle frende, (sayde mr. Througemertone,) I pray yow lett us goo in yff it maye be." He called to the cunestable within the gate, who opened the gate forthwith. " Now happye was I (sayde mr. Througemertone,) thatt I mett with you; I hadd byne lost eles."

When Wyatt was cume abowte,[a] notwithstandynge my discharge off the wache by mr. Norres, I putt on my armoure and wentt to the courte, where I founde all my felowes armed in the halle, wiche they weare apoynted to kepe that daye. Old syr John Gage[b] was apoynted withowte the utter gate, with sume off the garde and his sarvantes and others with hym; the rest off the garde weare in the greate courte, the gattes standynge opune. Sir Rychard Southwell had the charge off the bakesydes, as the woodeyarde and thatt waye, with v^c men. The quene was in the galary by the gatehowse. Then came Knevett[c] and Thomas Cobam,[d] with a company off the rebelles

---

[a] On Wednesday the 7th Feb. 1553-4, being Ash Wednesday,—having marched forward from Southwark the day before, and crossed the Thames at Kingston.

[b] Being lord chamberlain and constable of the Tower. See before, p. 139.

[c] William Knevett was one of the principal captains of the rebels: but two others of the family, Thomas and Anthony, were also among those committed to the Tower. See the Chronicle of Queen Jane and Queen Mary, pp. 51, 52, 53. At the end of the following

with them, thorow the gatehowse, frome Westmester,[a] uppon the sodene, wherewith syr John Gage and thre of the jugeis,[b] thatt weare menly armed in olde bryggantynes,[c] weare so fryghtede thatt they fledd in att the gattes in souche hast thatt old[d] Gage fell downe in the durte and was foule arayde; and so shutt the gates. Wheratt the rebelles shotte many arowes. By meanes off this greate hurleburle in shuttynge off the gattes, the garde thatt weare in the courte made as greate hast in att the halle doore, and wolde have cume into the halle amoungst us, wiche we wolde not suffer. Then they wentt

William and George were also committed to the Tower, and all three tried in the following February. (ibid. p. 62.) Thomas was condemned to death. The two latter were acquitted, or pardoned; and released, with their father lord Cobham, on the 24th of March. (ibid. p. 71, and Machyn, p. 58.) The particulars of lord Cobham's committal to the Tower on the 2nd of February are given in the same Chronicle, at p. 41.

[a] The rebels, on their way from Knightsbridge, were first attacked near St. James's palace, by the earl of Pembroke's horsemen; when some of them "which escaped the charge, passed by the backeside of Saint James towardes Westmynster, and from thence to the courte, and finding the gates shut agaynst them, stayed there a while, and shotte off many arrowes into the wyndowes and over into the gardeyne, neverthelesse without any hurt that was knowne. Whereupon the sayde rebelles, over whom one Knevett was captaine, perceyving themselves to be too fewe to doe any great feate there, departed from thence to followe Wyat, who was gone before towardes London." (Narrative by George Ferrers, included in Grafton's Chronicle, and copied by Holinshed.) Proctor, who published a separate narrative of Wyat's rebellion, erroneously imagined that the attack came from Charing cross: see a note on this point in the Chronicle of Queen Jane and Queen Mary, p. 131. The writer of that chronicle states (p. 48) that the party who turned down towards Westminster were commanded by "Cutbart Vaughan and about ij auncyentes."

[b] These judges were those of the common pleas. "This daye the judges in the common place at Westminster satte in armoure." (Proctor.) "Yea, this day, and other dayes, (says Stowe,) the justices, serjeants at the law, and other lawyers in Westminster hall pleaded in harnesse." Proctor adds that while the court gates were open, "one maister Nicolas Rockewod, being a gentleman of Lyncolnes inn, and in armour at the said court gate, was shotte through hys nose with an arrowe by the rebels. For the comminge of the said rebels was not loked for that way." See also the anecdote of Ralph Rokeby serjeant at law, pleading with a good coate-armour under his robes and playing a good part with his bow and a sheaf of arrows, quoted in the Chronicle of Queen Jane and Queen Mary, p. 40; also that (p. 41) of doctor Weston, who the same morning (being Ash Wednesday) sang mass before the queen "in harnesse under his vestments."

[c] Brigandines were jackets of quilted leather, covered with iron plates.   [d] *MS.* hold.

throungynge towardes the watergate, the kycheyns, and those ways.
Mr. Gage came in amoungst us alle durt, and so fryghted thatt he
coulde nott speke to us; then came the thre jugeis, so fryghted thatt
we coulde nott kepe them owte excepte we shulde beate them
downe. With thatt we issued owt off the halle into the courte to
se whatt the matter was; where ther was none lefte butt the porters,
and, the gattes beyng fast shutt, as we wentt towardes the gate,
meanynge to goo forthe, syr Rycharde Southwell came forthe off the
bake yardes into the courte. "Syr, (said wee,) commaunde the
gates to be opened thatt we maye goo to the quenes enemyes, we
wyll breake them opone eles; it is to mouche shame the gates shulde
be thus shutt for a few rebelles; the quene shalle se us felle downe
her enemys this daye before her face." "Masters," sayde he, and putt
off his muriane [a] off his heade, " I shalle desyer yow alle, as yow be
jentyllemen, to staye yourselves heare thatt I maye goo upe to the
quene to knowe her plesure, and yow shall have the gates oponed;
and, as I am a jentylleman, I wylle make spede." Uppon this we
stayde, and he made a spedie returne, and brought us worde the
quene was contentt we shulde have the gates opened. "Butt her
request is (sayde he,) that yow wyll not goo forthe off her syght, for
her only trust is in yow for the defence [of] her parsone this daye."
So the gate was opened, and we marched before the galary wyndowe,
wheare she spake unto us, requyrynge us, as we weare jentyllemen
in whome she only trusted, thatt we wolde nott goo from thatt place.[b]
Ther we marched upe and downe the space off an ower, and then
came a harrolde postynge to brynge newes that Wyatte was takone.
Immediately came syr Mores Barkeley [c] and Wyatte behynd hym,

[a] The morion was a scull-cap or hat of steel with a ridge on its top. See some representations in Meyrick's Ancient Arms and Armour, pl. lxviii., and Fosbroke's Encyclopedia of Antiquities, plate of Armour and Arms.

[b] Of the queen's personal demeanour on this alarming occasion see further particulars in the Chronicle of Queen Jane and Queen Mary, pp. 48, 49, 133, 188.

[c] Sir Maurice Berkeley, of Bruton, co. Somerset, was standard-bearer *(vexillifer)* to Henry VIII., Edward VI., and Elizabeth, according to the family pedigree. His

unto whome he dyde yelde att the Temple gate,a and Thomas Cobam behynde ane other jentylleman.b

Anane after we c weare alle brought unto the queues presentes, and every one kyssed her hande, off whome we haddo greate thankes and large promeses how goode she wolde be unto us; but few or none off us got any thynge, although she was very liberalle to many others d thatt weare enemyes unto God's worde, as fewe off us weare.

Thus wentt I home to my howse, wheare I kepte, and came litle abraude, untyll the maryage was concluded with kynge Phellippe. Then was ther preparynge to goo with the quene unto Wynchester; and all the bookes off the ordinarys weare parused by the beshope of Wynchester,e and the yearle of Arundelle, to consyder off every mane. Syr Houmphray Ratcleff, ower leffetenaunte, brought unto them the boke off the pencyonars, wiche when they overloked, and came unto my name, "Whatt dothe he heare?" sayde the yearle off Arundelle. "I knowe no cause why he shuld nott be heare, (sayde mr. Ratclyffe;) he is an onest mane; he bathe sarved from the begynnynge of the bande, and was as forwarde as any to sarve the quene in the tyme off Wyatt's rebellyon." "Lett hym pas then,"

name occurs as one of the knights of the king's privy chamber who signed the settlement of the crown on the lady Jane in 1553 (see Chronicle of Queen Jane and Queen Mary, p. 100). There was, however, at this time, besides sir Maurice of Bruton, another sir Maurice, the younger son of Thomas tenth lord Berkeley, and the uncle of Henry at this time the baron, and a minor. (Dugdale, Baronage, i. 368.)

a See the particulars of his surrender minutely described in The Chronicle of Queen Jane and Queen Mary, p. 50.

b "And another toke Thomas Cobham, and [a third] William Knevet, and so caryed them behind theym upon their horses to the courte." (Ibid.)

c *i. e.* the gentlemen pensioners.

d See the list of "The names of certaine lordes and gentlemen that were with hir majesties power against the rebelles," endorsed "to be rewardyd," printed from a MS. in the State-paper office, at the close of the Chronicle of Queen Jane and Queen Mary, p. 187. It may be remarked on that document that by "My lord Marshall" is meant lord Clinton, who was "Marshall of the field" or "of the camp" at Wyat's attack ; and by "My lord lieutenaunt" (p. 188) the earl of Pembroke, who had the chief command of the queen's forces.

e Gardiner, now the queen's chief minister.

sayde the beshope. " Well, (sayde the yearle,) you may do soo; butt I assure you, me lorde, he is an arche heritike." Thus I passed onst (once) agayne.

When we came to Wynchester, beynge in the chamber off presentts, with my fellowes, mr. Norres came for the off the quenes preve chamber, unto whome we dide reverance, as his place requyred. " Whatt! (saythe he unto me,) whatt do yow heare?" " Marry, sir, (sayde I,) whatt do yow heare?" " Ee, (sayde he,) are you so shourte with me?" " Syr, (sayde I,) I muste and wylle forbeare, for the place yow be in; butt yff you weare in the place yow weare in off the utter chamber, I wolde be shorter with yow. Yow weare then the doore-keper, when we wayted att the table. Your offyce is nott to fynde faulte att my beynge heare. I am att this tyme apoynted to sarve here by those thatt be in ottorytie, who know me as welle as yow doo." " They shalle know yow better, (sayde he,) and the quene also." With thatt sayde mr. John Calveley,[a] one off my felowes, brother unto syr Hewe Calveley off Cheshere, who sarved att the jurney to Laundersaye in the same bande thatt I dyde, " In goode faythe, mr. Norres, me thynke yow do nott welle. This jentyllemane ower fellow hathe sarved off lounge tyme, and was redy to venter his lyffe in defence off the quenes majestie att the laste sarvis, and as forwarde as any was ther; and also beynge apoynted and redy to sarve heare agayne now, to his greate chargeis, as it is unto us alle, methynkes you do moore then the parte off a jentyllemane thus to seke hym." " Whatt! (sayde he,) I parseave you wylle holde together." " Eles we weare worse then beastes, (sayde my fellow,) yff we wolde nott in alle leffulle causes so holde together thatt he thatt touchethe one off us shalle touche all." So wentt he from us into the preve chamber, and from thatt tyme never medled more with me.

[a] John Calveley, one of the younger sons of sir George Calveley, of Lea in Cheshire, by Elizabeth daughter of sir Piers Dutton, is in the family pedigree styled " valet to queen Mary." His elder brother sir Hugh was knighted at Leith in 1543. (Ormerod's History of Cheshire, vol. ii. p. 419.)

On the maryage daye,[a] the kynge and the quene dyned in the halle in the beshop's palice, sittynge under the clothe off estate, and none eles att thatt table. The nobilite satte att the syde tables. Wee weare the cheffe sarveters, to cary the meate, and the yearle off Sussex ower capetayne was the shewer (sewer).[b] The seconde course att the maryage off a kynge is gevyne unto the bearers; I meane the meate, butt nott the disshes, for they weare off golde. It was my chaunce to cary a greate pastie of a redde dere in a greate charger, very delicately baked; wiche for the weyght theroff dyvers refused; the wiche pastye I sentt unto London to my wyffe and her brother, who cherede therwith many off ther frendes. I wyll not take uppon me to wryte the maner off the maryage, off the feaste, nor off the daunssynge off the Spanyards thatt daye,[c] who weare greately owte off countenaunce, specyally kynge Phelip daunceynge with the quene, when they dide se me lorde Braye,[d] mr.

[a] At Winchester, on the 25th July 1554.

[b] "At the banquet, the earl of Arundel presented the ewer, the marquess of Winchester the napkin; none being seated except the king and queen; but, as to the rest of the entertainment, it was more after the English than the Spanish fashion. The dinner lasted till six in the evening, after which there was store of music; and before nine all had already retired." Narrative from the archives of Louvaine, in Tytler's Edward VI. and Mary, ii. 432.

[c] "And thus, shortly to conclude, there was for certain daies after this moste noble mariage such triumphing, bankating, singing, masking, and daunsing, as was never in Englande heretofore, by the reporte of all men. Wherfore, to see the kinges magestie and the queue sitting under the cloth of estate, in the hall where they dyned, and also in the chamber of presence at dansing tyme, where both their magesties dansed, and also to behold the dukes and noblemen of Spain daunse with the faire ladyes and the moste buetifull nimphes of England, it should seme to him that never did see suche, to be an other worlde." John Elder's Letter sent in to Scotlande to the bishop of Caithness, reprinted in the appendix to The Chronicle of Queen Jane and Queen Mary, p. 143. Mary had been always fond of dancing, and her brother king Edward once wrote to her to remonstrate with her on that score. (See Halliwell's Royal Letters, 1846, ii. 5; also Sir Fred. Madden's memoir of her prefixed to her Privy Purse Expenses.)

[d] John second lord Bray, who succeeded his father in 1539, had been lieutenant of the gentlemen pensioners before sir Humphrey Radclyffe, and was characterized as "a paragon in court, and of sweet entertainment." But, though he shone in the court of Mary, he did not agree in her policy, and in 1556 he suffered imprisonment in the Fleet

Carowe, and others so farre excede them; butt wyll leve it unto the learned, as it behovithe hym to be thatt shalle wryte a story off so greate a tryoumffe.

Wiche beyng ended, ther repare was to London, wheare shortlye after begane the cruelle parsecusyone off the prechers, and earnest professors and followers off the gospelle, and shearchynge off men's howses for ther bokes. Wherefore I goott olde Henry Daunce, the brekeleyer off Whytechappelle, who used to preche the gospelle in his gardene every halydaye, where I have sene a thowsande people, he dyde inclose my bokes in a bryke walle by the chemnyes syde in my chamber, where they weare presarved from moldynge or mice, untylle the fyrste yere off ower moste gracyouse quene Elisabeth, &c. notwithstandynge that I removed from thence, and wentt unto Coventry, and gott me a howse a myle owte off the citie in a woode syde. Butt before I removed from the sayde howse in London, I hadde too chyldearne [a] borne ther, a boye and a whence (wench).

It was a greate greffe to me to se so mouche innocentt bloode shede for the veritie. I was also thretened by John Avales and Bearde,[b] wiche I understoode by mr. Luke,[c] my very frende, off Colemane strete visissyone (physician), who was greate with sume thatt kepte them cumepany, and yett weare honeste mene; whome I caused to lett them understande thatt yf they dide attempte to take me excepte they hadd a warantt syngned with fore or fyve off the counceles bandes I wolde goo farther with them then Peter dide, who strake off butt the eare off Malcus, butt I wolde surely stryke off heade and alle; wiche was declared unto them; so thatt I oftene tymes mett them, but they wolde nott medle with me. So myghtilye

and in the Tower, on suspicion of connection with the conspiracy of Henry Dudley, in which his nephews Edward and Francis Verney were involved. The particulars of this trouble and his subsequent history until his early death in 1557 have been presented in detail to the Camden Society by Mr. Bruce in the Verney Papers, pp. 52, 56, 73, 77.

[a] Anne his fifth daughter, born the 4th of January 1554, and Edward his second son, born the 10th of February 1555. (See p. 135.)

[b] See before, p. 161.

[c] Luke Shepherd: see note in the Appendix.

the mercyfulle Lorde defendide me, as also frome beynge presentt att thatt blasphemus mase in alle the tyme off queue Mary.

This Luke wroote many proper bokes agaynst the papistes, for the wyche he was impresoned in the Flete; specially a boke called *John Boone and Mast Parsone*, who resoned together off the naturalle presense in the sakermentt; wiche boke he wroote in the tyme off kynge Edwarde, wherewithe the papist(s) weare soore greved, specyally syr John Gresam,[a] then beynge mayour. John Daye dide pryntt the same boke; whome the maior sentt for to knowe the maker theroff, saynge he shulde also goo to presone for pryntynge the same. It was my chaunce to cume in the same tyme, for thatt I badde founde oute wheare Alen the prophecyer hade a chamber, thorow whome ther was a brute in the citie thatt the kynge was deade, wiche I declared to the maior; requyrynge hym to have ane offycer to aprehende hym. "Mary, (sayde the maior,) I have receaved letters this nyght att mydnyght to make searche for the souche." He was goynge unto dynner, who wyllede me to take parte off the same. As we weare att dynner, he sayde ther was a boke putt forthe called *John Boone*, the maker wheroff he wolde also searche for. "Wy so? (sayde I,) thatt boke is a goode boke; I have one off them here, and ther is many off them in the courte." "Have yow so? (sayde he,) I praye you lett me se it; for I have nott sene any off them." So he toke it, and reade a litle off it, and laughed theratt, as it was bothe pythye and mery; by meanes wheroff John Daye, sittynge att the syde borde after dynnor, was biddene go whome, whoo badde eles goone to presone.

When we hade dyned, the maior sentt to (two) off his offycers with me to seke Alene; whome we mett withalle in Poles,[b] and toke hym with us unto his chamber, wheare we founde fygures sett to calke the

---

[a] Uncle to the celebrated sir Thomas Gresham. His mayoralty was in 1547-8. See memoirs of him in Burgon's Life of Gresham, pp. 11-21. Some particulars regarding him will be found in the notes to Machyn's Diary, p. 353; and as to his children in The Topographer and Genealogist, 1853, ii. 512.

[b] In the nave of Saint Paul's cathedral, then a place of general concourse.

nativetie off the kynge, and a jugementt gevyne off his deathe, wheroff this folyshe wreche thoughte hymselfe so sure thatt he and his conselars the papistes bruted it all over.ᵃ The kynge laye att Hamtone courte the same tyme, and me lord protector at the Syone;ᵇ unto whome I caryed this Alen, with his bokes off conejuracyons, cearkles, and many thynges beloungynge to thatt dylvyshe art,ᶜ wiche he affyrmed before me lorde was a lawfulle cyens (science), for the statute agaynst souche was repealed.ᵈ "Thow folyshe knave! (sayde me lorde,) yff thou and alle thatt be off thy cyens telle me what I shalle do to-morow I wylle geve the alle thatt I have;" commaundyuge me to cary hym unto the Tower: and wroote a letter unto syr John Markam thene beynge leffetenauntt,ᵉ to cause hym to be examyned by souche as weare learned. Mr. Markam, as he was bothe wyse and zelous in the Lorde, talked with hym; unto whome he dyde affirme thatt he kuewe more in the syence off astronomy then alle the unyversyties off Oxforde and Cambryge; wheruppone he sentt for my frende, before spokyne off, doctor Reccorde, who examined hym, and

ᵃ "In the mean season, bicause ther was a rumour that I was dead, I passed thorowgh London," writes king Edward in his Journal. "Item the xxiij. day of the same monyth (July 1549) the kynges grace came from the dewke of Suffolkes place in Sothwarke thorrow London, and soo to Whytte hall, goodly, with a goodly company." Chronicle of the Grey Friars of London, p. 60.

ᵇ Syon house, then belonging to the duke of Somerset.

ᶜ Some of these Underhill kept in his possession, and copies of them will be found in the Appendix, together with other notices of Allen.

ᵈ By the statute 1 Edw. VI. cap. 12, the act of 33 Henry VIII. cap. 8 (a copy of which will be found in the Appendix) was repealed, as being one of those constituting new felonies since the 1 Hen. VIII. See the Index to the Statutes of the Realm, *tit.* Witchcraft.

Sir John Markham was lieutenant of the Tower during the protectorate of the duke of Somerset, and was discharged from his office at the end of October 1551, because, during the duke's imprisonment, he had suffered him to walk abroad, and certain letters to be sent and answered, without making the council privy, as is recorded by king Edward in his Journal: see The Literary Remains of King Edward VI. pp. 233, 238, 328. He was head of the family seated at Cotham in Nottinghamshire, and his biography will be found in the History of the Markham Family, by the Rev. David Frederick Markham, 1854, 8vo. p. 19. See also a letter of archbishop Cranmer to Cromwell in 1537, highly commending sir John Markham both as an old soldier and as a favourer of God's word:

he kuewe nott the rules of astronamye, but was a very unlearned asse, and a sorcerer, for the wiche he was worthye hangynge, sayde mr. Recorde.

To have further matter unto hym we scntt for Thomas Robyns alias Morgane,[a] commonly called litle Morgane, or Tome Morgan, brother unto greate Morgane off Salisbury courte, the greate dycer, who when I was a companyone with them, told me many stories off this Alene, whatt a cunnynge mane he was, and whatt thynges he coulde do, as to make a womane love a mane,[b] to teache mene how to wyne att the dice,[c] whatt shulde become off this realme—nothynge butt he knewe it; so hadde his chambers in dyvers plases off the cittie, whether resorted many women for thynges stollene or lost,[d] to know ther fortunes, and ther chyldarnes fortunes; wheare the ruffelynge roysters the dicers made ther maches.[e] When this Morgane and Allen weare brought together, Morgane utterly denyed thatt ever he had sene hym or knowen hym. " Yes, (sayde Alene,) yow know me,

[a] The remainder of the MS. is now bound in the MS. Harl. 424, at f. 8.

[b] —"to provoke any person to unlawful love" was one of the objects of witchcraft enumerated in the Act 33 Hen. VIII. cap. 12, which will be found in the Appendix.

[c] See Allen's paper, No. 3, in the Appendix.

[d] The sorcerers were used to " take upon them to tell or declare where goodes stollen or lost shall become." (Act 33 Hen. VIII. cap. 12.) This was a branch of the " science" which formed too frequent a source of profit to be hastily relinquished. It was flourishing a century later, and is not yet entirely extinct. The famous Richard Baxter, in " The Certainty of the World of Spirits fully evinced, 1691," inquires " To what sort shall we rank those that tell men of things stolen and lost, and that shew men the face of a thief in a glass, and cause the goods to be brought back, who are commonly called *white witches?* We have had so many credible reports of such, as alloweth not reason to doubt of it." And he then proceeds to tell some stories of Hodges, one of these " white witches," whom he remembered, practising at Sedgley. See Allen's papers, Nos. 1 and 2.

[e] In the time of king Edward we read that " Dicing and carding are forbidden, but dicing and carding-houses are upholden. Some in their own houses, and in the king's majesty's court, (God save his noble grace, and grant that virtue and knowledge may meet in his royal heart!) give ensample to his subjects to break his statutes and laws. Prisons in London, where men lie for debt, be dicing-houses; places of correction and punishment be dens and schools of unthriftiness," &c. Epistle addressed to archbishop Cranmer, prefixed by Roger Hutchinson to " The Image of God, or laie man's booke," 1550. Hutchinson's Works, (Parker Society,) p. 7.

and I knowe yow," for he hadd confessed that beffore his comeynge. Upon this mr. leffetenauntt stayed litle Morgane also presonar in the Tower.

I caused also mr. Gastone the lawyare,[a] who was also a greate dicer, to be aprehendid; in whose howse Alene was mouche, and hadde a chamber ther, where was many thynges practesed. Gaston hadde an olde wyffe who was leyde under the borde alle nyght for deade, and when the womene in the mornynge came too wynde her, they founde thatt ther was lyffe in her, and so recovered her, and she lived aboute too yeres after.

By the resworte off souche as came to seke for thynges stollen and lost, wiche they wolde hyde for the nonst, to bleare ther husebandes' ies withalle, saynge " the wyse mane tolde them," off souche Gastone badde choyce for hym selffe and his frendes, younge lawers of the Temple. Thus became I so disspysed and odious unto the lawers, lordes and ladies, jentyllmene, marchantes, knaves, hoores, baudes, and theves, thatt I walked as daungerously as Daniell amoungest the lyons; yett from them alle the Lorde delivered me, nottwithstondynge ther oftone devices and consperices by vyolence to have shed my bloode, or with sorcery distroide me.

These affooresayde weare in the Tower about the space off a yere, and then by frendshipe delyvered. So scapithe alwayes the weked and souche as God commaundethe shulde nott lyve amounge the people; yea evyne now in these dayes also, so thatt me thynk I se the ruine off London and this hole realme to be evyn att hande, for God wylle nott suffer any longer. Love is cleane banished; no mane is sory for Joseffes hurte.

A prayer[b] tacon owt off the salmes off Davide, dayly and nyghtly used to be sayde off Edwarde Underhylle.

Lorde, teache me the understaundynge off thy commaundementes,

---

[a] This is probably the true name, and not Gascoigne. One of the knights of the Bath made at the coronation of queen Mary was sir Henry Gaston.

[b] Strype, in his Ecclesiastical Memorials, vol. iii., at the end of Chapter VI. has printed

thatt I maye aply myselfe for the kepynge off the same, as lounge as I lyve. Geve me souche wisedome thatt I maye understande and so to fulfylle the thinge thatt thy lawe devisethe; to kepe it also with my hoole harte, thatt I do nothynge agaynst it. Gyde me after the trew understaundynge off thy commaundementes, for thatt hath bynn alwayes my specyall desyer. Incline myne harte unto the love off thy statutes, and cause me utterly to aboure covetousnes. Turne myne ies asyde lest they be tangelede with the love off moste vayne thynges; butt leade me rather unto lyff thorow thy warnynges. Sett souche a worde befoore thy sarvantt as maye most cheffely further hym to worshipe the. Take awaye the shame thatt I am affrayde off, for thy jugementes are greatly myxed with mercy. As for me, verely I have loved thy commaundementtes; wherfore kepe me alyve accordynge to thy ryghtousnes.

Love God above all thynges, and thy neyghboure as thy selfe,
    Thatt this is Christes doctryne no mane cane it denye;
Wych litle is regarded in Yngland's common wealthe,
    Wherefore greate plages att hande be, the realme for to distroye.

Do as thow woldest be done unto, no place here he cane have;
    Of alle he is reffused, no mane wylle hym reseave;
Butt pryvate wealthe, thatt cursed wreche and most vyle slave,
    Over alle he is imbraced, and fast to hym they cleave.

He thatt hathe this worldes goode and seithe his neyghboure lake,
    And off hym hathe no campassyone, nor showith hym no love,
Nor relevithe his nesessite, butt suffres hym go to wrake,
    God dwellethe nott in thatt mane, the scriptures playnely prove.

Example we have by Dyves, that dayntelye dide fare,
    In worldely wealthe and ryches therin he dide excelle,
Off poore Lazarous' misery he hadde theroff no care,
    Therfore was sodenly takone and tormentide in helle.

EDWARDE UNDERHYLLE.

VII.

THE TROUBLES OF THOMAS MOWNTAYNE,

RECTOR OF ST. MICHAEL TOWER-RYALL, IN THE REIGN OF QUEEN MARY: WRITTEN BY HIMSELF.

THOMAS MOWNTAYNE was arrested for continuing to perform the Protestant communion after it had been prohibited: and then retained in prison as a traitor, having accompanied the duke of Northumberland in his journey to Cambridge when endeavouring to establish the title of queen Jane. Having lain for some months in prison, he was released through some legal informalities, and at length escaped to the continent.

Mowntayne himself informs us that he was the son of Richard Mowntayne a servant to king Henry the Eighth and king Edward. All that is further known of him, beyond what is related in the following narrative, is that on the dissolution of the college of the Holy Spirit and Saint Mary, founded by Richard Whittington, in connection with the church of Saint Michael in the Ryal, in the city of London, Thomas Mountein, clerk, was on the 29th Dec. 1550, presented to that church by the dean and chapter of Canterbury, and received institution from archbishop Cranmer, to whose jurisdiction the rectory belonged as a peculiar; but after the accession of queen Mary, Whittington's college being re-established, the former rector, Richard Smith, S.T.P. was reinstated. (Newcourt's Repertorium Ecclesiasticum Londinense, i. 494.)

Mowntayne was one of nine priests beneficed in London that pertained to the archbishop's jurisdiction, who (*sede vacante*) were by a citation dated March 7, 1553-4, ordered to appear before the vicar-general, Henry Harvey, LL.D. in Bow church, in order to be called to account as married men. Mowntayne was one of those who did not appear; and consequently, being pronounced contumacious, was deprived of his benefice. (Strype, Memorials of Cranmer, p. 327.)

Thomas Mowntayne, on his return from his continental exile, appears to have obtained the rectory of St. Pancras Soper-lane, to which his institution is not on record, but a successor was appointed on his res'gnation Oct. 4, 1561.

178 NARRATIVES OF THE REFORMATION.

Strype printed the whole of this narrative in his Ecclesiastical Memorials, with the exception of a few passages, but divided into five portions (vol. iii. chapters 7, 11, 20, 23, and 24,) and impaired by numerous errors. It is therefore thought that a complete and literal copy is not superfluous in the present collection.

(MS. Harl. 425, f. 106.)

In the yeare of Lorde God a thowsand fyffe hundrethe and iij quenc Marye was crownyd Quene of Ingeland, swche a daye of the monthe [a] beynge Sondaye; and the next Sondaye after, I Thomas Mowntayne, parson of Sent Myhellys in the towere ryall, otherwysse callyd Wythtyngeton college yn London, dyd ther mynystere al kyend of servys acordynge to the godly order than sett forthe by that moste grasyus and blessyd prence kynge Edward the syxte; and the hole paryshe, beynge than gatheryd togeather, dyd than and there moste joyfully communycate together with me the holly supper of the Lorde Jesus, and manye other godly sytysyns wher than partakers of the same, whoe, with byter terys [b] of repentance, dyd not onlye lament ther former wycked lyves, but also the lacke and lose of our moste dred sufferent lorde kynge Edward the syxte, whome we wher not worthye of, for our unthankefulnes and dyssobedyence bothe towardes Allmightye God and his magestie. Nowe, wyll I was even a brekynge of the bred at the table, sayenge to the communycants thes wordys, *Take and eate thys*, &c., and *Drynke thys*, &c., ther where standynge by, to see and here, sartayne sarvynge men belongyng to the bushope of Wynchester, amonge home, one of them most shamefully blasphemyd God, sayenge " Ye, Godys blud, standys thowe ther yet? sayenge *Take and eate, Take and drynke;* wyl not thys geare be lefte yet? yow shal be made to synge another songe withyn thys fewe dayes I trowe, or elys I have loste my marke."

The nexte Weddynsdaye followyng [c] the bushop of Wynchester sent one of hys servantes for me to come and speake with my lorde hys

[a] October 1, 1553.   [b] *Misprinted by Strype* bitterness.   [c] October 11.

master; to home I answeryd, that I wolde wayte one hys lordshyp after that I had done mornyng prayer. " Naye, (saythe hys man,) I maye not tarye so longe for yow. I ham commaundyd to take yow whersoever I fyend you, and to brynge yow with me; that ys my charge gevyn unto me by my lordys owne mowthe." " Wel than, (sayed I,) I wyll goo with yow owte of hande, and God be my comforde, and strengthyn me with hys holy spryte thys daye and ever, in that same truthe wher unto he hathe calyd me, that I may contynue theryn to the end. Amen!"

Nowe, whan I came ynto the greate chamber at Saint Marye Overy's, ther I fownd the bushop standyng at a baye wyndowe with a great companye aboute hym, and manye swters bothe men and wemen, for he was gooynge to the courte; amonge home ther was one mr. Sellinger, a knyghte and lord debytye of Iyerland,[a] beinge a swtter also to my lorde. Than the bushope callyd me unto hym and sayed, " Thou herytyke! how darste thow be so bowlde to use that sysmatycall service styll, of late set forthe? seynge that God hath sent us nowe a catholycke quene, whose lawys thow haste broken, as the rest of thy fellowse bathe don, and you shall knowe the pryse of yt yffe I do lyffe. Ther ys suche abomynable companye of yowe, as ys able to poyesyne a hole realme with your herysys."
" My lorde, (sayed I,) I ham none heretyke, for that waye that yow counte heresy, so worshupe we the lyvynge God; and as our forefathers hathe done and belevyd, I mene Habraham, Isaake, and Jacob, with the reste of the holly prophetes and apostyllys, even soo doo I believe to be savyd, and by no other meanes." " Godys pasyon! (sayd the bushop,) dyd not I tel yow, my lorde deby[ty], howe yow sholde knowe an heretyke? he ys up with the ' lyvynge

God,' as thoo ther were a dead God. They have nothynge yn ther mowthes, thes herytykys, but 'the Lord lyvythe, the lyvynge God rwlythe, the Lorde, the Lorde,' and nothyng but the Lorde." Here he chaffyed lyke a bushop, and, as his mannar was, many tymys he put of hys cape and rubbyd to and froo, up and done, the fore parte of hys heed, wher a locke of hare was alwayes standynge up, and that as some saye wase hys grace; but, to passyffye thys hastye bushop and cruell man, the lord debytye sayed, "My good lorde chaunseler, trobyl not yourselve with thys herytyke, I thynke all the worlde ys full of them, God bles me from them! but as your lordshyp sayed even now full well, havynge a chrystyan quene nowe raynynge over us, I truste ther wylbe shortly a reformasyon and an order taken for these herytykes, and I trust God hathe presarvyd your honorable lordshyp even for the very same porpoose." Than sayed mr. Selynger unto me, "Submyt yourselve unto my lorde, and so yow shall fynd favor at hys hand." "I thanke yow, syr, (sayd I,), plye your owne swete [suit], and I pray yow let me alone, for I never offendyd my lord, neyther yet wyll I make any suche submysyon has he wolde have me to doo, be assueryd of that, God wyllynge." "Wel, (sayed he,) you are a stuburne man." Than stode ther one by muche lyke unto docter Martyn,[a] and sayed, "My lorde, the tyme pasythe awaye; trubule your selve no longer with thys herytyke, for he ys not onlye an herytyke, but also a traytor to the quenes magesty, for he was one of them that wente forthe with the ducke of Northethumberland and was yn open felde agaynste here grace; and therfor as a traytor he ys one of them that ys exsemte owte of the generall pardon, and hathe loste the benyfytt of the same." "Ys yt even so? (saythe

[a] Thomas Martyn, D.C.L. one of the masters in chancery, who was actively engaged in the prosecution of archbishop Cranmer and many others, as appears in Foxe's pages, throughout the Marian period. He was author of a book published in 1554, on the Unlawfulness of Priests' Marriage. See memoirs of him in Wood's Athenæ Oxon. (edit. Bliss,) i. 500; and references to many particulars in the General Index to the Works of Strype.

the bushope,) feche me the boke that I maye see yt." Than was the boke broughte hym, weryn he loked a as one ingnorante what had bene done, and yet he beynge the cheffe doere hymselve therof. Than asked he of me what my name was. I sayed my name was Thomas Mownttayne. "Thow haste wronge," sathe he. "Why so, my lorde?" "That thow haste not *mowntyd* to Tyborne, or to soche a lyke place." Than sayed I unto hym, "I beseche your lordshyp be so good lord unto me, as to let me knowe myn acusars who they they be, for I truste that I have not desarvyd nether to be hangyd as a theffe, nor yet to be burnyd as [a] herytyke, for I onely beleve yn one God yn trinitye, and as for the lawes of the realme, I truste I have not offendyd or brokyn anye of them." "No? (sayd the bushop,) I wyll make thee to synge a newe songe or thow and I have done, for thes ij [b] be alwayes lynked together, treson and herysy, and thow haste lyke a shameles man offendyd in bothe, and that shalte thow knowe. I wyl scole thee myselve." Than he called for the marshall or some of his men, and ther was none of them ther. Than calyd he for one mr. Hungerford, one of his owne jentellemen; hyme he rowndyd yn the care a pretty whyele, and than openly the bushop sayed with a loude woysee, "I praye yow, mr. Hungerford, take thys trayterus herytike, and have hym to the Marshallsee, and remember wel whate I have sayed unto yow, for thys ys one of our new brochyd bretheryn that spekethe agaynste al good workes." "No, my lorde, (sayed I,) I never prechyd or spake agaynste anye of those good workys which be comawndyd of God yn the holy scryptures to be done; for yn those good workys every chrystyan man awghte to exsersys hymselve al the dayes of hys lyffe, and yet not to thynke hymselve to be justyffyed therby, but rather to cownte hymselve an unprovytable servant whan he bathe don the beste he can." "That ys true, (qothe the bushop;) ynded your fraternytye was, ys, and ever wyll be altogether unprophytabull yn al ages, and good for nothynge but

---

[a] *The words* **wherein he looked** *are omitted by Strype.*   [b] *ij omitted by Strype.*

for the fyere. Tel me, I praye the, whate good workes was ther done, other yn kynge Hary's days, or yn kyng Edward's days?" "Truely, my lorde, (sayd I,) ther was doone yn the dayes of these ij notable kynges, of moste worthye memorye, manye notable thynges moste worthye of perpetuall memory to the ende. Fyrste, the bushop of Rome was uterly abollyshyd owte of thys realme, with alle his usurpyd powre and auctor(it)ye over all crystyan prynsys; al idolatrye, superstysyon, and ipocrysye supressyd; all false and faynyd erelygyus[a] men and women dischargyd of ther longe lowtrynge yn cloysters, and thaute hence to serve God yn spirete and truthe, and no longer to worshup hym yn wayne, devoyrynge poore whydoose howsys under the pretence of longe prayers. Also, and that lyke your lordeshype, they did erecte many colegyes. Also the unyversytys of Cambryge and Oxforde fyrst by wyse men were vysytyd, than purgyd, wel furnyssyd with godly learnyd masters of every howse, and laste of all contynuallie relevyd and mayentaynyd from tyme to tyme by the good and well dysposyd people of thys sytye of London, that lernyd men myghte floryshe. Al these, my lord, were good workes. Further, they dyd erecte manye fayer ospytallys; one[b] for orfaynes and fatherlese chylderyn, wheryn they maye be towghte to knowe ther duety and obedyence bothe to God and man, havynge bothe a scolmaster and also an husher, to theche them ther grammer; these lykewaies also have meat, drynke, clothe, and logynge, lawnders, surgyns, and phisysyons, with al other nessesarys. Yn the other howsys,[c] my lorde, ther ys the blyend, the lame, the doume, the deaffe, and al kynd of syke, sore, and dessesyd peple; they have alwayes with them an honeste learnyd mynyster to comforte them, and to gyve them good cownsell that they myghte pasyently take yn good parte Godys vysytasyon. Thys they have: bysyed meate, drynke, lodgynge, surgyns, and physysyons. Are not al these good workes, my lord?" Than the bushop sayed unto me yn mokage, "Ser, you have made a greate

[a] Apparently a furtive jest, "irreligious" instead of "religious."
[b] Christ's Hospital. [c] St. Bartholomew's and St. Thomas's.

speke; for, wheras yow have set upe one begarlye howse, yow have pulde downe an C. prynsly howsys for yt; puttyng owte godly, lernyd, and devoyte men that sarvyd God daye and nyghte, and thurte [thrust] yn ther plase a sorte of scurvye and lowsye boyes. Wel, to be shorte with thee, whate sayeste thow to the blysyd sacramente of the alter? howe belevyste thow yn that?" "Not as yow beleve, my lord; for I never reed yn the scryptur of anye suche sacrament so callyd, and so unreverently to be hangyd up yn a rope, over a hepe of stones, and that same to [be] worshuppyd of the people as God. Woo be unto them that so dothe theache the people thus to beleve! for they be false prophetes,[a] beleve them who wyll; for trewlye I wyl not. Thus ham I tawghte to beleve." "By home?" saythe the bushope. "For sothe, even by Jesus Chryste, the hye bushop and pryest of our sowlys; who by the offerynge up of hys owne blysyd bodye on the crosse once for all, as saint Pawl sayth to Ebrwse, and ther shedynge hys moste presyus blude bathe clensyd us from al our synnes; and I trust only [b] by his deathe to have everlastynge lyffe." "What sayeste thow nowe, thow shameles heretike, unto the holy and blysyd mase?" "My lorde, suffer me to speake my consyence, I beseche yow; I nother beleve yt to be holly nor yet blyssyd, but rather to be abomynable before God and man, and the same to be acursyd;" and with that I knellyd doune and hylde up my handys, lokynge up unto hevyn, and sayed yn the presence of them all, "O Father of heaven and of earthe! I moost whomblye beseche thee to increase my faythe and to help my unbeleve, and shortly cast doune for ever that shameful idolle the mase, even [for] Jesus Chrystes sake I aske yt. Amen. God grawnte yt for hys marsy sake shortly to come to pase." "I crye you marsy, syr, (sayed the bushop,) howe holy you ar nowe! Dyd you never saye mase, I praye yow?" "Yese, my lorde, that I have, and I aske God marsy, and moost hartely forgyfenes for doynge so wycked a dede." "And wyll yow never saye yt agayne?" sayd the bushop. "No, my lord, God wylynge:

---

[a] "Priests" *in Strype*.   [b] only *omitted by Strype*.

never while I lyve, knoynge that I doo knowe; not to be drawne insunder with whyld horse. I trust that God wyll not so gyve me over and leve me to myselve." Than he cryed, "Awaye with hyme! yt ys the stoburnste knave that ever I talkyd with," etc.

Than mr. Hungerford callyd for iij or iiij of my lordys men to wayet apon hym to the Marshalsee; and by the waye as wee went he myghtyly persuadyd with me, that I showld gyve over myne herysys and wyckyd opynnyons as he termyd them; and he wolde be a mean for me unto my lord, and offeryd me to goo bake agayn. I thanked hym for hys good wyll, and dysyryd hyme that I myghte goo forward to the plase apoyentyd by my lorde. "Wel, (saythe he,) and ther be no remedye, come one. I ham sory for yow." Than cam we to the Marshallsee; and the porter, calyd Bryttyne, opynyd the doore, and let us yn, sayenge, "Whate have yow broughte here, mr. Hungerfurde, an herytyke?" He sayed "Ye, and a trayter to." "No, (sayed I,) I am none; I ham even as trwe a man bothe to God and to the crowne of Ingland as anye of yow bothe are, or my lorde your mastar other." "Well, (say'd the porter,) wee shall hamper yow wel inoughe. Come one with me." Then the jentelman rowndyd hyme yn the eare, and so went hys wayes. Than was I browghte unto [the] greate blocke. "Sete up your feete here, master herytyke, (sayed Bryttyne the porter,) and let me see howe thes cramp ryngynes wylle become yow." "I hame not to good (sayed I,) to were these for the truthe sake; seynge that Jesus Chryste dyed for my sake, they are welcome unto me, with all my harte: for by moche trybulasyon we muste enter ynto the kyngdome of God." Than he toke a greate hammer yn hys hand, and dyd set them one, and that surelye. Than he brughte me to my lodgynge, a place calyd Bonnares cool-house;[a] ther he put me yn and locked the dore apon me, sayeing that he was commandyd to keape me as a cloose prysonar, and that no man myghte speake with me. "Content, (sayd I,) and yete wyll I speake with one I truste every daye, and aske yow no beleve.[b]"

[a] Coal-house.   [b] *i. e.* by your leave.

"Whoo ys that? (sayed he,) I wolde I myghte knowe hym." "So wolde I trwely; than were yow a greate dell more nearar to the kyngdom of God than yow are nowe. Repent therfore your papestrye, mr. Brytyn, and beleve the Gospell; so shall yow be sucre to be savyd, or eles lost for ever." So he shuke hys hed at me, and whente hys wayes.

Withyn a ten dayes after, the bushopes amner came yn with hys mayster's awmese basketes, and thes woordys he sayed to the porter: "My lordys plesure is that none of thoos herytykes that ly here, sholde have anye parte of hys almes that he dothe send hether; for yef he maye knowe that they have anye of it, thys house shal never have yt agayne so longe as he lyffe." "Weel! (sayd Brytyn,) I wyll see to yt well inowght, mr. Broox[a]; and they have no meate tyl that theye have of that, some of them are lyke to starfe I warante you; and so tel my lorde, for anye favore they get at my hande." Than Broxe whent hys wayes; and, goynge owte, he behelde a peese of scrypture that was payentyd over the doore, yn the tyme of kyng Edwardes rayne, " Whate have we here? (saythe he,) a pecs of herysye! I command yow yn my lordys name that yt be clene put owte agaynst I come agayne; for if I fynd yt here my lord shall knowe yt, by the holy mase l"

Now, wylle I was prysonar yn the Marshallse, they came yn dayly thyke and threefold for relygyone, and than mr. Wyate was up yn Kente, and so comynge to London and lyenge yn Southewarke, he sent one of hys chaplaynes unto me and to the reste of my fellow prysonares, to knowe whether that we wolde be delyvered owte of pryson or no. Yf we wolde so doo, he wolde set us at libertye so manye as laye for relygyon; with the reste he wold not medylle. Than we all agreyd and sent hym thys answere, "Syr, wee gyve you moste hartye thankes for thys your jentell offer; but, for as mouche as we came yn for our consyences, and sent hether by the

[a] James Brooks, D.D. Oxon. 1546, master of Balliol college 1547, bishop of Gloucester 1554. He was one of the pope's delegates for the trial of Cranmer, Ridley, and Latimer. See other particulars of him in Wood's Athenæ Oxon. (edit. Bliss,) i. 314.

counsell, we thynke yt good here styll to remayne tyl yt please God to worke our delyverance as yt shall seme beste to hys glorye and owre lawfull dyscharge; whether yt [be] by lyffe or deathe we are contente, hys wyll be done apon us! and thus fayer you well." With this our answer he was very well content, as afterward reporte was made unto us.

That same Lente ther came unto me doctor Chadse,[a] doctor Penulton,[b] mr. Udalle,[c] parson Pyttyes,[d] and one Wackelyn a petye cannon of Powllys. Al these laboryd me very sore for to recant, and yf that I wolde grawnte so to doo, "my lorde chancelar wyll delyver yow, I dare saye, (sayed mr. Chadsey,) and yow shall have as good lyvynges as ever yow had and better." To whom I answeryd that "I wolde not by (buy) my libertye nor yet my lordys favore so dear, and to forsake my good God, as some of yow hafe done; the pryse wherof you are lyke one daye to feel yf that yow repent not yn tyme. God turne your harttys and make yow of a better myend! Fayer yow well. Yow have loste your marke, for I hame not he that yow loke for." And so we partyd.

[a] William Chadsey, D.D., prebendary of St. Paul's 1548, archdeacon of Middlesex 1550, canon of Windsor 1554, canon of Christchurch Oxford 1557, president of Corpus Christi college Oxford 1558, deprived of all his preferments 1559. In April 1554 dr. Chadsey took the lead in the disputation at Oxford with archbishop Cranmer. He preached the thanksgiving sermon Nov. 28, 1554, for queen Mary's supposed quickening, as fully described in Stowe's Chronicle; and others of his sermons are noticed by Machyn: see the index to that diary. Other particulars of him will be found in Wood's Athenæ Oxon. (edit. Bliss,) i. 322.

[b] Henry Pendleton, S.T.P., prebendary of St. Paul's 1554; rector of St. Martin's Outwich in the same year, and of St. Stephen's Walbrook 1556. Of his other preferments, and his religious principles, see Newcourt's Repertorium Eccles. Londinense, p. 204, and Wood's Athenæ Oxon. (edit. Bliss,) i. 325. He was the preacher at St. Paul's cross at whom a gun was fired on the 10th of June, 1554; and other occasions of his preaching will be found in the index to Machyn's Diary. His funeral, Sept. 21, 1557, at St. Stephen's Walbrook, "where he was parson," is described by Machyn, p. 152.

[c] Who this was does not appear: as it could scarcely be Nicholas Udall, once master of Eton school, who was ranged on the Protestant side.

[d] Probably the incumbent of a church in the borough of Southwark, as his name does not occur in Newcourt's Repertory of the diocese of London.

Doctor Martyn also dyd one tyme send for me lykewyse, to come speake with hyme at my lorde of Wynchester's howse, offerynge me good lyvynges, yf that I wolde submyte unto my lorde. I tolde hym that " yf I sholde goo abowghte to plese men, I knowe not howe sone my Maker wolde take me awaye, for a dubyle-hartyd man ys unconstante yn all hys wayes. I truste that your swete barmyse (balms) therfor shalle never break my hede; and, seynge that I have begone yn the spryte,[a] God forbyd that I sholde nowe end yn the fleshe!" And he herynge thys partyd from me yn a greate furye; and goynge out of hys chamber, he sware a great othe, sayinge that I was as craftye an herytyke knave as ever he talked with, and that I dyd nothynge but mocke my lorde. "Thow shalte gayne nothynge by it, I warrante ye. Kepar, have hyme awaye, and loke strayetly to hym, I counsell yow, tyl that yow knowe further of my lordys plesure."

So I returnyd to the Marshalse agayne withe my keapar; and within a whylle after, kynge Phyllyp beynge come yn to Ingland,[b] a sartayne dyscrypsyon was made of hys parson, queen Mary beynge joynyd yn the same, and somethynge sayed of her, as well as of the Spanyardes; and, because that I hade a copye of the same, yt was layed to my charge that I dyd make yt; wherupon sartayne jentelmen were apoyented to syte yn commysyon for the tryall theroff, and to examyne me and iij moo of my fellowse. The commysyonars wher these:[c] sir Jhon Baker,[d] sir Thomas Moyelle,[e] sir Rychard Sothwelle,[f] and mr. Brygys[g] the lefftenante, and sir Thomas Hold-

[a] Compare with the passage in Underhill's narrative, p. 159.

[b] He landed at Southampton, July 19, 1554.

[c] Strype, Eccles. Memorials, iii. 101, in giving these names, has printed "Sir Tho. Baker," instead of sir John, and has omitted Southwell and Brydges.

[d] A privy councillor, and chancellor of the exchequer.

[e] Sir Thomas Moyle was general receiver of the court of augmentations. Through his daughter and coheir Katharine, he was grandfather of sir Moyle Finch, the first baronet (1611), whose wife was created countess of Winchilsea, and from whom the subsequent earls of Winchilsea and Nottingham have descended.

[f] See before, pp. 8, 139.

[g] Thomas Brydges: see before, p. 144.

crofte,ᵃ beyng knyghte marshall. All thees sate yn comysyon withyn the Towere of London, yn a gallerye of the quenes syede; afore home we were commandyd to come, that ys I myselve one, Jamys Proctor,ᵇ Edmond Lawrance, and Thomas Stonynge, everye one of us beynge fyrste severally examynyd. We utterly denyinge that anye of us ever were the fyrste awctores theroff, "No, (sayd they,) that wyll be provyd the contrarye to some of your paynes.' Than sayed sir Rychard Sothewelle, "To the racke with them! to the racke with them! sarve them lyke erytyckes and traytors as they be; for one of these knavys ys able to undoo a hole syttye." Thys was spoken at afternone, and soudaynly he fell faste aslepe as he sate at the borde. Than sir Jhon Baker asked of me wer I had the coppy, and howe I came by yt. "For sothe, (sayed I,) ther was one Warter, cuerte (curate) of St. Bryedys yn Fletstrete, and he fyrste browghte yt yn amongste us, and so came I by the coppye of yt." "Whoo wryte yt?" sayd they. "That dyd I," sayed Tomas Stonynge. "And ys thys your hand?" "Ye, (sayed he,) and yt lyke your honors, I wyll never deny yt." "Onester man yow," sayd they. Than were we all commandyd to goo asyed. Than dyd they consulte togeather, and whan they hade done, we were calde yn agayne, and so commytyd unto the leftennant to be locked up, every man by hyme selve alone. Tomas Stonynge was stayed by hynde, and so had downe to the rake, and was layed on yt and so pulde that he began to crake under the armepytes and yn other partes of his bodye; and than was he takyn of and put yn a brake of iorne, hys necke, handys, and feet;ᶜ and so he stod al nyghte agaynste a walle, and the next day takyn owte agayne.

ᵃ Sir Thomas Holcroft, some time sewer to Henry VIII., made a knight of the Bath at the coronation of Edward VI. in 1547: imprisoned in the Tower in 1551 as an adherent of the duke of Somerset, and deprived of the office of receiver of the duchy of Lancaster in June, 1552. In his office of knight marshal, which he probably held for life by patent, he appears to have taken opportunities to act as a secret friend of the Protestants.

ᵇ There was one James Proctor who was procurator for the clergy of Sussex in the convocation of 1562: see Strype, Annals, i. 327, 338, 343.

ᶜ Both the rack and the brake of iron are shewn in operation in Foxe's cut, which re-

Thus dyd we contynywe prysonars yn the Tower a quarter of a yare or ther abowghte, and than, at the commandement of the counsel, we were sent to the Marshallse agayne, and ther I remaynyd untyl suche tyme as my lord chanseler sent a wryte to remove

presents the torturing of Cuthbert Symson in the Tower, in 1557. Of the iron brake we find it stated, early in Elizabeth's reign, "This engine is called *Skevyngton's Gives,* wherin the body standeth double, the head being drawen towards the feete. The forme and maner of these gyves, and of his (Cuthbert Symson's) rackyng, you may see in the booke of Martyrs, folio 1631." (Letters of the Martyrs, 1564, 4to. p. 686.) A few years later, the adherents of Rome had in their turn a personal acquaintance with these instruments of torture. Mathias Tanner, the martyrologist of the Jesuits, describes the Scavinger's Daughter (to which the name had been corrupted from that of Skeffington's Daughter) as inflicting torments the very reverse of that of the rack, but at the same time much more painful, producing in some victims a discharge of blood from the hands and feet, and in others from the nose and mouth. His words are: " Præcipua torturæ post equuleum *(the rack)* Anglis species est, *Filia Scavingeri* dicta, priori omnino postposita. Cùm enim ille membra, alligatis extractisque in diversa mannum pedumque articulis, ab invicem distrahat: hæc e contra illa violentè in unum veluti globum colligat et constipat. Trifariam hìc corpus complicatur, cruribus ad femora, femoribus ad ventrem appressis, atque ita arcubus ferreis duobus includitur, quorum extrema dum ad se invicem labore carnificum in circulum coguntur, corpus interim miseri inclusum informi compressione pene eliditur. Immane prorsus et dirius equuleo cruciamentum, cujus immanitate corpus totum ita arctatur, ut allis ex eo sanguis extremis manibus et pedibus exsudet, aliis ruptâ pectoris crate copiosus è naribus faucibusque sanguis effundatur, prout Cottamo etiam tum becticâ miserè laboranti evenit, amplius horâ integrâ anulo concluso." *(Societas Jesu usque ad Sanguinis et Vitæ profusionem Militans, &c. auctore Mathia Tanne*r, SS.T.D. *Pragæ*, 1675, folio, p. 18.) Thomas Cottam, the Jesuit here mentioned, suffered in the year 1582.

A committee of the House of Commons in 1604 reported that they found in the dungeon called *Little Ease* in the Tower, "an engine of torture devised by mr. Skevington sometime lieutenant of the Tower, called *Skevington's Daughters*, and that the place itself was very loathsome and unclean, and not used for a long time either for a prison or other cleanly purpose." Mr. David Jardine on this authority asserts, in his Reading on the Use of Torture in England, 1837, 8vo. p. 14, " In the same reign (Henry VIII.) we find sir William Skevington, a lieutenant of the Tower, immortalising himself by the invention of a new engine of torture, called Skevington's Irons," &c.; but sir William Skeffington was never lieutenant of the Tower. He was master of the ordnance, and in that capacity was probably required to supply these gyves. The length of this note will be excused the more readily from the circumstance that Skeffington's Daughter is still shewn among the historical curiosities of the Tower armoury.

me from thence to Cambryge castelle;[a] and over nyghte I had warnynge to prepare myselve agaynste the nexte daye yn the mornynge. Shorte warnynge I hade; but there was no remedye. In the mornynge I made me redy by tymes, and rekenyd with my keper;[b] went downe and toke my leve of al my felowe prysonars withe the reste of my frendys, movynge them and exortynge them, as the tyme dyd serve, " to be constante yn the truthe, to serve God and feare hyme, and to be obedyent unto the deathe, and not to resyst the hyere powers, havynge alwayes with yow the testymonye of a good consyence, belevynge that Jesus of Nazarethe was crusyfyed for your synnes, lettynge all other trache and trumperye goo. Yea and *thoo an angell sholde come from heven and preche anye other gospell unto yow than that which we have prechyd alredye*[c] yn the dayes of kynge Edward, beleve them not, but holde hyme acursyd, for *there ys a waye that some men thynke to be ryghte, but the end therof ledyth unto deathe.* (Prov. xiiij.) Chryst ys therfore the onely waye and meane unto God the Father: he is truthe and lyfe, he is alone our onlye medyator and advocate, sytynge at the ryghte hande of hys Father. Yt ys he, as S. Powle saythe,[d] that ys our onlye redempsion, salvasyon, justyffycasyon, and reconsylyation. Take yow heed therfore, my deare bretheryn, lest yow be abusyd and led awaye from the truthe by false prophetes; let them not make you to shute at a wronge marke, for they wyll onlye labore to make shypwrake of your faythe, and to brynge yow to pardysyon. Yow see whate a sort of greedie wolves are alredye enteryd yn amonge Christes flocke to devour them." " Staye there, syr, I pray yow, and make an end, (sayed the under marshall,) yow have talked long inowghe, I trowe, and that be good." To home (whom) I sayd, " Sir, I thanke yow moste hartely for your jentelnes, yn that yow have so pasyently sufferyd

---

[a] Mowntayne was removed to Cambridge because he was charged with high treason there committed when he accompanied the army of the duke of Northumberland.

[b] *i.e.* paid the fees, as Underhill did at Newgate (p. 153).

[c] Galatians, i. 8.

[d] 1 Corinthians, i. 30.

me freely thus to speake, and to take my leve of thys house. I truste I have not spoken anye thyng here yn your presens that bathe offended ether God or anye good man." "Well, (sayd he,) dyspache, I pray yow, for the wryte ys come, and they tarye for yow at the doore." With that I fell prostrate to the grownd, and sayed, "O hevenly Father, yf yt be thy blyssyd [will] and plesure, delyver me owte of thys trouble, and suffer me not to be temptyd above my strenght, I beseche the(e), but yn the mydyste of the temptasyon make suche a waye for my delyverance as shall be moste to thy glory, my comforde, and the edyfyenge of mye bretheryn. Never the lese, thy wyll be done, and not myne. Geve me pasyens, I beseche thee, O Father, for Christes sake!" To thys they all sayd Amen. So I kyssyd the earthe, and roose up, byddyng them all fayre well, and dyssyerynge them to praye for me, and not to forgete whate I had sayd unto them, as they wolde answer afor God.

Than wente I owte of the doores, fyendynge ther betwen the gates vj tale(tall)men yn blwe cottyes with swordys and buckelers and jauflynges yn ther handys, and one of them broughte unto me a geldynge, desyerynge me to lyghte on hym quyckely, "for the daye ys fare spente," sayde he. "Content I ham so to do." And, beynge on horsebake, one of good wyll broughte me a coup of wyne to comford me with; so I toke yt and dronke to all the peple that were present there, and thanked them al hartely for there jentelnes. The under-marshall than toke me faste by the hand, and roundyd me yn the eare, sayeng thus, "Syr, I ham commandyd by my lorde chanseler to charge yow in the kinge and quenes name, that yow doo keape your tongue as yow doo ryde throwe the syttye, and quietly to pase the same, as yow wyll answer to the contrye (contrary) before the counsel; and thus muche more I saye unto yow, I feare that I shall here of thys dayes worke for your sake. Never the lese, God strengthen yow yn that same truthe wherunto he hath callyd yow, for I parsave and also beleve that yow are yn the ryghte waye. Fayer yow well for I dare stand no longer with yow. Praye for me, and I wyll praye for yow." And thus we partyd at ix of the cloke yn the forenone.

Than iij of them ryd afor me, and the other iij behynde me, tyl I came to Ware, and there we alytyd at the syene of the Crowne[a]; and I was browghte yn to a fayer parlar, a greate fyer made afore me, and a tabulle coveryd. Than they asked me yf that I were not wery and a hungeryd. "Not gretly," sayd I. "Wel, (sayd they,) cal for whate yow wyll, and yow shall heve yt, yf yt be to be gotyn for gold, for so are we commawndyd; and be of good cheer, for Godys sake. I trust yow shall have none other cawse." So doune I sate at the borde, sayed grase, and made as I thoughte a good meale; and, so fare as I can remember, the reconynge came to a viij or ix^s., bysyed our horsemeate. So, grace beynge sayed, and the table taken up, the cheffyste of thes vj sarvynge men sayed unto me, "Sir, howe are yow myendyd nowe? anye other wyse than yow were whan yow came owte of London?" "No, trwelly, (sayed I,) I thanke God I ham even the same man nowe that I was than, and I truste yn God so to remayne unto the end, or els I wold be sory and also ashamyd; and I tell yow trwe, that *I hame not ashamyd of the gospell of Jesus Chryste, for yt ys the power of God unto salvasyon to as manye as doo beleve;*[b] and to tel you further, *yf thys gospell be hyde yt ys hyde from thoos that shall peryshe,*[c] for unto the good yt ys the savore of lyfe unto lyffe, and unto the wycked and ungodly yt ys the savore of deathe unto deathe.[d] Take yow all heed therefore, dearly belovyd; beware yn tyme, leste bothe yow and your teachers have your porsyon yn the fyerye lacke amonge the ipocrytes, wher there ys wepynge, wayllynge, and gnashynge of teethe[e]; weras the worme of consyence shall never dye,[f] but yow to dwell yn payne so longe as God raynythe yn glorye. O whate should yt prophyte a man to have thys whole worlde at wyll, and to leese hys owne sowle?[g] and whan yt ys lost wherwithall wyl you redeme yt agayne?

[a] Ware contained several large and ancient inns. It was not the Crown, but the Saracen's Head, which boasted of "the Great Bed of Ware," mentioned by sir Toby Belch in Shakspere's Twelfth Night, and represented in a plate of Clutterbuck's Hertfordshire.

[b] Romans, i. 16.   [c] 2 Corinthians, iv. 3.   [d] 2 Corinthians, ii. 18.
[e] Matthew, xxiv. 51.   [f] Mark, ix. 44.   [g] Matthew, xvi. 26.

I tel yow thys ys no maseynge [a] matter, neyther yet wyll any pardones, purgatorye, or pylgramagyes sarve your turne. No, and my lord chancelar, or the pope hymselve, shulde saye mass for one of yow, and synge iij^c tryntallys [b] for yow, yt wolde not goo for payement before God; for, as the prophet Davyd saythe yn the sphalme, *Ther ys no man that can make agrement to God for hys brother; he must let that alone, for yt coste moor than so:* [c] and *Yf one man syn agaynst another, dayes-men maye be judges; but yf a man synne agaynst the Lord, who wyl be hys dayes-man?* [d] *Yow ar dearly bought*, saythe sent Petter,[e] *not with coryptyble gold and silver, pearle or presyus stones, but by the moste presyus and ynnosent blude-shedinge of Jesus Chryste, the only begottyn son of God."* Than sayed they one to another, " Never let us talke any longer with hym, yt ys but lost labor. Yow see that he ys at a pownte; there ys no good to be done of hym, I perceive that he wylle dye yn hys opynyons." " Ye, (sayd I,) I truste yn God so; for yt ys wrytyn, *Happye and blessyd are al they that dye yn the Lorde,*[f] for they shall be sartayne and suer of a joyfull resurecsyon. Aryse therfor, I praye yow, and let us be gooynge."

So to horsbake we wente, a gret nomber of people beynge yn the yarde and yn the stretes, to see and behold me, the poore prysonar that came from London. Every man spake there fansy, and some broughte me wyne to comforde me with, for the which I gave them moste harty thankes, desyerynge them all to pray for me, and I wolde praye for them.

And thus with teres of all handys we partyd from Ware, and so came to Rayston [g] to our bed; wheras they made me good chere and spardo for no coste. Than they once ageyne dyd asawte me, desyerynge me to wryght my mynde to my lorde chansler, or to some other of the cownsell, to home I wolde, and they wolde del-

---

[a] Massing, *i. e.* pertaining to the Mass.
[b] The word iij^c is omitted by Strype
[c] Psalm cxlii. 4.   [d] 1 Samuel, ii. 25.   [e] 1 Peter, i. 18.   [f] Revelation, xiv. 13,
[g] Royston.

lyver yt wyth spede; " and yf that yow wyll so do, we wyl send one of our companye to cary the same, and wee wyll tarye here styll tyl that he bryng word agayne what the counsel's plesure ys." To home I answeryd, " I thanke yow for your good wyl. I yntend never to wryghte unto anye of the counsell whyll I lyve, for thys matter; and therfore I praye yow content yourselves, and ses (cease) your vayne swyte (suit) so oftyn atemptyd, for yow doo but stryve agaynste the streme, for I see that yow are not wyth Chryst, but agaynst Chryste. Yow savore of earthly thynges and not of hevenly. Yow goo aboughte to hynder my helthe and salvasyon layd up yn Chryst, and to plucke down whate God hathe byeldyd. Yow know not what yow doo. And therefore once agayne I praye yow hartely, lefve of, and take yn good part whate I have sayed alredy, and so judge al to the beeste (best)." " Wel, (sayed theye one to another,) yt were good that my lord chanseler dyd knowe all hys sayenges. One of us muste tel hym by mouthe as well as we can." They were not yet agreyd than whoo shold tel the tale. Than desyeryd they me to goo unto my lodgynge, wher there was a great fyer made redy agaynste I came, and al other thynges verye swett and cleane. So yn the name of God to bed I wente, and all they vj wachyd me that nyghte, all the doores [a] beynge faste locked apone me, and they kepynge the keyes themselves. They myghte goo owte, but no man colde come yn to them withowte there leve.

In the mornynge they calde me very carlye, and wylde me with speed to make me redye to horsbake; " for (sayd they) we muste ryed to the hye shyryff to dynnar." " Whoo ys that? (sayd I,) and where dothe he dwell?" " Viij myllys beyoned Huntyngton, (sayed they,) and hys name ys sir Ollyver Leader,[b] a man of muche

---

[a] *Misprinted by Strype* at the doors.

[b] Sir Oliver Leader was apparently of civic origin, as one of his name (and probably himself) occurs in the list of the Fishmongers' Company in 1537. (Herbert's City Companies, vol. ii. p. 6.) He was knighted by king Philip, Feb. 2, 1554. (MS. Harl. 6064.) He was twice sheriff of the county of Huntingdon, in 1541 and 1554, and one of its knights in parliament 1553. His funeral on the 6th March 1556-7 is noticed in

worshyp and one that keapyth a good howsse." " The poore shall fayer the better therby," sayed I.

So whan we came to Huntyngton they made me to drynke, and we came to the shyryffes howse[a] even as the tabull were coveryd. Than they herynge that the prysonar was come from London, ther was no small adoo. Worde was caryed to the churche, where syr Olyver was at mase,[b] and yt was no nede to yntrete hyme to come; for with speed bothe he and my lady hys whyffe[c] departyd owte of the churche, and the paryshe followyd them, lyk a sorte of shepe, stayryng and wonderynge at me. The shyryffe gently toke me by the hand and led me ynto a fayer parler, dyssyeryeng me to stand to the fyer and to warme me, for wee were all thorowe wet with rayne, snowe, and halle (hail). Than to dynnar we went, and greate cheare I had, with many welcomys; and oftyn tymes dronke to, bothe by the shyryffe hymselve and the reste hys freendys.

When dynar was done, yuto the parler I was callyd, and a great sorte of jentellmen beynge there set on the one syed, and jentelwomen on the other syed with my ladye the shyryffes wyffe, than mr. shyryffe sayed unto the knyghte marshalles men, " Where ys the wryte that yow have browghte as towchynge the resayte of thys prysonar?" " Here yt ys, syr," sayed one of them. So he reasavyd yt, and whan he had red yt, he toke me by the hand agayne and sayed that I was welcome. I thanked hyme for hys jentel frendshyp. Than callyd he for a payer of yndentores. So they were browghte yn and rede. That done, one of them was gyven to the knyghte marshalles man, and the other the shyryffe kepte. Than the knyghte marshalles man toke me by the hand, and sayed to the shyryffe, " Syr, I doo here, yn the presense of al these people, delyver thys prysonar unto you, and your mastarshyp from hence-

Machyn's Diary, p. 128, and more fully recorded in the College of Arms, I. 15, f. 272 b. Some notes from his will in the registry of the prerogative court of Canterbury will be found in Notes and Queries, Second Series, iv. 479, and some from his funeral, v. 96.

[a] At Beachampton in the parish of Great Stoughton.   [b] mass.
[c] Frances daughter of Francis Baldwin esquire of Beachampton.

forthe to stand chargyd with hyme, and my maystar sir Thomas Holdecrofftc, the kynght marshall, dyschargyth hymselve of the sayd prysonar callyd Thomas Mowntayne." And with that he dellyveryd hym bothe me and the yndentor. Than the shyryffe sayed unto hym, " I do here resave that same prysonar so callyd, and discharge your master of the same;" and so toke me by the hand, and delyveryd unto hym hys yndentor. All thys was done with greate sollemnytye.

Than was there a coupe of wyne calde for, and the shyryffe began unto me, and wylyd me to drynke to the marshales men, and so I dyd. Thane they toke their leve of the shyryffe, and so went their wayes, bedynge me fayerwell, sayenge unto me, " There ys remedy inowghte yet, mr. Mowntayne, yf that you wyll take heed yn tyme." " God be with yow all! (sayd I,) and I thanke yow. Have me commendyd I pray yow unto your master, and to the reste of all my frendys;" and so wee partyd. Than the shyryffe causyd iiij or v horse to be made redy. Yn the meane tyme he causyd one of hys men to make redye the warrant to the keapar of Cambrydge castylle. Never the lese, my lady hys wyffe laboryd very earnystly to her husband for me, that I myghte not goo to Cambridge castelle, beynge so vyle a pryson, but that I myghte remayne yn their owne howse as a prysonar. " Good^a madame, (sayed he,) I praye yow be contentyd; yf I shoulde so doo, I knowe not howe yt wolde be taken. Yow knowe not so mowche as I doo yn thys matter; but what fryndshyp I can shewe hyme he shall suerly have yt, for your sake, and for hys owne to, for I have known hyme longe, and ham very sory for hys truble." So I thanked hym for [his] jentelnes. By thys tyme all thynges were yn a redynes. Than he hymeselve and my lady browght me to the uter gate. He wyllyd me to be set one hys one (own) geldynge, gave me a cup of wyne, toke me by the hande, and bad me fayr wel; dyssyerynge me to be of good cheeare.

So to Cambryge I came; and at the townes ende there mete me one Kenrycke, who a lytell before hade been a prysonar yn the

---

[a] *This word* good *is omitted by Strype.*

marshallesee, as I myselve was; but our cawsys not lyke, for hys was playne fellonye, and so provyd, and myne was treson and herysye as they calde yt. " O mr. Mountayne, (sayde he, with a lowd voyce,) alase! what make yow here? I persave nowe that yt ys trwe that I have hard." "What ys that?" sayed I. " Trwely, (sayed he,) that yow be come hether to be burned." "This ys a sharpe sallutasyon, mr. Kenryke, (sayde I,) and yt ys more than I doo knowe of; and yf it be so, God strengthyne me yn hys trwthe, and hys wylle be done upon me, for I truste that I ham hys." Than ryd we yuto the towne to an yne called the Gryffyn, bycawse the kepar was not at home; where I alyghtyd, and went up to a chamber. My hed beynge than somewhate troublyd with Kenryckes sowdayne sallutasyon afore mensyonyd, I callyd mr. shyryffys men and sayed unto them, " Avoyed the peple, I praye yow, owte of the chamber, and loke (lock) the doores, for I have to saye unto yow." Whan thys was done I sate down, and sayed unto them, " Deare freyndys, a questyon I have here to move unto yow, wheryn I shall dyssyer yow to be playne with me, and note to dyesymble, even as yow wyll answer afore God at the laste daye; afore home bothe yow and I shall stand, and there to render up our accowntys. Tell me therefore, I praye yow, whate order bathe mr. shyryffe taken with yow as towchynge the daye and tyme whan I shall suffer, and whate kynde of deathe yt ys that I shall dye; and yn so doynge yow shall mowche plesure me, and cawse me to be yn a greate redynes, whansoever I shall be callyd." Than one of them, whose name was mr. Calton, sayed unto me, " Sir, yow need not to feare; for yf there were anye suche thyng, yow shulde have knolege of yt, as meet yt were; but our master wyllyd us, and also commaundyd us, that we shuld jentlye use yow, and also commaunde the kepar to do the same." Than called they for meate, and wyne; and when we had wel refreshyd us, we went up to the castell, where they callyd for the keaper, but he was not withyn. Than delyveryd they the warrante unto the kepares wyffe, sayenge thus, " Good wyffe Charlys, my master bathe sent your husband a prysonar here; and hys plesure ys, that you should yntreate hym well, and to see that he lake nothing, and also to have the lyberty of the yarde;" and so toke they their leve of me, and went their wayes. Than the kepares wyffe led me up throw the sessyones hall, and there she locked [me] up under iiij or v lokes, and at nyghte verye late the kepar came home, and up he came unto me, I beynge yn bed, and sayd unto me, " Syr, yow are wellcome byther. Are you come to me [to] be nursed?" To home I sayd, I hame sent hether unto thys jayell by the quenes cownsell, and whate yow are I knowe not as yet. I thynke that yow be the kepar." " So I ham yndeed, (sayd he,) and that shal yow knowe or yt be longe." " Well, I trust, mr. kepar, to fynd favor at your hand, and I beseche yow to be good unto me, for I have lyen longe in pryson." "What ys your name?" sayed he. " My name ys Thomas Mowntayne," sayed I. " Naye, (sayed he,) yow have another name " " Not that I doo knowe of," sayed I. Than he lokyd yn my purse whate monye I had, and toke yt with hyme; also my cote, my bottys, and spures, and so bad me good nyghte; and I sayed " Good nyghte, my nooste (mine host)." " I am content, (sayed he,) to be your oste to-nyghte; to morowe yow shall have a newe." Here I calyd to my rememberance the sallutasyons gyven unto me at the townes end, by the afore namyd Kyndrycke. So I ryse up, caste my cloke abowt me, and knellyd downe, cryenge owte unto Almyghtye God, dyssyerynge hyme of hys greate ynfynyte marsy and goodnes, for Jesus Chrystes sake, to comforde me with hys holye sprite yn that agonye, and not to forsake me yn my olde age, beynge so sore assaltyd of that sutyll dyvel the flatrynge worlde ᵃ and the weke fleshe, that I had well nye slypte, as Davyth that holy prophete sayed; and whan the dead tyme of the nyghte came, nature requyrynge reste, and I fellynge yn myselve yn shorte tyme yn so greate quyetnes, thorow the myghteye marsyes of my Lorde God, who had sent me so sweet a calme after so cruell and stormye a tempeste, sayd thus, " *Soli Deo honor et gloria*, &c., the Lordys name be praysyd from the rysynge up of the son untyl

ᵃ *Printed in Strype* the subtil Devil, flattering World, &c.

the goynge downe of the same! and unto thy marsyfull handes do I commend my souwlle, trustynge not to dye, but to lyffe for ever, yn the land of the lyvyng; for thy spryte, O Lorde, hathe so sartyffyed me, that whether I lyve or dye, stande or falle, that I ham thyne; and therefore thy blessyd wyll be done apon me!" Thys done, I layed me downe apone my bed, and slepte untyl v a clocke yn the mornynge; and than my kepar came and opynyd the dore, bade me good morowe, and askyd me and I were redye "Wherunto?" sayed I. "To suffer deathe," sayd the keapar. "Whate kyend of deathe?" sayed I, "and whan shall yt be." "Your tyme ys neare at hand, (sayed he,) and that ys to be hangyd and drawne [a] as a trayetor, and burnde as an herytyke; and thys muste be done even this foorenoone. Loke well to yourselve, therfore, and saye that yow be frendly usyd." "Your frendshyp, mr. Charlys, ys but hard and scares, yn gyvynge me thys *Scharborowe warnynge;* [b] but gyve me

[a] *In Strype* drawn and hanged.

[b] Dr. Thomas Fuller, in his "Worthies of England," after explaining the proverbial expression of "a Scarborough warning," that it implies no warning at all, but a sudden surprise, when a mischief is felt before it is suspected, adds, "This proverb is but of 104 years standing, taking its originall from Thomas Stafford, who in the reign of queen Mary, anno 1557, with a small company seized on Scarborough castle (utterly destitute of provisions for resistance) before the townsmen had the least notice of his approach." But before leaving the subject, Fuller adds, "But if any conceive this proverbe of more ancient original, fetching it from the custome of Scarborough castle in former times,— with which it was not *a word and a blow*, but a blow before and without a word, as using to shoot ships which passed by and strook not sail, and so warning and harming them both together,—I can retain my own, without opposing their opinion." Fuller's "own" notion of the origin of this saying has been adopted by Ray in his Proverbs, by Grose in his Provincial Glossary, and by others; but Nares in his Glossary has shown that the phrase was certainly older: for in a poem by John Heywood which was written and published at the time of the surprise of Scarborough castle by Thomas Stafford, (and which is reprinted in the Harleian Miscellany, vol. x. p. 258,) the phrase is not only employed, but the following attempt at its explanation occurs:

> This term *Scarborow warning* grew (some say)
> By hasty hanging for rank robbery theare,
> Who that was met but suspect in that way,
> Straight he was trust up, whatever he were.

According

leave, I praye yow frendly, to talke with you, and be not offendyd [with] whate I shall saye unto yow. Thys tale that yow have tolde me, ys yt trwe yn ded?" "Ye, (sayed he,) and that yow are lyke for to knowe. Dyspache therfor, I praye yow with speed." "Contentyd I hame with all my harte so to doo. Where ys the wryte of execusyon? let me see yt, I praye yow." "I have none, (sayed he;) thys ys moore and nydyes,[a] for I hame to be trustyd and yt were for a greater mater then thys." "Syr, I praye yow be contentyd; for yn thys thing I will not truste yow, bycawse yt ys a matter of lyve and deathe; it standythe me apon. Is the hye shyryffe sir Olyver Leadar come yn the towne to see the execusyon?" "No," sayed he. "Ys the undere shryffe hys debytye here to see yt?" "No," sayed he. "Is there anye probate[b] comawndemente come from the queenes counsell? or eles anye leteres sent of late for that porpose?" "No, (sayed he;) but yow doo all thys for no cawse eles then to prolonge the tyme." "No, (sayed I,) as I ham borne to dye, contentyd I ham so to doo whan God wyll; but to be made awaye after sowche slyghte, I wolde be verye lothe; and therfor, yfe that yow have nothynge to showe for your dyscharge, acordynge as I have requyryd of yow, I tel yow trwe that I wyll not dye. Take yow good heed therfor to your selve, and loke that I myscary not, for yfe that awghte come unto me but good, yow and yours are lyke to knowe the pryse of yt, be yow well assuryd therof. Whan dyd yow ever see anye man put to deathe, before he was condemnyd to dye?" "That ys trwe, (sayd he;) and are yow not condemnyd?" "No, (sayd I,) that I ham not, nether was yet ever araynyd

---

According to this supposition, the summary justice of Scarborough resembled the famous gibbet-law of Halifax: but whether this conjecture is more to be trusted than the preceding there is not sufficient evidence to determine. Foxe employs the phrase in one of his side-notes, and it was evidently of very current use throughout the sixteenth century. See a letter of Arthur lord Grey in 1580 appended to "A Commentary of the Services of William lord Grey of Wilton," (printed for the Camden Society, 1847,) p. 67; and a letter of archbishop Toby Matthew so late as 1603 quoted in Cardwell's Conferences, p. 166.

[a] *i.e.* than needs.
[b] private *in Strype.*

at anye sesyones." "Than, (sayed he,) I have been greatly myseynformyd. I crye yow marsy; for I hade thowghte that yow had been bothe araynyd, and also condemnyd to dye, beynge sent hether for to suffer yn thys plase, bycawse that yow were here agaynste the quene with the ducke of Northethomeberland." "Well, (sayed I,) thoos materes hathe bene alredye suffysyently answeryd before your betteres; but I praye yow, syr, and a man myghte aske yow, whoos man are yow, or to whome doo yow belonge?" "Marye! (sayd he,) I ham not ashamyd of my maister, I wolde thow showldest knowe yt, as thow arte. My lorde chaunsler of Ingland ys my master, and I ham hys man." " I thoughte sowche a mater; the olde proverbe ys trewe, I persave, for *soche a master, suche a sarvante ;* and ys thys my lord of Wynchesteres lyvere that yow were nowe?" "Ye," sayed he. " And ys thys the beeste servys that yow can doo my lorde your master? Fye, for shame, fye! wyl you folowe now the bludye stepes of that wyckyd man your master! whoo ys unworthye, before God I speake yt, bothe of the name and place that he hathe and ys calyd unto. What sholde moufe yow for to handyll me after thys sharpe sorte as yow have done, so spytefullye, beynge here not yet iij dayes under your kepyng? Wyl yow become a tormentor of Godys people and prophetes? wyl yow now seas from kyllynge of bolokes, calvys, and shepe, which ys your ockapasyon (being a bucher), and to gyve over your selfe moste crwellye to sarve your mastares tourne in sheddynge of ynnosente blode? O man, with what an avaye (heavy) harte maye yow laye your selve down to slepe at nyghte, yf that God of hys great marsy doo suffer yow to lyve so long yn thys your so wycked atempte and enterpryse! I speake not thys of anye hatryd that I bare unto yow, as God knowethe my harte, but I speake yt of good wyll, to thys end that yow myghte be callyd yn to a beter rememberance and knowlege of your duetye bothe towardys God and your chrysteyan brother. Let yt therfore repente yow, deare brother kepar, and knowe howe dangerus a thyng yt ys for a man to falle ynto the handys of the lyvynge God; and howe yt ys sayed that blud reqyryth blude. And yow wyl not be(le)ve me, set that teryble example of cursyd Cayen before your eyes, whoo slewe hys owne deare brother Abell, moste unnaturallye lyk a beastely man, and afterwarde wanderyd up and downe lyke a wacabound on the face of the earthe, seakynge reste, peece, and quyetnes, and cowlde never atayne unto yt, so that at the laste with mooste desperate wordys he burste forthe and sayde, 'O wreche that I ham, I sayed unto the Lorde, whan he callyd me to acownte for my brother's deathe, I answeryd that I was not hys keapar, but shortlye after I parsavyd that the shedynge hys blud cryed unto God for vengeancs to falle apon me for so doinge, and now I parsave that my synes be greater then the mersye of God ys able to forgyve.' Yf thys wyl not move your harde and stonye harte to repentaunce, than thynke of that trayetor Judas, which for lucare sake betrayed hys owne master, as he confessyd hym selve whan the worme of consyenes troublyd hyme, sayenge to the hye prestes, 'I have betrayed the ynnosent blude; take, there ys your mouye, for I wyll non of yt,' and that was too late; so to shortyne hys owne dayes, he moste desperately wente and bonge hym selve, so that he burste asunder yn the mydyste, hys bwellys hangynge abowte hys helys (heels [a]). O moste terryble examples, lefte wrytyn yn the holy scryptures, that wee therby myghte take hede and beware never to do the lyke, lest we sped yn reward as they dyd. From the which God defend us, for Jesus Chrystes sake!" "Amen! (sayed the kepar with wepynge teares,) and, syr, I beseche yow onenes (once) agayne, even for Godys sake, to forgyve me, and I aske God hartelly mersy for the great myschyffe that I porposyd yn my harte agaynste yow. I parsave that yow, and soche other, that yow be other maner of men than we and our beteres take yow to be; I parsave that *the blynd dothe eate manye a flye.* God, and yt be hys blyssyd wylle, make me one of your sorte! and loke, what that I can doo for yow, yow shalbe assueryd of yt. Come downe with me, I praye yow, ynto the yard." So I wente with hym, and when we [b]

---

[a] *Misread* belly *by Strype.*   [b] *Misprinted* he *by Strype.*

came downe, al the yarde was full of people. " Whate meanythe thys people?" sayd I to the keapar. " Al thes are come (sayde he,) to see yow suffer deathe; there ys some here that ys come as farre as Lyengkecon (Lincoln [a]), but I truste ther commynge shal be yn vayne. Be yow of good cheare." " Than goo your waye, (sayd I,) and gentlye dysyere them for to departe, and tell them yt ys no reason that anye man sholde suffer deathe before that he be condemnyd, and so yow shall eslye awoyed them, and I wyll goo up agayn tyl yow have don."

Whan theye were all gone, the kepar callyd me downe, to dyne with hym at hys owne table, and, dynnar beynge endyd, we fele yn talke agayne, and so, from tyme to tyme, had moche conferences together, and [I] began to growe yn greate credite with hym, insomuche that whansoever he ryd forthe aboughte anye busynes, he comytyd all the charge of hys hole house unto me, prysonares and all, and laboryd unto the hye shyryfe for me that I myght be delyveryd.

Notwithstandinge, I remaynyd ther prysonar halve a yeare, yn moche myserye, havynge some tyme meate and some tyme none, yea and manye tymes glad whan that I myghte gete a penye loffe and my glasse full of fayere water up to my lodgynge, beynge faste lockte up every nyghte, and at mydnyghte alwaye whan they searched the prysonars' iornys (irons [b]) than one shold come and knock at my dore and aske me yf I were withyn. To home I answeryd alwaye thus, " Here I ham, mr. kepar." " Good nyghte, than," sayed he; and so wold goo their wayes.

Now on a sartayne daye, beynge merye, he browghte home with hym to see me dyveres honeste men of the towne; amonge home there was one that I never sawe before, nor he me, callyd mr. Segare [c] a

---

[a] *Misread by Strype* Hengston.   [b] *Misread* rooms *by Strype*.

[c] This mr. Seager is mentioned by Foxe in his (second) account of the martyrdom of John Hullier (hereafter mentioned p. 206) as having supplied the sufferer with gunpowder for the usual purpose of shortening his torments when in the flames. Mr. C. H. Cooper, the historian of Cambridge, supposes him to have been the same person with Sygar Nicholson, who was one of the treasurers of the town of Cambridge for the year commencing at Michaelmas 1555, and one of the bailiffs for the year commencing Michaelmas 1557. He

berebruar, dwelynge at Madelyn bryge, whose harte God oppynyd above the reste to showe marsy unto me, for he knewe that the keapar wold doo muche at hys requeste, so that or ever he wente awaye he promysyd hyme payemante for my dyette, dyssyerynge hym to showe me favore for hys sake, "and I wyll be bound for hyme, that he shal be trwe prysonar." Al thys plesyd Charlys the kepar well, and yt was no greffe at all to me, to here thys bargayne made betwen them, "for otherwyse, (sayd I,) yt was not unlyke but that I sholde have here a peryshed for lacke of comforde. And her ys not to be forgotyn of my parte the myghtye and fatherlye provydence of God, who never fayellethe any man that trwelye putes hys truste yn hyme. Who can kylle hym, mr. Charlys, whome God wyll kepe alyve? maye I saye nowe, and who can dellyver hym whom God wyl destrowe? His greate powere delyveryd me ones owte of the lyones deen as he dyd hys holy prophet Danyell; so I truste that he wyll delyver me here owt of all my troubles, yf he so see yt good. Yf not, hys wyl be done!" And thus we partyd for that tyme, my keparc beynge glad of thys hys good assurance,[a] I takynge pasyently myne yndwerance, and my suertye hopynge for my dellyverance.

After thys, withyn short tyme, the hye shyryffe sent for me home to hys howse beyond Huntyngton, to see whether I woold relente or no; tellynge me that he hade wrytyn up to the counsell for me, and that yt was their plesure that I sholde be delyveryd yf that I wolde be a confyrmable man to the quenes prosedynges, and forsake herysy, or eles to remayne yn pryson untyll the nexte sessyons of gale delyvery. "For your good wyl, I doo thanke your mastership moste hartelye, and well contentyd I hame so to remayn as a prysonar, and rather than to gyve over my faythe

---

was probably a son of Sygar Nicholson, of Gonville hall, and one of the stationers of the university, noticed in Athenæ Cantabrigienses, p. 51, as having suffered a long and barbarous imprisonment in consequence of the works of Luther and other prohibited books having been found in his house.

[a] these good assurances *in Strype.*

for thys vayne lyfe which ys but shorte." "Wel! (sayde he,) I parsave than that yow are no chanlyng; yow shall therfore retorne to the place from whence yow came, and there abyed your tryall."

So wee toke our leve of hyme, and came our wayes bake agayne to Huntyngeton, and there we laye al that nyghte, I havynge apon one of myne armys a greate braslete of yeron iiij fingers brode, faste loked one, and a fyne chayne of iij yardys longe joynyd therunto; and beynge bed to supar of one Thomas Whype, marchante of London, with otheres, my keper was dyssyeryd to ease me for the tyme, and they wold be bound for me, and he to be well recompensyd for so doynge. Thys dyssyer of my frendyes was schares (scarce) well lyked of my keapar, bycawse they were Londoneres, and grawnte yt he wold not yn no wyse. So, when suppar was done, to our chamber wee wente, and anon comyse yn a smythe with a hammer and a greate stapyle. "Make yow redye, (sayd he,) I pray yow, and goo to bed." So I layed me downe apon my bed. Than he calde the smythe unto hym, and sayed, "Make faste the staple and the cheyne together, and dryffe them faste ynto some parte of the bedstead; for I have harde say, (saythe he,) *faste byend, faste fyend.*" Than he loked (looked) behyend all the payentyd clothes to see yf there were anye mo doores ynto the chamber than one. That done, he locked the dore and caste the keye owte of the wyndow, to the goodman of the house, dyssyeryng him to kepe yt save wylle the mornynge. Smale reste I toke that nyghte, I was so sore wronge aboughte my wreste that the blud was redy to spyn owte at my fyngeres endyes. So, early yn the mornynge we rys and toke our horse, and came to Cambrydge castelle to dynner, and then my braslete was taken of myne arme.

Yn Awguste followinge was the sessyones; unto the which there came my lorde chyffe justyes of Ingland, one that before was recordare of London and callyd mr. Broke[a]; with hym ther sate syr

---

[a] Sir Robert Brooke, appointed chief justice of the common pleas Oct. 28, 1554.

Thomas (James) Dyer[a], syr Clement Hyham[b], syr Olyver Leadare hy shyryffe, mr. Gryffyn the quenes sollysyter[c], mr. Burgone[d], with a number of jentellmen mo. Nowe, when they were come to the sessyones hall and there set, the kepar was commandyd to brynge yn hys prysonares. I, beynge fyrste callyd for by name, then on wente my braslet agayne, and there a preste callyd John Wllyard,[e] vycar o' Babram, he was faste loked unto me. We tayne (twain) went formoste, and stod at the bare. Than sayed my lord cheffe justyes unto me, "Syr, whate make yow here? are you not a Londynar?" "Yes, and yt lyke your lordshyp." "Howe longe have yow be here prysonar?" "Halve a yeare, my lorde." "Who sent yow hether?" "Forsothe, my lorde, that dyd the counsel." Than sayd the hye shyryffe, "My lorde, thys ys the man that I tolde your lordshyp of; I beseeche yow be good lord unto hyme, for he hathe bene as quyete a prysonar as ever came within thys gayell, and bathe usyd hymselve as honestly toward hys keapar." "Yow speake wel for hym," sayd my lorde; "stand asyed a whyell tyl yow be called." Yn the meane tyme mr. Gryffyn had a caste at me, sayenge thus, "Thou arte bothe a traytor and a herytyke."

[a] This should be sir James Dyer, a justice of the common pleas 1556, of the queen's bench 1557.

[b] Sir Clement Heigham, chief baron of the exchequer 1556-7. For his biography consult Gage's History of the Hundred of Thingoe, and Manning's Lives of the Speakers of the House of Commons.

[c] See before, p. 46.

[d] Probably Christopher Burgoyne, who was escheator of the shires of Cambridge and Huntingdon in 4 and 5 Edw. VI. He was either of Impington or Longstanton, at both which places there were families of Burgoyne.

[e] *Misprinted* Thomas Willyard *by Strype.* His real name was John Hullier. He was elected from Eton a scholar of King's college in 1538, and afterwards became conduct of Eton, vicar of Babraham near Cambridge, and preacher at King's Lynn. He was not so fortunate as Thomas Mowntayne in escaping from the persecutors, for he suffered at the stake on Jesus Green at Cambridge, on or about the 2d April 1556. Of this martyrdom Foxe inserts a full narrative in his Addenda, having previously given a shorter account, with some letters and a prayer of Hullier's composition (see edition by Townsend and Cattley, viii. 131-138, 378-380).

" No, and yt lyke your worshup, I ham nother of bothe." " Ys not thy name Mowntayne?" " Yes, forsothe, I wyll never deny yt." " And art not thow he that my lorde chansler sent hether with a wryte?" " I am the same man." " Wel! (sayed he,) and thow be not hangyd I have marvell. Thow wylte scape narrowly, I beleve." " Syr, I parsave that yow are my hevy freend. I besyche yow be good master unto me. I have lyen thys iij yeare [a] yn pryson yn yerons. Never was there anye man that layed anye thynge to my charge." Than he calde for the wryte. To home the hye shyryffe sayd that he had forgotyn to brynge yt with hyme. " O wel! (sayed [he [b]],) syr Olyver, yow are [a] good man I warant yow; thys man was not sent hether for byeldynge of churchys, I dare saye, nor yet for sayenge of our lady sawter. Yn dede, sir, these be thynges that I can not wel stylof (stifle [c])."

Than my lord cheffe justyce callyd me to the bare agayne, and cawsyd proclamasyon to be made, that whosoever colde laye awghte to my charge to come yn, and he shulde he hard, or elys (else) the prysonar to stand at hys dellyverance. Thys was done thryse, and no man came yn to gyve evydence agaynste me. Than sayed my lord cheef justyes unto the hole benche, " I see no cawse whye but that thys man maye be dellyveryd upon suertyes to be bound to apeare at the nexte sessyones here holdyn of gayell dellyverye; for yow see that there ys no man comythe yn to laye anye thynge to hys charge. Wee cannot but by the lawe dellyver hym, proclamacyon beynge ones made, and no man comynge yn agaynste hym. Whate saye yow, mr. Mowntayne, can yow put yn suertyes here, before the quenes justyssys, to apere before us here at the nexte sesyones? And yf that yow can so doo, paye your chargys of the howsse, and God

[a] Strype has here inserted between brackets the words " quarters of a " yeare: but Mowntayne included in his reckoning the time he had remained in prison in London, and he again in the closing paragraph of his narrative states that he lay three years in prison.

[b] This omission of the MS. not having been perceived by Strype, he has printed this passage very-confusedly.

[c] *Read* like of *by Strype.*

be with yow! Yfe not, than muste yow nedyes remayne here styll, untyll the next sesyones. Whate saye yow? have you anye suertyes redye?" "No, and that lyke your lordshype I have none redy; but yf yt please yow to be so good lorde unto me as to gyve me leve, I truste yn God to fyend suertyes." "Well! (sayd my lorde,) goo your ways; make as good speed as yow can, for wee muste awaye." Than he commaundyd the kepar to stryke of myne yerones.

That done, I was turned owte of the gate to seake my venter, without anye kepar at all, go where I wolde; and whan I came abrode I was so sore amasyd that I knew not where to be come. At laste, I toke the waye to the towne, and there I mete a man unknowen to me, whoo was not a lytle joyfull whan he see me at lybartye, sayeyng unto me, "Are yow clene dyschargyd from your bondys?" "No, (sayd I,) I lake ij shuertys." "Trwely, (sayd he,) I wyll be one, God wyllynge; and I wyll see yf that I can gete another to be bownd with me." So wee mete with another honest man callyd mr. Blunte; and havynge these tayne (twain) I gave thankes to God for them, and with speed returnyde bake agayne to the castell; and as I wente, there mete me ij Essex men which came to seake me, offrynge themselves to enter yuto bondys for me. I gave them moste hartye thankes for their jentil offer, and tolde them that God had raysyd up a couple for me alredy. "We are glad of yt, (sayed they;) yet we wyll goo with yow, lest yow doo lake;" and as I entryd ynto the castell yarde, the judgys were a rysynge, and they, seynge me comynge, sat downe agayne. Than sayed my lord chyffe justys, "Have you browghte yn your swertyes?" "Ye, and lyke your lordship here they be." "Let me see them," sayd he. Then they all iiij stood forthe, and shewyd themselves unto my lord: hoo sayed unto them, "Are yow contentyd to enter yuto bondys for thys man?" "Ye, my lord, (sayed they,) yf yt please yow to take us." "Well! (sayed he,) ij of yow shall sarve." There were standynge by ij bretheryn, and they, herynge my lord say that ij wolde sarve, went with sped to hym that wryt the band,

and cawsyd hym [to put ᵃ] in ther names [in the] fyne iijs. iiij d.ᵇ for [each of them], sayenge thus the one to the other, " Let us not onelye balle hym owte of bowndys; but also releve hyme with soche parte as God hathe lente us;" and so they dyd, I prayse God for yt. And whan the people sawe and understode that I was clearlye dyscharchyd owte of boundys, there was a greate showte made amongo them, suche joye and gladnes was yn their hartys, as myghte ryghte well apeare, for my dellyverance.

Than came mr. Segar, of whome I have spoken a lytell afore, and he payed all maner of charges that cowlde be dyssyerd of the keapar for the tyme of my beynge there; and, that done, he hade me home to hys owne howse, where as I had good yntertaynemente; and, after that I had remayned there a fortenight, I toke my leafe, and so came to London.

And withyn shorte tyme after, I, standynge yn Cheapesyed, sawe these iiij ryed throwe Chepe,ᶜ (that ys to saye,) kynge Phyllype, queno Marye, cardynall Poole, and Steven Gardynar chawnseller of Ingeland. Thys bushope ryde on the one syed before kynge Phyllyp, and the greate seall afore hyme; and on the other syede there ryde the quene, and the cardnall afore her, with a crose caryed afore hyme, he beynge all yn skarlette and blyssynge the people as he ryde throwe the syttye; for the wyche he was greatly laugyd to skorne, and Garduar beynge sore offendyd on the other syed, becawse the people dyd not pute off their capys, and make cursye to the croose that was caryed afore the cardnall, sayenge to hys sarvantes, " Marke that howse," " Take thys knave, and have hyme to the cownter," " Suche a sorte of herytykes ho ever sawe, that wyll nother reverence the croose of Chryste, nor yet ones saye so

---

ᵃ The paper is here torn: the sense is restored by the help of Strype.

ᵇ *Misprinted by Strype* iii*l*. iiii*d*.

ᶜ This was on the 26th of August 1555. King Philip was about to depart for the continent, and passed in state through London, taking barge at the Tower wharf for Greenwich. The event is noticed in Machyn's Diary at p. 93, and in the Chronicle of the Grey Friars of London, at p. 96.

muche as, God save the kynge and quene! I wyll teache them to doo bothe and I lyve." Thys dyd I here hym saye, I standynge at Sopar layne ende. And whan all thys syghte was paste, I wente my ways; for as yet I durste not goo home to my owne howse; and at nyghte, whan the bushope came home, one of hys spyallyes tolde hyme, that he sawe me stand yn Chepsyede whan the quene ryd throwe the sytye. Here he fell yuto suche a greate rage, as was tolde me by one of hys owne men, as was unsemyng for a bushop, and with great spede sent for the knyghte marshall; and whan he came he sayed unto hym, "Mr. Holcroffet, howe have yow handlyd yourselfe yn your offyse? dyd not I send unto yow one Mowntayne that was both a traytor and a herytyke, to thys ende that he shulde have sufferyd deathe? and thys daye the vylayne knave was not ashamyd to stand opynly yn the strete, lokynge the prence yn the ffasce. Myne owne men see hym. I wolde consell yow to loke hym upe, and that there be dyllygent searche made for hym thys nyghte, yn the sytye, as yow wyll answer afore the counsell." "All thys shal be done and yt lyke your honnor, and I truste there shal be no fawte fownd yn me." "Away than, (sayed the bushop,) abowte your bessyness." Than came one that was secrytorye unto the knyghte marshall, who wylled me with spede to departe owte of the sytye, "for thys nyghte (sayth he,) shal the sytye be searchyd for yow, and yf yow be taken, suerly ye dye for yt. Thus fayer yow well! God delyver yow out of their handys, and yt be hys wyll!"

Than wente I over yuto Sowthewarke, and there laye all nyghte. Yn the mornyng I roose up early, toke a bote and wente to Lymehouse, and so from thence to Colchester, and there toke shypynge, thynkynge to have gone ynto Seland, and so up ynto the hye countrye; but we were so whether-beatyn that of force we were glad to returne bake agayn; and thys vyage was tryshe (trice) attemptyd and always was pute bake; and at the laste tyme we were caste a land at sent Towhys,[a] wheras I durste not longe tary, bycawse of my lord

[a] Saint Osythe's, on the Essex coast, near Harwich.

Darsy,ᵃ whoo laye there, havynge a strayte comysyon sent unto hym from quene Marye, to make dyllygent searche for one beynge callyd *Trowge over the worlde*, and for all souche lyke begars as he was. So that I was fayne to flye to a lytle paryshe callyd Hemsted,ᵇ thynkynge ther for to have had some reste, but the schearch was so strayte, that at mydnyghte, I havynge almost to (too) shorte warnynge, was fayne with gret speed to flye unto Dedam heathe, and to take my cote yn my necke, havynge an noneste man with me, whoo had a foreste byll on hys bake, and with the same he cute downe a greate sorte of brakes, and that was my beed for a tyme, and whansoever I myghte geate ynto an haye-loffet, I thowghte myselve hapy and well to be logyd. At the laste I was howsyd, I thanke God, with an noneste man, and the same havynge a wycked sarvante, not lovynge the gospelle, went and complaynyd of hys master to the baylye and cownstablys; sayeyng unto them, that there was an herytyke yn hys mastares parler. "Howe knowe yow that? (sayd theye,) take hed whate thow sayeste; thy master ys an noneste man, and thow seaste howe trublesome tyme yt ys, and yf we apon thy report sholde goo searche hys howse, and not fyend yt so, whate arte thow worthye to have for sclawnderynge thy master?" "Inofe,ᶜ (saythe he,) I am suere yt ys so; for the howse ys never without one or other, and moste chyfly whan ther ys a fyer in the parler; and therfore I knowe by the smooke that there ys one yndeed." So the ofysars wyllyd hym to goo abowghte hys busynes, and to saye nothynge, "for (sayed they) we wold prove yt at nyghte." Yn the meane tyme they did hys master to understand whate hys man had sayed unto them, and frendly bad hym to take head, for they wolde searche hys howse that nyghte; and so they dyd yndeed, but the byrdes were flone. The nexte daye, the offysares toke hys man, and set hyme yn the [stocks, to teach him to

---

ᵃ Thomas first lord Darcy of Chiche, K.G. His seat was at Wivenhoe, between Colchester and St. Osythe's, at which latter place he was buried in 1560.

ᵇ Elmsted, four miles from Colchester.   ᶜ Enough. *Read by Strype* Tush!

speak[a]] good of hys master, and not to acwyse [him, and bring the] smoke [for a] wytnes agaynst hym.

Nowe, wyl I was seakynge a corner to hyd my hed yn, justyes Browne,[b] that dwellyth bysyed Borntewood, comys me downe to Colchester, and there played to dyvell,[c] by the counsell of one mr. Tyryll, and mr. Cossyne[d] inn holder of the same towne, and Gylbart the lawer, whoo cawsyd dyvers honeste men to be sent for, before the sayed justys, and sworne upon a boke to bryng yn the namys of all those that were suspectyd of heresy, as he term[ed]yt, and also gave unto the offysars a great charge, that from tyme to tyme dylygent search shoulde be made yn every howse for all strangers, and to take them and brynge them before a justyes; "for thys towne (sayed he) ys a harboror of all herytykes, and ever was." So whan he had bownd them all yn recounysanse, he wylyd them to departe, every man home to hys howse.

Than, apon ther returne, with speed was I convayed awaye to London warde forthewith, and whan I came there, I wente over ynto Sothewarke agayne, and there laye ij dayes and too nyghtys; and the thyrd nyghte, whan yt was somewhate darke, I entryd yuto shyp of Andwarpe, and so went downe to Graveseend. Ther they caste ankeer, and went al a lande, and lefte me aborde with a man and a boye. I, ferynge the sarchars,[e] that they wold have hade me to shoore, and there beynge so well knowyn as I was, I knewe yt

---

[a] Torn, and restored from Strype.

[b] Sir Anthony Browne, who purchased the manor of South Weald, in which parish the town of Brentwood is situate, was called to the degree of serjeant at law 1555, and appointed king and queen's serjeant on the 16th October in the same year. He was made chief justice of the common pleas in October 1558, but degraded by queen Elizabeth in 1559-60 (on account of his religion) to be a puisne judge of the same court. However, she knighted him in the parliament house in 1566. He died May 16, 1567, and has a monument in South Weald church. See Morant's History of Essex, vol. i. p. 118; and Foss's Lives of the Judges.

[c] *So the MS. Strype reads* played the devil.

[d] *Misprinted* Colson *in Strype*.

[e] searchers, as the officers of customs were then called.

was the next waye to brynge me before a justys to be examyned, and so to be returnyd bake agayne to London, and than suer I ham that I had dyed for yt, I loked yn my purse and there was iij pystolets. I toke one of them, and gave yt unto the man that was abord with me, and dysyeryd hym to goo ashore to the master of the shype, and he to be a meane unto the searchares for me whan they came a shypbord to searche; and trwely yt pleasyd God so to worke yn their hartys that I fownd greate favor at their handys, for when one of them had examynyd me, and that very straytly, he asked of me whate my name was. "Thomas Mowntayne ys my name, (sayed I,) I wyll never denye yt, nor never dyd, I prays God for yt." "Naye, (sayd he,) that ys not your name, for I knewe hym wel inoughe; his father and I were sarvantes to kyng Harye the viij. and also to kynge Edwarde, and I hame swere that Rychard Mowntaynes son was bornte, sence thys quene Marye came yn." "Syr, credyt me, I praye yow, for I ham the verye same man that nowe talkethe with yow. Yn dede God hatho myghtyllye delte with me, and most marsyfullye hathe dellyveryd me from the cruell handes of bludye men; and nowe beholde my lyffe ys yn your handys. I maye not ressyste yow, nor wyl not; but jentely submytynge myselve unto yow, dysyerynge your lawfull favore that I maye pase thys porte; and God I truste, that ys the hye searcher above, and knowethe the secrettes of all men's [hearts], shall one daye reward yow openlye, accordynge as he hathe promysyd.

Than begane he to water hys plantes, sayenge unto me, "Syr, I thowghte once never to have seene yow agayne; yow are grown owte of my knolledge; and, seynge that yt ys the wyll of God that yow shold not dye by ther crwelty, I truste that your blud shal never be requyryd at my handys. I wyl not molleste yow; but thys I warne yow of, yn anye wyse, that yow keep yourselve as cloose as yow can, for here ys one of the promotars,[a] that goythe yn the same shyp that yow goo yn." "Whoo ys that?" sayed I.

[a] See before, p. 161.

"Yt ys one mr. Bearde, (sayd he,) dwellynge yn Flet stret, a marchante tayeler." "I knowe hyme wel, (sayd I,) and he me." "Wel! (sayd he,) God be with yow! for yonder he commythe, and all the passyngeres with hym."

So we partyd, and I wente ynto the mastares cabbone, and there I laye tyl that wee were enteryd the mayne sease. Than came I forthe to refreche myselve, and Bearde seyenge me, began to blushe, saynge unto me, "Ser, whate make yow here?" "Trwely, (sayd I,) I hame of the same myend that yow are off." "Yow knowe not my myend," sayd he. "Whatesoever youres ys, I mean to goo to Andwarpe, God wyllynge, (sayd I,) and so doo yow I trowe." "Whate wyll yow doo there? (sayed he,) yow are no marchante man as I hame, and the reste that be here." "Mr. Bearde, whate the rest ys that be here, I knowe not; but as for your marchawntryes and myne, yn some poyntes I thynke they be mouche alyke; but whan that yow and I shall meet yn the Ingleshe burse together, yow shall see whate cheare that I can make yow. Yn the meane tyme, let us as frendys be mery together, I pray yow." "Naye, (sayd he,) I wolde I had mete yow at Gravysend, that I myghte have made yow some good chere there; but yt was not my fortone so to doo, and I ham verye sory for yt, beleve me and yow wyll." "Syr, I thanke God, yt ys better as yt ys. I knowe your cheare wel inowghte, and Jhon Avayellyes to.[a]" With that he wente downe under the hachys, and told all the pasyngars what an ranke herytyke I was, "for yt ys marvel (sayd he) that the shype dothe not synke, havynge so wyked a man yn yt as he ys; and therefore, good jentelmen, I praye yow hartely take heed and beware of hym. I hade rather than my welffete cote that he and I were at Grafsend agayn." Than came the marchawntes up to me, and callyd for meate and wyne, havynge good store there of their owne provysyon, and they made me great chere, bydynge me yn anye wyse to take head of Beard. These were marchantes of Danske, and hade to doo

---

[a] See p. 161. Strype has omitted the words "and John a Vales too."

here yn London with moste of the aldermen, unto home they gave a good reporte.ᵃ Now I, thynkynge to prevente Beard of further trouble that by hym and hys procuremente myght hape unto me apon my aryvall at Andwarp, whysperyd the master yn the care, and dysyeryd hym hartely to land us at Dounkerke, " for I wyll ryde the rest by waggon, God wyllynge, and so shall I be ryde of mr. Beardes companye." I ham content, (saythe the master of the shype,) for I ham werye alredye (saythe he,) of hys companye. The worson pape shall come no more yn myne sckepe!"

So to Downckerke we came, and Beard wente fyrste alände, and bade us all welcome, " for (sayd he) I wyll be our stuard, and we wyll fayer well and ther be anye good chear yn the towne." Than came we to our hoste's howse [and] supte altogether. That beynge done, we wente to our lodgyng, and so yt fel owte that Beard and I sholde lye togeather, and so dyd; but before he wente to bed, he knellyd hyme down at the bedsyed, and made apon hys bodye, as I thynke, xl. crossys, sayenge as manye *Ave Marya's*, but nother Crede nor Pater noster. Than he shewyd us whate monye he had: ther was bothe golde and sylver, and that plentye. At mydnyghte the master of the shype toke hys tyed, and wente hys waye. Mr. Beard, upe yn the mornynge by tyme, went downe to the water syed to loke for the shype; and when he sawe yt was goone he came and tolde us, swerynge and chaffynge lyke a made man, sayeing that kyng Phyllyp shold knowe of yt, howe he was usyd. Than sente he all abowghte, to knowe yf anye wente at the nexte tyed folowynge. Yn the meane tyme, I toke my waggon and wente my wayes, and that was the laste tyme that ever I sawe hym; but afterward I was ynformyd by credable parsones that he had spente all hys monye, bothe hys velffete cote and also hys lyvere cote that he had of quene Mary, and so came home poore and bare,

---

ᵃ " gave a good reporte." This phrase here means possessing credit and consideration, like " having a good report," which is frequently used in our authorised edition of the New Testament: Acts, xxii. 12, " Ananias having a good report of the Jews;" 1 Tim. iii. 7, " A bishop must have a good report of them," &c.

beynge verye syke and weake, and yn Holborne dyed moste myserably, full of lyse. Beholde hys end! God graunte he dyed hys sarvante. Amen!

Now whan as I came to Andwarpe, beynge never there afore, I was amasyd and knewe not where to become that nyghte. At laste I fownde owte the Inglyshe howse, and there I was realevyd[a] for a tyme. After that, I toke a howse yn the oxe-marte of a marchawnte callyd Adam Raner; hoo shewyd me muche favore, and there I thawghte a scoole for the space of a yeare and a halve quyetly; and than commyse over mr. Hussy, beynge than guvernor of the Inglyshe nasyon,[b] and yt was gyven owte that he wolde sodaynly shype and send awaye ynto Ingland al soche as were come over for relygyon, he namynge me hymselve for one. So with as mowche speed as I could make, [I] toke wagon, and wente up yuto Jarmanye, and there was at a place callyd Dwesborowe, a free sytye, beynge under the ducke of Clefveland, and there remaynyd untyl the death of quene Mary; and then came bake agayne to Andwarpe. And there whan I set all my doynges yn order, I returnyd home agayn with joy ynto Ingland, my natyffe contrye, yn the which God grawnte hys gospel to have free pasagge, and by the same owre lyves to be amendyd! Amen.

Thus hast thow harde, good crystyan reder, the paynful perygrynasyon of the aforenamed To. Mo., who, for the testymonye of the truthe, and keapynge of a good consyence, sufferyd al thys and a greate deale more not here expresyd; and, altho' that he laye iij yeare yn pryson, that ys yn the Tower of London, the Marshalsee, and Cambryge castyll, and moste of thys tyme yn yorons, bysyed the mysyerye that he sufferyd beynge beyond the secse for the spase

---

[a] *In Strype* received.

[b] There was one Anthony Hussey esquire, who, having been a master in chancery, chief registrar of the archbishop of Canterbury and of the chapter of St. Paul's, latterly resigned those functions, and became governor of the Muscovy merchants (see nôtes to Machyn's Diary, p. 380); and that he was the person to whom Mowntayne alludès in the text appears not improbable.

of ij yeares, the which ys v yeares ynn all; notwithstandynge, as the holy prophet Davythe sayth, God hath delyveryd hym owte of all hys trubles,[a] and hath promysyd that hosoever sufferythe parsecusion for hys name sake, and dothe contynue yn the same truthe unto the end, all those shall be moste sartayne and suere to be savyd, and to have their namys wrytyn yn the boke of lyffe, and after thys lyffe to be savyd by the only blud of Jesus Chryste, unto home, with the Father and the Holy Gooste, be all glory and prayse, nowe [and] for ever! Amen.

Wrytyn by me, THOMAS MOWNTAYNE.

At the head of Thomas Mowntayne's narrative is written, in his own hand, "God is my deffense." (which has been accidentally omitted in p. 178.)

---

[a] Psalm xxxiv. 6.

VIII.

THE LIFE AND DEATH OF ARCHBISHOP CRANMER.

In the present article, and that which will follow, are placed before the reader the materials from which Foxe composed that portion of his "Actes and Monuments" which is entitled "The life, state, (*or* actes *in the running head-lines,*) and storie of the Reverend Pastour and Prelate, Thomas Cranmer, archbishop of Caunterburie, Martyr," &c.

It was from the paper now before us that the martyrologist derived the substance of his chapter on Cranmer as it appeared in his first English edition of 1563, and as he had previously printed it in the Latin edition of 1559. It does not appear from what source it had proceeded: but the MS. is written in two very different hands, the first of which is of extraordinary accuracy both in penmanship and orthography, and the place where the second hand begins will be found indicated in p. 227. The second writer is by Strype (Memorials of Cranmer, p. 305,) conjectured to be either Scory or Becon: but the present editor has found no MS. of either Becon or Scory by which he could verify this conjecture.

In his second edition of 1576 Foxe interweaved with the present paper the greater portion of the succeeding one, written by Ralph Morice.

Various passages of this paper have been quoted by Todd and the other biographers of Cranmer as original statements of Strype.

THE LYFE AND DEATH OF THOMAS CRANMER, LATE ARCHEBUSHOPE OF CAUNTERBURY.

[MS. Harl. 417, fol. 90.]

Thomas Cranmer, the sonne of Thomas Cranmer of Aslocton esquier, and of Agnes Hatfeld his wyefe, doughter of Laurence Hatfeld of Wylloughby of lyke degre, was born (at the sayd Aslocton, within the county of Notingham,) the second of July .1489. and learned his gramar of a rude parishe clerke in that barbarus tyme, unto his age of .14. yeares, and then he was sent by his seyd mother to Cambrege, where he was nosseled in the grossest kynd of sophistry, logike, philosophy morall and naturall, (not in the text of the old philosophers, but chefely in the darke ridels and quidites of Duns and other subtile questionestes,) to his age of xxij yeares. After that, he gave hymselfe to Faber, Erasmus, good Laten authors, iiij or v yeares togyther, unto the tyme that Luther began to wryte; and then he, considering what great contraversie was in matters of religion (not only in tryfles but in the cheefest articles of our salvation,) bent himselfe to trye out the truthe herin: and, for as moche as he perceyved that he could not judge indifferently in so weyghty matters without the knowledge of the holy scriptures, (before he were enfected with any mannes opinions or errours,) he applyed his whole studye iij yeares unto the seyd scryptures. After this he gave his mynde to good wryters both newe and old, not rashely running over them, for he was a slowe reader, but a diligent marker of whatsoever he redd, for he seldom redd without pen in hand, and whatsoever made eyther for the one parte or the other, of thinges being in contraversy, he wrote it out yf it were short, or at the least noted the author and the place, that he might fynd it and wryte it out by leysure; which was a great helpe to hym in debating of matters ever after. This kynde of studie he used till he were made doctor of divinitie, which was about the 34 of his age.[a]

Not longe after kyng Henry the viij, being persuaded that the maryadge betwyxt hym and queue Katerine doughter to kynge Ferdinande of Spayn was unlefull and nought, by doctor Longland [b] bushop of Lincoln his confessor, and other of his clergy, sent for vj of the best learnd men of Cambredge and vj of Oxford to debate this question, whether it were lefull for one brother to mary his brother's wyfe, being knowen of his brother; of the which xij doctor Cranmer was apoynted for one, but because he was not then at Cambredge, there was an other chosen in his stead; which xij learned men agreed fully, with one consent, that it was lefull, with the pope's dispensation, so to do.

Shortly after, doctor Cranmer returning to Cambredge, dyverse

[a] In 1523.   [b] John Longland, bishop of Lincoln 1521; died 1547.

of the seyd learned men repayred to hym to knowe his opinion in the seyd mariadge, and, after longe reasoning therabout, he chaunged the myndes and judgmentes of v of them. Then almost in every disputation, bothe in privat houses and in the commen scholes, this was one question, Whether the pope might dispence with the brother to mary his brother's wyfe after carnall knouledge; and it was of many openly defended that he might not. Which thing Steven Gardener, then the kynges secretary and after bushop of Wynchester, hearing, shewed the king that doctor Cranmer had chaunged the myndes of v of the seyd learned men of Cambredge, and of many other besyde them; wherupon the king commaunded hym to be sent for. And after long reasonnyng with hym, he sent hym agayn to Cambrege, commanding him to pen the matter at large, and return agayn to hym with spede.[a]

Shortly after he sent him into Fraunce[b] with the erle of Wylshyre,[c] chefe ambassadour, doctor Lee[d] elect archebushop of Yorke, doctor Stockesley[e] elect bushop of London, dyvines, and doctor Trigonell,[f] doctor Karn,[g] and doctor Benet,[h] lawyers, to dispute this matter at

[a] Bale enumerated among the archbishop's works, "De non ducenda fratria, *lib. ii.*" but the work is not now extant. See Mr. Jenkyns's remarks on the subject, Remains of Cranmer, vol. i. p. vi.

[b] The several parties mentioned in the text were employed in various missions to the continent at the period in question: but it does not appear that they were ever placed all together in one embassy.

[c] Thomas earl of Wiltshire and Ormonde, the father of queen Anne Boleyne. He was sent ambassador to the emperor with doctor Stokisley and doctor Lee, in Jan. 1529-30, (see State Papers, 4to. 1849, vii. 230,) and was also in France about the same period, as well as his son George lord Rochford.

[d] Edward Lee, D.D. archbishop of York 1531; died 1544.

[e] John Stokisley, D.D. bishop of London 1530; died 1539. He was sent to France with George Boleyne, gentleman of the king's privy chamber (and presently viscount Rochford): see their instructions in State Papers, 1849, vii. 219.

[f] John Tregonwell, LL.D. afterwards knighted. He was a prebendary of Westminster as well as member of parliament.

Edward Carne, LL.D. afterwards knighted in 1541. He was appointed to the function of king Henry's excusator at Rome: see State Papers, 4to. 1849, vii. 269. He died in 1561 at Rome, where his monument still exists.

[h] William Benet, LL.D., archdeacon of Dorset 1530, dean of Salisbury 1531; died 1533.

Paris and other places in Fraunce. Wherin he behaved hym so learnedly, soberly, and wittely, that the sayd erle so commended hym by his letters to the king, that he sent hym a commission with enstructions to be his sole ambassadour to the emperour in the seyd cause of matrimony, when the emperour marched to Vienna agaynst the great Turke; and so he, traveling through Germany, fully satisfied many mennes mynd herin, which afor were of a contrary judgement; and in the emperor's court also. In so moch that Cornelius Agrippa confessed to the seyd ambassadour the maryage to be nought, but he durst not say so openly for feare bothe of the pope and the emperour. After which tyme the emperour wolde never heare the matter reasoned, but referred it to the court of Rome.

Wherfor the kyng called hyme home agayn, and shortly after sent hym ambassadour to the pope about the same cause; and there, after long disputation had, he so forced them that they graunted openly in the pope's chefe court of the rotta, that the seyd maryage was agaynst Goddes lawe, and they sayd morover that the pope might dispence with the lawe of God, which the sayd doctor Cranmer denyed utterly.

In the mean tyme dyed Wylliam Wharham, archebyshop of Canterbery[a]; wherfor the king called home the seyd doctor, and gave him the seyd archebyshopericke.

Not long after this, the usurped power of the bishop of Rome was propounded in the parliament, and then the old collections of the newe archebishop did him good service,[b] for the chefe and in manner the whole burden of this wayghty cause was layd upon his sholders; in so moche that he was forced to answer to all that ever the whole rable of the papistes could saye for the defence of the pope's supremisee; and he answerd so playnly, directly, and truly to all their argumentes, and proved so evydently and stoutly bothe by the word of God and consent of the primative churche, that this usurped power of the pope is a meare tiranny and directly agaynst the lawe of God, and that the power of emperours and kynges is the highest power here upon earth, unto the which byshoppes, priestes, popes, and cardinalles ought to submit themselves, and are as much bound to obey as their temporall subjectes or laymen (as the papistes call them), wherfore the pope's usurped supremisee was upon just causes abolished and utterly expelled out of this realme of Englonde by the full consent of the parliament.

After the which, bothe the kynge [and] the quene were cyted to appeare at Dunstable before Thomas Cranmer, archbyshop of Canterbury, and Stephen Gardiner, byshop of Wynchester, being judges to determine whether the forseyd mariage were good and laufull before God or not; before whom the kinge appeared at place and tyme apoynted, ready to make his answer by his proctour; but the quene refused to make answer before them as her judges, and stood to her appellation before made to the byshop of Rome; but for as muche as his usurped power was before abrogat by acte of parliament, and ordeyned that no person should appeale or prosecute any appeale to the pope or to any other person out of the kynges dominions, for the seyd causes, and the quenes contumacy in refusing to appeare and make answer before her laufull judges, they proceded to sen-

contents of which will be found in the Catalogue of the Lambeth MSS. folio, 1812, p. 255. There is further another large collection, formed by Cranmer, of extracts from the holy scripture and the fathers, which now forms the volumes 7 B XI. and XII. of the Royal MSS. in the British Museum. Its contents are given by Mr. Jenkyns in his vol. iv. pp. 147—150, and Cranmer's Works, (Parker Soc.) ii. 7, 8. (See in the Appendix hereafter the remarkable particulars of its history as a MS.) The writer of the text was probably aware of the existence of all these collections, of which he had previously given a general description (see p. 219).

tence, and, perceyving the maryage to be unlaufull and agaynst Goddes word, devorced the kynge and the quene.[a]

After this, the seyd Wynchester contynued still in his old popery secretly, allthough he had in open parliament renounced the same, bothe by word othe and subscribyng with his hand; but the seyd archbishop, judging it a thing impossible to make any reformation of religion under the pope's dominion, thought it now (the same being dispatched out of the realme,) a mete tyme to restore the true doctrine of Chryst, according to the word of God and the old primative churche, within his jurisdiction and cure, and with the seyd pope to abolishe also all false doctrine, errours, and heresyes by hyme brought into the churche, bothe by himselfe and by all other whom he judged earnestly to favour the truthe of the gospell, procured the kynge to appoynt certen bushoppes with other learned men, as Stockesley[b] byshop of London, Gardener of Wynchester,[c] Samson[d] of Ch[ich]ester, Reppes[e] of Norwyche, Goodrike[f] of Hely, Latymer[g] of Worcester, Shaxton[h] of Salisbury, and Barloo[i] of saynte Davides, to set forth a trueth of religion, being clean pourged from all popishe errours and heresy. In the whiche disputation Wynchester, the pope's chefe champion, with iij or iiij of the seyd byshoppes, went about with all subtill sophistry to maynteine all idolatry, heresy, and superstition wrytten in the canon lawe, or used in the church under the pope's tyranny; but at the last they, being convinced by the word of God and consent of the olde authors and primatyve church, agreed upon and set their handes to a godly booke of religion called

[a] The divorce was pronounced on the 23d May, 1533.
[b] John Stokisley, consecrated 1530, died 1539.
[c] Stephen Gardyner, bishop of Winchester 1531.
[d] Richard Sampson, bishop of Chichester 1536, translated to Lichfield and Coventry 1543, died 1554.
[e] William Repps, alias Rugge, bishop of Norwich 1536, died 1550.
[f] Thomas Goodrich, bishop of Ely 1534, died 1554.
[g] Hugh Latimer, bishop of Worcester 1535, resigned 1539.
[h] Nicholas Shaxton, bishop of Salisbury 1535, resigned 1539.
[i] William Barlow, consecrated bishop of St. Asaph 1533, translated to St. David's 1536, to Bath and Wells 1548, deprived 1553, appointed to Chichester 1559, died 1568.

the bishoppes' booke,[a] not muche unlyke the booke set forth by his sonne kyng Edward the vjth,[b] except in ij. poyntes; the one was the reall presence of our savyour Chrystes bodie in the sacrament of th'alltar, of the which opinion the seyd archebushop was at that tyme, and the most part of the other byshoppes and learned men; the other errour was of praying, kyssing [and] kneling before images, which was added by the kynge after the bysshoppes had set their handes to the contrary. This booke was estableshed by acte of parliament;[c] but not long after, the kynge, taking displeasure with the seyd archbushop and other byshoppes (as they term them) of the newe learnynge, because they would not gyve their consent in the parliament that the kyng should have all the monasteries suppressed to his own use, but would have had parte of them to have bene bestowed upon hospitalls, brynging up of youth in virtue and good learning, with other thinges profitable in the commen welth, being also stirred therunto by Winchester and other old dissembling papistes, in the next parliament made vj. newe articles[d] of our fayth, as well agreing with the word of God and the former booke of religion called the bysshoppes' booke as fier with water, light with darknes, and Chryst with Beliall. But after, the kyng perceyving that the seyd bisshoppes did this thing, not of malice or stubbornes, but of a zele that they had to Goddes glory and the commen wealth, reformed in parte the sayd vj. articles,[e] and doubtles he was mynded (yf he had lyved) to have set forth as good or a better booke as the first was.

[a] This was the name popularly given to *The Institution of a Christian Man*, issued in 1537. On the archbishop's share in its composition see Mr. Jenkyns's preface to the Remains of Cranmer, p. xvii.   [b] The Book of Common Prayer, afterwards mentioned.

[c] This does not appear to have been the fact, unless by the act already passed in 1536, for " extynguyshing the auctoryte of the bisshop of Rome," 28 Hen. VIII. cap. 10. Statutes of the Realm, iii. 663.

[d] The act of the Six Articles was passed in 1539, 31 Hen. VIII. cap. 14, and was entitled, " An Acte abolishinge of diversity of opinions in certen articles concerning Christian religion:" see Statutes of the Realm, iii. 739. The articles are given by Jenkyns, Pref. p. xxv.

[e] In 1543 appeared *A necessary Doctrine and Erudition for any Christen Man*, commonly called the King's Book. On its composition see Jenkyns, Pref. p. xxxvi.; Ridley's Works, (Parker Soc.) p. 511; and Morice's Anecdotes, hereafter, p. 248.

After whose death his sonne Edward, by the incyting of the foreseyd archbushop and the advice of the duke of Somerset the kynges uncle and protector of the realme, and the consent of the whole councell, stablished by acte of parliament so good and perfight a booke of religion,[a] and agreable with Goddes word (without disprayse of other be it spoken), as ever was used since the apostles' tyme. But when it pleased God, for our unthankfulnes and wycked lyvyng, to take from us this godly kyng, he, perceyving that he could not long lyve in this mortall lyfe, seing also his sister lady Mary, who by her father's wyll was heyr apparent to the crown after him, geven so moche to poprie, by the advyce and consent of his whole councell, and the cheffe judges of the realme, gave the crown with the realme to lady Jane, (doughter to the duke of Suffolke, begotten [of] kyng Henry the viijth's sister,) which lady Jane was bothe so virtuous and well learned as I thinke Englond never brought forth her peare. And when the whole councell and chefe judges had set theyr handes to the kynges wyll, last of all they sent for th'archbushop, requiring him also to subscribe the same wyll as they had done; who answerd that he might not without perjury, for so moche as he was before sworn to my lady Mary by kyng Henries wyll; to whom the councel answeryd that they had consciences as well as he, and were also as well sworn to the kynges wyll as he was. Then answerd he, "I am not judge over any mannes conscience but myne own only; for, as I wyll not condempn your fact, no more wyll I stay my fact upon your conscience,[b] seing that every man shall answer to God for his own dedes and not for other menues;" and so he refused to subscribe till he had spoken with the kyng herin; and then the king told him that the judges had enformed hyme that he might lefully bequethe the crown to lady Jane and his subjectes receyve her as quene, notwithstanding theyr former othe to kyng Henry's wyll. Then the seyd archbushop desired the kyng that he myght first speake with

[a] The Book of Common Prayer, first set forth in 1549, and amended in 1552.
[b] —" so he would not commit his conscience to other men's facts." *Foxe.*

the judges, which the king jently graunted him.a Then he spake with so many of the judges as were that tyme at the court, and with the kynges attornaye [b] also; who all agreed in one that he might lefully subscrybe to the kynges wyll by the lawes of the realme; wherupon he, returning to the kynge, by his commandment graunted to set his hand therto.

Shortly after this kynge Edward departed out of this transitory lyfe, I doubt not unto lyfe eternall with Chryst. After whose deathe the councell caused the seyd lady Jane to be proclaimed queue; but, partly for the right of her title and partly for the malice that the people bare to the duke of Northumberland (whose sone had maryed the seyd lady Jane) as well [as] for the death of [the] duke of Somerset and other cruelty by him used, the more part of the comens with certen of the nobilitie tooke part with lady Mary, who also proclamed herself quene. Wherfore the duke of Northumberland raysed an army, entending to subdue quene Mary; but shortly after his departure from London the councell caused lady Mary to be proclamed quene, and apprehended lady Jane in the Toure; wherupon much of the duke's army fled from him, and he was taken at Cambrege without any resistence, and sent to London to the Towre and dyverse other with him. Whyther queue Mary shortly after repayred: to whom the seyd archbushop by his frendes made humble sute for his pardon; but she, as well for his religion sake, as also because he had bene a worker in the devorce of her

---

[a] It will be recollected that Cranmer himself addressed to queen Mary an explanation of the circumstances under which he had been induced to consent to king Edward's settlement of the crown. It is to be found in Strype's Cranmer, Appx. No. LXXIV. Cranmer's Remains, i. 360; and Cranmer's Works, (Parker Soc.) ii. 442. It does not confirm the statements of the text in every particular. Cranmer had an interview with the king in the presence of the council, and desired to talk with him alone, but was not suffered to do so; nor did he personally consult the judges, but both the king and the privy council informed him of the opinions given by the lawyers, when "methought it became not me, being unlearned in the law, to stand against my prince," and then, at the king's personal requisition, he placed his signature to the will.

[b] Edward Gryffyn. He, however, disappeared from the scene between the 12th and 14th of June, and consequently retained his place under queen Mary. (See before, p. 46.)

father and mother,a wold nether here hym nor see hym. In the meane tyme yt was falslye bruted abrode that he offered hymselfe to synge the masse and requiem at the kynges burynge and also had restored the masse in hys cathedrall churche of Canturburye. To stay thys slaunder he wrote a letter to a frynd of hys, that he never made any suche promysse nor that he dyd erecte the masse at Canturburye, but that yt was a false flatteryng lyeng moncke,[b] doctor Thorden, a man havyng nether wytte, lernyng, nor honesty,[c] and yet hys wytt ys very ready, for he preacheth as well *extempore* as at a yeares warnyng, so learnedlye that no man can tell what he cheafly entendith or goeth aboute to prove, so aptlye that a grosse of poyntes ys not sufficiente to tye hys sermon together, a man not unlyke to Jodocus, a moncke of home Erasmus maketh mencion in hys Colloquies, who yff he were not garnysshed with these gloriouse tytells, Monck, Doctor, Vicedeane, and Suffragane, were worthye to walke openlye in the streates with a bell and cockscome.[d]

[a] Foxe has thus remoulded this passage,—"for as yet the old grudges agaynst the archbishop for the devorcement of her mother remayned hid in the bottom of her heart—

———— Manet alta mente repostum
Judicium Paridis spretæque injuria matris.—Virgil. Æneid i."

[It is at this point of the text in the MS. that the handwriting changes.]

[b] " Wherfore thes be to signifie to the world that it was not I that did sett up the masse at Canterbury, but it was a false, flatering, lyeng, and dissembling monke which causid the masse to be sett up ther, with out my advise or counsell." This is the passage of the archbishop's declaration (noticed in the next page) which is quoted in the text. In the MS. at this place the following side-note is annexed, in a different hand to the text, " These words folowing were not in the archbishop's letters, but they [are] very true, and added by the wryter of this history, who knoweth his [Thornden's] condition very well."

[c] Richard Thornden, alias le Stede, was vice-dean of Canterbury and suffragan bishop of Dover. Foxe tells us he was called " Dick of Dover," and describes his death as ensuing from a sudden attack of palsy, as he was one Sunday " vertuously occupied looking upon his men playing at the bowls," at Bourne, near Canterbury. Foxe's pages abound with instances of his " cruel tyranny upon many godly men at Canterbury." The cha-

Thys letter ᵃ was copyed by many men unto yt came to the handes of the counsell, where uppon he was sente for by them, and, confessyng thys letter to be made by hym, was therfore committed to the Tower, wher all other of the counsell which had wyllynglye subscrybed to the kynges wyll (the duke only except) had ther pardon, he beynge the last which hadd subscribed, beynge also seduced be gyvynge to muche credyte to the judges of the realme, in the lawes wherof he was ignorant, yea and in maner beynge enforced by the authorytye of the kynge and the consell, was condemned of hye treason.

And yet the quene, not therwyth contente, removed hym to Oxford, wher in a disputacion, doctor Weston ᵇ beynge judge, which was without all order, with hyssynge, haghyng, lawghyng, tauntynge, scoffynge, and quaffynge, speachynge some tyme x. or xij. at ones that none coulde be hard for another, thre questions aboute the sacrament beynge propounded, and but one of them beynge reasoned apone, he was in Goddes name with post hast condemned of all three; and so with gleves and bylls was agayne commytted to pryson, wher he remayned untyll Saturdaye the 21 of Marche, 1556, at what tyme he was brought into st. Maryes churche, beynge present lord Wylyams and lord Chandois, ᶜ with dyverse other judges,

---

ᵃ Here on the MS. are written these words, "It is good that the letter itselfe be sette in; the copie of it in prynte is annexed *:" and upon the printed copy, which is accordingly "sett in," are these words: "Joyne in yⁱˢ letter hoc signo *;" to which Strype appended, "Bp. Grindal's hand." The letter or declaration forms a small octavo leaf, "Imprynted 1557," evidently with foreign types. It is the "Declaration concerning the Mass," printed in vol. iv. p. 1, of Jenkyns's Remains of Cranmer; also in Strype's Memorials of Cranmer, p. 305, and Cranmer's Works, (Parker Soc.) i. 428. It was not published by the archbishop, but it is supposed to have been indiscreetly circulated by dr. Scory bishop of Chichester. A copy was publicly read in Cheapside on the 5th of September, 1553, which was nine days before Cranmer was committed to the Tower.

ᵇ Hugh Weston, dean of Westminster and Windsor.

ᶜ Above the name of lord Chandos is written in another hand "alias sir John Bridges." But this is altogether a mistake. Lord Chandos was not present: but his brother sir Thomas Brydges of Cornbury, in Oxfordshire. Cranmer was accompanied to the stake "by the mayre and alldermen, and my lord Wyllyams, with whom came dyvers gentyllmen of the shyre, sir T. Abryges, sir John Browne, and others." (Letter of J. A. mentioned in note ᶜ p. 229.)

knyghtes, and squyers, wher a sermon was made by doctor Cole,[a] durynge the which sermone he wepte very sore,[b] and the sermon beyng fynished he, beynge comaunded to declare hys mynd, sayd as foloweth[c] :—

"Good chrysten people, my deare beloved brethern and systern in Chryste, I beseche you moost hartlye to praye for me to Almighty Godd that he wyll forgeve me all my synnes and offences, which be many and without nomber and greate above measure. But yet one thynge greveth my conscience more then all the rest; wheroffe, Godd wyllynge, I intend to speake more herafter. But howe many and howe greate soever they be, I beseeche you to pray to God of hys marcye to pardon and forgeve them all."

And here kneeling downe [he] sayd, "O Father of heaven! O Son of God, Redemer of [the] worlde! O Holy Gost, [proceeding

[a] Henry Cole, warden of New college, and dean of St. Paul's.

[b] " I shall not nede, for the tyme of sarmon, to describe hys behavyour, hys sorrowfull countynance, his heyvye chere, his face bedewed with teares : sometyme lyftyng hys eyes to heaven in hope; sometyme castyng them downe to the earthe for shame: to be brefe, an image of sorowe, the dolore of hys hart burstyng owt at hys eyes in plentye of teares, retaynyng ever a quiet and grave behaveour, which incressed the pyttye in men's hartes, that they unfeynedly loved hym, hopyng yt had byn hys repentance for hys transgression and error." (Letter of J. A.)

[c] In the MS. Harl. 422 is preserved a contemporary account of the last hours of Cranmer, written by an eye-witness, and dated only two days after his execution. The writer, who signs J. A., though professedly condemning Cranmer, had an evident sympathy in his sufferings, and viewed his fate with deep commiseration, as the extract just given has shown. This document, highly important and interesting, is printed by Strype, Memorials of Cranmer, p. 384; and by Todd, in his Life of Cranmer, vol. ii. p. 493. The report it contains of the last prayers and exhortation made by the martyr is not only remarkable as coming from a quarter professedly unfavourable, but further as coinciding very closely with that given in the text, and which was published by Foxe. How is this close coincidence to be accounted for ? I am inclined to think that the letter of J. A. is in fact the original, and that the version in the text was written from it for publication in the Actes and Monuments, certain modifications being made, which will be shewn in the ensuing notes. Most of the incidents also of Cranmer's last hour, as the pertinacious conduct of the two Spanish friars, and of Ely of Brazenose, who refused to take the martyr by the hand when parting at the stake, and the final and most striking incident of all, that of the archbishop stretching forth his right hand, and exposing it first to the flames—all these are related by J. A., and confirm the supposition that Foxe's account was really founded upon the letter of J. A.

from them both,[a]] thre persons and one God! have mercye apon me moost wretched catyfe and miserable synner. I have offended bothe heaven and erthe more then my tounge[b] can expresse. Wether then may I goe, or wether shoulde I flee for succor? To heaven I am [c] ashamed to lyft upp my eyes, and in erthe I fynd no succoure or refuge. What shall [I] then doe? Shall I despayre? Godd forbydd! Oh, gode Godd! thou art mercyfull, and refusest none that come to thee for succoure. To thee therefore doe I come.[d] To thee I doe humble myselfe, saynge, O Lord [God], my synnes be greate, but yet have mercye apone me for thy greate mercye! [O God the Son, thou wast not made man,[a]] Thys mysterye was not wrought that Godd became man for fewe or lyttell offences. Thou dyddest not gyve thy sonne [unto death[a]], O Heavenly Father, for [our little and [a]] small synnes onlye, but for all and the greatest of the world, so that the synner returne and repente[e] unto thee with hys whole[f] harte, as I doe here at thys presente. Wherfore have mercye upon me, O Lord, whose property ys alwayes to have mercye and pytye,[g] for, although my synnes be great, yet ys thys mercye greater. Wherfore have mercye upon me, O Lord, after thy greate mercye. I crave nothyng, O Lord, for myne owne merits, but for thy name sake, that yt maye be halowed therbye. And for thy deare Sonne Jesus Christ's sake. And nowe therfore, O Father of Heaven, halowed be thy name."

And then standing up he sayd: "Every man, good people, desyreth at the tyme of hys death to geve some good exhortation that other may remember after hys deathe and be the better therby, for one word spoken of a man at hys last end wyll be more remembered then many sermones made of them that lyve and remayne;[h] so I beseche God grant me grace that I may speake that somethynge at [this] my departynge wherby God may be gloryfyed and you edyfied.

[a] Letter of J. A.   [b] — " more grievously than any tongue." *Letter of J. A.*
[c] may be. *Ib.*   [d] *Misprinted* run *by Strype and by Todd.*
[e] and repent *inserted.*   [f] a penitent. *Letter of J. A.*   [g] and pytye *inserted.*
[h] " for —— remayne," *not in the letter of J. A.*

"Fyrst, yt ys as hevy a case to see that many folkes be so doted upon the love of the false world and so carefull for yt, that of the love of God or the worlde to come they seme to care very lyttell or nothinge. Therfore thys shal be my fyrst exhortacion, that you set not overmuche by thys [false^a] glosynge worlde, but upon God and the worlde to come; and learne what thys leason meaneth which saint John teacheth, that *the love of the worlde ys hatred agaynst God.*

"The second exhortacion ys that next unto Godd you obey your kyng and quene, wyllyngly without murmur or grudgyng, not for feare of them onlye, but muche more for the feare of God, knowyng that they be Godes mynisters apoynted of Godd to rule and governe you, and therfore whosoever resisteth them resistethe Goddes ordinances.

"The thyrd exhortacion ys that you love altogether like brothren and systers. But alas! pitye ys to see what contentyons and hatred one man hath agaynst an other, not takyng eche other for bretherne and systers, but rather as strangers and mortall enymyes. But I pray you lerne and beare well away thys lesson, to doe good to all men as muche as in you lyeth, and hurte no man, no more then you wolde hurte your owne naturall brother^b or syster. For thys you may be sure that whosoever hateth hys brother or syster, and goeth about malyciouslye to hynder or hurte hym, surelye and without all doubte God ys not with that man, althoughe he thynck hymselfe never so muche in Goddes favor.

"The fourth exhortacion shal be to them that have great substance and ryches of thys worlde, that they may well consider and wey these iij saynges of the scripture. One ys of our Saviour Chryst hymselfe, who sayethe that yt ys a harde thynge for a ryche man to come ynto heaven, a sore saynge, and [yet] spoken of hym that knoweth the truthe. The second ys of saint John, whose saynge ys thys, He that bathe the substance of thys worlde, and seeth hys brother in necessytye, and shutteth up hys compassion and mercy

^a Letter of J. A.
^b *Written originally* bodye, *and corrected by a second hand to* brother.

from hym, howe can he saye that he loveth Godd? The thyrd of saint James,[a] who speaketh to the covetous and ryche men after thys manner: Weep and howle for the mysery which shall come uppon you. Your ryches doth rotte, your clothes be moth-eaten, your gold and sylver is cankered and rusty, and the rust therof shall beare wyttenes agaynst you, and consume you lycke fyer. You gather and hord up treasure of Goddes indignation against the last daye. Let them which be ryche ponder well theise sentences, for yff ever they hadd occasion to shewe theyr charytye they have yt nowe at thys present, the poore people beyng so many and victuells so deare; for, although I have been longe in pryson, yet have I harde of the greate penurye of the pore.[b]

"And nowe, forasmuche as I come unto [the] last ende of my lyfe, wheruppon hangethe all my lyfe passed and all my lyfe to come, ether to lyfe with my Savior Chryst in joye, or ells to be ever in paynes with wycked dyvells in hell; and I see before myne eyes presently eyther heaven (poyntyng hys fynger upward) redye to receave me, or elles hell (poyntyng downward) readye to swalowe me up, I shall therfor declare unto you my verye faythe, howe I believe, without coulour or dyssimulation, for nowe yt is no tyme to dyssemble, whatsoever I have sayd or wrytten in tymes past.

"Fyrst, I beleve in God the Father Almyghty, maker of heaven and earthe, &c. I beleve everye article of the catholike faythe, every worde and sentence taught by our Savior Chryst and hys apostelles and prophetes, in the newe and old testament.

"And nowe I come to the greate thynge that so muche troblethe my conscience more then anye other thynge that ever I dyd or sayd in my lyfe. And that ys settynge abrode in wrytynge contrarye to my conscience and the truthe; which nowe I here renounce and

---

[a] This is omitted in the letter of J. A.

[b] In Oxford itself the scarcity "was so great, that several societies, being scarce able to live, had leave from their governors to go into the country to their respective homes, to remain there till such time as bread-corn was more plentiful." Wood's Annals of the University of Oxford, under the year 1555.

refuse as thynges wrytten with my hand contrarye to the truthe which I thought in my harte, and wrytten for feare of deathe, to save my lyfe yf yt myght be. And that is all suche bylls or papers which I have wrytten and sygned with my hand sence my degradacion; wherin I have wrytten many thynges untrewe. And, forasmuche as my hand offendyd in wrytynge contrarye to my harte, my hand therfore shal be fyrste punished; for, yff I may come to the fyre, yt shall be fyrste burnte. And as for the pope, I utterly refuse hym as Chrystes enemy and Antechryst, with all hys false doctrine. And as for the sacrament, I beleve as I have taught in my booke agaynste the—

The rest of the original manuscript is lost: Foxe terminates the words of Cranmer's address thus:—

—bishop of Winchester, the which my book teacheth so true a doctrine of the Sacrament that it shall stand at the last day before the judgment of God, where the papistical doctrine contrary thereto shall be ashamed to shew her face."

This was certainly for the greater part an addition of Foxe, for his earlier Latin version of 1559 concludes thus:

— cujus libri assertionem tam firmam judico, ut omnes omnium Papistarum conatus nunquam sunt repulsuri.

The letter of J. A. probably presents the true circumstances under which the archbishop's mouth was stopped:—

"He added that, for the Sacrament, he believed as he had taught in his book against the bishop of Winchester. *And here he was suffered to say no more.*"

IX.

ANECDOTES AND CHARACTER OF ARCHBISHOP CRANMER,

BY RALPH MORICE, HIS SECRETARY.

This article has been added to the present collection on the suggestion of the Rev. J. E. B. Mayor, M.A., Fellow and Tutor of St. John's College, Cambridge, editor of the very interesting series of memoirs published under the title of "Cambridge in the Seventeenth Century:" who has also been at the trouble of transcribing it from the library of Bene't College. It is there preserved among the manuscripts of archbishop Parker: at whose request it was evidently written, as towards the conclusion he is twice addressed under the appellation of "your grace."

The propriety of attaching this document to the previous contents of the present volume will be acknowledged on finding that it formed part of the materials used by the historian Foxe; to whom Parker must have communicated it, previously to the publication of the second English edition of the Actes and Monuments in 1576, and of course subsequently to the first in 1563, to which the writer makes reference.

It will be found, on comparison with the present text of the Actes and Monuments, that Foxe, whilst interweaving this information with his former narrative of Cranmer (which had been formed from the MS. printed as the preceding article of this volume), remodelled and re-arranged the whole of Morice's anecdotes, greatly amplifying them in most parts, but retrenching them in others: generally changing Morice's language, but still retaining some of his most singular phrases and expressions. He gives Morice's name in one of his side-notes (where the archbishop's attendance outside the council door is mentioned:) "This secretary was mr. Ralph Morice, witnesse and drawer of this story."

I shall show in the notes some remarkable examples of the recastings made by Foxe, but they can be fully appreciated only by comparing the present pages with those of the Actes and Monuments.

Strype had the use of what he terms the "MS. Life of Cranmer in Bene't College;" but he did not discover that it had been previously worked up by Foxe. In chapters xxx. and xxxi. of his Memorials of Cranmer, Strype has inserted a great part of Morice's MS. verbatim. The introductory portions, which he omitted, were published by Mr. Mayor in the British Magazine in 1849 (vol. xxxvi. p. 165).

Ralph Morice, the writer of this paper, was the younger brother of William Morice esquire, of Chipping Ongar, in Essex,[a] who has been noticed at p. 45 of the present volume. Having graduated at Cambridge B.A. 1523 and M.A. 1526, he spent the best portion of his days as a faithful servant of archbishop Cranmer, of whose history, qualities, and actions he gives a cursory but effective sketch. So much has been written upon the biography and character of Cranmer that it appears unnecessary to burthen the following pages with much illustration or remark. The reader may drink elsewhere of more mixed streams: he must here imagine himself to be placed at the fountain-head.

Two undated supplications, or petitions, addressed by Ralph Morice to queen Elizabeth are still extant, and have been noticed by Strype.[b] In one of these[c] he thus describes his parentage:—

"Ralph Morice sonne unto James Morice late of Roydon in the countie of Essex esquier, some tyme servante unto that virtious and noble princesse of renowned memorie L. Margaret Countesse of Richmond and Derbie, your highnes' greate-graundemother, and to her grase also clercke of her kechin and mr. of her werkes, namelie of those ij colleges in Cambridge, Christes colledge and St. John's."

In the other petition Ralph Morice sets forth the extent of his services to Cranmer. They had been continued "for the space of 20 yeres and above, being reteyned in service with the said most reverend father in the rowme of a secretary," wherein he had "bestowed and spent both his time, youthe, and prosperitye of his life, not so much in writing of the private busynes of the said moost reverend father, as in travailing with his pen aboughte the serious affaires of the prince and the realme, commyted unto him by those most noble and worthie princes K. Henry the eighth and K. Edward the sixth, your majesties deare father and brother, concernyng aswel the writyng of those great and weightie matrimonyal causes of your highnes' said dere father, (the good effectes, successe, and benefits wherof to Godd's glory this hole realme with the subjectes therof in your highnes' most noble and royal personage do now most happilie enjoye,) as also aboute th'exstirpation of the bishop of Rome his usurped power

---

[a] The family of Morice of Chipping Ongar afterwards assumed the name of Poyntz, sir John Morice having married the daughter and heir of sir Gabriel Poyntz, and granddaughter of Thomas Poyntz esquire, the chief patron of William Tyndale. See Anderson's Annals of the English Bible, i. 525.

[b] See also the memoir of Morice in Athenæ Cantabrigienses, vol. i. p. 293.

[c] MS. Lansdowne 108, art. 8.

and authoritie, the reformation of corrupte religion and ecclesiastical lawes, th'alteration of divine service, and of divers and sundry conferences of lernid men for th'establishing and advancement of sincere religion, with such like: wherin your highnes' said orator most painfullie was occupied in writing of no small volumes, from tyme to tyme; as in that behalf divers lernid men now living can testifie, namely dr. Hethe,[a] dr. Thirleby,[b] the bishops of Elie,[c] Chichester[d] and Heriford."[e] (The rest of this petition will be found in Strype's Memorials of Cranmer, Appendix, No. CIII.)

Ralph Morice was register to the commissioners appointed in 1547 to visit the dioceses of Rochester, Canterbury, Chichester, and Winchester: who were sir John Hales, sir John Mason, sir Anthony Cope, dr. Cave (a lawyer), and mr. Briggs, preacher (of Pembroke college, Cambridge.) Strype's Memorials of Cranmer, p. 147.

Ralph Morice had his share of persecution and suffering in the reign of Mary. In the course of two years his house was thrice searched, by which he lost many valuable papers, and especially certain epistles of Edward VI. to archbishop Cranmer, and the archbishop's answers. When this occurred Morice had fled from his house; and was committed to custody, but escaped by breaking prison. His latter years were passed at Bekesbourn in Kent. He appears to have been living in 1570, but the date of his death has not been ascertained.

Morice made other communications to Foxe; one of which, relating to master Richard Turner preacher, follows the story of Cranmer in the Actes and Monuments. Another, (which appears to have been the earliest, and is addressed to Foxe's printer John Day,) is an account of Cranmer's patronage of doctor Thirlby afterwards bishop of Ely. This has been already laid before the Camden Society by Sir Henry Ellis in the "Letters of Eminent Literary Men," at p. 25. At its conclusion Morice tells Day that he " could say moche more concernyng the notable doinges of this worthie archebisshop which were worthie to be committed to perpetuall fame. And also sumwhat towching the progeny and advancement of the lorde Crumwell, which ys not attall towched in his storye." It was probably after writing this (which is dated " from Bekisborne, the xth of January, 1565,") that the old man was induced by archbishop Parker to indite the following anecdotes of Cranmer.

There can be no doubt that he also materially contributed to the portion of Foxe's work entitled " The life, actes, and death of the famous and worthy counsailour lord Thomas Cromwell earl of Essex," which is greatly enlarged

---

[a] The deprived archbishop of York.   [b] The deprived bishop of Ely.
[c] Richard Cox.   [d] William Barlow.   [e] John Scory.

in the second edition from what it was in the first. The story "How the lord Cromwell helped Cranmer's secretary," when the archbishop's manuscript arguments on the Six Articles fell into the river, and were detained by the lady Elizabeth's bearward who happened to pick them out, is evidently from the secretary's own pen; and so probably are several of the subsequent anecdotes. That relative to "The talke betwene the lorde Cromwel and certeine of the lordes at Lambeth," is acknowledged to be *ex testimonio Secretarij Cantuar.* (Second edition 1576, fol. 1160. The date 1540 there given to the anecdote was subsequently corrected to 1539.)

Again, the story of bishop Gardyner's exclusion from King Henry's will, as Morice had heard it told by sir Anthony Denny to Cranmer, is related by Foxe on the report of " the said archbishop's secretary, who is yet alive." (Edit. 1576.)

Ralph Morice likewise wrote an account of Hugh Latimer's first conversion at Cambridge, which is preserved among Foxe's papers, MS. Harl. 422, art. 12, and printed by Strype, in Eccles. Memorials, iii. 233, and in Latimer's Works, edit. Corrie, (Parker Soc.,) vol. ii. pp. xxvii—xxxi. On the same sheets are some anecdotes of mr. Thomas Lawney and bishop Stokesley, which will be found hereafter in the present volume.

Also a paper "concernyng mr. Latymer's communicacion with mr. Bayneham in the dungeon of Newgate," preserved in the same volume, MS. Harl. 422, art. 26. This has been printed in the Appendix to the fourth volume of the new edition of Foxe, (by Townsend and Cattley, 1846,) p. 770: and in a modernised version, by Strype, Eccl. Memorials, iii. p. [236], and Latimer's Works, (Parker Soc.) ii. 221.

A brief narrative, written by him, of "master Dusgate" burnt at Exeter, would have been appropriately placed in the present volume, had it not already appeared in one of the Camden Society's works, prefixed by Sir Henry Ellis to the letter before mentioned.

But, after all, perhaps the most valuable relic of the labours of Ralph Morice's pen is the MS. Harl. 6148, being a book in which he kept copies of a large number of letters on important matters of business, written for his master the archbishop. This volume was probably one of those of which his study was robbed during his troubles. It subsequently came into the possession of sir Richard St. George, who, filling up its blank pages with his heraldic collections, has nearly smothered the labours of Morice. Unfortunately, the letters are for the most part undated; but they have been published, first in the Christian Remembrancer, next edited by the Rev. Henry Jenkyns in his Remains of Archbishop Cranmer, and a third time in the Works of Cranmer, edited for the Parker Society by the Rev. John Edmund Cox. (Strype had made transcripts of them, which are now in the MS. Lansdowne 1045.)

[MS. Coll. Corp. Chr. Cantab. 128, f. 405.]

A declaration concernyng the Progeny, with the maner and trade of the lif and bryngyng upp, of that most Reverent Father in God, Thomas Cranmer, late archebisshopp of Canterbury, and by what order and meanes he came to his prefermente and dignitie.

First, it ys to be considered that the said Thomas Cranmer was borne [a] in a vilage named Arselacton, [b] in the countie of Notyngham, and the sonne of one Thomas Cranmer, gentilman, descending of an aunciente and famous famylie and progeny.[c] Insomoche as there yet remayneth an aunciente mansion house of antiquitie called Cranmer halle, in Lyncolne shere; whose armes at this present remayne there in the glasse wyndowes of the same house to be seene. And as it is thought by some men, the firste of that familie and name was one of the gentilmen that came into this realme with William Conqueror; whiche semeth something true, in that a gentilman being a Norman borne, and in kyng Henry the VIIIth his tyme assosiated in commission with a certeyne ambassador of France, gave the self-same armes in parte that the Cranmers do here in England, who was of the same name, whiche occasioned the same archebisshoppe to invite that noble gentilman unto his house at Lambeth, where he did banquett hym, so that after diner there was conference of both thair armes togethers, in divers poyntes nothing atall discrepaunte.

Secondlie, as towching his education and bryngyng upp in his youthe. I have harde hymselfe reporte, that his father did sett hym

[a] July 2, 1489.
[b] *First hand*, Arseleton. It is commonly written Aslacton.
Where *second hand* is mentioned in the ensuing notes it implies that the words so marked are above the line in paler ink, but it is believed written by the same hand as the text.
[c] *Progeny*, as is well known, was a word at this period applied rather to ancestry than posterity.

to scole with a mervelous severe and cruell scolemaster.[a] Whose tyranny towards youthe was suche, that, as he thoughte, the said scolemaster so appalled, dulled, and daunted the tender and fyne wittes of his scolers, that thei comonlie [more [b]] hated and aborred good litterature than favored or inbraced the same, w[hose] memories were also therby so mutulated and wounded, that for his p[arte] he loste moche of that benefitt of memorey and audacitie in his youthe that by nature was given unto hym, whiche he could never recover, as he divers tymes reported.

And albeit his father was very desirous to have hym lernyd, yet wolde he not that he shoulde be ignorante in civill and gentilman-like exercises, insomoche that he used hym to showte,[c] and many tymes permitted hym to hunte and hawke and to exercise and to ryde ronghe horsses. So that nowe being archebisshopp, he feared not to ryde the roughest horse that came into his stable. Whiche he wolde do very comblie, as otherwise at all tymes there was none in his house that wolde become his horse better. And when tyme served for recreation after studie he wolde both hawke and hunte, the game being preparid for hym beforehand. And wolde some-tyme showte in the longe bowe, but many tymes kille his dere with

---

[a] Who this was is not known. In the former biography he is termed "a rude parish clerk," and Foxe supposed Cranmer's master to have been the clerk, or priest, of Aslacton. The place of Cranmer's early education was probably a country school—indeed Morice presently speaks of his leaving a grammar-school for Cambridge. Thomas Tusser's verses on Nicholas Udall, the school-master of Eton, have been often quoted in illustration of the severity of the schoolmasters of that time.

> From Paul's I went to Eton sent,
> To learn straightways the Latin phrase,
> Where fifty-three stripes given to me
>   At once I had;
> For fault but small, or none at all,
> It came to pass thus beat I was.
> See, Udall, see the mercy of thee
>   To me poor lad.

[b] The margin is torn off.

[c] *i.e.* shoot with the long bow, as again mentioned a few lines lower.

the crosebow, and yet his sight was not perfayte, for he was pooreblinde.

Item, after this his bringing upp at gramer-scole he was sent to the universitie of Cambridge, where for the moste parte he remayned within Jesus colledge, being firste felowe of the same house; where he proceded in the degrees of the scole untill he was doctor of divinitie. But firste being mr. of arte, it chaunced hym to marye a wif,[a] by meanes wherof he was constraynyd to leave his felowshipp in the same colledge, and became the common reader at Buckingham colledge in Cambridge. And within one yere after that he was maried, his wif travailing with childe, both she and the childe died, so that incontynentlie after her decease, he contynuyng in the favor with the master and felowes of Jesus colledge, they choise hym again felowe of the same house, where he remaynid.

And then after, when cardynall Wolsey hadd begune his colledge at Oxforde, the said cardynall (emongs other of that universitie of Cambridge whiche he there procured to be of his newe foundation) wolde have hadd mr. Cranmer to be one of his felowes in his said new colledge, but he utterlie refused the same, abyding still in Jesus colledge where he proceded doctor of divinity, and there was admitted the reder of the divinitie lecture in the same colledge, untill he was preferred unto the king's service, whiche was after this sorte.

It chaunced that when cardinall Campagious and cardinall Wolsey, commissioners frome the bishopp in the king's cause of divorcemente betwene Katheren lady dowager of Spayne and his highnes, there was that yere a plague of pestilence in Cambridge, by meanes wherof doctor Cranmer, having ij scolers with hym at Cambridge the sonnes of one mr. Cressey of Walteham Abbey,

[a] The name of Cranmer's first wife has never been recovered: but she is said to have been a cousin of the good-wife of the Dolphin inn at Cambridge, with whom she lodged. On this subject see archdeacon Todd's Life of Cranmer, 1831, i. 4—8. Morice hereafter tells the story of a priest's slandering the archbishop as having been once " a hostler."

[b] " A name (remarks Dr. Thomas Fuller) utterly extinct in that town (where God hath fixed my present habitation) long before the memory of any alive. But, consulting

whose wyfe was of kyune unto the said doctor Cranmer, came frome Cambridge unto Walteham with the said scolers, to their father's house, to th'intente to remayne there during the plague tyme.

In the meane season, whiles he was thus abiding at Walteham in the house of the said mr. Cressey, and after the cardinalls had endid the tyme of thair commission, fynysshing no mattier according to the king's expectation, kyng Henry for a daie or twayne removid in great displeasure with the said cardinalles from London to Walteham Abbey. And so than, as it chaunced, doctor Stephens[a] the kinges secretarye and doctor Fox[b] almosyner (the great and onelie cheif doers of the kinges said cause at that tyme,) were by the harbengers lodged in the said mr. Cressey's house, where D. Cranmer was also lodged before thair comyng thether. By meanes wherof all thei three, being of olde acquayntaunce and metyng togethers, the firste night at supper, hadd familier talke concernyng the estate of the universitie of Cambridge, and so entering into farther communication, thei debatyd emongs themselfs that great and weightie cause of the king's divorcement, than of late ventulated before the said cardynalls. In whiche their communication and conference D. Cranmer uttered his opinion after this sorte: " I have nothing atall studied, (saied he,[c]) for the veritie of this cause, nor am not beaten therin as you have byn, howebeit I do thincke that you goo not the nexte wey to worke, as to bryng the mattier unto a perfecte conclusion and ende, speciallie for the satisfaction of the troubeled (*sic*) conscience of the king's highnes. For in observyng the common

---

Weaver's Funeral-Monuments of Waltham church (more truly then neatly by him composed), I finde therein this epitaph.

        Here lyeth Jon and Jone Cressy
        On whose soulys Jesu hav mercy. Amen.

Fuller's Church History, fol. 1655, book v. p. (179.)

[a] Afterwards better known by the name of Stephen Gardyner; appointed secretary to the king 1529; consecrated bishop of Winchester 1531.

[b] Edward Foxe, almoner 1531, bishop of Hereford 1535, died 1538.

[c] This speech or argument of Cranmer is very much abridged by Foxe: but the subsequent communication of Foxe and Gardyner with the king very considerably amplified.

processe and frustratory delaies of theis your courtes the mattier will lyngar longe enoughe, and peradventure in th'ende to come unto smalle effecte. And this is moost certeyne, (sayed he,) that there ys but one trueth in it, whiche no men ought or better can discusse than the divines. Whose sentence maie be sone knowne and brought so to passe with litle industrie and charges, that the king's conscience therby maie be quieted and pacified, whiche we all cheifelie ought to consider and regarde in this question and doubt. And than his highnes in conscience quieted maie determen with hymself that whiche shall seme good before God, and lett theis tumultuary processes give place unto a certeyne trueth." When he hadd thus spoken his advice, or like wourds in effecte, thei both liked well his counsaile therin. And within ij. daies after, D. Fox communyng with the king towching the farther prosecuting of that cause, declarid the conference thei hadd at Walteham with doctor Cranmer, whose device so pleasid the king's highnes, that he therapon commanded them to sende for D. Cranmer. And so by and by being sent for, he came to the king's presence at Grenewiche. And after some speciall communication with the said D. Cranmer, the king reteynyd hym to write his mynde in that his cause of divorcemente, and committid hym unto therle of Wilshere quene Annys father, to be enterteynyd of [him] at Durham place, where therle did lye, untill he hadd pennyd his mynde and opinion concernyng the said cause.

And when doctor Cranmer hadd accomplisshed the king's request in this behalf, he, with the secretary and the almosyner and other lernid men, hadd in commission to dispute that cause in question at both the universities of Cambridge and Oxforde, whiche being firste attempted at Cambridge, D. Cranmer by his authoritie and persuasions brought vj. or vij. lernyd men in one daie of the contrary parte and opinion on his parte.a Wherapon, after the determynation

---

a *i.e.* obviated their objections, and converted them to his opinion. This remarkable circumstance is unnoticed by Foxe, although it is asserted by the former biographer (p. 220) as well as by Morice.

of the said universities, (which both confirmyd the king's cause,) the king's majestie appoyntid the erle of Wilteshere, D. Cranmer, D. Stockisley, D. Bennett, and other lernid men ambassadors unto the bisshopp of Rome, to have the mattier there disputed and ventulatid.[a] And for that the king liked well D. Cranmer's travaile and industry in this mattier, he promotid hym before he wente forthe unto the deanery of Tanton in Devonshere,[b] and unto an other benefice named *(blank)*.

And when thei hadd accomplished thair ambassed with the bishopp of Rome, th'erle of Wilshere and th'other lernid men returnyd again into England, and D. Cranmer not being answered with the bisshopp of Rome, was sent forwardes[c] ambassador to th'emperor, than being in expedition againste the Turke at Vyenna And apon of *(sic)* th'emperor's returne homewarde thorough Germany he hadd in his jorney aswell conference with divers lernyd men in Germany as with certeyn lernyd of th'emperor's counsaile, who, being of the contrary opynion, was *(sic)* by hym alurid to favor the kingis cause; insomoche that, being by this meanes both well acquayntid and enterteynid emongs the lernyd men there, it was his chaunce to mary a kyniswoman of one of thairs,[d] this his laste wif, whome he secretelie sente home into Englande (before his returne *altered to*) within one yeer of his placing in his dignitye.

And whiles he was in this ambassage with th'emperor, th'archebisshopp of Canterbury William Warram being departid this transitory lif,[a] the said D. Cranmer was nominated and electid archebisshopp of Canterbury in his rowme.[b] Thusmoche concernyng his enteraunce towardes his dignitie.

Nowe, as towching his qualities wherewithall he was speciallie enduyd, like as some of them were very rare and notable, so oughte they not to be put in obblivion. Wherfore emonge other thinges it ys to be notid that he was a man of suche temperature of nature, or rather so mortified, that no maner of prosperitie or adversitie coulde alter or change his accustumed conditions: for, being the stormes never so terrible or odious, nor the prosperous estate of the tyme never so pleasante, joyous, or acceptable, to the face of [the] worlde his counteynance, diete, or sleape comonlie never altered or changed, so that thei whiche were mooste nerest and conversante aboute hym never or syldome perceyvid by no signe or token of counteynance howe th'affaires of the prince or the realme wente. Notwithstanding privatelie with his secrete and speciall frends he

Todd's Life of the archbishop she is named Anne, as she was by Strype, and so in the works of the Parker Society, and most other places in which she has been mentioned; but her name was Margaret. Her children by Cranmer were, one son, Thomas Cranmer esquire, and two daughters, Anne, who died before her father, and Margaret who survived him. After the archbishop's death she had two other husbands: the first of whom was Edward Whitchurch the printer, who had suffered imprisonment in 1540 for printing the Bible, and again in the beginning of Mary's reign, together with his partner Richard Grafton. His burial is supposed to be recorded in the register of Camberwell as "maister Wychurch," Dec. 1, 1561; and at the same place was celebrated on the 29th Nov. 1564, the third marriage of the archbishop's widow with Bartholomew Scott esquire, also of Camberwell, and a justice of the peace for Surrey; in whose epitaph (after he had survived her and married two other wives,) she was described as Margaret "ye wido of ye right reverend Prel: and Martyr Tho: Cranmer, Archbish: of Canterburie." (Collectanea Topogr. et Genealogica, iii. 145.)

[a] Warham died August 23, 1532.

[b] Nominated by bull dated Feb. 22, 1532-3. He was consecrated at Westminster on the 30th March following.

wolde shede forth many bitter teares, lamenting the miseries and calamities of the worlde.

Agayne, he so behavid hymself to the whole worlde, that in no maner of condition he wolde seme to have any enemy, although in verie ded he hadd both many greate and secrete enemyes, whome he alweys bare with such countenance and benivolence that thei coulde never take good oportunitie to practize thair malice againste hym but to thair greate displeasure and hinderaunce in th'ende. And as concernyng his awne regarde towardes slanders and reproche by any man to hym ymputid or ympinged, suche as entirelie kuewe hym can testifie that very litle he estemed or regarded the brute therof, by cause he altogether traivailed evermore frome gyvyng of juste occasion of detractione. Whereapon grewe and proceded that notable qualitie or virtue he hadd: to be beneficiall unto his enemyes, so that in that respecte he wolde not be acknowne to have anye enemy atall. For whosoever he hadd byn that hadd reportid evill of hym, or otherwaies wrought or done to hym displeasure, were the reconciliation never so meane or symple on the behalf of his adversarye, yf he hadd any thing attall relentid, the matter was both pardoned and clerelie forgotten, and so voluntarilie caste into the sachell of oblivion behinde the backe parte,[a] that it was more clere nowe oute of memorie, than it was in mynde before it was either commensid or committed: insomoche that if any suche person sholde have hadd any sute unto hym afterwardes, he might well recken and be as suer to obteyn (yf by any meanes he might lawfullie do it) as any other of his speciall frendes. So that on a tyme I do remember that D. Hethe late archebisshopp of Yorke, partelie mislyking this his overmoche lenitie by hym used, saied unto hym, "My lorde, I nowe knowe howe to wynne all thinges at your handes welenough." "Howe so?" (quoth my lorde.) "Mary, (saied D. Hethe,) I perceyve that I muste firste attempte to do unto you some notable displeasure, and than by a litle relenting obteyne of you

---

[a] Non videmus manticæ quod in tergo est. Catullus, xxii. 21.

what I can desire.[a]" Wherat my lord bitt his lippe, as his maner was when he was movid, and saied: "You saie well: but yet you maie be deceyvid. Howbeit, havyng some consideration so to do, I may not alter my mynde and accustumed condition, as some wolde have me to do."

Againe, one thing he comonlie used wherin many did discomende hym, whiche was this: he alwaies bare a good face and countenance unto the papistes, and wolde both in worde and dede do very moche for theym, pardonyng thair offences;[b] and on th'other side, somewhat over severe againste the protestants; whiche being perceyvid not to be don but apon some purpose, on a tyme a frende of his declarid unto hym that he therin did veraie moche harme, encoraging therby the papistes, and also therby in discoraging the protestants. Wherunto he made this answer, and saied, "What will ye have a man do to hym that ys not yet come to the knowledge of the trueth of the gospell, nor peradventure as yet callid, and whose vocation ys to me uncerteyne? Shall we perhapps, in his jorney comyng towards us, by severitie and cruell behaviour overthrowe hym, and as it were in his viage stoppe hym? I take not this the wey to alleure men to enbrace the doctrine of the gospell. And if it be a true rule of our Saviour Christe to do good for evill, than lett suche as are not yet come to favour our religion lerne to folowe the doctrine of the gos-

[a] Foxe suppressed the name of doctor Heath, but gives the same sentiment as "a common proverb," with the following introduction: "Few we shall find in whom the saying of our Saviour Christ so much prevailed as with him, who would not only have a man to forgive his enemies, but also to pray for them: that lesson never went out of his memory. For it was known that he had many cruel enemies; not for his own deserts, but only for his religion sake: and yet, whatsoever he was that sought his hinderance, either in goods, estimation, or life, and upon conference would seem never so slenderly any thing to relent or excuse himself, he would both forget the offence committed, and also evermore afterwards friendly entertain him, and shew such pleasure to him, as by any means possible he might perform or declare; insomuch that it came into a common proverb, Do unto my L. of Canterbury displeasure, or a shrewd turn, and then you may be sure to have him your friend whiles he liveth."

[b] His treatment of the quondam abbat of Tower hill, related by Underhill, (before, p. 157,) was an instance of such conduct.

pell by our example in using them frendlie and charitablie. On th'other side, suche as have tasted of syncere religion, and as it were taken holde of the gospell, and seme in wourdes to maynteyne the true doctrine therof, and than by the evill example of thair lyves moste pernitiously become stombeling blockes unto suche as are weake, and not attall as yet enterid into this vioage, what wolde you have me do with them? beare with them and wyncke at their faultes, and so willinglie suffer the gospell (by thair outeragious doinges) to be troden under our feete? neglecting herwith an other notable saying of our Saviour oute of our memorie, whiche saieth, *The servante knowing his Lorde and Master's pleasure and comandement, yf he regardith not the same is* (as a man might say, of all other) *wourthie of many plagues.*" And thus with theis ij. scriptures or doctrines of our Saviour Christe he answered myn eldeste brother, who was ernest with hym for the amendement of this his qualitie. Mr. Isaac, yett lyvyng, ys a witnes of the mattier.

Againe, if any matier of weighte (besides his awne cause, wherin evermore with all kinde of persones he was redie to relente and give place, according to the qualitie of the mattier, more than became his estate,) whiche towched Goddes cause or his prince, there was no man more stoughte or more inexorable, so fareforthe that neither feare of losing of promotion, nor hope of gaine or wynnyng of favour, coulde move hym to relente or give place unto the trueth of his conscience. As experience therof well apperid, aswell in the defence of the true religion againste the vj. Articles in the parliamente, as when he offered to combate with the duke of Northumberland in king Edward's time, speaking than on the behalf of his prince for the steying of the chauntries untyll his highnes hadd come unto lawfull age,[*] and that speciallie for the better maynteynance of his estate than.

[*] "An acte whereby certaine chauntries, colleges, free chapelles, and the possessions of the same, be given to the kinges majestie," was passed in 1 Edw. VI. cap. 14. (Statutes of the Realm, iv. 5.) A commission for their sale was issued in the summer of 1552, " for the payment of my dettes," as the king states in his Journal (Literary Remains of

But if at the prince's pleasure in cause of religion at any tyme he was forced to give place, that was don with suche humble protestation, and so knyt upp for the savegarde of his faithe and conscience, that it hadd byn better his good will had never byn requestid, than so to relente or give over. Which moste dangerouslie (besides sondrie tymes else) he speciallie attemptid when the vj. Articles by parliament passed, and when my lorde Crumwell was in the Tower, at what tyme the booke of articles of our religion was newlie pennyd; for even at that season, the hole rablemente, which he toke to be his frendes, being commissioners with hym, forsoke hym, and his opinion in doctrine, and so, leaving him post alone,[a] revolted altogethers on the parte of Stephen Gardyner bisshopp of Wynchester, as by name bisshopp Heathe,[b] Shaxton,[c]

Edward VI. p. 414.) It was probably on this occasion that Cranmer made the opposition which Morice describes: though his modern biographers refer to the earlier date. There is a chapter on Chantries in Fuller's Church History, book VI. § vi.

[a] Upon the occurrence of this phrase we may place in juxta-position with the text the passage of Foxe which is evidently founded upon it. "At the time of setting forth the Six Articles, mention was made before in the storie of king Henry the eighth, how adventurously this archbishop Thomas Cranmer did oppose himself, standing as it were *post alone* against the whole parliament, disputing and replying three days together against the said Articles. Insomuch that the king, when neither he could mislike his reasons, and yet would needs have those Articles to pass, required him to absent himself for the time out of the chamber while the act should pass, and so he did, and how the king afterward sent all the lords of the parliament to Lambeth to cheer his mind again, that he might not be discouraged." It will be observed that in this passage Foxe speaks largely of the stand made by Cranmer against the Six Articles, of which Morice says little; but borrows the singular phrase employed by Morice, where the archbishop is described as standing *post alone* in opposition to his fellow commissioners when revising "the book of Articles of our religion," and transfers it to his conduct in parliament upon the former occasion. By "the book of articles of our religion" is intended the manual entitled, "A necessary Doctrine and Erudition for any Christen Man," which was provided as a substitution for the "Institution of a Christian Man," before noticed in p. 224. It was promulgated in 1543.

[b] Nicholas Heath, afterwards archbishop of York, was elected bishop of Rochester, March 26, 1540.

[c] Nicholas Shaxton, consecrated bishop of Salisbury 1535, resigned that see in consequence of not subscribing to the Six Articles, 1539.

Thirlby,[a] *erased*) Daye,[b] and all other of the meaner sorte, by whome theis so named were cheifelie advaunced and preservid unto thair dignities.[c] And yet, this sodden invertion notwithstanding, God gave hym suche favour with his prince, that the booke altogethers passid by his assertion againste all thair myndes, more to be mervailed at, the tyme considered, than by any reason to compasse howe it shold so come to passe: for then wolde there have byn laied thousands of powndes to hundrethes in London, that he shoulde have, before that synode hadd byn endid, byn sett upp in the Tower beside his frende the lorde Crumwell. Howbeit, the kynges majestic, having an assurid and approvid affiance of his bothe deape knowledge in religion and fidelitie both to God and hym, susspected in that tyme other men in thair judgmentes not to walke uprightlie nor syncerlie, for that some of them swarved frome thair former opinion in doctrine. And having greate experience of the constancye of the L. Cranmer, it drave hym all alone to joyne with the said lorde Cranmer in the confirmation of his opinion and doctrine againste all the reste, to thair great admiration. For at all tymes when the kinges majestic wolde be resolved in any doubt or question he wolde but send wourde to my lorde overnighte, and by the next daie the king shoulde have in writyng breve notes of the doctors' mynds, aswell divines as lawers, both aunciente, olde, and new, with a conclusion of his owne mynde; whiche he coulde never gett in suche a redynes of none, no not of all his chapleyns and clergy aboute hym, in so shorte a tyme. For, being throughlie scene in all kinde of expositors, he coulde incontynentlie laye open xxx^{ti},

[a] Thomas Thirleby, afterwards bishop of Norwich and Ely, was consecrated bishop of Westminster in 1540.

[b] George Day, bishop of Chichester 1543.

[c] Foxe tells this story also, but quite in a different way. He does not mention the names of Shaxton, Thirleby, or Day: but he states that it was with bishop Heath and bishop Skip (John Skyppe, bishop of Hereford 1539-1552) that the archbishop had principally to contend: these two prelates (he says) had Cranmer down from the rest of the commissioners into his garden at Lambeth, and there by all manner of persuasions they endeavoured to alter his determination, but without success.

xl^{ti}, lx^{ti} or mo sumwhiles of authors, and so, reduceyng the notes of them altogethers, wolde advertise the kinge more in one daie than all his lernyd men coulde do in a moneth. And it was no marvaile: for it was well knowene that commonlie, yf he hadd not busynes of the prince's, or speciall urgent causes before hym, he spente iij partes of the daie in studie as effectuallie as he hadd byn at Cambridge, and therfore it was that the king saied on a tyme to the bisshopp of W[inchester?] (the king and my said lorde of W. defending togethers that the canons of the appostells were of as [a] good authoritie as the iiij evangelistes, contrarye to my lorde Cranmer's assertion) "My lorde of Canterburye (saied the king,) ys to olde a Trewante[b] for us twayne."

And emonges other thinges, this ys to be noted: that the kinge, afore hande perceyving that the said lorde Cranmer shoulde have moche adoo in the defence of christian religion, did alter his armes,[c] changeyng the iij cranes which were percell of his

[a] *MS.* as of.

[b] Trojan? See in Nares's Glossary various examples of the use of the word Trojan in a familiar way.

[c] The Rev. G. C. Gorham, in his Reformation Gleanings, 1857, 8vo., has stated, at p. 10, that the arms of Cranmer were probably first assumed when he was promoted to the see of Canterbury in 1533; and in a very singular way. He found on a seal of his prede-cessor Warham the coat of a chevron between three birds: these birds Cranmer chose to interpret as *cranes*, and therefore retained them on the seal, which he adopted for himself, adding on a second shield (which was plugged and re-engraved) his maternal coat of Aslacton. It is very probable that the Cranmers had previously used only the coat of the ancient family of Aslacton, whose property they had acquired by marriage in the reign of Henry VI. See the pedigree in Thoroton's Nottinghamshire. It was not until about the year 1540 that the archbishop changed the cranes into pelicans, which first appear on the title of the great bible printed in that year. (Gorham, p. 14.) The pelican in her piety was a favourite device in religious heraldry at this period; the arms of Richard Foxe bishop of Winchester, were, Azure, a pelican in her piety, and are still displayed as those of his foundation of Corpus Christi college, Oxford. "The like coat of arms, (remarks Strype,) or much resembling it, I find several of queen Elizabeth's first bishops took, whether to imitate Cranmer or to signify their zeal to the Gospel, and their readiness to suffer for it, I do not determine." Memorials of Cranmer, p. 390.

aunciters' armes into iij pellicanes, declaryng unto th'archebisshopp, that those birdes shoulde signifie ᵃ to hym, that he oughte to be redie as the pellicane ys to shede his bloode for his yonge ones brought upp in the faith of Christe; for (saied the king) you arr like to be tasted (tested) yf you stand to your tacklyng ᵇ at length; as in veraie dede many and sondrie tymes he was sholdered att by his secret enemys the papistes, aswell suche as were of the counsaile as gentilmen and justices of the shere of Kente, and elswhere, insomoche that the prebendaries and certeyn gentilmen of Kente at one tyme conspired againste hym, complaynyng of hym unto the kinges majestie of the doctrine by hym and his chaplens tawghte in Kente. An other tyme one sir John Gostewyke knighte of Bedfordeshere,ᶜ a man of greate service in his tyme, but yett papisticall, accusid hym openly in a parliament for his preaching and reading att Sandewhiche and at Canterburye. At the length the confederacye of the papistes in the counsaile (as king Henry the viij^th hadd of both sectes aswell papistes as protestantes,) accusid hym moste grevouslie unto the kinge, that he with his lernyd men hadd infectid so the hoole realme with thair unsavery doctrine, that iij partes of the realme were become abominable heritiques. And therfore desired of the kyng that he might come to examination and triall, and to be committed unto the Tower for that purpose. But the said L. Cranmer

---

ᵃ *Parker has in the Manuscript underlined with his red pencil the words* shoulde have moche adoo —— signifie.

ᵇ Foxe borrows this phrase, though not in the same place. He says that "many wagers would have been laid in London, that he should have been laid up with Cromwell, at that time in the Tower, for his *stiff standing to his tackle.*"

ᶜ Sir John Gostwick was for many years treasurer and receiver-general of the first fruits and tenths; but the information of his descendant sir William Gostwick (quoted in Wotton's English Baronetage, 1741, i. 289, and thence copied by various other writers,) that he was afterwards master of the horse to Henry VIII. is surely erroneous. He was knight in parliament for Bedfordshire in 1539, and sheriff of Beds and Bucks in 1541. Leland says of him, when noticing Willington in Bedfordshire, (where the family was settled as early as the year 1209,) "Mr. Gostewik, beyng borne at Willington, boute (bought) this lordship of the duke of Northfolk now living, and hath made a sumptuus new building of brike and tymbre *a fundamentis* in it, with a conduit of water derived in leaden pipes."

was so growne in estymation with the kinges highnes, that none of theis complayntes colde prevaile.

For as concernyng the firste attempte of the prebendaries and justices of Kente, the kinge on an evenyng rowing on the Thames in his barge,[a] came to Lambeth bridge and there receyvid my L. Cranmer into his barge, saying unto hym merily, "Ah, my chaplen, I have newis for you: I knowe nowe who is the gretest heretique in Kente." And so pulled oute of his sleve a paper, wherin was conteynid his accusation artycled againste hym and his chaplens and other preachers in Kente and subscribed with thandes (the hands) of certeyn prebendaries and justices of the shere.[b] Wherunto my L. Cranmer made answer, and besought his highnes to appoynte suche commissioners as wolde effectuallie try oute the trueth of those articles, so that frome the highest to the loweste thei might be well punisshed in example of others, yff thei hadd don otherwise then it became theym. "Marye, (saied the king,) so will I doo; for I have suche affiaunce and confidence in your fidelitie, that I will committ th'examination herof wholie unto you, and suche as you will appoynt." Than saied my L. Cranmer, "That will not (if it please your grace,) seme indifferent." "Well, (saied the kinge,) it shalbe none otherwise; for suerlie I reken, that you will tell me the trueth: yea of yourself, yf you have offendid. And therfore make no more adoo, but lett a commission be made oute to you and suche other as you shall name, wherby I maye understande how this

---

[a] Foxe has enlarged this into a more finished picture—"The king finding occasion to solace himself upon the Thames, came with his barge furnished with his musicians along by Lambeth Bridge, towards Chelsey. The noise of the musicians provoked the archbishop to resort to the bridge to do his duty, and to salute his prince: whom when the king had perceived to stand at the bridge, eftsoons he commanded the watermen to draw towards the shore, and so came straight to the bridge. 'Ah, my chaplain,' (said the king to the archbishop,) come into the barge to me.' The archbishop declared to his highness that he would take his own barge, and wait upon his Majesty. 'No, (said the king,) you must come into my barge, for I have to talke with you.' When the king and the archbishop all alone in the barge were set together, said the king to the archbishop, 'I have news out of Kent,'" &c. &c. but much amplified from the text.

[b] See note in the Addenda.

confederacie came to passe." And so a commission was made oute to my lorde Cranmer, dr. Coxe his chancellor, dr. Belhowsis,[a] and to mr. Hussey [b] his regester, who came immediatelie downe to Canterburye, and satte there to enquire of theis maticrs. By meanes wherof every one that hadd medeled in thos detections shroncke backe and gave over thair holde. And than his chaunceller and register were suche fautours of the papistes, that nothing wolde be disclosid and espied, but every thing colorablie was hidd. Insomoche that uppon lettres by me written unto D. Buttes [c] and mr. Deny,[d] D. Lee [e] was sent downe (after thei had satt vj wekes) by the king. And he by the kinges advice did appoynte to the nombre of ix or x of my lordes gentilmen, to serche both the pursses, chestes, and houses of certeyn prebendaries and gentilmen, all in one momente, by meanes wherof suche letters and writinges were founde, and that a great nombre, that all the confederacy was utterlie knowen and disclosed, to the defaceyng of a greate sorte of their dishonesties. And so, a parliament being at hande, great labour was made by thair frendes for a generall pardon, which wyped awaie all punisshement and correction for the same, specially my L. Cranmer being a man that delighted not in revengyng.

As towching mr. Gostewycke's accusation, the kinge, perceyving that the same cam of mere malice, for that he was a stranger in Kente and had not harde my lorde neither preache nor reade there, knowyng therby that he was sett on and made an instrumente to serve

---

[a] Anthony Bellasis, LL.D. a master in Chancery, prebendary of Westminster 1540, of Lincoln 1543-4, of Wells 1546, of York 1549; archdeacon of Colchester 1543; died 1553.

[b] See a note before in p. 216.

[c] Dr. William Butts, the king's favourite physician; see Athenæ Cantabrigienses, i. 87.

[d] Sir Anthony Denny, another favourite attendant of Henry VIII. See his memoir in the same work, i. 99.

Foxe states that the king sent to York for doctor Lee, in order that he might proceed into Kent for this business. This was Thomas Legh, a master in chancery, who was much employed as one of the visitors of religious houses. He was knighted before his death, which occurred in 1545: see Athenæ Cantabrigienses, i. 87.

other mennys purposes, his highnes mervelously stormed at the matter, calling openly Gostwyke *verlett*, and saied that he hadd plied a vilonyous parte so to abuse in open parliamente the primate of the realme, speciallie being in favour with his prince as he was; "what will thei (quod the king,) do with hym yf I were gon?" Wherapon the king sent wourde unto mr. Gostewycke after this sorte: "Tell that varlett Gostwycke, that if he do nott acknowlege his faulte unto my lorde of Canterbury, and so reconcile hymself towardes hym that he maie become his good lorde, I will suer both make hym a poore Gostewycke, and otherwise punishe hym, to th'example of others." Nowe Gostewycke, hearing of this heynous threate frome the kinges majestic, came with all possible spede unto Lambeth, and there submittid hymself in suche sorrowfull caase, that my lorde oute of hande not onelie forgave all th'offence, but also went directlie unto the king for th'obteynyng of the kinges favour againe, which he obteynyd very hardelie apon condition that the king might here no more of his medeling that weye.

As to the thirde accusation, wherin the counsaile required that the L. Cranmer might be committed unto the Tower, while he were examined, the kinge was veraie straight in grauntyng therof. Notwithstanding, when thei tolde the kinge, that, the archebisshopp being of his privie counsaile, none man durst objecte matter against hym oneles he were firste committed unto indurance, whiche being don, men wolde be bolde to tell the trueth and sey thair consciences: appon this persuasion of thairs, the kinge grauntid unto them, that they shoulde call hym the next daie before them, and as thei sawe cause so to committ hym to the Tower. At nighte about xj of the clocko, the same night before the daie he should appere before the counsaile, the kinge sent mr. Deny [a] to my lorde at Lambeth, willing hym incontynently to come unto Westminster to speake with hym. My lorde being abedd rose straight waie, and wente to the king into his galery att Whitehall at Westminster; and there the

---

[a] Sir Anthony Denny.

king declaird unto hym what he had don in gyvyng libertie unto the counsaile to committe hym to prison, for that they bare hym in hande^a that he and his lernyd men hadd sowne suche doctrine in the realme that all men almoste were infectid with heresie, and that no man durste bring in matter against hym being at libertie and one of the counsaile oneles he were comitted to prison, "and therfore I have grauntid to thair requeste, (quod the king,) but whither I have don well or noo, what sey you, my lord?" My lorde answered and mooste humblie thancked the king that it wolde please his highnes to give hym that warnyng aforehande, saying that he was very well contente to be committed to the Tower, for the triall of his doctrine, so that he mighte be indifferentlie harde (heard), as he doubted not but that his majestie wolde see hym so to be used. "Oh Lorde God! (quod the king,^b) what fonde symplicitie have you: so to permitt yourself to be ymprisoned, that every enemy of yours may take vantage againste you. Doo not you thincke that yf thei have you ones in prison, iij or iiij false knaves wilbe sone procured to witnes againste you and to condempne you, whiche els now being at your libertie dare not ones open thair lipps or appere before your face. Noo, not so, my lorde, (quod the king,) I have better regarde unto you than to permitte your enemyes so to overthrowe you. And therfore I will that you tomorow come to the counsaile, who no

---

^a This phrase, which was one in frequent use, was equivalent to "tried to persuade him." I beare hym in hand, *Je luy fais accroyre.* Palsgrave, Lesclarcissement de la Langue Francoyse, 1530.

^b Foxe's version of this speech affords a good example of the liberties he took with Morice's narrative, and certainly often with little or no improvement either in force or probability of expression :—" The king perceiving the man's uprightness, joined with such simplicity, said, ' O Lord! what maner of man be you! what simplicity is in you! I had thought that you would rather have sued to us to have taken the pains to have heard you and your accusers together for your trial, without any such indurance (*i. e.* imprisonment). Do you not know what state you be in with the whole world, and how many great enemies you have? Do you not consider what an easy thing it is to procure three or four false knaves to witness against you? Think you to have better luck that way than your master Christ had? I see by it you will run headlong to your undoing if I would suffer you. Your enemies shall not so prevail against you; for I have otherwise devised with myself to keep you

doubte will sende for you, and when thei breake this mattier unto yow, require theym that, being one of theym, you maie have thus moche favour as thei wolde have themselves, that ys, to have your accusers brought before you, and if thei stande with you withoüten regarde of your allegations, and will in no condition condiscende unto your requestes, but will nedes committe you to the Tower, than appele you frome them to our person, and give to them this rynge,[a] (which he delivered unto my L. Cranmer than,) by the whiche (saied the kyng,) thei shall well understande that I have taken your cause into my hande frome theym, which ryng thei well knowe that I use it to none other purpose butt to call mattiers frome the counsaile into myn awne handes to be orderid and determy[ni]d." And with this good advice my L. Cranmer, after mooste humble thanckes, departid from the kinges majestie.

The nexte mornyng, according to the kynges monition and my lorde Cranmer's expectation, the counsaile sent for hym by viij of the clocke in the mornyng; and when he came to the counsaile chamber doore, he was not permitted to enter into the counsaile chamber, but stode withoute the doore emonges servyng men and lackeis above thre quarters of an hower, many counsellers and other men nowe and than going in and oute. The matter semed strange, as I than thoughte, and therfore I wente to doctor Buttes and tolde hym the

out of their hands. Yet notwithstanding, tomorrow, when the council shall sit, and send for you, resort unto them, and if in charging you with this matter they do commit you to the Tower, require of them, because you are one of them, a counsellor, that you may have your accusers brought before them without any further indurance, and use for yourself as good perswasions that way as you may devise, and if no entreaty or reasonable request will serve, then deliver unto them this my ring (which then the king delivered unto the archbishop), and say unto them, 'If there be no remedy, my lords, but I must needs go to the Tower, then I revoke my cause from you, and appeal to the king's own person by this his token unto you all;' for (said the king then unto the archbishop) so soon as they shall see this my ring, they know it so well that they shall understand that I have resumed the whole cause into mine own hands and determination, and that I have discharged them thereof."

[a] Of the custom of sending a ring by way of token some examples have been before given in p. 56. The present passage is still more remarkable: "and so incontinently, (as Foxe words it,) upon the receipt of the king's token, they all rose, and carried to the king his ring, surrendering that matter, as the order and use was, into his own hands."

maner of the thing, who by and by came and kepe my lorde company. And yet, or that he was called into the counsaile, D. Buttes wente to the king, and tolde hym that he had sene a strange sighte. "What ys that?" quod the kyng, "Mary! (saied he,) my lorde of Canterbury ys become a lackey or a servyng man; for well I woott he hath stande emonges them this hower almoste at the counsaile chamber doore, so that I was ashamed to kepe hym company there any lenger." "What! (quod the king,) standeth he withoute the counsaile chamber doore? Have thei servid me so? (saied the king.) It is well enough, (saied he,) I shall talke with theym by and bye."

Anon my lorde Cranmer was callid into the counsaile. And it was declaird unto hym, that a great complaynte was made of hym both to the king and to them, that he and other by his permission had infectid the hole realme with heresie, and therfore it was the kinges pleasure that thei shoulde committ hym to the Towre, and there for his triall to be examined. My lorde Cranmer required, as is before declaird, with many other both reasons and persuations, that he might have his accusares come there before hym, before thei used any suche extremity againste hym. In fyne, there was no entreatie colde serve, but that he muste nedes departe [to] the Tower. "I am sorye, my lordes, (quod my L. Cranmer,) that you dryve me unto this exigente, to apple (appeal) frome you to the kinges majestie, who by this token bathe resumed this mattier into his awne bandes, and dischargeth you therof;" and so delivered the kinges ryng unto them. By and by the lorde Russell [a] sware a greate othe and saied, "Did not I tell you, my lordes, what wolde come of this matter? I kuewe right well that the king wolde never permitte my lorde of Canterbury to have suche a blemyshe as to be ymprisoned, oncles it were for high treason." And as the maner was, when thei hadd ones receyvid that ryng, they lefte of thair mattier, and wente all unto the kinges person both with his token and the cause.

[a] John Russell, afterwards earl of Bedford.

When thei came unto his highnes the king saied unto theym, "Ah! my lordes, I hadd thoughte that I had hadd a discrete and wise counsaile, but nowe I perceyve that I am deceyvid. Howe have ye handeled here my L. of Canterbury? What make ye of him a slave, shitting hym oute of the councell-chamber emonges servyng men? Wolde ye be so handeled yourselfes?" and after suche tanting wourdes saied, "I wold you shoulde well understande, that I accompte my L. of Canterbury as faithfull a man towardes me as ever was prelate in this realme, and one to whome I am many waies beholding, by the faith I owe unto God (and so laied his hand uppon his breste) and therfore who so loveth me (saied he,) will regarde hym therafter." And with theis wourdes all, and specially my lorde of Northfolke,[a] answered and saied, "We mente no maner hurte unto my lorde of Canterburye in that we requested to have hym in durance, that we only did bycause he might after his triall be sett at libertie to his more glorye." "Well, (saied the king,) I praie you use not my frendes so. I perceyve nowe wellenough howe the worlde goeth amonge you. There remayneth malice emonge you one to an other; lett yt be avoyded oute of hande, I wolde advice you." And so the king departid, and the lordes shoke bandes every man with my lorde Cranmer, against whome nevermore after no man durste spurne duryng the kyng Henry's life.

And for bycause the kyng wolde have amitie alwaies nurrisshed betwene the lordes of the counsaile and hym, the king wolde sende theym divers tymes to dyner unto my lorde of Canterbury's, as he did after this reconciliation, and also after the parliamente endid wherin the vj articles were grauntid.[b] And at that diner I harde the lorde Crumwell saye to my lorde Cranmer, "You were borne in a happie hower I suppose, (saied he,) ffor, do or sey what you will, the kyng will alwaies well take it at your hande. And I must nedes confesse that in some thinges I have complaynyd of you unto

[a] Thomas Howard, second duke of Norfolk, at this time the leading man of the king's councıl: see Athenæ Cantabrigienses, i. 118.

[b] In the year 1539.

his majestie, but all in vayne, for he will never give credite againste you, what soever is laied to your charge; but lett me or any other of the counsaile be complayned of, his grace will moste seriously chide and falle oute with us. And therfore you arr moste happy, yf you can kepe you in this estate."

Againe his estymation was suche with his prince, that in matters of greate ymportance wherin no creature durste once move the king, for feare of displeasure or moving the kinges pacience or otherwise for troubeling his mynde, than was my lorde Cranmer moste violentelie by the hole counsaile obtruded and thruste oute, to undertake that danger and perill in hande; as, besides many tymes, I remember twise he servid the counsailes expectation withoute all hope.

The firste tyme was when he stayed the king's determinate mynde and sentence, in that he fullie purposed to sende the ladye Mary his daughter unto the Tower, and there to suffer as a subjecte, by cause she wolde not obey unto the lawes of the realme in refusyng the bishopp of Rome's authoritie and religion.[a] Whose stey in that behalf, the kinge than saied unto the L. Cranmer, shoulde be to his utter confusion at the lengethe.[b]

Th'other dangerous attemptate was in the disclosing the unlawfull behaviour of quene Katheren Howarde towardes the king in keping unlawfull[c] company with Durrante her servante;[d] for the kinges affection was so mervelously sett appon that gentilwoman as it was never knowne that he had the like to any woman, so that no man durste take in hande to open to hym that wounde, being in greate

---

[a] The lady Mary's overt act of disobedience to her father consisted in her refusal to relinquish the title of Princess, with which he had previously invested her. The struggle occurred soon after queen Anne Boleyne had given birth to the lady Elizabeth, in the year 1533.

[b] to his—lengethe *in second hand over an erasure. The words erased seem to have been:* one of theym shoulde see cause to repente.

[c] unlawfull *in second hand.*

[d] Francis Derham.

perple[x]itie howe he wolde take yt. And than the counsaile hadd noo other refuge but unto my lorde Cranmer, who with overmoche ymportunitie gave the charge, which was done with suche circumspection, that the king gave over his affections unto reason, and wraught mervelous colorablie for the triall of the same.

Nowe, as concernyng the maner and order of his hospitalitie and house-keping. As he was a man abandoned from all kynde of avarice, so was he contente to maynteyne hospitalitie both liberallie and honorablie, and yet not surmountyng the limites of his revenewes, having more respecte and foresighte unto the iniquitie of the tyme, than (then) being inclynyd to pull and spoile frome the clergie, than to his owne private commoditie. For els, yf he hadd not so don, he was right suer that his successors sholde have hadd asmoche revenewes lefte unto theym, as were lefte unto the late abbeys; specially considering that the landes and revenewis of the said abbeys being nowe utterlie consumed and spredd abrode, and for that there remaynid no more exercise to set on wourcke our newe officers, both surveyors, auditors, and receyvors, it was high tyme to shewe an example of liberall hospitalitie; for, although theis said wourkemen, onelie brought upp and practized in subverting of monasteriall possessions, hadd brought that kinde of hospitalitie unto utter confusion, yet ceasesid not thei also to untermynde (undermine) the prince by divers persuasions, for hym also to overthrowe the honorable estate of the clergie. And, bycause thei wolde lay a suer foundation to buylde thair purpose apon, thei founde meanes to putt into the kinges headde, that th'archebisshopp of Canterbury kepte no hospitalitie or house correspondente unto his revenewis and dignitie, but solde his wooddes, and by greate incombes and fynes maketh money to purches landes for his wife and his children. And to th'intente the king shoulde with more facilitie beleve this information sir Thomas Semer, the duke of Somerset's brother, being of the privie chambre, (took *altered to*) was procured to take this mattier in hande. And before he informyd the king therof, he blastid it abrode in the courte, insomoche that [myne eldeste brother, being one of [a]] the gentilmen ussers, and he fell oute for the same, my brother declaring that his reporte was manifeste false, aswell for the keping of his house as for purchasyng of landes for his wife and children. This notwithstanding, mr. Semour went thoroughe with his said information, and declaird unto the king as is before declaird. The kinge, heringe this tale, with the sequele (that was that it was mete for the bisshopps nott to be troubeled ne vexed with temporall affaires in ruling thair honours, lordeshipps, and manours, but rather, they having an honeste pension of money yerlie alowed unto theym for thair hospitalitie, shoulde surrender unto the kinges majestie all thair royalties and temporalties,) saied, "I do mervaile that it ys saied that my lorde of Canterbury shoulde kepe no good hospitalitie, for I have harde the contrary." And so with a fewe wourdes moo in commendation of my L., as one that litle regardid the sute, but yet, as it appered afterwards, something smelling what thei wente aboute, lefte of any farther to talke of that mattier, and convertid his communication to another purpose. Notwithstanding, within a moneth after, whither it was of chaunce or of purpose it ys unknowne, the king, going to dyner, callid mr. Seymour unto hym and said, "Goo ye straight waies unto Lambeth, and bydd my lorde of Canterbury come and speake with me, at ij of the clocke at after noone." Incontynently mr. Seymour cam to Lambeth, and being brought into the halle by the porter, it chaunced the halle was sett to dyner, and when he was at the skrene, and perceyvid the hall furnisshed with iij principall messes, besides the reste of the tables thoroughlie sett, [b] having a giltie conscience of his untrue reporte made to the king, [c] recoylid backe and wolde

---

[a] These words have been erased in the MS. and the words "my brother" in the next line altered to "they," in order to suppress the name of mr. William Morice.

[b] Foxe has rewritten this passage thus—"the hall, which was thoroughly furnished and set, both with the household servants and strangers, with *four* principall head messes of officers, as daily it was accustomed to be." The MS. had originally iiij, but the first i. has been erased with a knife.

[c] made to the king *in second hand*.

have gone into my lorde by the chapell awaie. Mr. Nevill[a] being stewarde, perceyving that, rose uppe and wente after hym, and declaird unto hym that he could not goom [sic] that wey, and so brought hym backe unto my lorde thoroute the halle; and when he came to my lorde, and had don his message, my lorde caused hym to sit downe and dyne with hym. But, making a shorte dyner bycause he would bring the kinge wourde againe of his message, he departid and[b] came to the king before he was rysen frome the table. When he came to the kinges presence, saied the kinge, "Will my lorde of Canterbury come to us?" "He will wayte on your majestie, (saied mr. Seimour,) at ij of the clocke." Than saied the king, "Had my lorde dyned before ye came?[c]" "Noo forsothe, (saied mr. S.) for I founde hym at dyner." "Well, (saied the king,) what chere made he you?" With those wourdes mr. Seymour knelid downe and besought the kingis majestie of pardon. "What is the matter?" (saied the king.) "I do remember (saied mr. Seymour,) that I tolde your highnes that my lorde of Canterburye kepte no hospitalitie correspondent unto his dignitie; and nowe I perceyve that I did abuse your highnes with an untroth, for, besides your grace's house, I thincke he be not in the realme of none estate or degre that hath suche a halle furnysshed, or that fareth more honorablie at his awne table." "Ah! (quod the king,) have you espied your awne faulte nowe?" "I assuer your highnes, (said mr. S.) it is not somoche my faulte as other mennys who semed to be honeste men that enformede me herof, but I shall hensforthe the woursse truste theym whiles thei lyve." Than saied the king, "I knowe your purposes well enoughe; you have hadd emonge you the commodities of the abbeis, whiche you have consumed some with superfluous apparell, some at dice and cardes and other ungratious

---

[a] "Richard Nevel, gentleman, the steward of the houshold." (Foxe) He was the son of sir Alexander Neville of Nottinghamshire, and brother to sir Anthony Neville; and his son Thomas Neville, D. D., became dean of Canterbury in 1597. See Hasted, History of Kent, folio edit. iv. 534, 591.

[b] he departid and, *in second hand.* [c] before ye came, *in second hand.*

rule, and nowe you wolde have the bishopp landes and revenewes to abuse likewise.[a] Yf my lorde of Canterbury kepe suche a halle as you sey, neither being terme nor parliament, he ys metelie well visited at those tymes I warrante you. And if th'other bisshopps kepe the like for thair degre, thei had not nede to have any thing taken frome theym, but rather to be aided and holpen. And therfore sett your harte at reste; there shall no suche alteration be made whiles I lyve" (quod the kinge). So that in very dede, where some had pennyd certeyn bookes for the altering of that estate in the nexte parliamente, thei durste never bring them forthe to be redde. Wherapon also it came to passe that when the kinge understode that, contrary unto the reporte, my lorde C. hadd purchasid no maner of landes, his highnes was contente apon th'onelie motion of D. Buttes, without my L. C. knowledge, that he shoulde have that abbey in Notynghamshere whiche his wife nowe enjoyeth,[b] to hym and his beires.[c]

Thusmoche I have declarid concernyng mr. Seymour's practise, to th'intente men may understande that my lord C. hospitalitie was[d] a meane to stcye the estate of the clergie in thair possessions.

And here I muste answer for my lorde C. againste certeyne objections whiche arr in divers mennys heddes, that by his meanes all the prefermentes, offices, and fermes arr so given and lett oute, that his successours have nothing to give or bestowe appon thair frendes and servantes, nor that suche hospitalitie can be kepte by reason of his decay in letting goo suche thinges as shoulde have

[a] Parker has marked this paragraph (*Than —— likewise*) with a stroke of his red pencil down the margin. Foxe has translated the latter clause—"and now that all is gone, you would fain have me make another chevance with the bishops' lands, to accomplish your greedy appetites."

[b] Todd thinks this was a mistake, and that Cranmer's widow enjoyed no abbey in Nottinghamshire, but merely the rectories of Aslacton and Whatton, which had belonged to the abbey of Welbeck. Life of Cranmer, ii. 513. There is, however, extant a petition of Thomas Cranmer, son of the archbishop, stating that his father had purchased of Henry VIII. and Edward VI. the monastery of Kirkstall and nunnery of Arthington (Ibid. p. 515,) which is perhaps the purchase to which Morice refers.

[c] This paragraph also is scored with the red pencil.

[d] was *in second hand*.

maynteynid provision of houscholde. But to answer this in a fewe wourdes before I descend to any particular declaration: It is mooste true, that yf he hadd[a] nott well behavid hymself towards his prince and the worlde, his successours shold not [have] byn combered with any pece of temporall revenewe, either in landes, wooddes, or other revenewes. And I praie God that thei may maynteyne, in this mylde and quiete tyme, that whiche he in a moste dangerous worlde did upholde and lefte to his successours. Yet for better declaration in answering those objections, it ys to be considerid that when he enterid unto his dignitie, every man aboute the kinge made meanes to get some reversion of ferme or of other office of hym; insomoche, the king hymself made meanes to hym for one or ij thinges before he was consecratid, as for the ferme of Wyngham barton,[b] whiche was grauntid unto sir Edwarde Baynton knight[c] for iiij^{xx}xix yeres. When my lorde perceyvid that suche sutes as he grauntid to the king and the quene men wolde nedes have a hundreth yere save one, he wrote to the chapiter of Christes churche,[d] and willed them in any condition nott to confirme any moo of his grauntes of leaces which were above xxj yeres. By this meanes moche sute was stopped, so that in very dede he gave oute his leaces but for xxj yeres, whiche wolde not satisfie the gredie appetites of some men. And therfore thei founde a provision for it; for, when my lorde hadd let oute certeyne goodlie farmes at Pynner, Heyes, Harrow-on-the-hill, Mortelake, &c., to the nombre of x or xij fermes, for xxj yere, taking no maner of fyne for theym, all theis fermes by and by were put into an exchange for the kinge. And the kinge hadd nott them in his poss[ess]ion vj daies, but thei were my lorde Northes and other

[a] hadd *in second hand.*

[b] The manor of Wingham was one of the residences of the archbishops of Canterbury (see Hasted, History of Kent, folio edit. iii. 695), but was one of those exchanged to the crown in 29 Hen. VIII., as mentioned in a subsequent note.

[c] Sir Edward Baynton was vice-chamberlain to queen Anne Boleyne, and it is said to two others of king Henry VIII.'s queens. See Latimer's Works, (Parker Society,) ii. 322. He is mentioned in a letter of Hooper in 1546 as one of the chief supporters of the Gospel in England then recently deceased. Zurich Letters, 1846, iii 36.

[d] *i. e.* Canterbury.

mennys;[a] and thei were not paste one yere in thair possessions but that the reversion of every [of] theym was solde for more yers, some for c^{li}, some for cc^{li}, and some for more and some for lesse, making swepestake of altogethers.

And so was my lorde used in all thinges almoste that he did lett oute for xxj^{ti} yeres, by meanes wherof justice Hales[b] and other of his counsaile lernid in the lawe adviced him to let oute his fermes for many yeres, whiche might be a meanes that thei shoulde not be so moche desired in exchanges as thei be, for thos fermes as came to my lorde came with yeres enough apon thair backes. And so uppon this consideration my lorde was fayne to alter his purpose in letting of his fermes. Wherapon he did lett S. Gregoris[c] in Canterbury to mr. Nevill, the Priory of Dover, Chislett Parke, and Curleswood Parke, with other, for so many yeres as he did; of purpose to stay them, or els he had gon withoute theym one tyme [or] other. And as I harde sey syns your grace[d] was electe Curleswood Parke was in exchange, and the rente therof paied for one halfe yere unto the quenys use; but so sone as thei understode that thei were so many yere to come in it, it was reversid to the archebisshopricke againe. So that herby partelie maie be perceivd in what estate my lorde Cranmer stoode with his landes. And as towching the diminisshing

[a] Edward lord North, sometime treasurer and afterwards chancellor of the court of augmentations, was one of the greatest traffickers in church lands.

[b] Sir James Hales, of the Dungeon, Canterbury, (see Hasted, iv. 440,) made one of the judges of the common pleas and knighted 1547. He suffered persecution for his religious principles under Mary, after having been especially signalised among the judges for his loyalty at her accession; and, his mind becoming impaired, committed suicide in the Fleet prison. See the treatise on this catastrophe written by bishop Hooper, printed by Strype, Eccles. Memorials, iii. Appendix xxiv. Hooper's Works, (Parker Soc.) ii. 374; and for the judge's biography see Foss's Judges, vol. v. p. 370.

[c] The archbishop became possessed of the late priory of St. Gregory's in Canterbury in exchange for the late abbey of St. Radegund near Dover. Richard Neville of Canterbury esquire, (see before, p. 262,) died possessed of the lease in 5 Edw. VI., and by his will gave it, after his wife's death, to Alexander Neville esquire his son. Hasted, iv. 634.

[d] *i. e.* archbishop Parker, to whom these anecdotes were addressed by Morice. He was elected archbishop Aug. 1, 1559.

of his rentes, houses, and other comodities for the provision of his hospitalitie, if all thinges be well pondered, he hath lefte the same in better estate then he fonde it.

For as towching his exchanges, men ought to consider with whome he had to do, specially with suche a prince as wolde not be brydeled, nor be againste-said[a] in any of his requeste, oneles men wolde danger altogethers.[b] I was by when Otteford and Knolle was given hym.[c] My lorde, mynding to have reteynid Knoll unto hymself, saied that it was to small a house for his majestie. "Marye, (saied the king,) I had rather have it than this house, (meanyng Otteforde,) for it standith of a better soile. This house standith lowe, and is rewmatike, like unto Croydon, where I colde never be withoute sycknes. And as for Knoll standeth on a sounde, perfaite, holsome grounde.[d] And if I should make myne abode here, as I do suerlie mynde to do nowe and than, I myself will lye at Knolle, and moste of my house shall lye at Otteforde." And so by this meanes bothe those houses were delivered upp into the kingis handes; and as for Otteforde,[e] it ys a notable greate and ample house, whose reparations yerlie stode my lorde in more than men wolde

[a] *Against-said*, hence the word *gainsay*.

[b] oneles —— altogethers, *in second hand*.

[c] By indenture, dated 30 Nov. 29 Hen. VIII. (1537) the archbishop and the prior and convent of Christ church in Canterbury conveyed to the king and his successors all those his manors of Otford, Wrotham, Bexley, Northflete, Maidstone, and Knoll, with other lands and appurtenances, as particularised by Hasted in his History of Kent, folio edition, i. 340 See a letter of Cranmer to Cromwell on this exchange, in Jenkyns, i. 203.

[d] Knole was granted in the reign of Edward VI. successively to the duke of Somerset and the duke of Northumberland. By queen Mary it was restored to the archbishop of Canterbury, then cardinal Pole; but, being conveyed to him personally, it returned to the crown on his death, and when queen Elizabeth stayed there for five days in 1573 it was called her own house. (Progresses of Queen Elizabeth, i. 333, 347.) She granted it first to her favourite Leicester, and it afterwards became the property of the Sackvilles, under whose care this interesting specimen of ancient magnificence has been handed down little altered to our own times.

[e] The palace of Otford had been largely repaired by Cranmer's immediate predecessors Deane and Warham; but soon after it came into lay hands, it was allowed to fall into total ruin. The Duke of Northumberland was resident there towards the close of the reign of Edward VI.; and it became the property of his son-in-law sir Henry Sidney.

thincke. And so likewise did Maidestone, which had no maner of comoditie to belonge unto yt. And I am suer that after certeyn exchanges past betwene the kinge and hym, there was aboute a c. merke a yere, or thereaboute, alowid unto hym in his latter exchanges for recompence of his parckes and chaces. And yet those parkes and chases, besides the provision of his venson, stode hym yerely in moche more money, by reason of the patentes and fees belonging unto them, than he by any meanes els gate by theym; for, as for Curleswoode, it stode hym in xxt^j nobles a yere fee, and yet there was no gaine in yt, but only coneys, whiche the keper had also in his patente, so that the archebisshopp by suppressing of that, and raising that smale rente it paieth, may spende therby vij^{li} a yere more than it was accustumed to paie towardes [the revenue] of the archebisshoppricke. And towching Chislet Parcke,[a] it came to my lorde in exchange for viij^{li} a yere, and the fe[r]mour paieth x^{li}, so that therby is gotten xl^s a yere, wherefore it cannot be indifferentlie gathered that my lorde in preferryng his friendes unto theis thinges hath any whitte hindered the revenewe of the bisshoppricke.

And as towching pasture and medowe for the provision of his house both at Croydon and aboute Canterbury, Forde, and Cheslett, there arr thrise so moche medowe, pasture, and mersshe, than was lefte unto hym.

And as for the sale of his woodes,[b] like as he was dryven to exchange theym and sell theym for to maynteyne his hospitalitie, specially having almoste xxti yeres togethers lernyd men contynu-allie sytting with hym in commission for the trying oute and setting

---

[a] Chislet Park, seven miles from Canterbury, had belonged to the abbat of St. Augustine's. It was granted in 29 Hen. VIII., in exchange for other lands, to the archbishop and his successors. Hasted, iii. 627.

[b] Aylmer bishop of London was afterwards, from necessity or choice, a great destroyer of timber, and in consequence acquired the punning nickname of *Mar-elm*. Such satirical transpositions were not unusual. Archbishop Grindal's name was converted, by no less a person than the poet Spenser, into *Al-grind;* and sir Richard Sackville, chancellor of the augmentations, the careful father of the lord treasurer Dorset, was thought to be properly characterised when his name was inverted into *Fill-sack*.

forthe of the religion receyvid, and for the discussing of other mattiers in controvercie, some of them dailie at diete with hym, and some evermore lying in his house, so provided he againe like wooddes more commodious for his houses; as the Blene woodes [a] belonging to St. Austen's, and Pyne woodde, and others, whiche be knowne well enough.

As towching provision for corne oute of Chislett Courte and in other places, yt is uncredeble what a busynes he hadd, and [b] ado with sir Christopher Hales [c] for that ferme and corne, who c[h]alenged it of the king by promise, and so wolde have defeatid my lorde therof, had not the kinge very benignelie stande of his syde, and it ys no smale revenewe to have yerlie so moche corne, bothe wheate, malte, and ottes, of so meane a price.

And therfore lett men leave of that reporte of hym that he was not beneficiall unto his successours. Other bisshopps some of them loste hole manours and lordeshipps, withouten any exchaunce attall. Thusmoche my conscience hath compellid me to sey in defence of my lorde and mr. his good name, whome I knewe to take as moche care for his successours in th'archebisshoppricke as ever did archebisshopp or shall do, and wolde asmoche have advaunced the same, yf the iniquitie of the worlde wolde have permitted hym.

Nowe, finallie, concernyng his behaviour towardes his familie, I thincke there was never suche a maister emonges men, both fearid and entierlie belovid; for, as he was a man of moste gentill nature, voide of all crabbed and churlishe conditions, so he coulde abide no suche qualities in any of his servantes. But if any suche outeragiousness were in any of his men or familie, the correction of thos enormyties he alwaies lefte to the ordering of his officers, who wekelie kepte

[a] The forest of Blean was given to the church of Canterbury by Richard I. in the first year of his reign. (Somner's Canterbury, 4to., 1640, p. 221.) It extended from the suburbs of the city, where there is a church named St. Cosmos and Damian of the Blean, to the neighbourhood of Feversham, where lies the parish of Boughton under the Blean.

[b] and *in second hand*.

[c] Sir Christopher Hales, solicitor-general 1525, attorney-general 1529, master of the rolls 1536, died 1541. Hasted, History of Kent, ii. 576; Foss, History of the Judges, v. 183.

a counting-house. And if any thing universallie were to be reformed or talked of on that daie, whiche comonlie was Friday, the same was putt to admonition. And if it were a faulte of any particuler man, he was callid forthe before the company, to whome warnyng was given, that if he so used hymself after iij monitions he should lose his service.[a]

There was an infamy of hym, that he shoulde have byn an osteler, whiche the ignorante popishe preistes for very malice hadd published againste hym, saying that he had no maner of lernyng attalle more than ostelers arr woute to have; and this rumour sprange of that, that when he hadd maried his firste wife, being reader than of Buckingham colledge,[b] he did putt his wif to borde in an inne at Cambridge. And he resorting thether unto her in the inne, some ignorante preiste named hym to be the osteler, and his wif the tapster.[c] This brute than began. But it moche more was quickened when he was archebisshopp than before. Insomoche that a preiste farr northe, about Scarbarowe, syttyng emonges his neighbours at the alehouse and talking of the archebisshopp Cranmer, divers men there moche commending hym, "What! (saied the preiste,) make ye somoche of hym? he was but an osteler, and hath as moche lernyng as the gooslynges of the grene that goo yender," quod the preiste. Appon whiche wourdes the honest[d] men of the parishe, whiche

[a] Here the remainder of the MS. page 436 is covered by a strip of paper containing six lines, which is all that has been preserved of the leaf which in Morice's original came between the pages numbered (by Parker) 436 and 437. Probably Parker cut away the the parts now wanting, as thinking them of little general interest. Some rash hand has partially raised the patch, so that one can read a few words beneath. The text ran: "And suerlie there [was never any?] committed to the porter's lodge oneles it were [for?] sheding of bloodde, picking, or stealing." The same subject seems to have been continued at the bottom of the opposite page.

[b] Now Magdalene college.

[c] It may be presumed that originally an *hosteler* was the master of on hostel or inn, of which term *host* was an abbreviation. At the period before us the hosteler appears to have been the principal servant or chamberlain, (see a former note in p. 100,)—whilst the function of serving liquor was usually performed by a woman, whence we read so much of alewives. In a third stage, the term ostler was transferred exclusively to servants in the stable.

[d] honest *second hand*.

harde theis wourdes, gave information to my lorde Crumwell of that his slanderous wourdes. The preiste was sent for before the counsaile, and caste into the Fleete. My L. Cranmer not being that daie emong the counsaile nor hearing no maner of wourde of the preistes accusation, it chaunced the preiste to lie in the Fleete viij or ix weekes, and nothing saied unto hym. He than made sute (by one named Chercey, a grocer dwelling within Ludgate, nowe yet alyve, and uncle as I suppose to the preiste,) unto my lorde C. for his deliverance. This Charcy brought the copie of the preist's accusation frome my lorde Crumwell's house, wherby it planly appered that there was nothing laied unto the preiste but those wourdes againste my lorde Cranmer: and therfore besoughte my L. C. to helpe hym oute of prison, for it hadd putt hym to greate chargis lying there, and he had a benefice whiche was unservid in his absence, and saied that he was very sory that he hadd so unhonestlie abusid hymself towardes his grace. Wherapon my lorde Cranmer sent to the Fleete for the preist.[b] Whan he became before my lorde, saied my lorde to hym, "It is tolde me that you be prisoner in the Fleete for calling me an osteler, and reporting that I have no more lernyng than a goseling. Did you ever see me before this daie?" "No, forsothe," quod the preiste. "What ment you than to call me an osteler, and so to deface me emonge your neighbours?" The preiste made his excuse, and saied he was overseen with drincke. "Well, (saied my L. C.,) now ye be come, you may appose me, to knowe what lernyng I have; begynne in gramar yf you will, or els in philosophie and other sciences, or divinitie." "I beseche your grace to pardon me, (quod the preist,) I have no maner of lernyng in the Laten tongue, but altogether in Englishe." "Wel, than, (saied my lorde,) yf you will not appose me, I will appose you.

---

[a] Foxe says that the archbishop "*sent his ring* to the warden of the Fleet, willing him to send the prisoner unto him, with his keeper, at afternoon," and that the parson was brought into the garden at Lambeth, where the archbishop received him, sitting under the vine. This tale, like other parts of the original, is considerably worked up and amplified by Foxe.

Arr you not wonte to reade the Bible?" quod my lorde. "Yes, that wee do dailie," saied the prieste. "I praie you tell me, (quod my lorde than,) who was Davides father?" The preiste stode still, and saied, "I cannot suerlie tell your grace." Than saied my lord againe, "Yf you cannott tell me, yet declare unto me who was Salamon's father." " Suerly, (quod the preiste,) I am nothing attall seene in those geneolagies." " Than I perceyve (quod my L.) howsoever you have reported of me that I hadd no lernyng, I can nowe beare you witnes that you have none attall. There arr suche a sorte of you in this realme that knowith nothing, nor will knowe nothing, butt sitt appon your alebenche and slander all honeste and lernyd men. Yf you hadd butt common reason in your headdes, you, that have named me an osteler, you might well knowe, that the king, having in hand one of the hardeste questions that was movid oute of the scriptures theis many yeres, wolde not sende an osteler unto the b. of [Rome][a] and to the emperour's counsaile, and other princes, to answer and dispute in that so harde a question, even emonges the hoole collidge of cardynalls and the Roote [b] of Rome. By all likelyhodd the king lacked moche the helpe of lernid men, that was thus dryven to sende an osteler on suche a vioage, or els his majestie hath many idle preistes withoute witt or reason, that can so judge of the prince and the counsaile and of the waightie mattiers of the realme. God amende ye! (said he,) and gett ye home to your cure, and frome hensforth lerne to be an honeste man, or at leaste a reasonable man." The preiste, lamenting his folie, went his waie into the countrie, and my L. C. dischargid hym [c] oute of the Fleet, bycause there was no mattier against hym but that whiche onelie concernyd my L. C. My lorde Crumwell within iiij daies after cam to my L. C., and sware by a great othe that the popisshe knaves shoulde pycke oute his eies and cutt his throote before he wolde any more rebuke theym for slanderyng of hym. " I hadd thought

[a] The *Rota*.
[b] Either R has been hidden by the binding, or Rome omitted altogether.
[c] hym *second hand*.

that the knave preiste whiche you have dischargid and sente home shoulde have recantid at Paules crosse on Sunday nexte." "Yea, mary, (quod my L. C.,) you wolde have all the worlde knowe by that meanes that I was an osteler in deede." "What maner of blockeheddes wolde so thinck?" quod my lorde Crumwell. "To(o) many papistes, (quod my L. C.) Howbeit, (quod he,) you have caused the poore preiste to spend all that he hath in prison, and wolde you nowe put hym to open[a] shame too? He ys not the firste, not by v^c of them, that hath callid me so, and therefore I will nott nowe begynne to use extremitie againste this prieste.[b] I perceyve he ys sory for yt." "Well, (quod my lorde Crumwell,) yf you [do] not care for it[c] no more doo I; but I warrante you one daie, yf thei may, they will make you and me both as vile as ostelers." This I repeted to declare his lenytie and promptnes to remitte notable offences; howbeit, it should have byn placed before yf I hadd rememberid it.

Thus I have hastelie pennyd suche thinges as came to my memory synce Satterdaie laste, beseching your grace to take it in good parte, being certeynlie assuryd that I have devised nothing of myn hedde as concernyng the very mattier.

I have lefte oute here where he was maried, and the hole ende of his lif and doinges concernyng King Henry's divorcement, by cause it ys at large towched in the boke of the Actes and Monumentes of the Churche, speciallie from his begyninge, fo. 1470.[d] And of his trouble and vexation for religion, and the maner of his death, &c.

[a] open *in second hand*. [b] this preiste *in second hand*. [c] for it *in second hand*.
[d] This refers to the first edition of Foxe's great work, printed in 1563.

X.

CRANMER AND CANTERBURY SCHOOL.
BY RALPH MORICE.

This is another of the communications made by Ralph Morice to Foxe, in addition to those already enumerated. It was not published by the martyrologist: but is introduced (in a modernised form) into Strype's Memorials of Cranmer, p. 88. Strype was not aware of its authorship.

[MS. Harl. 419, fol. 115.]

At what tyme the cathedral churche of Canterburye, newlie erected, altered and changed frome monckes to seculer men of the clergie, in the time of kinge Henry the viij[th], as to prebendaries, canons, peticanons, queresters, and scholers, there were present at that erection Thomas Cranmer archebisshopp of Canterbury, the L. Riche chaunceller of the courte of the Augmentacion of the revenewes of the crown, sir Christopher Hallis knight the kynges attorney, sir Anthony Sencteleger knight, with dyvers other commissioners; and taking upon them to nominate and electe suche conveniente and apte persons as sholde serve for the furnyture of the said cathedrall churche according to the newe foundacion, it came to passe that when thei sholde electe the children of the grammer scole, there were of the commissioners mo than one or twoo whiche wolde have none admitted but younger brethren and gentilmenys sonnes; as for other husbende mennys children, thei were more mete (thei saied) for the plough and to be artificers than to occupie the place of the lernyd sorte. So that thei wisshed none els to be putt to scole but onelie gentilmennys children. Whereunto that moste reverend trary mynde, saied that "he thought it not indifferent[a] so to order the mattier, for (saied he) pore mennys children arr many tymes enduyd with more synguler giftes of nature, which are also the giftes of God, as with eloquence, memorie, apte pronunciacion, sobrictie, with suche like, and also commonly more gyven to applie thair studie, than ys the gentilmannys sonne delicatelie educated." Whereunto it was on the other parte replied, that it was mete for the plowe mannys sonne to go to plowe, and the artificer's sonne to applie the trade of his parentes vocation, and the gentilmenys children arr mete to have the knowledge of govermente and rule in the common welth; for we have as moche nede of plowe men as on any other state, and all sortes of men maie not goo to scole. "I graunte (quod th'archebisshopp,) moche of your meanyng herin, as nedefull in a common wealth; but yet utterlie to exclude the plowe mannys sonne and the poore manys sonne from the benefite of lernyng, as though thei were unworthie to have the gyftes of the holie Goste bestowed apon them as well as apon others, ys asmoche to sey as that almightie God sholde not be at libertie to bestowe his greate giftes of grace apon any person, nor no where els but as we and other men shall appoynte them to be enployed according to our fansey, and not according to his most godlie will and pleasure; who gyveth his giftes both of lernyng and other perfections in all sciences, unto all kinde and states of people indifferentelie; even so doeth he many tymes withdrawe frome theym and thair posteritie againe those beneciall giftes, yf thei be not thanckefull. Yf we sholde shitt up into a straite corner the bountifull grace of the holie Goste, and therapon attempte to buylde our fanseis, we shold make as perfaite a worke therof as those that toke apon them to buylde the Tower of Babelon; for God wolde so provide that the ospring of our best borne children sholde peradventure become moste unapte to lerne, and very doltes, as I myself have seene no smalle nombre of them verie dull and withoute almaner of capacitie; and, to saie the trueth, I take it that none of us all here being gentilmen borne (as I thincke) but hadd

[a] *i. e.* fair or equitable.

our begynnyng that wey from a lowe and base parentage; and thorough the benefite of lernyng and other civile knowledge for the moste parte all gentil ascende to thair estate." Than it was againe answered, that the moste parte of the nobilitie came up by feate of armes and martiall actes. "As though (quod the archebısshopp,) that the noble captayne was always unfurnisshed of good lernyng and knowledge to persuade and dissuade his army rethorically, whiche rather that wey is broughte unto authoritie than els his manly lokes. To conclude, the [a] pore mannys sonne by paynestaking for the moste parte wilbe lernyd, when the gentilman's sonne will not take the payne to gett yt; and we arr taught by the scriptures, that almightie God raiseth upp from the dongehill and setteth hym in high authoritie; and, when so it pleaseth hym of his divine providence, deposeth princes unto a right humble and poore estate. Wherfore yf the gentilman's sonne be apte to lernyng, lett hym be admitted; yf not apte, lett the poore mannys childe apte enter his rowme—" with such like wordes in effecte.

[a] *MS.* to.

XI.

THE ANSWERS OF MR. THOMAS LAWNEY.

These anecdotes are written by Ralph Morice upon the same sheet with his account of the conversion of Latimer, as already stated in p. 237.

Little is known of the witty master Lawney: but that little is to the effect that he was one of the party of students of New college at Oxford, who were among the earliest welcomers of the Protestant doctrines. Foxe mentions him as "Thomas Lawney, chaplain of the house, prisoner with John Frith." He is said to have afterwards enjoyed preferment in Kent.

[MS. Harl. 422, f. 87.]

Concerning the vj. Articles. The answer of mr. Thomas Lawney unto my olde lord of Northfolke, concernyng preistes' wyves.

At what tyme the vj. articles were paste by acte of parliament, more by the authoritie of a parliament than by the authoritie of the worrde of God, it chaunced that my lord of Northfolke mett with mr. Lawe(ney), a preacher at that tyme in Kent, whose chapleyn he was in tymes paste. "Ah! mr.[a] Lawney, (quod the duke, knowing hym of olde moche to favour priestes' matrymoneys,) whither may preistes nowe have wyfes or noo?" quod the duke. "Yf it please your grace, (quod Lawney,) I cannott well tell whither preistes maie have wyfes or noo; but well I woott, and I am suer of it, for all your acte, that wifes will have preestes." "Harken, maisters, (quod the ducke,) howe this knave scorneth our acte, and maketh it not worthe a flie! Well, I see by yt that thou wilt never forgett thyne olde tryckes." And so the duke, and such gentilmen as were with him, went awaie merelie lawghing at mr. Lawny's sodden and apte answer.

[a] *Misprinted* my *in Strype's Memorials of Cranmer, p.* 35.

Concerning Bishop Stokisley, bisshop of London.[a]

The lyke fyne answer he made of the busshopp Stokisley's answer made to my lorde of Canterbury his lettres requiryng his parte of the translation of the New Testament.

My lorde Cranmer, mynding to have the New Testament thoroughlie corrected, devided the same into ix or x partes,[b] and caused it to be written at large in paper bokes and sent unto the best lernyd bishopps, and other lernyd men, to th' intent they sholde make a perfect correction therof, and when thei hadd done to sende them unto hym at Lambeth by a day lymyted for that purpose. It chanced that the Actes of the Apostelles were sent to bisshopp Stokisley to oversee and correcte, than bisshopp of London. When the day came every man hadd sentt to Lambeth thair partes correcte,[c] onlie Stokisley's portion wanted.[d] My lorde of Canterbury wrote to the bisshopp lettres for his parte, requiring to delyver them unto the bringer therof his secretary.[e] Bisshopp Stokisley being at Fulham receyved the lettres, unto the whiche he made this answer, "I marvaile what my lorde of Canterbury meaneth, that thus abuseth the people in gyvyng them libertie to reade the scriptures, which doith nothing else but infecte them with heryses. I have bestowed

[a] John Stokisley, bishop of London from 1530 until his death in 1539, a great persecutor of heretics. See memoirs of him in Wood's Athenæ Oxon. (edit. Bliss,) ii. 747. There is a speaking portrait of him by Holbein in the possession of Her Majesty at Windsor castle: see Waagen, Treasures of Art in Great Britain, 1854, ii. 431. It has not been engraved.

[b] " Cranmer took an existing translation—Tyndale's, of course, for as yet there was no other." The Annals of the English Bible, by Christopher Anderson, 1845, i. 453.

[c] i. e. (in m dern grammar) corrected.

[d] " With regard to the portions actually returned to Cranmer, they must have formed a singular medley, and, had they remained in existence, must have forcibly illustrated the character of Cranmer's associates. But not one fragment remains, and it is well. They have been consigned to oblivion, with the vain efforts, in ancient times, of many who had taken in hand that for which they were not competent, and that of which God did not approve. Luke, i. 1." (Anderson's Annals of the English Bible, i. 454.) Bishop Gardyner, by his own account, on the 10th of June 1535, had finished the translation of Saint Luke and Saint John, " wherein I have spent a great labour." (Ibid. p. 446.)

[e] Namely, to Morice, the writer of this story.

never an hower apon my portion, nor never will; and therfore my lorde shall have his boke agame, for I will never be gyltie to bring the symple people into errour." My lord of Canterbury's servante toke the boke, and brought the same to Lambeth unto my lord, declaring my lord of London's answer. When my lord had perceyved that the bisshop hadd done nothing therm, " I marvaile (quod my lorde of Canterbury,) that my lorde of London ys so frowarde, that he will not do as other men do." Mr. Lawney stode by, and hearyng my lorde speake so moche of the bisshopp's untowardnes, saied, "I can tell your grace whie my lorde of London will not bestowe any labour or payne this wey. Your grace knoweth well (quod Lawney,) that his portion ys a pece of Newe Testament; and than he, being persuaded Christe had bequeth hym nothing in his testament, thought it mere madnes to bestowe any labour or payne where no gayne was to be gotten. And besides this, it is the Actes of the Apostells, whiche were symple poore felowes; and therfore my lord of London disdayned to have to do with any of thair actes." My lord of Canterbury and other that stode by coulde not forbere frome lawghter, to here mr. Lawney's accute invensyon, in answeryng to the bisshopp of London's frowarde answer to my lorde of Canterbury's lettres.

XII.

CHRONICLE OF THE YEARS 1532—1537, WRITTEN BY A MONK OF ST. AUGUSTINE'S, CANTERBURY.

The following brief Chronicle is that which Strype has mentioned in the Preface to his Memorials of Cranmer, as "Annals writ by an Augustine Monk of Canterbury," and cited in his Chapter V. and elsewhere in that work, as "an old Journal made by a monk of St. Augustine's, Canterbury;" also in his Ecclesiastical Memorials, vol. i. p. 206.

It gives a summary view of the leading events of our ecclesiastical history during the years above specified, combining with occurrences of which we have much fuller accounts the particulars of several transactions in the city of Canterbury, particularly the dissolution and dispersion of its religious communities, which are not elsewhere recorded. It may be noticed that Hasted in his "Remarkable Occurrences" in the history of Canterbury, Hist. of Kent, folio edit. iv. 433, has recorded none between the years 1520 and 1573.

[MS. Harl. 419, f. 112.]

. y well seene. (*The MS. is torn.*)

[The] year of our Lord 1532 Henry viij came to Canterb[ur]y the ix day [of October], who [the] xjth day of the same month sayled towardes Calice with [the n]obles of his kingdom[a]; and from thence went to Boloyne, wher of the king of Fraunce,[b] the king of Navary[c] and of the cardinalle of Rotomage[d] and the dolphin, and other famous men of France, with great reverence he was receaved; wher when he had remayned 2 dayes[e] he went againe to Calice, being accompanyed with the kinges of Fraunce and Navayre and other noble men of Fraunce, wher with kingly pompe they remayned.

---

[a] See the company enumerated particularly in The Chronicle of Calais, p. 41.
[b] Francis I.   [c] Henry d'Albret II.
[d] The cardinal of Lorraine, archbishop of Rouen.
[e] According to The Chronicle of Calais, p. 43, the King was nine days at Boulogne, from the 21st to 30th of October.

In this jorney peace and tranquilyty was concluded betwene these kings by a perpetualle league.

In the year of our Lorde 1533 the daughter of the earle of Wilshier, An Boleine, was proclaymed queene and crowned at Westminster the seconde day of Penticoast in the presence of the nobles of the kingdome, whear (as it was mete) a great feast was made, with great joy and gladnes.

The same yeare mr. Thomas Cranmer was made archbishop of Canterbury, who did forbyd that the worde of God shold be preached in the churches throwghout his dioces, and warned the rest of the bishops throwghout England to do the same.

The same year the 3 day of December Thomas Cranmer arch bishop of Canter[bury] receaved the pontificalle seat[a] in the monasterye of St. Trinety.

The same year a certayn nonne, called Elisabeth Barten,[b] by marveylows hipocrysy moked alle Kent and almost alle England, for which cause she was put into prison in London, wher she confessed many horrible thinges agaynst the king and the quene. This forenamed Elisabeth had many adherentes, but specialli doctor Bocking monke of Christes church in Canterbyry, which was her chiefe author in her dissimulation: which alle[c] at the last were accused of treason, heresye, and conspiracy, and so before the open crosse of St. Poule in London, and here also in the churchyard of the monastery [of] the Holy Trinitye, at the sermon time, they stode over the high seate, wher of the preacher they were grevosly rebuked for theyr horrible fact.

[a] *i. e.* was inthroned in the cathedral church, according to ancient usage.

[b] A summary of this well-known matter will be found in the volume of "Letters relating to the Suppression of the Monasteries," edited for the Camden Society by Mr. Thomas Wright, at p. 13, followed by several original papers relating to it.

[c] The culprits were altogether six in number: Elizabeth Barton, a nun of the house of St. Sepulchre at Canterbury; doctor Edward Bocking and Richard Dering, monks of the house of the Holy Trinity, or Christ church, Canterbury; Henry Gold, rector of St. Mary Aldermary in London; Hugh Rich, warden of the friars observants at Canterbury; and Richard Rigby, one of his brethren. See another account of their penance in the Chronicle of the Grey Friars of London, p. 37.

The same year Thomas Cranmer, archbishop, the ix day of Decembre began to go on visitation throughout alle his diocese.

In the year of our Lorde 1534 a certay.[a] . . . . . the xx day of Aprill the fifth day[b] call . . . . . . prison of London through all the streates . . . Bocking and his brother Jhon [Richard] Dering monkes of the Holy Trinitye at the place of execution called Tiburne, wher she and these monkes and also two brothers of the Minors suffered with the rest uppon the gallhouse for treason and heresye.

The same year of our [Lord] 1534, the brethren friers[c] wear expulsed from their conservance, from their seates and from their places throughout all England, for their disobedience towardes the kinges majestye.

The same year also, as well religiows as laymen bound themselves by an othe concernyng the succession of [issue born] betwene the queene Anne and our king (*altered to* K. Henry).

The same year thear were many heretiques in sundry places of England which did blaspheme the saintes and the worshipping of them, barking agaynst tithes, which neyther wold have fastinges nor pilgramagies.

The same year abowt Christmas it was graunted to the king in the parlyament, that the clergy showld paye to him yerely 30 thowsand markes for ever.

In the year of our Lord 1535 it was ordayned[d] and confirmed that the king showlde be the Supreme Head of the whole Church of Englande.

The same year, the clergy of England was admonished by the

[a] The paper is here torn.

[b] The execution of the holy maid and her followers was on the 5th of May, according to the Chronicle of the Grey Friars, p. 37. Mr. Wright *(ubi supra)* places it on the 20th of April, probably in consequence of Strype (Memorials of Cranmer, p. 22) having misapprehended the purport of this imperfect paragraph.

[c] The words "friers" is written above "brethren." It is probable that these notes were at first written in Latin, and translated.

[d] By act 26 Hen. VIII. cap. 1; Statutes of the Realm, iii. 492.

kinges commaundement[a] for to put forth altogether the name of Pope out of the canon and other places wher that name was written, and yet no man durst once name this word Pope, i. neyther to geve place to his authority, but with all theyr power in all thinges to resiste him, and also in sermons to bark agaynst his power, whiche hath been used many yeares before this time in this our kingdom.[b]

And also the same yeare Jhon Fisher, bishop of Rochester, and master Thomas More, being excellent well learned men, suffered death.

The same year also many Cartulienses suffered deth for disobedience towardes the kinges majestye.

[The sa]me yere, being 1534 (1535), the king sent many docteurs [of divini]tie and others throughout all England to visite all the [houses] of saynct Benedictes order, and all the monasteries [and nunneries] of every order, hospitalls, colledges, and chanteries, &c.; amongst whome, doctour Layghton,[c] being a professeur in the lawes, and the chiefest,[d] did visite this our house, mr. Bartlet[e] being hys scribe and of counsayll wyth hym, the 20 day of October.

In thys visitation, all men utterly renownced the name of the Pope, hys privilegies and exempt places, &c.

The same tyme the newe house of the prior of the church of saynct Saviour's[f] was set on fier and burnt, doctor Layghton the visitour, and mr. Bartlet the scribe, with others, being present, the xvj day of October at mydnight.

---

[a] By proclamation dated the 9th of June, which is printed in Foxe's Actes and Monuments.

[b] Some of the brethren of the writer's house, countenanced by the prior (Goldwell), were specially charged with resisting this change: "the sayde pryour badde takyne a collette ffor the bysshoppe of Rome by name of Pope, contrarye to his othe and a lawe made in that behalfe." Christopher Levyns to Crumwell, in Wright's collection, p. 90.

[c] Dr. Richard Layton, the writer of many of the "Letters relative to the Suppression of the Monasteries," edited by Mr. Wright.

[d] The principal visitors, under the direction of Crumwell the King's vicegerent or vicar-general, were doctors Layton, Legh, Petre, and London. See Strype, Eccles. Memorials, i. 206: and Mr. Wright's volume, *passim*.

[e] Richard Bartelot, who occurs in Mr. Wright's volume at pp. 59, 75.

[f] Or the Holy Trinity, Canterbury.

In the yere of our Lorde 1536, all the monasteries and religious howses through all England, that were not above the yerly revenew of 300 li. (all chardges deducted) were by acte of parliament given to the King's majestie to the amplifieng of hys crowne, and to hys successours for ever.

The same yeere was quene Anne Bulleine, the lorde Rochford hyr brother, mr. Norrice, mr. Weston, mr. Bruton,[a] and Marcas[b] committed to prison; and the xvij. daye of Maye, fyve of them were for treason put to execution.

The same yeere, Jane Semer, the daughter of the lorde Semer,[e] was maried to kynge Henry and crowned queene.

The same yere the fyrst and second mariages of the kynge, by the assent of all the parliament howse, were annichilate and made unlawfulle. But thys the thurde mariage was confirmed by them all to be good and lawfulle.

The same yere, the xxj. daye of July, kyng Henry came to Canterburie with the lady Jane the qweene, who in the monastery of Saynct Augustine was very honorably reseaved, the reverend father Thomas Goldwell[d] prior of Christes churche being present. Who from thence went to Dover to se the peere, to hys great charge and coste begonne.[e]

---

[a] Randle Brereton. [b] Mark Smeaton. [c] Sir John Seymour, a knight only.

[d] Thomas Goldwell, prior of Christ church, Canterbury, from 1515 until its dissolution in 1539, when a yearly pension of 80*l*. was assigned to him, together " with the office of one of the prebendaries there." He was the prior who received Erasmus on his visit to Canterbury, and is thus mentioned in the Colloquy on Pilgrimage for Religion's sake. " He appeared to me to be a man equally pious and judicious, nor unskilled in the Scotian theology (*i. e.* of the school of Duns Scotus.)"

A letter written by him to Crumwell relative to Elizabeth Barton is printed in Mr. Wright's collection, at p. 19. In another letter in the same volume (p. 90) addressed to Crumwell by Christopher Levyns, there are many grave charges against Goldwell, among the rest that he had murdered divers monks of his house.

[e] William Lambarde in his Perambulation of Kent, written in 1570, speaking of Dover, says that " now in our memorie, what by decay of the haven, which king Henrie the eight with the cost of 63,000 pounds upon a piere, but all in vaine, sought

284   NARRATIVES OF THE REFORMATION.

The same yere, the 20 and 21 daye of September, doctour Peter,[a] being sent of the lorde Cromwell to visite all the clergie throughout all Kent, dyd visite this abbey of Saynt Agustine; making inquierie of the observinge of the Injunctions which we in the fyrst visitation receved by doctour Leyghton.

The same yeare in the moneth of September was there a conspira[cy in the county] of Lincolne and in the North partes:[b] [to subdue which] were sent the duke of Norfolke, the [duke of Suf]folke, the earle of Derby, and the noble earle [of] Shrewsbury [with] an armie: who after that they had commoned of the matter, lyking the condicions of peace offered, were reconsiled to the kynges favour wythout any battayle stroken.

In the yere of our Lorde 1537 the xxiij day of February, the monasterie of Seynct Gregories[c] was suppressed and the chanons were expulsed: mr. Spilman and mr. Candish [d] being the kynges commissioners herunto appointed.

The same day, the church of Saynct Sepulchre,[e] by the autoritie of the same commission, and by the same commissioners, was

was brought in manner to miserable nakednesse and decay." (Edit. 1596, p. 147.) In the History of Dover, by the Rev. John Lyon, 4to. 1813, vol. i. p. 153, will be found an account of the works carried on in the reign of Henry VIII. for erecting a pier at Dover, which were commenced on St. Anne's day (July 26) 1533. See also a discourse written by Thomas Digges, esq. about 1582, in the Archæologia, vol. xi.; and " A Discourse of Sea Ports, principally of the Port and Haven of Dover, by Sir Walter Raleigh, published by Sir Henry Shears, 1700." 4to.

[a] William Petre, " who was then, if I mistake not, master of the faculties to the vicegerent, lord Crumwell, and afterwards secretary of state." Strype's Cranmer, p. 55. See Wright's Letters relating to the Suppression of the Monasteries.

[b] See Chronicle of the Grey Friars of London, p. 39.

[c] A priory of Black canons in Canterbury; see the Monasticon Anglic. new edit. vi. 614.

[d] Misprinted by Strype (Eccles. Memorials, i. 472) "mr. Spitman and mr. Candel." Thomas Spilman, of Canterbury, gentleman, was the grantee of the house of Grey Friars in that city, and of other church lands. The latter was William Cavendish, afterwards treasurer of the chamber, and a knight; see Collins's Peerage, *tit.* Devonshire.

[e] A house of Bénédictine nuns in Canterbury: see Monasticon Anglicanum, new edition, iv. 413; Hasted's Kent, folio edit. iv. 449. Elizabeth Barton had been a member of this house.

suppressed. The moinalls [a] notwithstandyng at that tyme were not removed, for they obtayned lycence to abyde there untill Easter, which notwithstanding scarlsly (scarcely) remayned one moneth afterwardes: so at the last the weeke before Easter they were expulsed.

The same yere, divers persons of Lincolneshire, which made the forenamed insurrection, and allso many persons of Yorkshiere, were put to death both there and allso at London about the tyme of Lent and Whitsontyde.[b] The captaynes of that conspiracie were the lorde Hussey, the lorde Darcie sonne of the lorde Tommas,[c] with other gentelmen of those parteis. The chiefest notwithstanding in that conspiracie was a certen lawyer whose name was Aske; a man of base parentage, yet of mervelous stomack and boldnes.

The same yere was it forbidden by the parlament and by the bishops, that the feast of S. Thomas the martyr should not be celebrated, nor of S. Lawrence, nor of divers others, the feastes of the xij Apostells excepted and of our Ladye, S. Michaell, and Mary Magdalen. Allso the feast of the Holy Crosse was forbydden to be celebrated, and that none should presume to kepe any of thease feastes holy, that is, they should rynge no bells, nor adorne theyr churches, [nor go in] procession, nor other such thinges as belong to festiv[als.]

The same yere dyed the noble lady Ka[therine.[d]]

The same yere the archbishop of Canterbury did not fast [on S. Thomas] even, but dyd eate fleshe, and dyd suppe in his [parlour with [e]] hys famulye, whiche was never seene before in all the coo..

The same yere [f] died the most noble qweene Jane, and was buried at Windsor.

---

[a] *i. e.* the nuns: misprinted " monks " by Strype, *ubi supra.*

[b] See the Chronicle of the Grey Friars of London, pp. 40, 41.

[c] The words " sonne of the lorde Tommas " must be a mistranscript. Lord Darcy's own name was Thomas. Strype printed these words as " son of the Lord L."

[d] Katharine of Arragon, then styled " princess dowager."

[e] These words are supplied from Strype, Mem. of Cranmer, p. 61.

[f] On the 24th of October, twelve days after the birth of Edward VI.

The yere of our Lorde 1538, the archbishop of Canterbury dyd reade the epistell of S. Paull to the Hebrues halfe the Lent in the chapter howse of the monasterie of the Holy Trinitie.

The same yere the monasterie of Abindon, by the consent of the abbot,[a] was given unto the kynges majestie, the moonkes therof being expulsed because of theyr slowthfulnes.

The same yere was the monasterie of Boxley suppressed,[b] and the fygure of the crosse called Roodrooffe (*blank in MS.*[c]) before all the people for certen slayghtes and false inv[entions] that were fownde in the same, was at Paul's crosse broken and cut in peaces, the bishop of Rochester [d] at the tyme making the sermon.

[a] The abbat of Abingdon, Thomas Pentecost alias Rowland, who had been one of the first to acknowledge the King's supremacy in 1534, surrendered his monastery on the 9th Feb. 1537-8, and for his ready compliance was allowed to retain for life his manor of Cumnor, where he died in the reign of Edward VI.

[b] Surrendered on the 29th June, 29 Hen. VIII. 1537-8.

[c] This shows the MS. to be a transcript, a word here not having been understood by the transcriber. The original no doubt read "the rood of grace," which was the name by which this celebrated idol was known. It is described at some length in Lambarde's Perambulation of Kent: see also references to several contemporary letters upon its destruction in Gorham's Reformation Gleanings, 1857, p. 17.

[d] John Hilsey.

XIII.

SUMMARY OF ECCLESIASTICAL EVENTS IN 1554.

THIS is another MS. among John Foxe's papers. It is valuable, because evidently contemporary; and it contains some facts and circumstances which are not noticed elsewhere, except as Strype may have retailed them from this source. The document therefore deserves to be printed in its entirety.

It appears most probable that all the events it contains belong to the year 1554, though 1555 is prefixed to most of the latter paragraphs. Such of them, however, as are elsewhere recorded, will be found to belong to 1554.

[MS. Harl. 419, f. 131.]

1554. This yeare was comaundement gyven, that in all churchis in London, the sepulcre should be had upp agayn, and that every man should beare palmes, and goo to shrifte.[a]

On Ashe weddinsday that Wyat was at Charing crosse,[b] did docter Weston singe masse before the quene in harnesse, under his vestmentes:[c] this Weston reportid himself unto one mr. Robardes.

1555. On Hallowe thursdaie[d] the quene went [in] procession about the courte at Seinct James by London. And Burne busshopp of Bath dyd ther were a myter in procession, and a paier of slyppers of sylver and gilte, and a paier of riche gloves, with great owches of sylver uppon them, being very riche.

---

[a] *i. e.* the holy sepulchre to be made for Good Friday, palms to be carried on Palm Sunday, and confession made on Shrove Tuesday. Of these ancient usages, with that of distributing ashes on Ash Wednesday, ample particulars will be found in Brand's Popular Antiquities. They had been abandoned in the 1st of Edw. VI. and were now revived in the diocese of London by bishop Bonner's injunctions, upon which John Bale published a "Declaration" and commentary. There also appeared " A Dialogue, or familiar Talke between two neighbours concernyng the chyefest ceremonyes that were, by the mightie power of God's most holie pure word, suppressed in England, and nowe for our unworthines set up agayne by the bishoppes the impes of Antichrist, &c. From Roane the 20. of February, A.D. 1554." 12mo.

1555.[a] This yeare, the xix daie of Maye, came my lady Elizabeth out of the Tower by water, and so went westward unto Woodstock. At her comyng out of the Tower there were uppon the Teames a number of botes, full of people, which greatly rejoysed to se her, and heavy also for her trouble, that she went under safe-keping.

1555 (*read* 1554). The second daie of Aprill this yeare beganne the postle masse againe at Poules.[b]

1555. This yeare the xxiiij daie of June a preist was put into Newgate for synging the Englishe letany in his parishe church at Charing crosse.

1555.[c] This yeare the ix worthies at Graces churche was paynted,

[a] Certainly 1554. See the Chronicle of Queen Jane and Queen Mary, p. 76, and Machyn's Diary, p. 63.

[b] The apostles' mass was one of the three masses which were daily performed by the minor canons of St. Paul's cathedral—Missa Beatæ Mariæ, Missa Apostolorum, Missa Capitularum. (Consuetudines Eccl. S. Pauli Lond., printed in Dugdale's History of St. Paul's, edit. Ellis, p. 353.) It appears to have derived its name from having been performed at the apostles' altar, (Ibid. edit. Ellis, p. 333,) and had been stopped in 1549. By a letter addressed to bishop Bonner dated the 24th June in that year, the council, "having very credible notice that within your cathedral church there be as yet *the Apostles masse* and *our Ladies masse* and other masses of such peculiar name, under the defence and nomination of *our Ladies communion* and *the Apostles communion,* used in private chappels and other remote places of the same and not in the chauncell, contrary to the King's majesties proceedings," &c. direct the immediate discontinuance of the same. This letter is printed by Foxe, together with Bonner's letter written on the 26th, forwarding the same to the dean and chapter. This prohibition will be found noticed in the Chronicle of the Grey Friars of London, at p. 59, and at p. 88 its revival, under the misnomer of " the epestylle masse," at the same date as in the text, " the ij day of Aprille," 1554, not 1555. Machyn, in his Diary, under the same year, says "The xxx. day of Aprell begun the postyll mass at Powles at the v. of the cloke in the mornyng evere day :" which means, perhaps, that during the summer months the mass was at an earlier hour than in the winter. Again, after the accession of Elizabeth, Machyn says, " The xxx day of September (1559) begane the mornyng [prayer] at Poulles at that owr (*i.e.* at the same hour) as the postylles masse." The Rev. Dr. Rock (who obligingly answered an inquiry of mine on this subject, in Notes and Queries, 2nd series, vol. v. p. 297,) suggests that the ritual used for this mass was probably that to be found both in the Roman and Salisbury missals for June 29 ; on which day of the month, though not in the same year, St. Peter and St. Paul suffered martyrdom at Rome.

[c] This date, again, should be 1554.

and king Henry the eight emongest them with a bible in his hand, written uppon it VERBUM DEI, but commaundement was geven ymmediatlye that it should be put out, and so it was, and a paier of gloves put in the place.a

1555 [4?]. This yeare the xj or xij daie of September in Ypswich, beinge a xj parishe churches, there was but ij preistes to serve them, and in all Suffolk very fewe in comparison to the towens.

This yeare, the Sondaie [b] after All-ballowe daie, did certene prestes ther penaunce at Poules, and went before the procession, ech of them in a whit shirt, with a tapere in one hand, and a whit rode in the other. In the procession, the busshopp came and displed them, and then kyssed them. Then they stode before the preacher at Poules Crosse till the praiers were made; then dyd the preacher disple them, and so they put of ther whit vesture, and stode all the reast of the sermond in ther clothes.

1555.[c] This yeare, the xxvij daie of November, did the parliament sit at the courte at Whit-hall in the chamber of presence, where the quene sat highest, rychlye aparelid, and her belly laid out, that all men might see that she was with child. At this parliament they said laboure was made to have the kinge crowned, and some thought that the quene for that cause dyd lay out her belly the more.[d] On the right hand of the quene sat the king; and on the other hand of him the cardinall,[e] with his capp on his head: who made an

[a] See other versions of this story in the Chronicle of Queen Jane and Queen Mary, p. 78.

[b] Nov. 4, 1554. See another account of this ceremony in the Chronicle of the Grey Friars of London, p. 92 : and a third in Machyn's Diary, p. 73. The priests were some of those who were now compelled to relinquish their wives. Strype, Memorials of Cranmer, p. 326, has given a list of those priests in the diocese of London who were called to account on this head, and specifies those who performed the required penance.

[c] Also 1554 : see Machyn's Diary, p. 76.

[d] The tenure in an earldom or barony possessed by the husband of an heiress was considered to be confirmed by the birth of a child, before which it was incomplete. The passage in the text is suggested by the application of this doctrine to the crown. Had king Philip been crowned he would have continued king of England after queen Mary's death.

[e] Cardinal Pole. His oration is given at full in John Elder's letter, reprinted in the Chronicle of Queen Jane and Queen Mary, p. 154.

oracion, that pope Julius the thirde had sent them his benediction and blessing, uppon their reconsileacion againe; willing them to knele all dowen uppon their knees, to receyve the pope's blessing and benediction,[a] for ther falling from the pope and his lawes and statutes, and in hope that they will turne to ther ould use and custome againe, the pope by him offerith them his blessing: and so they all kneled dowen and receyved it, all save one[b] sir Raulf Bagnall,[c] who said he was sworne the contrary to king Henry the

---

[a] *Read* absolution.

[b] The circumstance that there was *one* member of the lower house of parliament that ventured to open his mouth at this crisis, is mentioned, but without naming him, by bishop Gardyner, in the course of his examination of the martyr John Rogers, on the 22nd Jan. 1554-5. On that occasion Gardyner (then lord chancellor) said to Rogers: " Ye have heard of my lord cardinal's (Pole) commyng, and that the parliament hath receyved his blessing, not one resisting unto it, *but one man which did speake against it.* Such a unitie, and such a myracle, hath not been seen. And all they, of which there are eyght score in one house, *save* (1) *one that was by, whose name I know not,* have with one assent receyved pardon of their offences, for the schism that we have had in England, in refusing the holy father of Rome to be head of the Catholicke Church." (Foxe.)

(1) This word has been misprinted " said " in all the editions of Foxe before the last; but it was pointed out to be an error for " save " in the errata to the first edition of 1563.

[c] Sir Ralph Bagenal was evidently an extraordinary personage in his day. The editor of the last edition of Foxe, (1846, vi. 776,) has termed him " this noble-minded individual " in reference to the passage in Strype (Memorials, iii. 204,) derived from the statement in the text: but, from what we elsewhere find of him, he was more probably a reckless dissolute courtier, who chose to adopt the Protestant party, and, having but little to lose, did not stop short, from any scruples of sobriety or caution, in doing or saying whatever the impulse of the moment dictated. Underhill in a passage already printed (p. 158) has classed him with the gamblers and "ruffling roysters" of the reign of Henry VIII. His name occurs as one of the defenders in the justs holden on the morrow of king Edward's coronation Feb. 21, 1546-7. In 6 Edw. VI. he obtained a grant of Dieulacres abbey in Staffordshire, with various dependent manors, as thus related by Sampson Erdeswick : " The said house, with the most things belonging to it, was given, in king Edward the Sixth's time, to sir Raufe Bagenholt, for his advancement. But sir Raufe (good-fellow like) dispersed it *et dedit pauperibus,* for he sold it to the tenants, for the most part to every man his own, at so reasonable a rate, that they were well able to perform the purchase thereof, and [he] spent the money he received, gentleman-like, leaving his son sir Samuel Bagenhall (now lately knighted at Cales, anno 1596) to advance himself by his valour, as he had done before." (Survey of Staffordshire, edit. 1844, p. 493.) The same author, when treating of the village of Bagenhall, had previously (p. 15) thus noticed the family,

eight, "which was a worthy prince, and labourid xxv^{ti} yeres before he could abolish him, and to say that I will nowe agree to it, I will not."

after stating that they occurred in records of the time of Henry III. : "but since then all the names of them have been brought down, I know not how, unto the plebeian estate, until this our present age, that two brethren of that surname, sons of John Bagenhall, born at Barleston [*other copies say* Newcastle], the one Ralfe, the other Nicholas, were for their valour, Raufe at Musselborough [1551] and Nicholas in Ireland [1565] both of them adorned with the honour of knighthood ; the son of which sir Nicholas, Henry by name, tracing his father's steps, is also advanced to the same dignity [1578], as was also Samuel the son of Ralph, knighted for his military services [as in the preceding paragraph]." It does not appear for what place sir Ralph was sitting at the time of his memorable speech in parliament ; but in 1 Eliz. he represented the county of Stafford, his brother sir Nicholas then sitting for Newcastle-under-Lyme. In 5 Eliz. sir Ralph sat for Newcastle, in 13 Eliz. sir John [qu. sir Ralph again ?] Sir Ralph was sheriff of Staffordshire in 2 Eliz. His name occurs so late as 1572 as being one of the commissioners for concealed lands, whose conduct (according to Strype) had become "so odious, so unjust, and so oppressive, that, by the lord treasurer's means, the queen by proclamation revoked her commission, and forced them to restore the things they had wrongfully taken. But they stood upon their justification, and laboured again to get their commission renewed : and particularly one sir Richard [*read* Ralph] Bagnal did so, who was very severe, especially upon the clergy, being also in commission (either with George Delves and Lancelot Bostock esquires, or concurrently with them,) to compound for offences against the statute of non-residence, and other offences of the clergy, and to take the whole commodity thence arising." (See Strype's Annals, ii. 313, and his Life of Archbishop Parker, book iv. chapters 21 and 42 ; also Archbishop Parker's Correspondence, printed for the Parker Society, pp. 413, 424.) Sir Ralph Bagenal's arms were, Sable, within an orle of martlets argent an inescocheon ermine charged with a leopard's face gules ; and his crest, On a wreath or and sable a dragon's head erased gules charged with two bars or. (MS. Cotton. Claudius, C. III.) Sir Nicholas Bagenal above mentioned occurs as marshal of Ireland, 28 Jan. 1550-1. (Privy-council register.)

In Ward's History of Stoke-upon-Trent, 1843, 8vo., p. 346, there is a pedigree of this family, extending from William Bagenhall of Newcastle-under-Lyme, 1 Edw. IV. (the great-grandfather of sir Ralph) to Anna-Maria and Frances the daughters and coheirs of John Bagnall esq. of Early Court, Berks, who were married respectively to William Scott, Lord Stowell, and the Hon. Thomas Windsor.

APPENDIX

OF

ADDITIONAL NOTES AND DOCUMENTS.

REMINISCENCES OF JOHN LOUTHE.

Page 1. *Inquisition on the death of Lionel Louthe esquire.*—By inquisition taken at Stilton on the 10th May, 13 Edw. IV. it was found that Lionel Louthe esquire held no lands in the county of Huntingdon of the King in chief or in service; but that Thomas Wesynham esquire, Thomas Thorpe esquire, and William Horwode, being seised in fee of the manor of Bealmes in Sawtre, and the advowson of the church of saint Andrew, had by charter dated 20th Sept. 23 Hen. VI. demised the same to Lionel Louthe and Katharine his wife, and the survivor of them, with remainder to the right heirs of Lionel: and that, on his dying so seised, his widow was left in possession. Lionel died on the feast of saint Andrew (30 Nov.) 11 Edw. IV. (1471), and Thomas his son and heir was of the age of twenty-four and more at the date of the inquisition. The manor, &c. were held by Henry duke of Buckingham, as of his manor of Southo, and were worth per annum twenty marks. (Inq. p. mort. 12 Edw. IV. No. 31.)

Page 4. *The inquisition on the death of Thomas Louthe* is preserved, but in an injured and obliterated state. It was taken at St. Ive's on the 28th May, 26 Hen. VIII. He had settled the manor, &c. of Sawtrey, so that on his death Thomasine his widow became seised thereof. It was valued at xx li. and held of Henry Nores, esquire of the King's body, as of his manor of Sowthoo, as the fourth part of a knight's fee. Thomas Louthe died on the 26th Oct. 1533, leaving his great-granddaughter Margaret his heir, she being the daughter of Lionel, son of Edmund, son of the said Thomas, and at the death of the deceased four years old and more.

Page 14. It is worthy of remark that doctor Robert Lowth, bishop of London 1777-1787, bore the same arms as our archdeacon (without the crescent), and was probably descended from the same family. He was not only, like John Louthe, a scholar of Winchester college, but a native of that city, where his father was a prebendary. He published the Life of William of Wykeham in 1758. His great-grandfather Simon Lowth was rector of Tilehurst, in Berkshire. There was another Simon Lowth, rector of Dingley in Northamptonshire, in 1633, who was father of Simon Lowth, D.D. a nonjuror, nominated dean of Rochester by James the Second (a memoir of whom is given in Chalmers's Biographical Dictionary).

Page 22. *The first Protestants at Oxford.*—The following members of the university of Oxford are named in the narrative of Anthony Dalaber (given by Foxe), among those who, besides himself, then a scholar of St. Alban hall, were in 1528 suspected to be infected of heresy, from having purchased such books of God's truth as were brought to Oxford by Thomas Garret, fellow of Magdalen college, and curate of Honey-lane in London :—

1. Maister John Clarke, which died in his chambre, and could not be suffered to receyve the communion, being in prison, and saying [in substitution for the elements] these woordes, *Crede et manducasti.*

2. Maister Somner, and

3. Maister Bettes, fellows and canons of Friswith's college.

4. Richard Taverner, then organist at Friswith's. He was charged with concealing some of the books under the boards of his school, but Wolsey excused him, by saying that he was but a musician (see Athenæ Cantabrigienses, i. 338).

5. Radley. These five all of Friswith's or Cardinal college.

6. Nicholas Udall, of Corpus Christi college, afterwards master of Eton school.

7. Sir Diet or Dyott, also of Corpus Christi college.

8. Maister Edon, fellow of Magdalen college.

9. A black monk of S. Austines of Canterbury, named Langporte.

10. Another black monk of S. Edmondes Bury, named John Salisbury, afterwards suffragan bishop of Thetford, dean of Norwich, and bishop of Sodor and Man (see Athenæ Cantab. i. 318).

11, 12. Two white monks of Barnard college.

13, 14. Two canons of S. Maries college, one of them named Robert Ferrar, afterwards bishop of S. Davies, and burned in quene Maries time.

"— with divers other." In a letter of John (Longland), bishop of Lincoln, to cardinal Wolsey, "wryten in Holborn the thyrd day of March," 1527-8, it it stated that " The chefe that were famylyarly acquainted in this mater with master Garrott was master Clarke, master Freer, sir Fryth, sir Dyott, Anthony Delabere." And in another letter of the same writer to the cardinal, written

London, upon the commaundement, immediately after your departure. This Garrott, Clerke, and Freer are thre perylous men, and have bene occasion of corruption of the yougthe. They have doon moche mischeve; and for the love of God latt them [be] handeled therafter, for I feare me soore they have infecte many other partes of England, which will appere if they be strately handeled and examyned." See the letters in Appendix VI to the vth volume of Foxe's Actes and Monuments, edit. Townsend and Cattley.

In 1532 Thomas Garret and Anthony Dalaber did penance at Oxford, "carrying a fagot in open procession from saint Maries church to Friswides, Garret having his red hoode on his shoulders like a maistre of arte."

Bearing a fagot was part of the penance performed by heretics in the public ceremony of their recantation. Among the articles laid to Richard (or Robert) Bayfield in 1531, is this:—

"8. Item, after your abjuration it was enjoyned to you for penance, that you should go before the cross in procession, in the parish church of S. Buttolf at Billinges gate, and to beare a fagot of wood upon your shoulders." (Foxe, 1st edit. 1563, p. 481.)

The ceremony is circumstantially described by Foxe in his story of doctor Robert Barnes, when prosecuted in 1540:—

"Then they (bishops Gardiner and Foxe—the former then secretary to cardinal Wolsey and the latter master of the wards)—commaunded the warden of the Fleete to carye hym with his fellowes to the place from whence he came, and to be kept in close pryson; and in the morning to provide 5 fagots for doctour Barnes and the 4. Stilliard men. The 5. Stilliard man was commanded to have a taper of 5 pound weight to be provided for him, to offer to the roode of Northen* in Paules, and all these things to be ready by 8. of the clocke in the morning; and that hee with all that he could make, with bils and gleaves, and the knight marshall with his tipstaves that he could make, should bring them to Paules and conduct them home again. In the morning they were all readye by theyr houre appoynted in Paules church, the church being so full that no man coulde get in. The cardinal [Wolsey] had a scaffold made on the top of the staires for himselfe, with 36 abbots, mitred priors and byshops, and he in his whole pompe mitred (which Barnes spake against) sate there inthronized, his chapleins and spirituall doctors in gownes of damaske and satine, and he hymselfe in purple, even like a bloudye Antichriste. And there was a new pulpit erected on the top of the staires also, for the bishop of Rochester

---

* This was a favourite object of devotion at the North door of St. Paul's church. It is mentioned as a place of great resort by archbishop Arundel in his examination of Thomas Thorpe in 1457. It was taken down in the year 1537.

[Heath] to preache against Luther and doctor Barnes: and great baskets full of bookes standing before them within the railes, which was commaunded after the great fire was made afore the roode of Northen there to be burned, and these heretikes after the sermon to goe thryse about the fire, and to cast in theyr fagots."

Latimer writes, in a letter to sir Edward Baynton,—" Good saint Paul must have borne a fagot, my lord of London [Bonner] being his judge. Oh, it had beene a goodly sight to have seene saint Paul with a fagot on his backe, even at Paul's crosse, my lord of London, bishop of the same, sitting under the crosse!"

In the reign of Edward VI. the same course was still pursued towards the anabaptists. On low sunday (1549) one of them named Champenes bare a fagot at Paul's cross, where Miles Coverdale preached the rehearsal sermon; and on the following sunday a farmer of Colchester named Putto, who had recanted, bare a fagot at Paul's cross, and after that at Colchester. (Stowe's Chronicle, and the Chronicle of the Grey Friars of London, p. 58.)

Sometimes the memory of the penance was perpetuated by a badge representing a fagot being sown upon the offender's dress. In 1505, we read of one William Brewster, who, " after other penaunce done at Colchester, was enjoyned to weare a fagot upon his upper garment during his life: whiche badge he did beare upon his left shoulder neare the space of two yeares, till the controller of the earle of Oxforde pluckt it way, because he was labouring in the workes of the earle."

In 1530 Thomas Cornwell or Ansty, who had been injoyned by bishop Fitzjames for his penance to wear a fagot brodered upon his sleeve, under pain of relapse, having failed to keep the same, was condemned to perpetual custody in the house of S. Bartholemew.

Page 25. *John Petit.*—Since the note in this page was written, a persevering research has recovered some memorials of John Petit. The records of the Grocers' company are ancient, but not at present accessible. In those of the city of London at Guildhall, which are in an admirable state of preservation, Petit's election to parliament is recorded; but it does not appear that he occupied that position more than once, instead of for " twenty years," as stated by archdeacon Louthe. The ancient mode of election for the city was that two out of the four representative citizens should be returned by the aldermen, and two by the commoners; and the result in 1529, when Petit was chosen, was as follows:

Et postea ad hustingas tentas die martis viz. quinto die Octobris anno regni regis Henrici octavi xxj°, in magna aula, immensa communitate tunc presente,

Johannes Baker recordator,

— per majorem et aldermannos nominati in interiori camera Guyhalde, et postea per dictam communitatem in aula confirmati et ratificati,

Johannes Petyte grocerus,

Paulus Wythypolle mercator scissor,

cives civitatis prædictæ, cominarii elceti per dictam communitatem. (Journal Rudston, f. 149.)

The probate of Petit's will, which is recorded in the prerogative court of Canterbury (22 Thower), shows he was dead in little more than three years after his election to parliament. It was proved on the 24th Jan. 1532-3, before dr. Richard Gwent, then commissary of the vacant see, and is as follows:

" In the name of God, amen. The xxij^t day of August, in the xxiij^t yere of king Henry the vilj^t, I, John Petyt, of London, grocer, beinge hole of mynde, make this my last wille and testament, in maner and forme followinge: First, I bequeth my soule to Almighty God and my bodye to the erth in cristen buriall; also I bequeth my yeres and termes of my house and kaye to Luce nowe my wife. Item, I bequeth and wille that my detts be paide to every persone that I owe money unto. Item, I wille and geve all the residue of my goodes moveable and unmoveable to my wife and children indifferently to be devided, that is to say, the oon halfe thereof to my wife and th'other halfe to my children equally to be devided amonge them whan they come of lawfull age or mariage, accordinge to the custume of the citie of London thereof longe tyme used, and I make and ordeyne my sole executrice of this my last wille Luce my wife. In wittnesse whereof I have written this present wille with myne owne hand the daye and yere abovesaide."

The name of "John Petit alias Petye" occurs in a list given by Foxe (first edit. 1563, p. 418) of those forced to abjure in king Henry's days, but in uncertain years.

John Petit was not the only representative of the city of London in parliament who at this period fell a victim to his patriotism and honesty. *Robert Packington*, mercer, was in the year 1536 [a] murdered in Cheapside; and his death, according to the report of Hall, Grafton, Bale, and Foxe, was generally attributed to the malice of the clergy. Hall's narrative of the story is as follows: " In this yere one Robert Packyngton mercer of London, a man of good substaunce, and yet not so riche as honest and wise, this man dwelled in Chepeside at the signe of the Legg, and used daily at foure of the clock winter and sommer to rise and go to masse at a churche—then called saint Thomas of Acres, but now named the Mercers' chapel, and one mornyng emong all other,

---

[a] Foxe says 1538, but Hall places the murder in 28 Hen. VIII. *i. e.* 1536 or 7.

beyng a great mistie mornyng such as hath seldome beseene, even as he was crossyng the strete from his house to the churche, he was sodenly murdered with a gonne, whiche of the neighbors was playnly hard; and by a great nombre of laborers at the same tyme standyng at Soper lane end he was both sene go furth of his house, and also the clap of the gonne was hard, but the dede-doer was never espied nor knowen. Many were suspected, but none could be found fauty: howbeit it is true that, forasmuch as he was knowen to be a man of a great courage, and one that could both speake, and also would be harde: and that the same tyme he was one of the burgesses of the parliament for the citie of London, and had talked somewhat against the covetousnes and crueltie of the clergie, he was had in contempte with theim, and therefore mooste lykely by one of theim thus shamefully murdered, as you perceive that master Honne was in the sixte yere of the reigne of this kyng." (Hall's Chronicle, edit. 1548, fol. CCxxxi, *v*.)

To this account Holinshed adds, "At length the murtherer in deed was condemned at Banburie in Oxfordshire, to die for a fellonie which he afterwards committed; and when he came to the gallowes on which he suffered, he confessed that he did this murther, and till that time he was never had in anie suspicion therefore." (Chronicle, folio, 1586, p. 944.)

This passage, it may be hoped, is an answer to the assertion of John Foxe, who in his Actes and Monuments (edit. 1563, p. 525) told the story, in the same words as above, but with this addition:—" although many in the meane time were suspected [one of whom, Foxe elsewhere tells us, was Singleton, chaplain some time to queen Anne Boleyne, and who suffered death as a traitor in 1544,] yet none could be found faultie therin, the murtherer so covertly was concealed, tyll at length by the confession of doctour Incent deane of Paules in his deathbed it was knowne, and by him confessed that he was the author therof, by hiring an Italian for lx. crownes, or thereabout, to do the feate. For the testimonie whereof, and also of the repentaunt wordes of the said Incent, the names both of them which heard him confesse it, and of them which heard the witnesses report it, remayne yet in memorie to be produced, if neede required." This serious accusation against dean Incent has continued uncontradicted in the pages of Foxe until this day.

Foxe adds that Robert Packington was brother to Austen or Augustine Packington, mercer, mentioned in a former place of his book, as having been employed by Tunstall when bishop of London, about the year 1529, to buy up at Antwerp all the unsold copies of Tyndale's New Testament, with the object of burning them at Paul's cross: but the result of which transaction was that the translator was thereby provided with the funds to print a new and more accurate edition.

298   APPENDIX.

There was still another alderman of London, who suffered imprisonment in the Tower, for the favour he had shown to the Reformers,—*Humphrey Mummuth*, or *Monmouth*, some account of whose troubles will be found in the Actes and Monuments. Among the charges brought against him by bishop Stokesley were these,—for having and reading heretical books and treatises; for giving exhibition to William Tindal, Roy, and such others, for helping them over the sea to Luther; for ministering privy help to translate as well the Testament as other books into English, &c. &c. Monmouth served sheriff in 1535-6, but but he did not live to be lord mayor. Foxe erroneously states that he was knighted. He was buried in the churchyard of Allhallows Barking, where by his will, made in 1537, he directed thirty sermons to be preached by bishop Latimer, dr. Barnes, dr. Crome, and mr. Taylor, in lieu of the trental of masses which had been customary: see Strype's edition of Stowe's Survey.

Subsequently, in the reign of Mary, there were several aldermen who were supposed to favour the Protestant doctrines, and suffered some persecution in consequence. Foxe enumerates their names, "as master Lodge, master Hawes, master Machel, master Chester, &c." The first of these was afterwards sir Thomas Lodge, sheriff in 1559-60, lord mayor in 1563-4 (of whom see further in the notes to Machyn's Diary, p. 375). The second, John Hals, or Hawes, was sheriff in 1558-9, but did not arrive at the mayoralty. The third, John Machell, was sheriff in 1555-6, but also died below the mayoralty, on the 12th Aug. 1558 (see Machyn's Diary, p. 170). The last, sir William Chester, sheriff in 1554-5, lord mayor in 1560-1, is noticed in Machyn's Diary, p. 381, and there is a memoir of him in the Athenæ Cantabrigienses, i. 311.

Page 27. The *martyrdom of Thomas Bilney* took place on the 19th of August, 1531 (see Anderson's Annals of the English Bible, vol. i. p. 300). It is remarkable that Petit's will (already given) is dated only three days later: and it may therefore have been made whilst he was still in the Tower, where we are told he was Bilney's fellow-prisoner. There is some inconsistency in what Louth afterwards relates of Petit being secretly visited by Frith, whilst the latter was a prisoner in the Tower; for that was not until the year 1533, after Petit's death. Frith's visits must have been at an earlier period.

Page 28. *In his debte booke these desperatte debtes he entered thus,—Lent unto Chryste*. This mode of remitting debts is paralleled in the instance of another citizen of London, John Petit's contemporary. Sir William FitzWilliam, in his will made in 1534, " remits and forgives all such poor as be in his debt, whose names appeareth in his seventh book of debts, under whose names he had written these words, *Amore Dei remitto*." (Collins's Peerage.) It was customary for executors and others to class the debts of an estate under the heads *Sperate* and *Desperate*.

Page 28. *William Bolles, the second husband of Lucy Petit.*—He was the son of William Bolles esquire, of Wortham in Suffolk, descended from the family living at Haugh in Lincolnshire. He received the royal license to purchase the manor of Osberton, in the parish of Worksop, in 32 Hen. VIII., and thus brought his wife Lucy, the widow of John Petit, into the sphere of archdeacon Louth's acquaintance. He died March 2, 1582, and his will was proved on the 30th May, 1583, "giving his soul to God almighty, hoping through Jesus Christ to be saved, and his body to be buried in the south side of the quere or chancel of the parish church of Wyrksop, and to have a fair and large marble, with his arms and cognizance of his wife Lucye Bolles graven in mettle called lattin, and set forth in their right colours. As also, on the same to be graven or written the day and year of both their deaths, whose wife's death was 28th November, 1558, whose bones he will have taken up where they lye, in the body of the said church of Wirksop, and laid by his and his last wife Agnes Bolles, who departed this life 2d Nov. 1569." No remembrance of the proposed fair marble and its commemorative engravings is preserved: and we are consequently not acquainted with "the cognizance of his wife Lucye." His posterity, descended from her, continued at Osberton until the middle of the seventeenth century, when their heiress was married into the family of Leeke. (History of Worksop, by John Holland, 1826, 4to. pp. 184, 185.)

Page 31, note, *Lady Parry.*—Anne, daughter of sir William Read, of Borestall in Buckinghamshire, was married successively to sir Giles Greville, sir Adrian Fortescue, and sir Thomas Parry, comptroller of the household to queue Elizabeth, who died Dec. 15, 1604, and was buried in Westminster abbey. See a biographical note on sir Thomas Parry in Lodge's Illustrations of British History, vol. i. p. 302. Lady Parry died Jan. 5, 1585: see her epitaph at Welford, in Ashmole's Berkshire.

Page 39. *Family history of Anne Askew.*—The parentage of Anne Askew is undisputed. She was the second daughter of sir William Askew, or Ayscough, of South Kelsey, county Lincoln, by his first wife Elizabeth, daughter of Thomas Wrottesley.

But the identity of her husband has not been ascertained. Mr. Pishey Thompson, in his History of Boston, folio edition, 1856, at p. 388, remarks, "Everything relating to this martyr for conscience sake appears to be involved in impenetrable mystery;" but at p. 385, Mr. Thompson conjectures that her husband was of the Stickford branch of the Kyme family, upon the evidence of an armorial coat (a chevron between three trefoils), supposed to be that of Kyme of Stickford, impaled with Ayscough in the Ayscough chapel at Kelsey. But as the same bearings were those of Robert Williamson of Nottinghamshire, who married Faith, daughter of sir Edward Ayscough,[a] this conjecture is not improbably based upon unsubstantial evidence.

In the History of Sleaford, 1825, 8vo. p. 289, Anne Askew is said to have resided at Austhorpe, or Ewerby Thorpe, till her imprisonment; but no authority is alleged for that statement.[b]

Even her husband's christian name is uncertain, for whilst Speed calls him John Kyme, he appears by the name of Thomas in the register of the privy council.

In the hope of solving this difficulty I have had recourse to the inquisitions post mortem; but the result is still ambiguous and unsatisfactory. Thomas Kyme esquire, who died 9th August, 1 Edw. VI. seized of Hilstall and other lands in Fryskney, Waynflet, Wrangle, and Thorp, left a son and heir named *Thomas*, aged thirty years and more, who may have been Anne Askew's husband. There was also a *John* Kyme, who had a small estate of 3*l* 16*s*. yearly value in Fryskney and Waynflete, and died 17th Oct. 1 and 2 Phil. and Mary, leaving *Thomas* his cousin and heir, aged forty years and more. This Thomas is stated to have been buried at Friskney in 1591, in Oldfield's History of Wainfleet and Candleshoe, p. 170.

The circumstances of Anne Askew's unhappy marriage are thus described by Bale: "Concerning master Kyme [her husband] this should seem to be the matter. Her father sir William Askewe, knight, and his father old master Kyme, were sometime of familiarity and neighbours within the county of Lincolnshire. Whereupon the said sir William covenanted with him for lucre to have his eldest daughter [Martha] married with his son and heir—as, in an ungodly manner, it is in England much used among noble men, and it was her chance to die afore the time of marriage. To save the money he constrained this [daughter Anne] to supply her room, so that, in the end, she was compelled against her will or free consent to marry with him. Notwithstanding, the marriage once passed, she demeaned herself like a Christian wife, and had by him (as I am informed) two children. In process of time, by oft reading the sacred Bible, she fell clearly from all old superstitions of papistry to a perfect belief in Jesus Christ; whereby she so offended the priests, that he, at at their suggestion, violently drove her out of his house. * * * * Upon this occasion (I hear say) she sought of the law a divorcement from him. * * * * Of this matter was she first examined (I think) at his labour and suit."

That is to say, when brought before the council at Greenwich, she was (as

---

[a] I am favoured with this suggestion by the Right Hon. Lord Monson.

[b] The Rev. Dr. Yerburgh, Vicar of Sleaford, a gentleman attached to genealogy, is upposed to have been the chief contributor to this work.

she herself relates) first "asked of master Kyme. I answered that my lord chancellor knew already my mind on that matter. They with that answer were not contented, but said it was the King's pleasure that I should open the matter to them. I answered them plainly that I would not so do; but if it were the King's pleasure to hear me, I would shew him the truth. Then they said it was not meet for the King with me to be troubled. I answered, that Solomon was reckoned the wisest king that ever lived, yet mislik'd he not to hear two poor common women; much more his grace a simple woman and a faithful subject. So in conclusion I made them none other answer in that matter."

Thus in this as subsequently in her religious examinations this self-possessed and intrepid woman had ever an answer ready for her persecutors; and the result of her examination before the council was, that they deemed her very heady, self-willed, and obstinate, and consequently determined that she should be left to the cruel provisions of the act of the Six Articles.

The entry in the register of the privy council is as follows:—

"At Greenwiche, June 19th, 1546.—*Thomas* Keyme, of Lincolnshire, who had married one Anne Aseue, called hether, and likewise his wiffe, who refused him to be her hosbande without any honeste allegacion, was appointed to returne to his countrey tyll he shoulde be eftesoones sente for; and for that shee was very obstynate and headdy in reasonyng of matters of relygeone, wherein she shewed herselfe to be of a naughty oppinyon, seeinge no perswasione of good reason could take place, she was sent to Newegate, to remaine there to answere to the lawe; like as also one [Christopher] White,* who attempted to make an erronyous booke, was sente to Newgate, after debatyng with him of the matter, who shewed himself of a wrong oppinyon concernynge the blessed Sacrament."

There are many incidents in this sad history that on examination invest it with additional interest. Anne Askew was an orphan; her own mother had long been dead; her father died between August 1540 and May 1541, five years before the catastrophe. Her bitterest persecutors were of her own family; and, from the omission of her name in genealogical records, it seems that after her death they ignored all memory of her.

Page 40. *Mr. Disney*, who married Anne Askew's sister, was probably a strong favourer of the doctrines of the Reformation, if we may judge from the Old-Testament names which he bestowed on his children. They are thus stated in his epitaph at Norton-Disney: "Ric'us Disney et Nele uxor ejus

---

* Styled Christopher White, of the Inner Temple, in the Chronicle of the Grey Friars of London, p. 51.

filia Will'i Hussey militis, ex qua procreavit Will'um, Humfridum, Joh'em, Danielem, Ciriacum, Zachariam et Isaac filios, et Saram, Esther, Judith, Judeh, et Susannam filias. Jana uxor altera, filia Gulielmi Aiscough militis, per quam nulla soboles." (MS. Harl. 6829, f. 341.) It was, however, probably long after her sister Anne Askew's death that Jane (by her first marriage lady St. Paul) became mrs. Disney. Mr. Disney died in 1578.

Lionel Throckmorton was nephew of archdeacon Louthe, being the son of Simon Throckmorton (son of John of South Elmham, Norf. younger brother to sir Robert of Coughton, co. Warw.), by Anne, daughter of Edmund Louthe of Sautrey; which Anne was remarried to John Duke of Bungay, gentleman, who died s. p. s. in 1559, leaving her surviving. Lionel Throckmorton was under twenty-one in 1540. He died in 1599, having married first Elizabeth, daughter of Bartholomew Kempe of Gissing, Norfolk, and secondly Elizabeth, daughter of John Blenerhasset of Barsham, by the latter of whom he left issue. (Davy's Suffolk Collections, MS. Addit. 19,151.)

Page 42. *Sir George Blaage* was not knighted until the expedition in Scotland in 1547, in which he served as joint commissioner of the musters with sir John Holcroft. (Patten's Narrative of that Expedicion, p. xxvi.) He was then one of the knights made by the duke of Somerset in the camp at Roxburgh on the 28th of September. He represented the city of Westminster in the parliament which began Nov. 8, 1547. His death in 1551 is mentioned in one of Roger Ascham's letters as the loss of one of the brightest ornaments of the court.

Ibid. note [c]. *Kenelm Throckmorton* is mentioned in 1563 as having the custody of a French hostage or prisoner detained in England. (Strype's Annals, i. 433.)

Page 43. *John Lascelles.* He is mentioned with others in the following entry of the Register of the Privy Council:—

"At St. James's, the vij day of June, 1546. Weston the luteplayer, for his sedityous conference at sondrie tymes with one Barber and one Latham (*sic*) and Lascelles, with others, upon proffecyes and other thinges styrringe to commotion against the Kinges ma[tie], after his briefe examination, wherein he (*i.e.* Weston) would confesse small matter in respect of that he had spoken, was comitted to the porter's lodge to be further examined." (MS. Harl. 256, fol. 217.)

(Same day.) " Lanam (*sic*) a prophesier was comitted this day to the Tower for prof[esy]inge, according to Weston's and Barber's depositions, and a letter was addressed to the lieftenante for his saufe kepinge theire accordingly." (Ibid. f. 217 b.)

Page 43. *The Racking of Anne Askew.*—The application of torture in the case of Anne Askew was so irregular and so illegal, that some eminent writers have pronounced it to have been impossible. Because such a barbarity ought not to have been perpetrated, they have argued that it could not have been attempted. This conclusion has not hitherto materially affected the general stream of our historical and biographical literature, but the following passage is an instance of its doing so:—

" The popular story that she was tortured previously to her death, and that the chancellor with his own hands stretched her on the rack, seems unworthy of credit. See Jardine's Reading on the use of Torture." (Women of Christianity exemplary for acts of Piety and Charity. By Julia Kavanagh. 1852.)

Dr. Lingard also has published the following note:—

" In the narrative transmitted to us by Foxe as the composition of this unfortunate woman, she is made to say: My lord chancellor and master Rich [why the name of bishop Gardiner has since been substituted for master Rich in several editions, I know not,] took pains to rack me with their own hands, till I was nigh dead. (Foxe, ii. 578.) Foxe himself adds that when Knivet the lieutenant, in compassion to the sufferer, refused to order additional torture, the chancellor and Rich worked the rack themselves. To me neither story appears worthy of credit. For, 1. Torture was contrary to law, and therefore was never inflicted without a written order subscribed by the lords of the council. 2. The person who attended on such occasions to receive the confession of the sufferer was always some inferior officer appointed by the council, and not the lord chancellor or other members of that body. 3. There is no instance of a female being stretched on the rack, or subjected to any of those inflictions which come under the denomination of torture. See Mr. Jardine's Reading on the use of Torture." (History of England, fifth edition, 1849, vol. v. p. 201.)

We now turn to Mr. Jardine's essay, where, in lieu of any detailed examination of Anne Askew's case, we find it summarily dismissed in the following passage. After stating that he had not discovered a single instance of the application of torture to any persons of noble blood, Mr. Jardine adds, "Nor are there during the five reigns to which I have referred (Edward VI. to Charles I.) any instances of women being exposed to regular torture; but bishop Burnet, in the History of the Reformation (vol. i. p. 342) mentions that Anne Askew, the celebrated Protestant martyr, was tortured in the Tower in 1546, and states that the 'lord chancellor, finding the rack-keeper falter in his operations, threw off his gown and drew the rack himself so severely that he almost tore her body asunder.' Burnet says there is no doubt that she was tortured, as he had seen a relation of the fact in an original journal of the transactions in the Tower. What the authority of this journal might be is uncertain, and there is no authentic record of the fact. The story of the chancellor's barbarity is treated by Burnet himself as one of the fables of Foxe's Martyrology, and entitled to no credit whatever."

Thus Dr. Lingard's incredulity rests on the dictum of Mr. Jardine, and Mr. Jardine's on that of bishop Burnet, the "original journal" which bishop Burnet cited as his authority being set aside. But, on further investigation, it appears that Mr. Jardine has materially misrepresented the sentiments of Burnet, whose phrase is "no entire credit," instead of "no credit whatever." His words are: "Foxe does not vouch any warrant for this; so that, though I have set it down, yet I give no entire credit to it. If it was true, it shows the strange influence of that religion, and that it corrupts the noblest natures." We further find, that after the publication of the first part of the History of the Reformation, the rev. William Pulman pointed out to its author, that the statement did not rest simply on the authority of Foxe, but that Anne Askew (whose narrative was originally edited by Bale,) had herself[a] related this circumstance of the lord chancellor and master Rich racking her with their own hands; "so (continues Burnet) there is no reason to question the truth of

[a] As quoted in p. 43. The fact is also alluded to in her letter to John Lascelles, (written whilst under sentence of death,) in which she remarks:—

"I understand the council is not a little displeased that it should be reported abroad that I was racked in the Tower. They say now, that they did there was but to fear me; whereby I perceive they are ashamed of their own uncomely doings, and fear much lest the king's majesty should have information thereof: wherefore they would no man to noise it. Well! their cruelty God forgive them!" Foxe relates that sir Anthony Knyvett, the lieutenant of the Tower, actually went to inform the king, the councillors having threatened him for his repugnance to the torturing: "Which when the king had understood, he seemed not very well to like their extreme handling of the woman, and also granted to the lieutenant his pardon, willing him to return and see to his charge." The MS. original of this passage is still preserved, in Foxe's own handwriting, in the MS. Harl. 419, f. 2, and, to place before the reader all the known evidence upon this matter, it is here appended:—

"Anne Askew.

"Syr Anth. Knevyt, lieuetenant of the Tower and of the privy chamber in kynge Henry's tyme, because at the commandement of Wrysley and syr John Baker he would not racke so extremely as they required, they put of their gownes, and racked her themselves, and fell out with mr. Knevet. He mystrustyng their thretes, went fyrst to the kyng, and shewed hym the whole matter, and obteined so much favour of hym, that [he] came a glad man home."

[This note is followed by some on the loss of Calais, written in the same way and probably at the same time: consequently the preceding would not be written before the reign of Elizabeth.]

it; and Parsons, who detracts as much from Foxe's credit as he can, does not question this particular." [a]

So that, instead of giving the story "no credit whatever," Burnet's conclusion was that "there is no reason to question the truth of it;" which very materially invalidates Mr. Jardine's arguments, upon which Dr. Lingard has relied.

It is evident that the fact can only be disputed on the supposition that "the narrative transmitted to us by Foxe as the composition of this unfortunate woman" is a forgery, as Dr. Lingard appears to insinuate; in which case not Foxe, but bishop Bale, its first editor, must be responsible for its contents.

How far such a suspicion can be fairly entertained, every reader of the narrative must judge for himself; but the general verdict may be anticipated to be, that it is too simple, natural, circumstantial, and consistent, to be a fabrication. And Dr. Lingard's suggestion appears the less probable, when we remember that it was published whilst the incidents were still recent, and their actors still surviving. Anne Askew suffered in 1546, and her narrative was edited by Bale in the very next year.[b]

Nor is there a total absence of collateral evidence. The journal cited by bishop Burnet and ignored by Mr. Jardine has a claim to consideration as the production of a contemporary of known station and respectability. The writer Anthony Anthony was a man whose name continually occurs in the council register and elsewhere as that of an officer of the ordnance in the Tower of London, and who would have good opportunities of information.[c]

Besides that, a contemporary letter written by Ottiwell Johnson, a merchant in London, to his brother John Johnson in Calais, testifies to the report

[a] Parsons, in fact, directly asserts that king Henry himself "caused her to be apprehended, and putt to the racke," in order to ascertain how far she had conversed with the queen and " corrupted " his nieces of Suffolk. Parsons's version of the story is so remarkable, and has been so entirely ignored by recent writers, even of his own communion, including Dr. Lingard, that I have thought it desirable to extract it in the subsequent pages. It will be seen that he connects Anne Askew with queen Katharine Parr much more decidedly than Foxe had done; and positively asserts that " the said Anne Askue was putt to the racke, for the discovery of the truthe."

[b] It is noticed as a new book in a letter of bishop Gardyner to the protector Somerset dated May 21, 1547, printed by Foxe, in the Actes and Monuments.

[c] Anthony's journal is again quoted by Burnet as giving some important particulars towards the history of Anna Boleyne. It is to be regretted that Burnet did not print it among his Records, or at least state where it was preserved. In the MSS. at the Ashmolean museum, Nos. 861 and 863, are " Divers things excerpted out of a book of collections made by mr. Anthony Anthony, surveyour of the ordinance to Hen. 8, Edw. 6, and queen

current in London immediately after Anne Askew's visit to the Tower. This gentleman, after describing dr. Crome's sermon, which was delivered on Trinity Sunday the 27th of June, (and which was the occasion of sir George Blagge's trouble: see p. 42,) proceeds to state that on the next day, that is, "On Monday following, *quondam* bishopp Saxon (Shaxton), maistres Askewe, Christopher White, one of maister Fayres sons, and a tailiour that come from Colchester or therabout, wer arraigned at the Guyldhall and received theyar judgement of the lord chauncelor and the counseil to be burned, and so wer committed to Newegate again. But sins that time th'aforsaid Saxon and White have renounced thayr opinions, and the talle goeth that they shall chaunce to escape the fyer for this viage: but the gentilwoman and th'other men remayne in stedfast mynd, and *yet she hath ben rakked sins her condempnacion,* (as men say,) which is a straunge thing, in my understanding. The Lord be mercifull to us all!" Letter dated "At London the ij^{de} in July, 1546," printed in Ellis's Original Letters, second series, ii. 177.

Lastly, we have the description of Anne Askew's enfeebled condition at her execution, in consequence of her frame having been racked. Foxe relates that "she was brought into Smithfield in a chair, because she could not go on her feet, by means of her great torments from the extremity she suffered on the rack." Louthe, who was present, states that she sat in a chair, supported by two serjeants. The racking had been done in secret; but its effects were made known in the great public market-place.

The object of torture, as practised in this country, was not to punish, but to elicit information from unwilling witnesses. We may therefore admit that, when Anne Askew was placed upon the rack, it was not to vent a malicious spite, or to gratify any sentiments of revenge or gratuitous cruelty, but we find that, as she herself has related, it was to force her to betray her friends.[a] In burning the king's servant John Lascelles, in endeavouring to subject the courtier Blagge to the like doom, and in exacting from Anne Askew the penalty of her sincerity and enthusiasm, notwithstanding the favour and countenance she had received from many ladies of high rank and station, the object was evidently to intimidate persons in the highest position; and Wriothesley and the Romanist party were so anxious to push their advantage that they would gladly at this period have struck at "the head game," and found some pretence for attacking ladies that might have afforded a still more terrible example.[b] The queen herself, who had been raised to the throne

---

[a] Who some of these friends were, or were suspected to be, will be shown in a subsequent note (p. 311).

[b] The proclamation for the discovery of heretical books, which is dated on the 8th

from a comparatively low condition, was not above their mark—unless we are also to disbelieve some other very remarkable passages both of Foxe's history and of Parsons's commentary upon it; and from recent successful experience the statesmen of that day assailed as confidently an obnoxious queen as they would a rival minister. Under the provocation of such motives Wriothesley and Rich may have ventured to exceed the bounds of constitutional law in examining Anne Askew upon the rack, and they were such influential members of the council that they can scarcely be supposed to have wanted its authority. There is therefore no necessity to suppose that the narrative left by the victim of this act of inquisitional cruelty was either fabricated or interpolated.

Extract from Robert Parsons's "Examen of I. Fox his Calendar-Saints. The moneth of June." Published in " The Third Part of a Treatise intituled : of Three Conversions of England. By N. D. 1604." 8vo. p. 491.

"After this, upon the second day of the same [moneth of June] there ensue foure other burned togeather at one fyre in Smithfield, upon the last yeare of the raigne of king Henry the eyght, for Zuinglianisme, Calvinisme, and denying the reall presence in the Sacrament of the Altar. Three were men; to witt, Nicolas Belenian, priest, of Salopshire, John Lacells, gentleman of the house of king Henry the eyght, [and] John Adams, taylor, of London. But the captayne of all was a yong woman of some 24 or 25 yeres old, named Anne Askue; who, havinge left the company of her husband John Kime, a gentleman of Lincolneshire, did follow the liberty of the new ghospell, goinge up and downe at her pleasure, to make new ghospellers and proselits of her religion, untill king Henry restrayned her by imprisonment. This yonge woman's story is so pittifully related by John Fox, as he would moove compassion on her side, and hatred against the king and his councell, that particularly handled this matter, and sought to save her, yf yt had byn possible. And twise she recanted publikely, once upon the 20. of March 1545, which Fox himselfe doth relate out of the register, subscribed with her owne hand, and testifyed by two bishopps, three doctors of divinity, and seaven other credible witnesses. Wherin she protesteth and sweareth amongst other words:—'I Anne Askue, otherwise called Anne Kime, do truly and perfectly beleve, that after the words of consecration be spoken by the priest,

July 1546, and therefore only five days before the racking of Anne Askew, was evidently aimed to involve the same parties whom she was urged to betray. It required that " from henceforth no man, *woman*, or other person, *of what estate, condition, or degree he or they may be*, shall, after the last day of August next ensuing, receive, have, take, or keep in his or their possession the text of the New Testament of Tyndale's or Coverdale's," &c. &c. See Anderson's Annals of the English Bible, ii. 202.

accordinge to the common usage of the Church of England, there is present really the body and blond of our Saviour Jesus Christ, &c.'

"Another recantation also she made, or at least an abnegation, upon the 13. of June next followinge in the very same yeare in the Guyld Hall of London. Where Holinshed declareth, 'that she was arraigned before the king's justices for speakinge words against the Sacrament of the Altar, contrary to the statute of Six Articles,' togeather with one Robert Luken, and Joane Sawtry. And that she was quitt and dismissed thence, for that there was no witnesse to prove the accusation against her. Which in such matters of heresy is not likely would have happened, except there also shee had made profession of her faith to the contrary. But yet the next yeare followinge, king Henry being informed that, contrary to her oathes and protestations, she did in secrett seeke to corrupt divers people, but especially weomen, with whome she had conversed; and that she had found meanes to enter with the principall of the land, namely with queene Catherine Parre herselfe, and with his neeces the daughters of the duke of Suffolke, and others: *he caused her to be apprehended and putt to the racke*, to know the truth therof. And findinge her guilty, he commanded her also to be burned. And by her confession he learned so much of queene Catherine Parre, as he had purposed to have burned her also, yf he had lyved. As may appeare by that which Fox relateth himselfe of her daunger, presently after the burninge of Anne Askue, in the same yeare 1546, which was the last of king Henry: prefixinge this title before his treatise thereof, 'The Story of Queene Catherine Parre, late Queene and wife to K. Henry the Eyght, wherin appeareth in what daunger she was for the ghospell, &c.' In which narration, though Fox, according to his fraudulent fashion, doth disguise many things, and lay the cause of all her trouble upon bishop Gardener and others, and that the king did kindly and lovingly perdon her, yet the truth is, that the king's sicknesse and death shortly ensuynge was the cheefe cause of her escape. And the error of the lord chauncelour Wriothesley, (afterward earle of Southampton,) who lett fall out of his bosome the king's hand and comission for carryinge her to the Tower, gave her occasion (the paper being found and brought to her,) to go and humble her selfe to the king. At what tyme Fox confesseth, that the king said unto her, 'Yow are become a doctor, Kate,' &c. And the truth is, that the principall occasion against her was for hereticall books found in her closett, brought or sent her in by Anne Askue. Wherof the witnesses were, the lady Herbert, lady Lane, lady Tyrwitt, and others. *And by that occasion was the said Anne Askue putt to the racke*, for the discovery of the truth.

"And this is the story of Anne Askue, whome John Bale describeth in these wanton words, 'Anna Ascua, præclari generis juvencula, eleganti forma atque ingenio prædita, &c.—Anne Askue, a yong wench of a worshippfull house, and of elegant bewty and rare witt,' &c. And then he placeth her among the famous wryters of her age, for that perhapps she wrote some 4 or 5 sheets of paper in private letters, which yow may see sett downe in Fox. As also by the like reasons he maketh the lord Seamer duke of Somersett a renowned wryter, for settinge his hand perhaps to some proclamations, whilst he was Protector: and namely to a treatise of peace, printed and sent to Scotland from Mustleborow field. Wheras otherwise he is knowne to have bin scarse able to write or read. And for that Bale calleth Anne Askue *juvencula*, a yong heaffer or steere that abideth no yoke, he seemeth not to be farre amisse. For that she was a coy dame, and of very evill fame for wantonnesse: in that she left the company of her husband, maister Kyme, to gad up and downe the countrey a ghospelling and ghossipinge where she might, and ought not. And this for divers yeares before her imprisonment; but especially she delighted to be in London neere the court. And for so much as Jo. Bale so highly commendeth her bewty and youth, affirminge besides that she was but 25 years of age when she was putt to death, yt is easily seene what may be suspected of her lyfe, and that the mysticall speaches and demaunds, which herselfe relateth in Fox to have byn used to her by the king's councell, aboute the leavinge of her husband, were grounded in somwhat. Especially, seing that she seemed in a sort to disdayne the bearing of his name, calling herselfe Anne Askue alias Kime. And Bale in his description of her never so much as nameth her husband, or the name Kime: but only calleth her Askue, after her fathername.

" By all which, and by the publike opinion and fame that was of her lightnesse and liberty in that behalfe, every man may ghesse what a *juvencula* she was, and how fitt for Bale his pen, and for Fox his Calendar. And the proud and presumptuons answers, quips, and nips, which she gave both in matter of religion, and otherwise, to the king's councell and bishops, when they examined her, and dealt with her seriously for her amendment, do well shew her intollerable arrogancy. And yf she had lived but few yeares longer, yt is very likely she would have come to the point that her dear sister, disciple, and handmayd, Joane of Kent, (alias Knell, alias Butcher,) did. Whome she used most confidently in sendinge hereticall books hither and thither, but especially into the court. Who denyed openly within foure years after that our Savior tooke flesh of the blessed Virgin. And being condemned to the fire by Cranmer and other bishops and councelors in king Edward's dayes for the same, (as in some other places also I have related, havinge receaved yt from him that was present, and heard her speake the words,) she said scornfully unto them, 'Yt is not long agoe since yow condemned and burned that notable holy woman Anne

Askue for a peece of bread. And now yow will burne me for a peece of flesh. But as yow are now come to beleeve that your selfes which yow condemned in her, and are sory for her burning, so will the time come quicklie that yow will beleeve that which now yow condemne in me, and be sory also for this wronge done unto me,' &c. And this was a nipp given by her to bishopp Cranmer especially, who had given sentence against Anne Askue and others of the Zuinglian sect: and yet now would seeme to be of yt himselfe. And so he is affirmed heere by John Fox, and put for a saint in the same Calendar with Anne Askue, whome he burned. And so much of her, I meane both of Anne Askue, of whome we have wryten also largely in the *Certamen,* as also of Joane of Kent, of whose notable resolute spiritt, in standinge against both Cranmer, Ridley, and other preachers after her condemnation, in my lord Rich his house for a whole weeke togeather, you may read a testimony of the said lord Rich afterward, in the story of John Philpott, December 3.

"As for the other three, her companions, burnt in Smithfield at the same fyre, (to witt, Nicholas Belenian, the priest of Saloppshire, John Addams, the taylor of London, and John Lacells, the king's servant,) all schollers and disciples of this yong mistresse, nothinge is recorded of their acts and gests by Fox, but only the copy of a letter sett downe of Lacells, treating against the reall presence in the blessed Sacrament of the Altar. Wherin he discovereth himselfe to agree neyther with Luther, Zuinglius, nor Calvyn therin, nor in the expositiou of those words, *Hoc est corpus meum,* but rather followeth the fancy and devise of Carolstadius, treated by us before in the third chapter of this part. Who, desiring to be singular, affirmed that Christ when he said, 'This is my body,' pointed not to the bread in his hand, but to his body sitting at the table. Of which opinion also Lacells heere sheweth himself to be, in the discourse of his said letter. Where, amonge other things, he writeth thus, 'These words, *Hoc est corpus meum,* this is my body, were spoken (by Christ) of his naturall presence. Which no man is able to deny, because the act was finished on the crosse, as the story doth plainly manifest yt to them that have eyes,' &c.

"So as Lacells will not have the words, 'This is my body,' to be applied to the bread, nor meant by Christ of the bread:[a] but of his naturall body there present at the table, which was a peculiar devise of Carolstadius, as before we

[a] Though the letter of Lacells is well known, and of easy reference, it would be unjust to him to print Parsons's misrepresentation without at least one extract: "Furthermore, I doe stedfastly beleeve that where the bread is broken according to the ordinance of Christ, the blessed and immaculate Lambe is present to the eyes of our fayth, and so we eate his flesh and drinke hys bloude, which is to dwell with God, and God with us." This seems to comprehend the full meaning of the sacrament of the Lord's Supper, as established in the Articles of the Church of England.

have signified, and mayntayned afterward by Anne Askue and this man; accordinge to whose interpretation the sense is, that when Christ is said by the Evangelists to have taken bread in his hand, blessed and broken the same, and given it to his disciples, saying, 'This is my body,' he pointed not to the bread, but to his body; as yf he had said, this is bread, (holdinge yt out in his right hand,) and this is my body, poyntinge to his brest with his left hand; which how well it hangeth togeather every man may see. And yet was he so confident in this devise as he would needs dy for yt, assuringe himselfe that he should presently (as a martyr) go to heaven, for so he concludeth his forsaid letter in these words, 'I doubt not but to enter into the holy tabernacle which is above, yea, and there to be with God for ever.' And thus much of Lacells.

"But of the other two, Belenian and Addams, Foxe wryteth nothing at all, but only in generall of all three he saith thus, 'It happened well for them that they died togeather with Anne Askue, for, albeit that of themselves they were strong and stout men, yet through the example and exhortation of her they were more boldened and styrryed upp through her persuasions to sett apart all kind of fear,' &c. Lo, what the persuasion and example of a woman could do, to draw them to this vayne glory of dyinge for defence of their own particular opinions!"

Protestant Ladies of the Court of Henry VIII.

The ladies of rank who were suspected to be favourable to the Protestant doctrines are named in the following passage of Anne Askew's narrative.

"Then came Rich and one of the council (from Foxe's account this appears to have been sir John Baker), charging me upon my obedience to show unto them if I knew man or woman of my sect. My answer was, that I knew none. Then they asked me of my lady of Suffolk, my lady of Sussex, my lady of Hertford, my lady Denny, and my lady Fitzwilliams. I said if I should pronounce anything against them I should not be able to prove it. Then said they unto me, that the King was informed that I could name if I would a great number of my sect. I answered that the King was as well deceived in that behalf as dissembled with in other matters." Being further pressed to state from whom she had received relief whilst in prison, on their saying that there were divers ladies who had sent her money, she admitted "that there was a man in a blue coat which delivered me ten shillings, and said that my lady of Hertford sent it me; and another in a violet coat gave me eight shillings, and said my lady Denny sent it me. Whether it were true or no I cannot tell; for I am not sure who sent it me, but as the men did say."

The five ladies, whose names are thus disclosed as persons of high rank that favoured the Protestant doctrines, were—

1. *Katharine (baroness Willoughby d'Eresby) duchess of Suffolk*, the last wife of Charles Brandon duke of Suffolk. She is well known from the history of her subsequent exile with her husband Mr. Bertie, related by Holinshed and Foxe, and in a ballad version, which is reprinted in Evans's collection, vol. iii. and as a broadside, 1806. See also Lady Georgina Bertie's "Five Generations of a Loyal House, 1845," pp. 21 et seq., and references to various incidents connected with her religious sentiments in the Index to the Parker Society's Works, *voce* Brandon.

2. The *countess of Sussex* was Anne, daughter of Sir Philip Calthrop, and second wife of Henry Ratcliffe, second earl of Sussex, K.G. Like Anne Askew, she was unfortunate in her marriage; for, whilst the earl of Southampton was chancellor, *i.e.* between May 1547 and June 1549, she had separated from her husband, and was charged with wishing to marry sir Edmond Knyvett (see a long letter of her writing in Miss Wood's Letters of Royal and Illustrious Ladies, iii. 236). In 1552 she was imprisoned in the Tower, on a charge of sorcery (some particulars of which are appended in p. 314). After the triumph of the Roman faith she was barred from jointure and dower by act of parliament 2 and 3 Phil. and Mar. (Journal of the House of Lords, i. 499.)

3. *Anne (Stanhope) countess of Hertford*, afterwards duchess of Somerset: a lady whose history is well known. It was said of her in 1550 that her chiefest study was the holy Bible: see Ames's History of Printing (edit. Herbert), p. 754. (The author of the Index to the Parker Society's Works, p. 699, has questioned whether the lady who relieved Anne Askew was not Katharine Fillol, the earl of Hertford's first wife: but she was dead before sir Edward Seymour became a peer, for in 1536 he was created viscount Beauchamp, with remainder to the children of his then wife, Anne Stanhope.)

4. *Joan lady Denny* was the daughter of sir Philip Champernoun, of Modbury, co. Devon, and wife of sir Anthony Denny, a privy councillor, and groom of the stole to Henry VIII. He died on the 10th Sept. 1549; and she on the 15th May, 1553. (Topographer and Genealogist, vol. iii. p. 210.)

5. *Lady Fitzwilliam.* The Rev. Christopher Anderson (Annals of the English Bible, ii. 195) has altered the designation of this lady to countess of Southampton,[a] evidently on the mistaken presumption that she was the wife of sir William FitzWilliam, who was created earl of Southampton in 1537, and died in 1543. This is clearly wrong, as that lady was always called the countess of Hampton or Southampton. On the other hand, the compiler of the Index to the Parker Society's Works identifies the Protestant "lady Fitzwilliams" with Anne, sister to sir Henry Sidney, K.G. and wife of sir William Fitz-

---

[a] The error previously appears in the General Index to Strype's Works.

William, of Milton, co. Northampton, marshal of the King's bench.[a] It appears more probable that she was the widow of that sir William's grandfather, sir William FitzWilliam, the first of Milton, and an alderman of London, who died in 1534. This was his third wife Jane, daughter and coheir of John Ormond or Urmond: and it must have been to the same person that Anne Cooke, afterwards lady Bacon, dedicated her translation of the Sermons of Barnardine Ochyne (printed about 1550),—" To the right worshipful and worthily beloved mother the Lady F.—for that I have well known your chief delight to rest in the destroying of man's glory and exalting wholly the glory of God." Anne Cooke the translator, who is described in the editor's preface as "a well occupied gentlewoman and virtuous maiden, that never gadded further than her father's house to learn the (Italian) language," was one of the accomplished daughters of the learned sir Anthony Cooke by his wife Anne FitzWilliam; who was a daughter of sir William FitzWilliam, the alderman, by his first wife: thus "the Lady F." addressed as "mother," was really the widow of the grandfather of the young authoress.[b] Sir William FitzWilliam left as his executors John Baker esquire, recorder of London (afterwards sir John Baker, and a privy councillor), Anthony Cooke the younger esquire (his son-in-law), and his cousins Richard Waddington and Richard Ogle the younger. (Collins's Peerage.)

Anne Hartipole and the Countess of Sussex (see p. 312).

The name of Anne Hartipole has been hitherto known from a letter written to her by John Philpot, which is printed among "The Letters of the Martyrs," expostulating with her on having "fallen from the sincerity of the Gospel, which she had before long known and professed." Philpot acknowledges that he had himself received strength from her good and godly example, " at such time as that blessed woman Ann Askew (now a glorious martyr in the fight of Jesus Christ) was harboured in your house."

It appears from the following entries in the register of the privy council that she was subsequently involved in the troubles of the countess of Sussex.

[a] It is true that this gentleman and his wife are in the list which Strype has given (Eccles. Memorials, iii. 142) of those who were charitable towards the religious sufferers in the reign of Mary; a list formed from the Letters of the Martyrs.

[b] Such a form of relationship was something beyond the apprehension of Mr. George Ballard, who, in his "Learned Ladies," 8vo. 1752, imagined that Anne Cooke was thus addressing her own "mother" by her maiden name,—a very untenable supposition, as in her maidenhood Anne FitzWilliam could have had no claim to the title of "lady." The terms of relationship, it will be remembered, were in those days much more widely applied than now; and, besides their natural mother, persons might have several others in the degrees of stepmother, mother-in-law, and grandmother, or wife's grandmother, &c.

APPENDIX.

"iv. April, 1552. A letter to the lord chamberlaine to gyve ordre to suche as his lordshipp shall think good to goo to the howse of Hartlepoole, and there to make serche of wrytings, and suche other things as his lordeship shall thinke good to gyve them instructions for.

"5 April, 1552. This day one Clerke, sometimes servaunt and secretarie to the duke of Norfolke, being accused to be a reporter abroade of certein lewde prophecies, and other slaunderous mattiers concerning the King's Matie, and dyvers noblemen of his counsell, was brought before the lordes, and burdened with the same, and allso with certaine carracts (characters?) and books of nigromancie and conjuracion found in his lodging, which were brought before them, whereunto being unable to make any other aunswer but styff denyall of the hole, he was by their lordshipps committed to the Tower tyll the mattier might be better examyned, and ordre taken for the woorthy punishment thereof accordingly.

"One Hartlepoole was allso this day committed to the Flecte for being privie and a doer with the sayd Clerk in his lewd demeanour.

"A letter to the lieutenaunt of the Tower to receyve the body of Clerke, and to se hym salfly and severally kept, so as none be suffered to have conference wyth hym but by ordre from hence.

"13 April, 1552. A letter to the lieutenaunt of the Tower to receyve the bodyes of the countes of Sussex and mistres Hartlepoole, and to se them salfly and severally kept, so as neither they have conference together nor any other with them.

"A letter to mr. Hobby and the lieutenant of the Tower, that they with Armigill Waade shall examyne the countesse of Sussex uppon articles delyvered unto them by the sayde Armigill Wade.

"To the sayd lieutenaunt tò lodge the sayd lady in his lodging, and to suffer her wooman t'attend uppon her.

"10 July, 1552. A letter to the lieutenant of the Tower to suffer Richard Hartlepole to have accesse to his wyef, prisoner in the Tower, at convenyent tymes.

"27 Sept. 1552. To the master of the rolls, and the lieuetenant of the Tower, to set the lady of Sussex and Hartlepoole's wyfe at lybertye, gyving them a lesson to beware of sorceries, &c." (MS. Addit. Brit. Mus. 14,026.)

Extract from a letter of the duke of Northumberland to the lord chamberlain (Darcy), from Oxford, May 30, 1552:—

"And as touching the settinge at lybertye of the countesse of Sussex and Hartypooles wyffe, me thinketh by your lordship's better advyse that matter wolde be some whate better tryed and searchyd, the rather for that she ys chardged to have spoken and sayde that oone of kinge Edwardes sonnes [*i.e.*

a son of Edward IV.] sholde be yet lyvinge." (State-paper Office, Domestic Edw. VI. vol. xiv. art. 33.)

Imprisonment of John Davis, of Worcester.

Page 65, note. *Richard Dabitote.*—" There is yet one of the Abetots, a man of 20li. land in Worcester toune." Leland's Itinerary, vol. viii. f. 112 b.

Page 67. *Henry Joliffe, B.D.*—See a memoir of him in Athenæ Cantabrigienses, i. 320.

Ibid. *Richard Euer, B.D.*—Instead of M. (*i.e.* mr.) Yewer, Foxe printed N. Yewer, and so it appears in the last edition by Townsend and Cattley, viii. 554, and its index, whereby the real name of Richard Ewer, or Eure, is quite concealed. Foxe, in the same article of John Davis, misprinted the name of Yowle as " Yowld," and that of Howbrough as " Hawborough."

Biographical Narrative of Thomas Hancock.

Page 71. Hancock's description of the obstinate resistance made by the inhabitants of Hampshire, in the diocese of bishop Gardyner, to the progress of the Reformation, is confirmed by one of the rarest productions of bishop Bale, entitled "An Expostulacion or complaynte agaynste the blasphemyes of a franticke papyst of Hamshyre. Cōpiled by Johan Bale." It is without date, but was certainly published in 1552,[a] being dedicated to " Johan Duke of Northumberlande, Lorde greate Maister of the Kinges most honourable housholde, and Lorde presydent of his Maiestyes most honourable prevye Counsell."

Early in the book Bale asserts that " the rage at thys present is horryble and fearce, whych the stought sturdy satellytes of Antichrist in dyverse partes of the realme, *chefely within Hamshire*, do bluster abroade in their mad furyes to blemyshe the Evangelycal veryte of the Lorde now revelated."

The report of the speeches made by the Hampshire papist against the King's proceedings in religious matters is as follows :—

" And nowe, last of all, by unlearned loyterers and desperate ruffyanes, as Braba

---

[a] The incident which occasioned it occurred " on the xxix daye of Decembre last past " (see p. 316). Before that date, in the year 1552, Bale had already left Hampshire to take possession of the bishopric of Ossory; and, as Dudley was not advanced to the dukedom of Northumberland before October, 1551, it is clear the offence given by the " franticke papyst " was during the Christmas of that year, and the publication no doubt very shortly after.

he of whom I have written this treatise followynge is one.[a] Of thys latter sort are some become farmers of benefyces, some blynde brokers in the lawe, some scribes, some pharysees, some flatterers for faver, some lyngerers for lucre, some cloynars for advauntage, menpleasers, and make-shyftes. These gyve the preachers most uncomly reportes to deface their godly preachynges, and most odyble names, to brynge them in contempte of the people. Their croked counsels, persuasyons, illusyons, provocacyons, and promyses of ayde in wythstandynge the mynysters, are such, for a welthie lyvynge in ydelnesse, that the truth of the Lord can take no place. These are, as were Elymas the sorcerer, Hymeneus, Philetus, and Alexander the copper smythe, enemyes of all truthe, withstanders of all ryghtousnesse, and chyldren of the devyl. Men of corrupt myndes, resysters of the veryte, and lewde as concernynge faythe (2 Tim. iii.); and all these are set a wurke by the pope's late masmongers, by olde pylgrymage goers, by crafty cathedralystes, mynster men, and collygeners,[b] lokinge yet for a daye of mayntenaunce in theire olde sorceryes."

Bale prays the duke of Northumberland—

"Lete them be restrayned from doynge suche vyolence, ravyne, and excesse, as they have done now of late to Christes mynysters in Hamshire. Lete them be inhybyted of dagger-drawynge and of fyste-lyftynge in the open strete, when no man hath ones offended them. Lete them leave their pullynges by the bearde and bosom in the presence of people, starynge like wylde oxen, whan no evyl at all is meant to them. Lete them no longer bragge afore the justyces in the open sessyons of castynge their glove and of wagynge battayle uncorrected, whan no thynge is eyther done, sayde, or yet thought agaynst them. Lete them be well stayed from ragynge and raylynge, oblocutynge and slaunderynge, withoute cause reasonable, for upholdyng the wicked tradycyons of Antichrist. Permyt them no longer to counsell in corners, to have wycked persuasyons, and to drawe people after them. Lete them from hensfourth be charged, under payne of sore punyshment, not lycencyously to do all their lewde lykynges, as they have done hertofore, lyke men that are lawles. We desyre not the evyll of thys frowarde sort, but their good. We covete not their losse, but their winning; not their utter destruccion, as they do ours, but their spedye amendement, if such angels of reprobacyon as they are may amende, which I scarsely beleve. Chiefly our request is to lyve in peace," &c.

"Now to thys frantyck papyst than, whych on the xxix. daye of Decembre

---

[a] In the margin is the word Braban. Whether this was the name of "the desperate papist" is not apparent.

[b] The term "Styngers," added in the margin, is one I am unable to explain.

last past [1551] in the house[a] of a gentylman of hys affynyte within Hamshire beynge in the full beate of hys frenesye, brast out into thys unreverent, blasphemouse, and contemptuouse talke of the Kinges Maiestie, and of hys mooste godly procedynges. Alas poore chyld! (sayd he) unknowne is it to hym what actes are made now a dayes. But whan he cometh ones of age, he wyll se an other rule, and hange up a hondred of such heretyke knaves, meanynge the preachers of our tyme, and their maynteyners, by lyke. For at the same season he had most spyghtfully rayled of one of them, beynge absent [here Bale probably means himself], whych never in hys lyfe did hym dyspleasure, nether in dede nor in wurd, that he was able to burden hym wyth. The fyrst part of this blasphemouse clause toucheth the Kynges hyghnes, the second hys honourable counsell, and the thyrd the true ministers of God's wurde."

Bale then proceeds to discuss each of these divisions at length; and in the course of his arguments, in reply to the papist's speech concerning the King, he thus speaks of the excellence of Edward's education :—

"Hys wurthie educacion in liberall letters and godly vertues, and hys naturall aptenesse in retaynyng the same, plenteously declareth him to be no *pore child*, but a manifest Salomon in princely wisdom. Hys sober admonicions and open examples of godlines at this day sheweth him mindfully to prefer the welthe of his commens, as well gostly as bodyly, above all foren matters. Marke what his majestie hath done already in religion, in abolishing the most shameful idolatries of Antichrist, besides his other actes for publyque affayres, and ye shal find at this day no christen prynce lyke to hym."

Returning to the papist, Bale declares—

"The propyrtie which he hath of that father and mother [the Pope and Babylon] is to blaspheme God, and in that he hath shewed hymselfe plenteouse. First, by a chaplayne, whych popyshly mynystred in hys hyred benefyce; secondly, by conveyaunce of certen ymages in hope of a change; and thirdly, in judgyng it a fowle heresye to write any thynge in reproche of the Byshopp of Rome.

"Concernynge the first. Upon the .xx. day of September last past I was (as he well knoweth) at service there,[b] to beholde the workemanly conveyaunce of hym and that popyshe chaplayne of his, and to know what wholesome frutes I shulde fynde after that tyme of their .ii. plantinges. Such an other ape of Antichriste as that prest was never sawe I afore in my lyfe, for he coulde not reade a psalme, nether yet speake Englyshe, beynge an allyen, an

[a] I have not discovered any allusion that might identify the parties, but they were doubtless in the vicinity of Bale's own residence, which was at the rectory of Bishop's Stoke, five miles from Southampton.

[b] The place is not mentioned.

Armoricall or Frenche Britayne*; and to excuse his beastly igrtoraunce, his own selfe was compelled, I being there present, to slaver out the .ii. lessons of the Byble with no small stutting and stamberyng, turnyng his arse to the people after the old popysh maner, to helpe forward the Kynges most godly procedynges. More apysh toyes and gawdysh feates could never a dysard in England have plaied (I think) then that apysh prest showed there at the communyon. He turned and tossed, lurked and lowted, snored and snurted, gaped and gasped, kneled and knocked, loked and lycked, with both hys thombes at hys eares, and other tryckes more, that he made me .xx. tymes to remember Wylle Somer.[b] Yet of them both that prest semed the more foole a great deale; and, to amende the matter, he had than a new shaven crowne, which I rebuked him for. By thys I prove hys maistre a mocker of God, a deceyver of the people, and a contempner of the Kynges just procedynges."

The third offence of the papist was that—

"In the weke afore Christmas last past, as he chaunced to be in the house of the forseyd gentylman of his owne affinyte, where he might alwayes be bolde to do hys lewde feates, hys accustomed frenesie came sodenly upon him. In the heat wherof he most shamefuly revyled a servant of that house, calling hym heretyke and knave, because he had begonne to studie a parte[c] in suche a comedie as myghtely rebuked the abomynacyons and fowle fylthie occupienges of the bishopp of Rome. Moreover, he requyred hym in hys own stought maner to do a lewd massage, whych was to call the compiler of that comedie [Bale himself] both heretike and knave, concludynge that it was a boke of most perniciouse heresie. That boke was imprynted about .vj. years ago, and hath bene abroad ever sens, to be both seane and judged of men what it contayneth. And thys is the name therof, 'A Comedie concerning iii. lawes, of Nature, Moyses, and Christ, etc.'"

Page 73. *The Proclamation concerning irreverent talkers of the Sacrament,* dated 27th Dec. 1 Edw. VI. is inserted by Strype in the Repository of original documents at the end of vol. ii. of his Ecclesiastical Memorials, under letter M. It declared that whosoever should "revile, contempne, or despise the said sacrament by calling it an *Idol*, (as Hancock did,) or other vile names, shal incur the Kyng's high indignation, and suffre imprisonment, or be otherwise grievously punished at his Majesties wil and pleasure."

 It seems not improbable that this was the very "sir Brysse," mentioned by Thomas Hancock (p. 81).

[b] The favourite fool of the King's court.

[c] This passage is remarkable, as showing that Bale's comedies (as he chose to term them) were really enacted, as well in Hampshire, as he states in his "Vocacyon" they were at Kilkenny.

The Defence of Thomas Thackham.

Page 95. *Clement Burdet.*—In a list of recusant clergy in 1561 we read: " Clement Burdet, late of Bath : to remain at Crondal in Hampshire, or else at Sonning in Barkshire. *(Contemporary side-note,)* An unlearned priest." Strype, Annals of the Reformation, i. 277, from a document in the State-paper office.

Page 129. The following were the letters patent for the mastership of Reading School, granted in 1541 to Leonard Coxe and his deputies or assigns during his life, and which were successively transferred to Thackham, Palmer, and other parties, as stated in p. 108. With this copy I have been favoured by the Rev. Robert T. Appleton, M.A., the present master of Reading School, through the kind assistance of William Hobbs, esq. F.S.A.

De concessione ad vitam pro Coxe.—Rex omnibus ad quos, etc. salutem. Sciatis quod nos de gratia nostra speciali ac ex certa scientia et mero motu nostris, et ob specialem amorem et zelum quos pro erudicione et educacione puerorum hujus regni nostri Angliæ in arte et sciencia grammaticali et honestis literis diu ante hæc tempora habuimus et adhuc gerimus, volentes pro hujusmodi educacione et erudicione puerorum aliqualiter providere et augmentari; et pro eo quod dilectus subditus noster Leonardus Coxe, qui in arte et sciencia grammaticali satis peritus et eruditus existit, ut certam habemus noticiam, nullum officium neque stipendium a nobis pro hujusmodi educacione puerorum adhuc habet neque percepit, ut certam habemus scienciam, dedimus et concessimus ac per presentes damus et concedimus eidem Leonardo officium Magistri sive Præceptoris Scholæ Grammaticalis sive Ludi Literarii villæ nostræ de Reading, in comitatu nostro Berkshire, ac ipsum Leonardum Magistrum et præceptorem scholæ sive ludi prædicti facimus constituimus et ordinamus per præsentes; et ulterius de uberiori gratia nostra et pro consideracionibus prædictis dedimus et concessimus ac per præsentes damus et concedimus præfato Leonardo totum illud mesuagium in Reading prædicta cum suis pertinenciis in quo prædictus Leonardus modo inhabitat, una cum quadam parva venella sive pecia terræ jacente ex parte australi ejusdem mesuagii, ac etiam quoddam aliud mesuagium sive domum in Reading prædicta modo in tenura et occupacione prædicti Leonardi vocatum *a Schole House* in quo pueri modo erudiuntur et docentur in arte et sciencia prædictis; habendum et tenendum gaudendum et exercendum tam officium prædictum præfato Leonardo per se vel per sufficientem deputatum suum sive sufficientes deputatos suos, quàm prædictum mesuagium domum venellam et cetera præmissa cum corum pertinentiis eidem Leonardo et assignatis suis durante vita ejusdem Leonardi absque compoto seu aliquo alio proinde nobis heredibus et successoribus nostris reddendo solvendo seu faciendo. Et ulterius sciatis quod nos de ampliori gratia nostra ac ex certa sciencia et mero motu nostris prædictis et pro consideracionibus prædictis dedimus et concessimus ac per præsentes damus et concedimus præfato Leonardo Coxe de et pro exercicio et occupacione officii prædicti ac pro diligencia laboribus et expensis suis circa idem officium habendis et sustinendis quandam annuitatem sive annualem redditum decem librarum, habendum gaudendum et recipiendum prædictam annuitatem sive annualem redditum decem librarum sterlingorum præfato Leonardo Coxe durante vita sua de exitibus proficuis firmis et revencionibus manerii nostri de Cholsey in dicto comitatu nostro Berkshiræ, tam per manus receptoris et ballivorum ejusdem manerii quàm per manus generalis receptoris terrarum nuper monasterii pertinentium pro tempore existentium ad festa Paschæ et Sancti Michaelis archangeli equis porcionibus solvendis. Et insuper de uberiori gratia nostra prædicta dedimus et concessimus ac per præsentes damus et concedimus præfato Leonardo Coxe tot et tantas denariorum summas ad quot et quantas prædicta annuitas sive annualis redditus decem librarum a festo Sancti Michaelis archangeli quod erat in anno regni nostri tricesimo primo se attingit, habendum percipiendum et gaudendum eidem Leonardo Coxe ex dono et regardo nostris de exitibus firmis revencionibus et proficuis prædicti manerii nostri de Cholsey per manus generalis receptoris terrarum dicti nuper monasterii pertinentium absque compoto seu aliquo alio proinde nobis heredibus et successoribus nostris reddendo solvendo seu faciendo. Eo quod expressa mencio, &c. In cujus rei, etc. Teste Rege apud Westmonasterium decimo die Februarij.

Per breve de Privato Sigillo, etc.

(Rot. Pat. 32 Hen. VIII. pars 5.)

The Autobiography of Edward Underhill.

Page 132. *The band of Gentlemen Pensioners.*—Although sir Humphrey Ratcliffe (in page 168) roundly asserted that Underhill had served from the beginning of the band, it is probable that such was not literally the case, but that he received his appointment on returning from the French campaign in 1544, where he had been one of the King's body-guard, as described in page 148. The band of Gentlemen Pensioners was formed in December, 1539, as is distinctly recorded by the chronicler Hall. He states that Henry VIII. had first instituted this force at the commencement of his reign; but, being formed on too sumptuous a scale, it fell into disuse, until revived thirty years after, shortly before the reception of the lady Anna of Cleves. Mr. Pegge, who read a memoir upon this honourable Band before the Society of Antiquaries in 1782, and afterwards published it as the Second Part of his Curialia, 4to. 1784;

imagined that he had discovered that the band was existing in 1526, and that consequently Hall's account was fallacious; but Mr. Pegge was misled by the circumstance that the documents upon which he relied, being themselves undated, followed in the same MS. the household statutes made at Eltham in 1526 (as they do in the volume of Household Ordinances, printed for the Society of Antiquaries, 4to. 1790). But the names which occur in those documents prove them to be of the latter years of Henry's reign, whilst Katharine Parr was queen and Wriothesley was chancellor; and consequently Mr. Pegge was led into a material error, which affects several passages of his memoir.

The date mentioned by Hall would derive confirmation, were it requisite, from a letter of archbishop Cranmer, who on the 28th Dec. 1539, thus addressed the lord privy seal (Crumwell) on behalf of one of his servants, a brother of the martyr Anne Askew:

"Whereas I am informed that this bearer Edward Askew my servant, son unto sir William Askew knight, is by some nobleman preferred unto the room of one of these *new speres in the court*, which because it is done without my knowledge and his, I shall beseech you, my Lord, inasmuch as I have no friend to sue unto for me and mine but only unto your lordship, that you will at this my request bear unto him your lawful favour and furtherance in the same; assuring your lordship that he, the young man, is of a very gentil nature, right forward, and of good activity, so that I think he shall be meet to furnish such a room, and to do to the King's majestic diligent and faithful service. At Forde, 28th Decembre, 1539." Works of Cranmer (Parker Soc.) ii. 399.

In the original ordinances for the constitution of the band (which Mr. Pegge has introduced into his memoir) the members are not termed Pensioners, but " Speres, called Men of Armes," and they were to be chosen from gentlemen of noble blood. They were, in fact, upon the same footing as the force which composed the garrison of Calais, who were also called indifferently Spears, or Men of Arms, and were usually of good families: see the list of those who held office in 1539 (not 1533) in the Chronicle of Calais, p. 136. At the coronation of Edward the Sixth they are called "the pencioners," and king Edward mentions them as "the gentlemen pensioners" in his Journal, Oct. 31, 1551. The annual pension received by each man was seventy marks (16l. 13s. 4d.),—in 1509, according to Hall, it had been fixed at fifty pounds. The captain received two hundred marks, the lieutenant and standard-bearer each one hundred. These officers were also reckoned of " the ordinary of the King's chamber, which have bouche of court, and also theire dietts within the court." (Household Ordinances, p. 165.)

In the list printed in Mr. Pegge's memoir sir Anthony Browne is captain, sir Ralph Fane lieutenant, and Edward Bellingham standard-bearer. After sir Anthony Browne's death in 1548 the marquess of Northampton became captain; and in king Edward's reign sir Humphrey Radcliffe was lieutenant and sir William Stafford standard-bearer.

It is evident that this band of Spears was suggested by the French *Garde du Corps*, which was instituted by Louis XI. in 1474: and which was a band of one hundred Lances, each attended by a man of arms and two archers. The English Spears, in like manner, were to be attended each by a page, and a coustrell[a] or servant armed with a javelin or demi-lance, and by two archers well horsed and harnessed. When on foot the Spears adopted the battle-axe as their weapon, which was also in imitation of the French band, who were sometimes called the *Gentilhommes du Bec de Corbin:* "Ils avoient, outre la lance, la hache d'armes, dont ils se servoient lorsqu'ils etoient de guet ou de garde aupres de la personne du roy." (Père Daniel)

When Edward VI. proceeded through London to his coronation "the pensioners and men at armes, with their pole-axes, went on either side the way on foote;" and on the King's landing on the day of the coronation at the privy stairs, they awaited him there, "apparelled all in red damaske, with their pole-axes in their hands."[b]

The band of Pensioners maintained its credit and estimation through the reign of Elizabeth, and at her death their Captain, lord Hunsdon, recommended them to the notice of her successor in the following terms: "They are in all fifty gentlemen,—besides myself, the Lieutenant, Standard-bearer, Clerk of the Cheque, and Gentleman Harbinger,—chosen out of the best and antientest families of England, and some of them sons to earls, barons, knights, and esquires, men thereunto specially recommended for their worthyness and sufficiency, without any stain or taint of dishonour, or disparagement in blood. Her Majesty and other princes her predecessors have found great use of their service, as well in the guard and defence of their royall persons, as also in

---

[a] Mr. Pegge (p. 5) makes a note that this word is "uniformly miswritten throughout these ordinances; for it should evidently be *coustill*, an abbreviate of the French word *coustillier*." He quotes lord Herbert and Lloyd (the author of the Worthies) in favour of this view; and says that Père Daniel derived the term from *coútille*, a cutlass, in Latin *cultellus*. I am rather inclined to derive the term from *costé*, and to understand it for one who kept close by the side of his master, in which sense it would answer to the English *henchman* or *launchman*. The term in use in English was certainly *costerell*. (See Machyn's Diary, p. 13.) The name of Cotterell is probably derived from this source.

[b] So, Underhill says (p. 161), "we came up into the chambre of presence with our poll-axes in our hands." It was only when the gentleman pensioner was on special duty that he carried his pole-axe in person. At other times it was "borne after him with a sufficient man, the axe being cleane and bright," as required in the ordinances.

sundry other employments, as well civil as military, at home and abroad, insomuch as it hath served them always as a nursery to breed up deputies of Ireland, ambassadors into foreign parts, counsellors of state, captains of the guard, governors of places, and commanders in the wars, both by land and sea." This was high boasting; but the captain might have added that, in the person of sir Christopher Hatton, the band had bred not only a captain of the guard, but a lord chancellor.

For fuller and subsequent particulars in the history of the Band the reader will turn to Mr. Pegge's memoir. In the Collectanea Topogr. et Geneal. vol. vi. p. 192, will be found a roll of the band in the year 1618 (erroneously headed 1608).

Page 134. The anecdote of king Edward the Sixth's inquiries respecting Saint George, communicated by Underhill to Foxe, is as follows,—" being notified to me by one mr. Edward Underhill, who, waiting the same time with the rest of his fellowes, pensioners and men at arms, as sir Henry Gates, mr. Robert Hall, mr. Henry Harston, and mr. Stafforton, heard these wordes betwene the Kinge and his counsaile. The 4. yeare of his raigne, being then but 13 yeares old and upward, at Greenwich upon S. George's day, when he was come from the sermon into the presence-chamber, there being his uncle the duke of Somerset, the duke of Northumberland, with other lords and knights of that order, called the order of the Garter, he said unto them, ' My Lords, I pray you what saint is S. George that we heere so honour him?' At which question the other lords being all astonied, the lord treasurer that then was (the marques of Winchester), perceiving this, gave answer and said, ' If it please your Majestie, I did never reade in any historie of S. George* but

---

* In the King's scheme for remodelling the order of the Garter, made shortly after, (and printed in his Literary Remains, 4to. 1859,) the very name of Saint George was to be suppressed, and the order called merely "The Order of the Garter, or Defence of the Truth as contained in holy scripture." The annual feast was to be removed from St. George's day, and kept early in December. In 1630 the fair fame of our national saint was vindicated by Dr. Peter Heylyn in his "History of the famous Saint and Soldier of Christ Jesus, St. George of Cappadocia," a book respecting which some curious particulars will be found in Dr. Heylyn's Life, prefixed to the edition of his History of the Reformation, by J. C. Robertson, M.A. 1849, pp. lxx—lxxiv. Heylyn remarks that "the memory of this saint shines in our calendar prefixed before the public liturgy of the church of England, where he is specially honoured with the name of *Saint*, as is no other not being an apostle or evangelist but Saint Martin only." (History of St. George, edit. 2, p. 208.) But at the last review of the Prayer-book that designation was prefixed to some other names. In the Archæologia, vol. v. the history of Saint George was investigated at some length by the Rev. Samuel Pegge, LL.D., F.S.A.

onely in *Legenda Aurea*, where it is thus set downe, that S. George out with his sword, and ran the dragon through with his speare.' The King, when he could not a great while speake for laughing, at length said, ' I pray you, my lord, and what did he with his sword the while?' ' That I cannot tell your Majestie,' said he. And so an end of that question of good S. George."

Page 150. *High price of wood in London.*—In William Baldwin's poem, entitled, " The Funeralles of King Edward the syxt," (reprinted for the Roxburghe club in 1817, and also as an appendix to Trollope's History of Christ's Hospital,) is the following passage,—the personification being " crasy Cold:"

> He passed Yorke, and came to London strayt,
> And there alight to geve his horse a bayt,
> Where, ere he had three days in stable stood,
> He eat so much, the poore could get no wood,
> Except they would pay after double price
> For billet treble under common cise.

Page 152. *Underhill's committal to Newgate* is not noticed in the register of the privy council: but his discharge is thus recorded:—

"At Richmount, the 21st August, 1553. A letter to the keeper of Newgate for the deliverie of Edwarde Underhill, in consideracion of his extreame sickenes, out of prison, to mr. Thomas White and John Throgmorton esquires, maisters of the quenes highnes' requests, whome the lords have ordred to take bands of the said Underhill for his appearaunce herafter before them, beinge called therunto." (Council Register, as printed in the Cecill Papers, by Haines, p. 172.) Underhill is wrong in stating that his release passed the council when his enemies were absent: the board was very fully attended on this day, by no less than twenty-seven members.

Page 158 note. Sir Thomas Palmer would probably be called *long Palmer*, in distinction to another of the name, whom we find mentioned as *little Palmer* in a list of the defenders at the Justes held on the morrow of the Coronation of Edward the Sixth.

Page 159. *Hot gospellers*—this appears to have been a cant term in common use. Attached to one of Latimer's sermons we find this side-note, " Hot gospellers are no sufferers of persecution." It is placed against this following passage: " Others, that began so *hot* at first, are quite gone. And truely I fear me that a great many of those are as the seed sown upon stones, which speak now fair, and make a goodly shew of the gospel; but if there come persecution or affliction, then they are gone." Latimer's Works, (Parker Soc.) ii. 213.

Page 163. *When we came to Ludegate, the gate was fast locked, and a greate wache within the gate off Londonars, but noone withowte* Page 165. *So to New-*

gate we wentt, where was a greate wache withowte the gate.—This was the course taken on occasions of extraordinary alarm. In the previous year, upon the accession of queen Mary, we read: " Item the xxij day of the same monyth (July, 1553) began the wache at every gatte in London in harnes, viij be syde the viij comoners." Chronicle of the Grey Friars of London, p. 81.

Page 172. The *doctor Luke* of Underhill's narrative, author of *John Bon and mast Person*, is certainly to be identified with an author mentioned by Holinshed, among the learned men who flourished in the reign of Mary, as " Lucas Shepherd, born in Colchester in Essex, an English poet;" and of whom the fuller account given by Bale is as follows:—

" Lucas Opilio, Colcestriæ ut ferunt in Essexia natus, poeta valde facetus erat, qui in poematibus ac rhythmis Skeltono non inferior, in patrio sermone eleganter edidit, honestis jocis ac salibus plenos,

Adversus veritatis osores libellos aliquot.—Quosdam etiam Psalmos in rhythmos Anglicos vertit, tractatulosque fecit plures. Claruit anno Christi 1554."

Warton, in his History of English Poetry, remarks—

"Luke Shepherd, mentioned by Holinshed, iii. 1168, appears to have been nothing more than a petty pamphleteer in the cause of Calvinism, and to have acquired the character of a poet from a metrical translation of some of David's Psalms about the year 1554. I believe one or two of Shepherd's pieces in prose are among bishop Tanner's books at Oxford."

Strype, in his notice of doctor Luke (Ecclesiastical Memorials, ii. 116), states that he had been imprisoned in the Fleet for former pamphlets written in king Henry's time: but Underhill (see p. 172) does not say that his imprisonment was in Henry's reign, and from the context it may rather be concluded that it occurred in the reign of Mary.

Doctor Luke Shepherd's productions having been all published anonymously, they have still to be ascertained, with the exception of *John Bon and Mast Person*, to which Underhill's story has helped us. This was a quarto pamphlet of four leaves, imprinted at London by John Daye and William Seres. It was reprinted (250 copies) in 1807, by G. Smeaton, accompanied only by a few lines of not very accurate remarks, which had been written in it by Richard Forster, esq. to whom the original had belonged—no second copy being known. It is reviewed in Censura Literaria, v. 277-280, by Mr. Joseph Haslewood, who ridicules the name of "Interlude," given to it by Mr. Forster. It is, however, a conversation (in 164 rhyming lines) more resembling the religious plays of John Bale than the poetry of Skelton. John Bon, a ploughman, and Mast Person, a parson or priest, meet upon the eve of the feast of Corpus Christi, and discuss the observances then celebrated, and the doctrine of transubstantiation, upon which many coarse jests are passed. The term

326   APPENDIX.

Mast, as an abbreviation of Master, occurs again in some doggrel verses of Stephen Staple to Mast Camell, mentioned in Ames's History of Printing, (edit. Dibdin,) vol. iii. p. 582. In 1852 "John Bon and Mast Person" was re-edited for the Percy Society, by Mr. W. H. Black, who remarks: "John Bon is the Piers Ploughman of the sixteenth century. So characteristic and spirited is his part of the dialogue,—so popular and forcible is his argument,—so justly severe are the rebukes administered to the Parson, that John Bon may be read more than once without disrelish."

Page 174. *Allen the prophesyer.*—In the records of the Tower prisoners the name of this person twice occurs. In a return made on the 11th Feb. 1551-2, is mentioned "Robert Allen, who hath been there xij monethes and more, for matters of astronomie and suspicion of calculation." (MS. Harl. 419.) Again (also in 1551-2), "Robert Alen, rated by the weke, for all charges, viij s. vj d." (Bayley, Hist. of the Tower, Appx. XLVI.)

The following are the papers which were found upon Allen's person, and preserved by mr. Underhill.

[MS. Harl. 424, f. 1.]

No. 1. On parchment.

Iu a man haue stoleñ any thyng̃ of thyne.

Take & wryte in pchement. ✠ Agios ✠ Agios ✠ Agios ✠ Crux Crux Crux Spiritus scūs Spiritus scus spiritus be wᵗ the Su"nt of God. & putt yt ouer thy hed, & in the same nyght thow shalt knowe who yt ys.

No. 2. On another piece of parchment.

If any man⁹ of woman haue doñ the thefte.

Take & wryte thes names in vyrgen waxe. ✠ Agios ✠ Agios ✠ Agios ✠. & holde yt in thy lefte hand vnder thy ryght eyre, & lay the to slepe, and thow shalt haue a vysyon & knowlege who hathe thy thyng̃.

No. 3. On paper folded and soiled from carriage in the pocket.

Wheñ thowe wylte goe fourthe to playe att the Carde & Dyse lett the Ascendent be in a sygne moveable as ♈/♋/♎/♑/. And lett the lord of the Ascendent be well dysposed in a good place.

And lett the 7 house be feble and impedyte: And yf ytt maye be lett the lord of the 8 house be in the second or in the fyrste house recevyd of the lord of the second or the fyrste house, nor lett nott hym̃ receve the lord of the second. And lett the ☽ be fre sepate from a fortune & joynyng̃ to añ other fortune for tunate & strong̃, & lett nott her be upon the Earthe. And the breste of the player toward the ☽ & hys face. And yf att these thyngẹ cannott be done, Att the leaste see ytt be a moveable sygne. Whan thow goest owt for to playe, and the ☽ uppon thy breste when thow playest, or att the leste see that thy breste and thy face be toward the ☽.

No. 4. On paper.

And yff thow weylt wette whether a man tell ye a false tatte or a trewe, take the letters of hes name & of hes surname & of that daye, & putto all the nowmbere xxx· & than depart alle that hotte nowmbere be xxv^{ti}, & yf ther leve euen nowmbere at the laste ende, yt ys falss that he tellett, and yff yt be oode yt ys trwe.

And yf thow welt wette a gowynge a pelgremage, whethe[r] they shall well go & com̃ harmelles or nott, take the nowmbere of the letters of her names, & of the daye & of the age of the mowne, & the name of the place that they goo to, and putto att thes xxx & than depart all the hotte nowmbere be xxv^{ti} as long as ye maye, & yf ther leve even nowmber they shall goo and come withoute hort or harme, & yff the nowmbere be oode they shatt nott spede well.

And of thes manere ye maye wette att manere of thyngẹ that ye dessyre.

Also yf ye well wette of a man that purpowsyth hem̃ to have a benefyce, or to go to Relygyoñ, take the letters of hes name and of the beneffece, & of the daye, and depart them be xxx. and yf ther lene eveñ nownber he shatt spede, & yf ther leue oode he shatt nott spede, & yf ther leve ix he shatt be Relygyous.

No. 5. On paper.

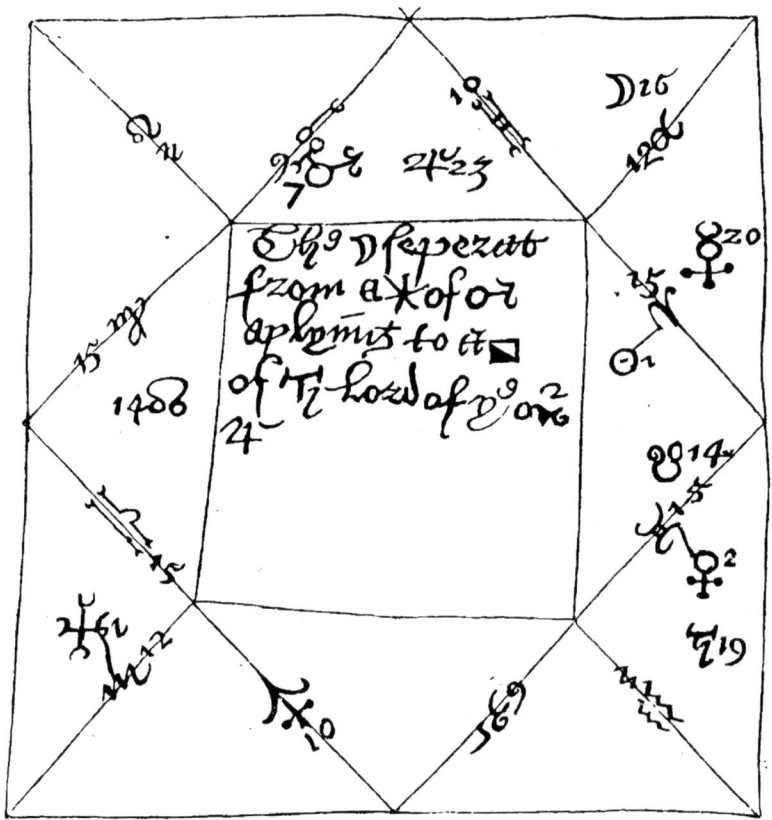

Whythir it is better to remove or to contynew wher the qwerāt do dwell styll, and whether they be past dawngar of burnyng of ther hows or godws, or nat.

No. 6. On paper.

Yf thow wylt take yei iornay to do any thyng.

    The ☽ being in ♈ go in the ow^r of ♂

    The ☽ in ♉ go in ye ow^r of ♀

    The ☽ be in ♊ go in ye ow^r ☿

    The ☽ in ♋ go in the ow^r ☽

The ☽ in ♌ go in yͤ owʳ of yͤ ☉
The ☽ in ♍ go in the owr of ☿
The ☽ in ♎ go in yͤ owʳ of ♀
The ☽ in ♏ go in yͤ owʳ of ☊
The ☽ in ♐ go in the owʳ of ♃
The ☽ in ♑ go in the owʳ of ♄
The ☽ in ♒ go in the owʳ of ♄
The ☽ in ♓ go in the owʳ of ♑

Nota.—When the ☽ is in ♎ go nat in yͤ owʳ ☉
When the ☽ is in ♓ go not in yͤ owʳ ☿
When the ☽ is in ♍ go not in the owʳ of ♀
When the ☽ is in ♋ go nat in yͤ owʳ ♂
and so ferthe of all other.

Examination of Allen.
(MS. Harl. 424, Art. 7.)

Memorandum.—That Alleyn requireth to talke with one of the counselle, sayinge yf he were unburdened of that he wold then saye, he cared not what came of hym.

Also he saithe afore the commissioners that he can make the grett alyxor.

Also he stode earnestly before the saide commissioners that he cowld saye more concerning astrologie and astronomy than all the lerned men within the universities of Oxford or Cambridge, and yet understandeth no parte of the Lattyn tonge.

Item, sir John Godsalve* required the commissioners to demaund whether that Alleyn did not saye unto ij men yet lyvinge, that x daies before the apprehension of the lord Cromwell, that the said lord Cromwell should be in the towre within xiiij daies followinge.

* Sir John Godsalve was of a Norfolk family. He was clerk of the signet in the reign of Henry VIII., was knighted at Edward's coronation, Feb. 22, 1547-8, and soon after appointed a commissioner of visitation (see the Return, 1 Edw. VI. printed in Appendix to Dugdale's St. Paul's, (edit. Ellis,) No. 4). He held the office of comptroller of the mint; and died Nov. 20, 1557. There is a portrait of him by Holbein engraved in Chamberlain's series; where also will be found further notices of sir John and his family, by Mr. Lodge. Another portrait and memoir will be found in Harding's Biographical Mirrour, p. 37. See also a note to the Privy-purse Expenses of the Princess Mary, p. 234.

APPENDIX.

Item, the question beinge demaunded of him, he denied not that he said so, but said that he spake it not of his owne knowelege, but of otheres.

Item, sir John Godsalve saythe that he was borne in Northefolke, and that he bathe ben a gret doer in judgementes of dyvers matters there.

Note in Underhill's hand.—This Alen was called *the god of Northefolke* beffore they reaceaved the light of the gospelle.

The statute against conjurations, upon the repeal of which Allen is said to have relied (p. 173), is as follows:—

(MS. Lansdowne 2, art. 15.)

"The bill against conjuracions, and wichecraftes. and sorcery, and enchantments.

"Whereas dyvers and sundrie persons unlawfully have devised and practised invocacions and conjuracions of sprites, pretending by suche meanes to understande and get knowlege, for their own lucre, in what place treasure of golde and silver shoulde or mought be founde or had in the earthe or other secrete places, and also have used and occupied wichecraftes, inchantments, and sorceries, to the distruccion of their neighboures personnes and goodes. And for execucion of their saide falce devises and practises have made or caused to be made diverse images and pictures of men, women, children, angelles, and develles, beastes, or fowlles; and also have made crownes, septures, swordes, rynges, glasses, and other things, and, gyving faithe and credit to suche fantasticall practises, have dygged up and pulled down an infinite nombre of crosses within this realme, and taken upon them to declare and tell where thinges lost or stollen should become; wych thinges cannot be used and exercised but to the greate offence of God's lawe, hurte and damage of the Kinges subjectes, and losse of the sowlės of such offenders, to the greate dishonor of God, infamy and disquietnes of the realme. For reformacion whereof be it enacted by the Kynge oure Sovereigne Lord, with th'assent of the lordes spirituall and temporall, and the commons, in this present parliament assembled, and by auctoritie of the same, that if any persone or persones, after the firste day of Maye next comyng, use, devise, practise, or exercise any invocacions or conjuracions of sprites, wichecraftes, enchantments, or sorceries, to th'intent to get or fynde money or treasure, or to waste, consume, or destroy any person in his bodie, membres, or goodes, to provoke any persone to unlawfull love, or for any other unlawfull intente or purpose, or by occasion or colour of such thinges or any of them, or for dispite of Christe, or for lucre of money, dygge up or pull downe any crosse, or crosses, or by suche invocacions, or conjuracions of sprites, wichcraftes, enchantments, or sorcerie, or any of them, take upon them to tell or declare where goodes stolen or lost shall become, that then all and every suche offence and offences, from the saide first day of Maye next comynge, shall be demyd accepted and adjuged felony; and that all and every persone and persones offendyng as is above said, their councellors, abettors and procurors, and every of them, from the saide first day of Maye shall be demyde, accepted, and adjuged a felon and felones, and the offender or offenders contrarie to this Acte, being thereof lawfullie convicted before suche as shall have power and auctoritie to here and determyne felonyes, shall have and suffer suche paynes of deathe, losse and forfaytures of their landes, tenements, goodes, and catalles, as in cases of felonye, by the course of the common lawes of this realme, and also shall lose privilege of clergie and sayntuarie."

Indorsed, Bill against conjuracion, wichecraftes, &c. an⁰ 33 H. 8, No. 8. Repealed 1⁰ Edw. 6.

From the number of prophesyers, conjurers, and pretenders to supernatural powers, whose names occur about the same time as that of Robert Allen, we may conclude that the profession was not unprofitable, though great efforts were made to check it by severe punishments. One is thus noticed by Stowe: "Also in the month of September (1550) Grig, a poulter of Surrey, taken among the people for a prophet, in curing of divers diseases by words and prayers, and saying he would take no money, &c. was, by commandement of the earle of Warwick and other of the councill, set on a scaffold in the towne of Croydon, in Surrey, with a paper on his breast, wherein was written his deceiptfull and hypocriticall dealings. And after that, on the 8 of Septembre, set on the pillorie in Southwarke, being then our Ladies faire there kept, and, the maior of London with his brethren the aldermen riding thorow the faire, the said Grig asked them and all the citizens forgivenesse. Thus much for Grig." (Stowe's Chronicle.)

The following particulars respecting some other conjurers, in the reign of Edward the Sixth, are very curious, and hitherto unpublished. Among other extraordinary assertions here made are these, that the conjurer's art had been employed to recover the protector Somerset's stolen plate, as well as the money of a servant of secretary Paget, with the consent of both those statesmen; and another, that there were supposed to be five hundred conjurers practising in England. The confessions of Wycherley's ill-success are so ludicrous and absurd that it is difficult to realise the fact that they were gravely extracted by a privy councillor. Every page is signed by the hand of the deponent:—

(MS. Lansdowne 2, art. 26.)

[*Modern title*, An examination taken by Sir Thomas Smith of Wm. Wicherly, conjurer, and his complice, a⁰ 1549.]

William Wicherley, of Saint Sepulchre's parishe, in Charterhouse-lane, taylor, where he hath dwelt for the space of twoo yeres and more, being examyned upon certain articles, he saith as followeth:—

To the first he saith that he hath been theis three monethes acquaynted with John Clerke, of Westminster.

To the seconde he saith that about Easter last one of the gromes of the King's slaughter-house wife, whose name he knoweth not, had her purse picked of tenne shillinges, and the forsaid Clerck brought the said slaughterman's wife to this deponent, to lerne who had picked her purse. At which tyme she delivered to this deponent the names in writing of suche persons as she had in suspicion. Which names he put severally into the pipe of a kay, and laying the kay apon the verse [a] of the spalter (psalter) in the spalter book, viz. *Si videbis furem, &c.* did say, *Si videbis furem, correbas cum eo, et cum adulterem portionem tuam ponebas.* And whan this verse was said over one of the names, which was a woman, the book and key tourned rounde, and therapon this deponent said to the abovesaid Clerke, and the slaughterman's wife, that the same woman had the money whose name was on the kay, as farr as this deponent could judge, because the kay and boke did tourne at her name and at none others. And he saith that he hath used this practise[b] so often that he (dothe not remembre *altered to*) cannot expresse how many the tymes; for people ar so importune upon hym dayly for this purpose, that he is not able to avoyde them, but kepeth hymself within his doores.

Per me, Wylla^m Wycherle.

Item, to the third and iiijth articles he saith that John Clerke was with hym apon Saturday last in this deponent's house, and moved hym to use his forsaid practise for a kercher, a placard, and a double rayle[c] which a woman of Westminster, as the said Clarke said, was stolne (*sic*), and then named to this deponent vj wymmen and a man which was then in the house when it was stolne; and this deponent aunswered and said that he wolde not meddle withall, except he had the counsail's lettre or commaundement. And he saith that mr. Paget servant about hallantide last came to this respondent with his maister's lettre, desiring and willing hym to help his man the best he could to mony that he had lost; yet notwithstanding he saith that he wolde not, nor did not medle anything in the mater. And otherwise he denyeth the articles.

Per me, Wylla^{m.} Wycherley.

xxiij° Augusti.

Item, he saith that about ten years past he used a circule called *Circulus Salamonis*, at a place called Pembsam[d] in Sussex, to calle up *Baro*, whom

---

[a] Psalm l. v. 18. It is printed above as written in the MS.

[b] The same mode of divination is described in the Athenian Oracle about 1704; see Brand's Popular Antiquities, (edit. Ellis,) ii. 641.

[c] *i.e.* a kerchief, a placket or under-petticoat, and a rail or over-petticoat.

[d] Perhaps Pepplesham, between Hastings and Bexhill.

he taketh an orientalle or septentrialle spirit. Where was also one Robert Bayly the scryer of the cristalle stone, syr John Anderson the *magister operator*, syr John Hickley, and Thomas Goslyng, in the which their practise they had sworde, ring, and hallywater. Where they were frustrated, for *Baro* did not appere, nor other vision of spirit, but there was a terrible wynde and tempest for the tyme of the circulation. And sithens that tyme he used no consecrat cyrcule, but hath used the cristalle to invocate the spirit called *Scariot*, which he called dyvers tymes into the cristall, to have knowledge of thyngs stolne, which spirit hath geven hym knowledge an C. tymes, and thereby men have been restored to their goodes.

And this practise by the cristalle he hath at the commaundement of my lord protector executed in the presence of mr. Thynne, mr. Whalley, mr. George Blage, and mr. Challoner, and one Weldon. And by this meane my lord protector's plate was founde, where this deponent told his grace that it was hidd.

And about a moneth past, at the chaunge of the mone, he did use this praetise with the cristalle, and invocation of the spirite, to know whither he could fynde things that were lost; and about twoo monethes, likewise at Haleoke, for treasure hid, but he hath founde none by his art.

Per me, WYLLIᴬ· WYCHERLEY.

Item, he saith that he can invocate the spirite into the cristalle glasse assone as any man, but he cannot hynde the spirit so sure as other from their lyinge lyes.

Item, as concernyng the sword and the use therof he saith that he hath not used the same, save only about twoo monethes past he used hallywater, a sworde unconsecrated, and therefore was uneffectuouse, at Hale oke beside Fullam, where they digged for treasure and found none. But as they were working in the feat, ther came by them alongst the highway a black blynde horse, and made this deponent and other with hym to ronne their wayes, for it was in the nighte.

Otherwise he hath not wrought with sworde, sceptre, crowne, ring, or any other thing.

Item, he saith that within this sevenight one Humfray Locke, about Wyndsore forest, and one Potter, of St. Clement's parish without Temple barre, came to this deponent for a sworde and a sceptre going apon joynctes, which hath been consecrated and now are polluted; and a ring with the great name of God written thrise, *Tetragrammaton*, which this deponent delivered them;

334   APPENDIX.

and they twoo with a preest entend at this or the next lunation to conjure for treasure hid betwene Newbury and Reading.

Item, he saith that about ix yeres past he did conjure at Yarmouth in the great circule, with the sworde and ring consecrated; but nothing appeared unto hym, because that an old preest being there was so sore afraide that he ran away before the spirit called *Ambrose Waterduke* could appere.

Scryers.—Item, he knoweth that one Lowth, in Flete-strete, a broderer, useth the cristall stone, and goeth about daily to dygge for treasure.

Thomas Malfrey of Goldstone besides Yarmouth, [and] a woman besides Stoke Clare, whose name [he] knoweth not, are skryers of the glasse.

Conjurors.—Maier, a preest, and now say-master of the mynt at Durham house, hath conjured for treasure and their stolne goods.

Sir John Lloyd, a preest, that somtyme dwelt at Godstone besides Croydon, hath used it likewyse.

Thomas Owldring, of Yarmouth, is a conjurer, and hath very good bookes of conjuring, and that a great nomber.

Sir Robert Brian, of Hiegh-gate, preest, some tyme an armyt,[a] conjureth with a syve and a pair of sheeres,[b] invocating saint Paule and Saint Peter. And he also useth the psalter and the key with a psalme, *Deus humani generis,* or *Deus deorum.*[c]

One Thomas Shakilton occupieth the syve and sheeres, and he dwellith in Aldersgate-strete, a laborer, but he saith by saint Saviour that the man hath doone therwith many praty feates, and many trouthes tryed out.

One Christopher Morgan, a plaisterer, and his wife, dwelling in Beehe-lane, besides the Barbicane, occupieth the syve and sheeres also.

Item, one Croxton's wife, in Golding-lane in Saint Giles parishe, occupieth the syve and sheeres, and she only speaketh with the fayrayes.

John Davye, a Welshman, late dwelling with my lord protector's grace, is a prophesier, and a great teller of thinges lost.

[a] Near the bishop of London's toll-house at Highgate, in the parish of Hornsey, was a hermitage, with a chapel,—the nucleus around which the present town of Highgate was formed. See Newcourt's Repertorium Eccles. Londinense, i. 654.

[b] A mode of divination described by Theocritus: see several passages collected about it in Brand's Popular Antiquities, (edit. Ellis,) ii. 639. The points of the shears were fixed in the wood of the sieve, which was balanced upright by two persons, on a finger of each; on the real thief being named, the sieve suddenly turned round.

> The oracle of sieve and shears,
> That turns as certain as the spheres.
>   Hudibras, Part II. Canto iii. l. 569.

[c] *Deus deorum* is the 50th Psalm, of which the 18th verse, alluding to "a thief," has been already cited in p. 332. I do not recognise *Deus humani generis.*

John Turnour, dwelling at a place within twoo miles of Lynne, and his son, conjureth a spirite.

One Durant, a paynter in Norwich, doth use invocation of spirites.

And this deponent saith that there be within England above v hundred conjurers as he thinketh, but he knoweth not their names; and specially in Norfolk, Hartfordshire, and Wourcestershire and Gloucestershire a great nomber.

WYLLA^{A.} WYCHERLEY.

On the 24th of May, 1551, we find " William Tassell committed to the custodie of the master of th'orses for casting of figures and prophesieng." On the next day, " William Tassell, of Balsam, neare Cambridge, bounde by recognisaunce of xl li. t'appeare from daie to daie before the counsaill." (Register of the Privy Council, MS. Addit. 14,025, f. 199.)

On the 7th June, 1552, there was "a letter to sir Anthony Auchier to cause one Rogers to be set in the pillorie for his sedicious reporting of lewde prophecies, according to the minute." (MS. Addit. 14,026, f. 130.)

It would be easy to extend this note into a volume, if we went on from the reign of Edward the Sixth into those of his successors, for the same struggle with credulity and imposture was continued during the sixteenth century, and with little abatement during the seventeenth.

Page 175. *Gastone the lawyer.*—The authors of the Athenæ Cantabrigienses, vol. i. p. 374, are inclined to "fear" that this was George Gascoigne, afterwards distinguished as a poet. Still there is room to hope to the contrary, not only because Gascoigne's flowers of poesy did not begin to bud until 1562, whereas poets generally show themselves at an early age; but further, because " Gastone the lawyer" had " an old wife" as early as the date of Underhill's anecdotes, that is, about 1551.

THE AUTOBIOGRAPHY OF THOMAS MOWNTAYNE.

Page 177. *Whittington College.*— Stowe relates, respecting the monument of the founder of this college, and great city benefactor, sir Richard Whittington, that his remains had been three times buried in the church of St. Michael in the Ryal: "first, by his executors, under a faire monument; then in the reigne of Edward the Sixth, the parson of that church, thinking some great riches (as he said) to be buried with him, caused his monument to be broken, his body to be spoiled of his leaden sheet, and againe the second time to be buried; and, in the reigne of quene Mary, the parishioners were forced to take him up, to lap him in lead as afore, to bury him the third time, and to place his monument, or the like, over him againe " The spoliating parson was, of course, our over-zealous friend Thomas Mowntayne.

Page 180. *The living God.*—Mowntayne represents bishop Gardyner to say, " They have nothing in their mouths, these heretics, but *The Lord liveth, the living God*," &c. and that heretics might be recognised by their constant use of such expressions. There is a corresponding statement in Foxe's account of the examination of Richard Woodman in 1556. One of his answers was, " No, I praise the living God." On which doctor Story remarked, " This is a heretic indeed! He hath the right terms of all heretics, *the living God*. I pray you, be there dead Gods? that you say *the living God*." Woodman quoted Baruk, chapter vi., to prove both that there is a living God, and that there be dead gods; and afterwards the 84th Psalm. After which, doctor Story, addressing bishop Christopherson, said, " My lord, I will tell you how you shall know a heretic by his words, because I have been more used to them than you have been; that is, they will say *the Lord*, and *we praise God*, and *the living God*. By these words you shall know a heretick." (See the conversation at length in Foxe's story of Richard Woodman.)

Page 194. *Funeral of Sir Oliver Leader.*—On Thursday mornynge, beinge the xviijth of Februarye, A⁰ 1556, betweene iij and iiij in the mornynge, dyed sir Olyver Leader knight, at his howsse at Greate Stolton, in the countye of Huntyngton, wheras he was buryed the t'xvᵉ (25th?) of the same moneth.

  Morners, Mr. Wylsone, one of the clerkes of the chauncerye.
    Gerarde Harvye.
    George Symper.
    Edward Butler.
    Roberte Tonfyeld.
      Standerd, Rychard Mylsent.
      Pennon, Edmond Ogle.

His woorde, *Now thus, thankyd be Jhs*'. (MS. Coll. Arm. I. 15, f. 272 b.)

Page 211. *Trudge-over-the-world* was the soubriquet given to one George Eagles, a tailor, whose martyrdom is related at some length by Foxe, under the title of "The story and death of George Eagles, otherwise *Trudgeover*, a most painfull travailer in Christ's Gospel,"—" for he, wandering abroad into divers and far countreys, where he could finde any of his brethren, did there most earnestly encourage and comfort them, now tarrying in this town, and some time abiding in that, certain moneths together, as occasion served, lodging sometime in the countrey, and sometime for fear living in fields and woods, who, for his immoderate and unreasonable going abroad, was called *Trudgeover*. Often times he did lie abroad in the night without covert, spending the most part in devout and earnest prayer.... In the queen's name a grievous edict was proclaimed thorowout foure shires, Essex, Suffolke, Kent, and Northfolke, promising the partie that took him twentie pounds for his pains." At last he was seen at Colchester, at the fair time on Mary Magdalen's day, and soon after caught hiding in a corn-field. His indictment "did runne much after this fashion: George Eagles, thou art indicted by the name of

George Eagles, otherwise *Trudgeover the world*, for that thou didst such a day make thy prayer, that God should turne queen Maries heart, or else take her away." He suffered at Chelmsford the barbarous death of a traitor, being hung, cut down alive, beheaded, and quartered. His head was placed on the market cross at Chelmsford, and his quarters exposed at Colchester, Harwich, Chelmsford, and S. Rouses (*i e.* St. Osythe's).

The following passage occurs in the register of the privy council under the 3rd August, 1556: "Where sondrie letters had been before directed to divers justices for the apprehension of one *Trudgeover*, he being taken and executed by mr. Anthony Browne, sergeant-at-law, in Essex, a letter as this day was directed to the said sergeant Browne, geving hym thanks for his diligent proceding against the said *Trudge*, willing hym to distribute his head and quarters according to his and his colleagues' former determinations, and to procede with his complices according to the qualities of their offences."

In Foxe's story of Ralfe Allerton, who was apprehended by the lord Darcy of Chiche, and burnt at Colchester Sept. 17, 1557, we read that the bishop of Rochester (Maurice Griffin), in his examination on the 19th May, 1557, asked him, "Were you a companion of George Eagles, otherwise called *Trudgeover?* My lord of London tells me that you were his fellow companion." Ralfe answered, "I knew him very well, my lord." The bishop remarked, "By my faith, I had him once, and then he was as drunke as an ape, for he stanke so of drinke that I could not abide him, and so sent him away." Ralfe boldly replied, "My lord, I dare say you tooke your marke amisse. It was either yourselfe, or some of your company; for he did neither drinke wine, ale, nor beere, in a quarter of a yeere before that time; and therefore it was not he, forsooth." Foxe affirms of Eagles, "His diets was so above measure spare and slender, that for the space of three yeers he used for the most part to drink nothing but very water; whereunto he was compelled through necessitie of the time of persecution; and after, when he perceived that his bodie by God's providence proved well enough with this diet, he thought best to inure himself therewithall against all necessities."

Page 212. *Mr. Tyrell.*—See in Foxe a letter of Edmund Tyrel esquire, dated from Raimesdon park, the 12th of June, 1555, reporting his capture of John Denley and John Newman, who were afterwards burned; also, a letter of sir John Mordaunt and Edmund Tyrel esquire, justices of the peace for Essex, sending up to London certain heretics from Great Berstede, 2 March, 1556. His name occurs frequently in Foxe as a cruel persecutor in Essex: see the Index to Cattley's edition. One of Foxe's larger cuts represents this Edmund Tyrell, of Saynt Osythe's, burning the hand of Rose Allin, of Much Bentley. (On such tentative burning see a former note in p. 65.)

The Life and Death of Archbishop Cranmer.

Page 220. Cranmer's book, *De non ducenda Fratria,* supposed by Jenkyns to be lost, is by W. H. C. in Notes and Queries, Second Series, vol. vi. p. 92, identified with the article in Ames's History of Printing, p. 1133, entitled *Gravissimæ, &c. censuræ.*

Page 222, note. The literary history of *Cranmer's Collections from the Holy Scriptures and the Fathers,* now the Royal MSS. 7 B. XI and XII, is preserved in the following very remarkable correspondence of archbishop Parker:—

To the right honorable Sir William Cecyl, Knight,
Principal Secretary to the Q. Majestie. At the court.

(*Extract*)—Now, Sir, with spying and serching, I have found out bi very credible enformation, among other things, in whose bandes the grete notable wryten bokes of my predecessour, dr. Cranmer, shuld remayne: the partyes yet denying the same; and therupon despayre to discover them, except I maye be ayded bi the councell's letters to obtayne them. I pray your honor to procure ther letters to authorise me to enquire and serch for such monuments by al wayes, as bi mi pore discretion shal be thought good: whether it be bi deferryng an othe to the parties, or veweng ther studies, &c. This opportunytie of enformation being suche, I wold wyshe I coud recover these bokes, to be afterward at the Q[ueen's] commandment. I wold as moche rejoyce whyle I am in the countreye to wynne them, as I wold to restore an old chancel to reparation. Because I am not acqueynted with the stile of the councel's letters in this case, I send you no minute, trusting that your goodnes will think the lauber wel bestowed to cause the clarke of the councel to devise the forme.

At my house, from Bekesborne, this 22 of August [1563].

Your honor's assured,   Matthue Cant.

(Strype's Memorials of Cranmer, Appendix, p. 217.)

Sir William Cecill's reply, written from Windsor, Aug. 25:—

"May it please your grace, I thank the same for your lettres. I am gladd that you have herd of such hidd treasures, as I take the bookes of the holly archbishop Cranmer to be. I have of late recovered of his wrytten bookes v. or vj., which I had of one mr. Herd from Lyncoln. Your grace wryteth to have lettres from the counsell: but to whom they shuld be wrytten, or who the persons be of whom the wrytinges shuld be demanded, your grace's lettre maketh no mention. And therfor, knowing no such ernestnes here or care of such matters, I forbeare to press the counsell therwith, specially being not hable[*]

---

[*] *Printed by Strype* liable.

to render them an accompt who hath the wrytinges. But upon advertissment therof, I will not fayle but procure such lettres. From Wyndsor, where we ar yet in helth, thanked be Almighty God. On tewsdaye the Spa: ebascador dyed with in ij myles of a burning agew. 25 Aug. 1563. Your graceës at command W. CECILL." (Autograph in MS. Reg. 7 B. XI.)

Archbishop Parker, in reply (from the original draft, MS. Reg. 7 B. XI.):

"Where I dyd wright to your honor to procure the councell's letters for the obteyning of certen auncyent wryten bokes of the late lord Cranmer, and belike dyd not express particularly eyther to whom these letters shuld be directed, nor the persons of whom thei shuld be demanded, your honor shal understand that the partye to whom belongeth these bokes, suyd to me to recover them out of D. Nevyson's handes,[a] in whose studye the owner playnly avoucheth that he sawe them with his owne eyes there: who after that dyd require them of hym, beyng conveyd away from hym the sayd owner; but the said Nevison denyeth to have them; and I am persuaded he wold do the same to myself yf I shuld de[mand] them; and thereupon desired to have the councell's letters which he might better regard, eyther directed to me to require them of hym, or ellis to hym to delyver them to me, beyng none of his own but usurped in secrecye, for the which I have made moch long enquirye, tyl nowe the partye who owneth them detected so moche to me. I refer the consideration of this my desire eyther to be satysfyed by the meanes of such letters aforsaid, or ellys by yours privately, as yor gentle prudence shal thinke best. Indeed the mater is of ernest importance, and nedeth your helpe. Yf gratitude the sayd Nevyson to me ware not to seke.[b] Eynally I praye your honour onys again helpe forward mr. Manwood's good entent,[c] as conscyence with the reason[d] your office may convenyently beare yt. 7 Sept."

[a] Stephen Nevynson, LL.D. commissary-general of the diocese of Canterbury 1561, and a canon of Canterbury about 1570. See a memoir of him in Athenæ Cantab. i. 426.

[b] *So the MS. Probably the archbishop intended to write,* "In gratitude to me the said Nevynson were not to seek," *i. e.* doctor Nevynson was in gratitude bound to accede to his wishes without much solicitation.

[c] Mr. Manwood was apparently the person whom Parker calls the owner of the manuscripts, and who was prepared to transfer them to him upon recovering possession. Strype (Life of Parker, p. 136) conjectures that the rightful owner could only be archbishop Cranmer's son Thomas, as his father's heir; but other arrangements might have transferred the books to mr. Manwood. This was no doubt Roger Manwood, serjeant-at-law 1567, justice of the queen's bench 1572, and chief baron of the exchequer 1578, the founder of Sandwich Grammar-school: see Boys's History of Sandwich, 1792, 4to, pp. 200, 248, and Foss's Lives of the Judges.

[d] *So the MS.*

The council's letter (from the original in 7 B. XI.):—

After our verie bartie commendations to your good lordshippe. Being given t'understand that certaine written bokes containeng matters of divinytie, sometime belonging to archebisshop Cranmer, your L.'s predecessour, are come to th'andes of Doctor. Neveson, being verie necessary to be sene at this tyme; we have somwhat earnestlye writ to the said Mr. Neveson to deliver those bookes unto your L. And like as we doubt not but he will furthwith deliver the same unto you, considering they are for so good a purpose required of him; So, if he shall deny the delivery thereof, we thinke mete that your L. by your owne authoritye, do cause his studye, and suche other places where you thinke the said bokes do remayne, to be sought: and if the same bokes may be founde, to take them into your L. custody. And thus we bid your good L. moste hartely farewelle. From Windesore Castle, the xxiijth of September, 1563.

Your good L. most assured lovinge frendes,

N. Bacon, C.S.	W. Northt.	Penbroke.
R. Duddeley.	E. Clynton.	F. Knollys.
Willm. Petre, S.		W. Cecill.

When archbishop Parker obtained the MSS. he caused transcripts to be made of them, which Strype saw in the library of dr. Compton bishop of London 1675-1713; and he has printed the contents of the chapters in Appendix XXIII. to his Life of Parker. Another table of contents is given by Casley in his Catalogue of the Royal Manuscripts.

The original volumes, now the Royal MSS. 7 B. XI. XII., passed again into private hands. "I find (says Casley), in a Catalogue of MSS. formerly mr. Theyer's of Cooper's Hill,* but which were bought for the King's library of mr. Scott, that these two volumes were valued at 100*l.*; but bishop Beveridge and dr. Jane, appraisers for the King, brought down the price to 50*l.*" (Casley, Catalogue of the Royal MSS. p. 125.) They must therefore have been acquired for the Royal Collection in the reign of queen Anne, dr. Beveridge being bishop of St. Asaph from 1704 to 1708.

Page 227. *Ricd. Thornden, suffragan bishop of Dover.*—Foxe has published a letter to Thornden bishop of Dover, from Thomas Goldwell, prior of Christchurch (noticed in p. 283), which was written from Brussels on the 16th of June, 1554, by direction of cardinal Pole, then in that city. It severely censures the suffragan for his conduct and doctrine in the days of King Edward, and again for having recently presumed to sing mass *in pontificalibus* before he had

---

* On the fly-leaf of 7 B. XI. is written: "This is the first volume of Bp. Cranmer's Common-place book.—John Theyer. 4 *September*, 1659."

received absolution; but at the same time conveys to him faculties for the continuance of his functions as suffragan. (Edition by Cattley, vii. 297.)

Page 228. On the posting of Cranmer's *Declaration* in London and in Canterbury, see the Zurich Letters, i. 371.

Ibid. *Sir Thomas Brydges* —In 1548 Thomas Brydges, next brother to John first lord Chandos, was steward of the King's hundred of Chadlington, and of his manors of Burford and Minster Lovell, and keeper of his forest of Whichwood, and of his parks of Langley and Cornbury, at which last he resided, and was buried in the church of Chadlington. Through the reign of Edward VI. he had large grants of abbey lands. (Topographical Miscellanies, 1792. 4to.)

Sir Richard a Brydges (another brother ?) was, when sheriff of Berkshire, one of the commissioners for the trial of Julins Palmer at Newbury, July 16, 1556; and, in order to induce Palmer to renounce his opinions, made what Foxe terms a "gentle offer" to him of meat and drink, and books, and ten pounds yearly, so long as he would live with him.

Morice's Anecdotes, &c. of Cranmer.

Page 235. *The Family of Ralph Morice* —In one of his supplications to queen Elizabeth, Ralph Morice represents that he had four daughters all marriageable, and not wherewithal to bestow them according to their quality; and he prays to be relieved with the pension that had been allowed in the time of the late prior Wildbore of St. Augustine's abbey in Canterbury, from his estate at Beakesbourne, as it would be a good furtherance to his said daughters' marriage.

I have been favoured by the Rev. James Craigie Robertson, M.A. the present Vicar of Beaksbourne, with the following extracts from his parish register, which appear to show that when the means arrived three out of Morice's four daughters went off at double quick time. Let us hope that the fourth remained to close her father's eyes in peace.

1570-1. Edward Vanwylder and Margaret Moryce, Jan. 25.
James Cryppyn and Mary Morice, Jan. 29.
John Hart and Anne Morrice, Feb. 8.

Under 1561-2 occurs the burial of Alyce Morrys, Feb. 25.

Page 236. *Commission to visit the dioceses of Rochester, &c. in 1547.*—In Foxe, edit. 15 , p. , is another communication of Morice, relating the conversation which took place between the archbishop and "the said register his man," *i.e.* Morice, at Hampton Court, "touching the good effect and success of the same visitation." Mr. Jenkyns has extracted it in his Memorials of Cranmer, vol. i. p. 320.

Mr. Briggs, the "preacher" to the visitors, was Simon Briggs, fellow of Pembroke hall, Cambridge, 1538, and of Trinity college, by the foundation charter, 1546; D.D. 1547. See Athenæ Cantabrigienses, i. 93.

Page 237. *Ralph Morice* further contributed to Foxe " A discourse touching a certain policy used by Stephen Gardiner, bishop of Winchester, in staying King Henry the Eighth from redressing of certain abuses of ceremonies in the Church; being ambassador beyond the seas. Also the communication of King Henry the Eighth had with the ambassador of France at Hampton court concerning the reformation of Religion as well in France as in England, A.D. 1546, in the month of August." (Edit. 1570, p. 1425; Cattley's edition, v. 561—564.) I should in p. 234 and p. 237 have spoken of the second edition of Foxe as dated 1570, not 1576.

Morice also wrote the recantation of one master Barber, M.A. of Oxford. Cattley's edit. v. 454.

Page 247. *Mr. Isaac.*—" Edward Isaac of the parishe of Well in the countie of Kent," as he is described in Morice's paper respecting Latymer and Bayneham (mentioned in p. 237), but which should be corrected to " Well court in the parish of Ickham, near Littlebourn." When doctor Sandys (afterwards archbishop of York) went into exile, mr. Isaac met him at Milton-shore in Kent, and sent his eldest son with him to Antwerp. Isaac was afterwards himself a refugee, resident some time at Strasburg, and afterwards at Frankfort, where his eldest son died. When Dr. Sandys was at Strasburg, "his sustentation there was chiefly from one master Isaac, who loved him most dearly, and was ever more ready to give than he to take." (Foxe, not improbably from Morice's information.) Mr. Isaac appears to have lived chiefly at Frankfort during his exile, and his name occurs among those who were strongly opposed to John Knox. (See the Troubles of Frankfort; Hasted, History of Kent, iii. 666, 722; Strype, Memorials, III. i. 231, 406; Annals, I. i. 153; Latimer's Works, Parker Soc. ii. 221.)

Page 250. *The Pelican.*—Over the figure in brass-plate of John Prestwick, dean of Hastings, in Warbleton church, Sussex, is a canopy terminating in a finial, which is composed of the pelican feeding her young with her blood, and this motto Sic Xpus dilexit nos. The date of this design is 1436. It is engraved in Boutell's Monumental Brasses, and in the Sussex Archæological Collections, vol. ii. p. 307. There was an old distich which thus declared the meaning of this emblem—

> Ut pelicanus fit matris sanguine sanus,
> Sic sumus sanati nos omnes sanguine nati, *i. e.* Christi.

Page 251. *Sir John Gostwyck.*—How Gostwyck was capable of acting is shown by a memorandum under his own hand addressed to the King after Crumwell's disgrace: " May it please your most excellent majestic to be advertised that I, your most humble servaunt, John Gostwyck, have in my hands, whiche I treasaured from tyme to tyme unknowne unto th'erl of Essex, whiche if I had declared unto hym he would have caused me to disburse by commaundement, without warraunt, as heretofore I have done ...... x M li." (Ellis's Original Letters, II. ii. 162, from MS. Cotton. Append. xxviii. fol. 125.) Sir Henry Ellis considers that this statement may have done Crumwell essential harm, as counteracting his asseveration that he had never deceived the King in any of his treasure.

Page 252. *Certain prebendaries and justices of the shire.*—In Morice's paper, which was inserted by Foxe in his Actes and Monuments, concerning "the trouble of Richard Turner, preacher, at Chatham," he has given some other particulars of the doings of the popish justices of Kent; and thus mentions their names—" the justices, such as then favoured their cause and faction, and such as are no small fools, as sir John Baker, sir Christopher Hales, sir Thomas Moile [of Westwell], knights, with other justices." In Jenkyns's Remains of Cranmer, the archbishop's letters cxcvi. and cxcviii. are addressed to a justice who had publicly impugned his doctrines, and letters cxcvii. and cxcix. are the justice's replies, written in October 1537. The last letter is dated from Raynham, but it is not clear from Hasted's History of Kent who was the justice then there resident. Possibly it was sir Anthony St. Leger, whose fluctuating religious sentiments have been elsewhere discussed (p. 179).

Page 256. —*but stode withoute the doore emonges servyngmen and lackeis above thre quarters of an hower.*—This anecdote of Cranmer is the original of a passage in Shakspere's *Henry the Eighth*, in which Dr. Butts tells the King:—

> *Dr. Butts.* I'll shew your Grace the strangest sight
> I think your Highness saw this many a day,
> There, my Lord,—
> The high promotion of his Grace of Canterbury,
> Who holds his state at door, 'mongst pursuivants,
> Pages, and footboys.

Page 2. *Mary of Henawde and queen Philippa.*—In the pedigree of Moyne we read that sir John Moyne, who died about 1408, married Joan daughter and heir of John Belvale, by Katharine, *nurse* to Philippa queen of Edward III. (Hutchins, Hist. of Dorsetshire, first edit. iii. 407.) This sir John Moyne had two coheiresses,—Elizabeth, married to William Stourton esquire, father of the first lord Stourton; and Hester, married to sir William Bonville of Somersetshire. Sir William Moyne, lord of Sawtrey in Huntingdonshire, living 20 Ric. II. was a brother to sir John; and, dying in 1404, was the subject of the epitaph in Sawtrey church (p. 3). To this sir William Moyne was made the remarkable surrender of the arms of Beaumeys, (Argent, on a cross azure five garbs or,) which is printed in the Visitation of Huntingdonshire, at p. 16. It was made by Thomas Grendale of Fenton in the same county, the cousin and heir of John (or Nicholas) Beaumeys, and was dated at Sawtrey on the 22d Nov. 15 Ric. II. This was very shortly after the same Thomas atte Hethe, otherwise called Thomas Grendale of Fenton, had been found the nearest heir of Nicholas Beaumeys, who had died without heirs of his body on the 24th Jan. 14 Ric. II. Thomas Grendale was the son of Cecilia, daughter of Margaret, daughter of Robert Beaumeys, father of William, father of John, father of Robert, father of Nicholas.* The estates in question were one virgate and a half in Copmanford, and ten shillings rent of assize in Upton, held of the King as of the honour of Huntingdon as one twentieth part of a knight's fee, and then in the King's hand on account of the minority of Nicholas Beaumeys. (Inq. p. mort. held at Huntingdon on Saturday after the feast of the Circumcision 15 Ric. II.)

Whether Moyne inherited any blood of Beaumeys does not appear; but, as we find the family of Louthe quartering both Moyne and Beaumeys—on the monument at Cretingham, p. 6, it might be presumed that they had formed a marriage with an heiress of Moyne, particularly as they also assumed the Moyne crest. And yet no such marriage is represented by the impalements in pp. 2, 3, though it would seem that sir William Moyne and a Louthe married sisters (Somayne?).

One is also led to suspect some connection between "Mary of Henawde," the wife of Roger Louthe, and Katharine, wife of John Belvale before-mentioned, "nurse to queen Philippa." Could the consanguinity (as it was termed) with Lionel duke of Clarence, be that supposed to exist between the child of a nurse and her foster-child? If Louthe had married a coheir of Belvale, the family would probably have quartered the Belvale coat, which was Argent, a chevron between ten billets sable.

* In the Visitation of Huntingdonshire, p. 16, these names will be found, drawn into a tabular pedigree, but Margaret is made the daughter of Nicholas, who really died s. p.

The two families of Beaumeys and Le Moyne had been co-existent on the two manors of Sawtrey from very early times. In an ancient feodary they were thus described :—

"Dominus Robertus de Beaumes tenet capitale manerium de Beaumes in villa de Salteria de domino comite Gloverniæ, et est de feodo de Lovetot,* &c.

"Dominus Willielmus le Moyne tenet manerium de Salteria le Moyne de abbate de Ramesey, et dominus abbas de Rege."

The two manors continued in subsequent times to be named after their former owners; the former being also called Sawtrey Juett, from the countess Judith widow of Waltheof earl of Huntingdon, temp. Will. Conq.

In Philipot's Stemmata, Coll. Arm. 75, is a pedigree of Moyne drawn for William lord Stourton in 1575, upon which is tricked a very remarkable seal, copied with the following memorandum: "Willielmus Moigne de com' Huntingdon' miles, per chartam suam datam anno quinto Ricardi secundi, dedit Ricardo Revenshere clerico, Simoni Burle militi et aliis seisinam de maneriis suis de Sautre, Ravele, Gyddyng, Luddington, et Reweye, &c. et dictæ chartæ apposuit sigillum suum ad arma talem qualem hic depinxi." The arms of Moigne on this seal are the two bars and three mullets on chief: by the side of which is the crest, placed on a helmet, which covers the head of a lion sejant; the crest is in this instance a tall monk at whole length, holding his whip of penance over the shield: behind him is a long-legged bird. The legend: SIGILLVM WILLIELMI MOINE. It will be remembered that the Stourtons (like the Louths) adopted this crest of a monk, and still continue to use a device which now appears peculiarly appropriate to that eminent Roman Catholic family.

Page 26. It was from *Lyon key* that Katharine duchess of Suffolk, having left her house called the Barbican, between four and five of the clock in the morning, embarked on her flight to the continent on the first of January, 1554-5. See the narrative in Foxe's Actes and Monuments.

Pages 43, 302. *John Lascelles.*—The first arrest of this gentleman is thus mentioned in a letter of the council to secretary Petre, dated May 11, 1546: " Ye shall perceive that Mr. Crome notith in his aunswer, to be comeforted by oon Lasselles, whome we have in examination,—nat called apon Crome's detection, but because himself boosted abrode that he was desirous to be called to the counseill, and he would answer to the pricke." (State Papers, 1830, i. 844.) A few days after, according to the same reporter, his confidence had

---

* Hence the coat of Lovetoft in Sawtrey church (p. 2). See also the Testa de Neville, pp. 354, 355 b.

left him: for, under the date of the 14th of May, it is stated that "Lasselles wil not answere to that parte of his conference with Crome that toucheth Scripture matier, withoute he have the Kinges majestes expresse commandement, with his protection; for he sayeth it is neither wisdom nor equitie that he shuld kyll himself. Thus you see his Highnes must pardon, before he knowe if Mr. Lasselles may have his will; and in dede his answeres be therafter." (p. 850.) It is one of many instances that occur of persons having been intrapped by an incautious expression of their sentiments, from the perils of which the majority escaped by retractation or denial; but the honest and conscientious were made to suffer the penalty of their "obstinacy."

Page 94. "*The Lady Elizabeth Fane's* 21 *Psalms and* 102 *Proverbs*," were printed by Robert Crowley in 1550, 8vo. (Ames, Typographical Antiquities, p. 760). I have not traced any remaining copy of this book.—Ames, p. 1103, states that in 1563 John Charlwood had licence to print "a book of serten Godly Prayers of Lady Fane's;" but on examining the entry Mr. Payne Collier found that the "lady Fane" was there a misreading for the lady Jane (Grey). Registers of the Stationers' Company, (Shakespeare Soc.) i. 85.

Page 107. *Banbury Gloss.*—This phrase is used by bishop Latimer in his letter to king Henry, printed by Foxe (edit. 1596, p. 1590); when speaking of the pharisaical prelates, he declares, " they have sore blinded your liege people and subjects with their lawes, customs, ceremonyes, and *Banbury glosses*, and furnished them with cursings, excommunications, and other corruptions— corrections I would say," &c.

Page 127, note. *Desperate Dick.*—This term occurs in doctor Thomas Wilson's Art of Rhetorique, 1553, "Though men kept their goodes never so close, and locke them up never so fast, yet often times, either by some mischaunce of fyre or other thinge, they are lost, or els *desperate Dickes* borowe now and then, against the owner's wille, all that ever he bathe." (f. 101.) Thomas Nash, in his contest with Gabriel Hervey, calls Richard Hervey *desperate Dick:* and in 1568-9 Robert Ealie had license " to prynte a ballad intituled *Desperate Dycke*." (Collier's Registers of the Stationers' Company, ii. 195.)

Page 151. The *Seven Sciences Liberall* were personified in one of the pageants presented to King Edward VI. in his passage through London the day before his Coronation. See the description, with their poetical speeches, in The Literary Remains of King Edward VI., pp. cclxxxiv. *et seq.* Their names agree with the list cited in p. 151 from the title-page of James Howell's Familiar Letters, and with those represented in the annexed fac-simile, which is copied from a woodcut used by Richard Grafton, printer to King Edward the Sixth, in several of his works, particularly in Marbeck's Concordance of the Bible 1550, Wilson's Arte of Logique 1551 and 1553, and probably others (see Dibdin's edition of Ames's Typographical Antiquities, vol. iii. pp. 471, 474, 480.)

Page 328. *Prophecies on going a journey.*—" The people were grown unto such a folly that scant would they ride or go any journey unlesse they consulted either with their blind prophets, or at the least with their prophesies, which yearly to no little hurt, both to the faith of Christ and wealth of the realm, were without all shame divulged." A short treatise, declaring the detestable wickednesse of magicall sciences, as necromancie, conjuration of spirites, curiouse astrologie, and such lyke: by Francis Coxe; supposed to have been first published in 1561. (Herbert's Ames, ii. 889.)

THE CRUEL TREATMENT OF WILLIAM MALDON WHEN A BOY, AT CHELMSFORD, BY HIS FATHER.

Among the supplementary matter at the end of Foxe's work, under the head of "God's punishment upon Persecutors and Contemners of the Gospel," are some anecdotes communicated by William Maldon, then of Newington, which are thus introduced : " Mention was made, not long before, of one William Maldon, who in king Henry's time suffered stripes and scourgings for confessing the verity of God's true religion." But no previous mention of William Maldon is to be found. This shows that it had been Foxe's intention to insert the following paper, written by Maldon, but that it was accidentally omitted. Had that course been taken designedly, it might have been deemed more to the credit of Foxe's discrimination, for as a record of personal suffering or of persecution this narrative will by many be considered as trifling and insignificant. It is the ordinary case of an arbitrary and passionate parent, exceeding the bounds of parental discipline, and defeating his own object, by undue violence. The lapse of three centuries, however, has given it a different value: for many circumstances are incidentally noticed that are highly characteristic of the manners of the times, and particularly of the humbler ranks of the early Protestants. The description of their flocking to hear the reading of the holy scriptures, when first promulgated in the vulgar tongue, is especially remarkable.

This document has hitherto appeared only in an abridged form in Strype's Memorials of Cranmer, p. 64. The original is in a detached portion of Foxe's papers (see the Preface). The handwriting is above mediocrity, showing William Maldon to have been a person of some education.

(MS. Harl. 590, fol. 77.)

Grace, peace, and mercy from God our Father and from our lord Jesus Christ be with all them that love the gospell of Jesus Christ unfeignedly (so be it)! Not unto us, Lord, not unto us, but unto thy name be all honour and glory! Jentyll reder, understand that I do not take in hande to wryte this lytyll tratys as followeth of myne owne provoking, but I with another ,chanced to goe in the company of mr. Foxe, the gatherer together of this grete boke, and he desired us to tell hym if wee knewe of any man that had suffered persecution for the gospell of Jesus Christ, to that end he myght add it unto the boke of marters.[a] Then said I that I knewe one that was whipped in king Henryes time for it, of his father. Then he enquired of me his name. Then I bewrayed and said it was I myself, and tould him a pece of it. Then was he desirous to have the whole surcomstance of it. Then I promysed him to wryght it, and as I said to him, "Not for any vayne glory I will speke, but unto the prayse and honour of our God, that worketh all in all men of all good gyftes that cometh from above, unto whom be all honour and glory for ever in this lyfe and for ever in the lyfe to come (so be it)!" As I find by the brefe crownakill [b] that the bibill of the sacred schrypteures was set forth [c] to be rede in all churches in Ingelande by the late worthy king Henry the viij[th], (then was I about a xx yeares of age,) and imedyately after dyveres poore men in the towne of Chelmysford in the county of Essex, where my father dwelled and I borne, and with him brought up, the sayd poore men bought the Newe Testament of Jesus Christ,[d] and on sundays dyd set redinge in lower ende of the church, and many wolde floke about them to heare theyr redinge. Then I came amonge the sayd reders, to here their redyng of that glad and sweet tydyngs of the gospell. Then my father seying this, that I lystened unto them everie sundaye, then cam he and sought me amonge them, and brought me awaye from the hering of them, and wolde have me to say the Lattin mattyns with hym, the which greved me very mych, and thus dyd fete me awaye divers times. Then I see I could not be in reste. Then thought I, I will learne to rede Englyshe, and then will I have the Newe Testament and rede ther on myself; and then had I learned of an English [e] prymmer as far as *Patris sapyentia*, and then on sundays I plyed my Engelysh prymmer.

The Maye tide following, I and my father's prentys Thomas Jeffrey layed our mony together and bought the Newe Testament in Engelish, and hydde it in our bed strawe, and so exersised it at convenient times. Then shortly after my father set me to the kepyng of a shop of haberdashery and grosary

[a] This is one of several proofs that "The Book of Martyrs" acquired its familiar title at an early period of its existence, of which others are noticed in the preface.

[b] Perhaps "A Breviate Chronicle," printed by John Mychell, 1552.

[c] In the year 1538.

[d] "No man can come unto me except it be geven hym of my Father. John vj." *Side note.*

[e] *So the MS.* qu. Latin? In a primer printed at Rouen in 1555, entitled "Hereafter foloweth the Prymer in Englysshe and in Latin sette out along; after the vse of Sarū. In edibus Roberti Valentini. M.D.lv." the place of which Maldon speaks will be found under the head of Matyns of the Crosse. *Patris sapientia, veritas divina, Deus homo, captus est hora matutina,* &c.

wares, beyng a bowe shott from his howse, and there I plyed my boke. Then shortly after I wolde begyn to speke of the schriptures, and on a nyghte about eight acloke my father sate sleepyng in a chayr, and my mother and I fell on resonyng of the crucifyx, and of the knelyng downe to it, and knokeynge on the breste, and holding up our bandes to it when it cam by on procession. Then sayd I, it was plain idolatry, and playnely againste the commandement of God (when he sayeth) Thow shalt not make to thyself anye graven image, thou shalt not bow downe to it, nor worshyppe it. Then sayed she, "Thou thefe! if thy father knewe this, he would hange the. Wilte not thou worshippe the crosse? and it was about the when thou weare cristened, and must be layed on the when thou art deade," with other talke. Then I went and hidde Frythes boke on the Sacrament,* and then I went to bede. And then my father awakyd, and my mother toulde him of our communycatyon. Then came he up to our chamber, with a greate rodde, and as I harde hym coming up I blessed me saying, "In the name of the Father, and of the Sonne, and of the Holy Ghoste, so be it." Then sayd my father to me, "Serra, who is your scholmaster? tell me." "Forsouthe, father, (said I,) I have no scholmaster but God, wher he sayth in his commandment, Thou shalt not make to thyself any graven image, thou shalt not bow downe to it, nor worshyppe it." Then he took me by the heare of my heade, with bothe his handes, pullyd me out of the bede, behynd Thomas Jeffrey's bake, he syttyng up in his bedde. Then he bestowed his rodde on my body, and style wolde knowe my scholmaster; and other then I sayd before he had none of me. And he sayd I spake againste the King's injuntyons, and as trewely as the Lord liveth I rejoiced that I was betten for Christ's sake, and wepte not one taare out of mine eyes, and I thynke I felte not the strypes, my rejoysyng was so much. And then my father sawe that wen he had betten me inofe, he let me goo, and I went to bedde agayne and shed not one tare out of myne eyes. "Surely (sayde my father,) he is past grace, for he wepeth not for all this." Then was he in twyse so much rage, and said, "Fette me an haulter, I will surely hange him up, for as good I hange him up as another shoulde." And when he sawe that nobody wolde goe, he went downe into his shopp, and brought up an haulter, and the whyles he went, "A thou thefe! (sayd my mother,) howe haste thou angeryd thy father! I never sawe hym so angary." "Mother, (said I,) I am the more sorreyer he shoulde be so angary for this

* Probably "A boke made by John Frith, prisoner in the Tower of London, answeringe unto M. More's letter which he wrote ayenst the first litle treatyse that John Frith made concerninge the Sacrament and the body and bloode of Christe," &c first printed in 1533, and repeatedly for some years after.

matter," and then began I to weepe for the grefe of the lake of knowledge in them.[a] Then sayd my mother, " Thomas Jeffary, aryse, and make the reddy, for I cannot tell what he will doe in his anger;" and he sat up in his bede puttynge on of his clothys, and my father cometh up with the haulter, and my mother entretyd him to lett me alone, but in no wyse he wolde be intretyd, but putte the haulter aboute my neke, I lying in my bede: he putte the haulter about my neke, and pulled me with the haulter behynd the sayd Thomas Jeffaryes' bake, almoste elene oute of the bede.[b] Then my mother cryed out, and pullyed hym by the armes awaye; and my brother Rycherd cryed out that laye on the other syde of me, and then my father let go his houlde, and let me alone and wente to bede.

    Henr. 8.
(*Indorsed,*) Receaved of W. Maldon, of Newyngton.

 [a] " Wepyng tares I wrete this, to thynk the lake of knowledge in my father and mother; they had thought they had done God good servise at that tyme. I troste he hath forgeven them."—*Side note.*

 [b] " I thynke vj. dayes after my neke greved me with the pullyng of the haulter." *Side note.*

ERRATA.

Page 5, line 11, *for* here *read* there.
Page 149, line 22, *for* ther *read* then (than).

GLOSSARIAL INDEX.

I. WORDS.   II. PHRASES.   III. PROVERBS.   IV. OATHS.
V. RELIGIOUS NAMES OF REPROACH.   VI. SOBRIQUETS.

I. WORDS.
advoutrey, 50
ale-bench, 271
along (together), 349 note
altogethers, 248
armyt (hermit), 334
assoile, 40 note
axe (ask), 34, 45, 48, 56
bards (of horses), 148
beleve (by your leave), 184
belyke (by like), 156
a bowed (bent) groat, 121
brast (burst), 155, 317
bridge (a landing place), 252
brigandine, 167
brokers in the law, 316
calculation, 326
to calke (calculate), 172
calker, 159
catchpole, 104
chanlyng (changeling), 205
chevance, 263
cise, 324
cloynars, 316
collygeners (members of colleges), 316
comoditie (advantage), 267
constable, 38, 104

I. Words—*continued.*
 horse-litter, 153
 hosteler, 100, 269
 howgh hoo, 67
 howse-end, 23
 impeach, 137 note
 indifferent (impartial), 274
 indurance (imprisonment), 255
 infamy (an), 269
 jugelar (juggler), 158
 kercher, 332
 knowen (carnally), 219, 220
 laches, 38
 lancequenets, 137
 lattin (metal called), 299
 legerdemayn, 109 note
 lord lieutenant, 168 note
 lovetyckes (love-tricks), 52
 lowtryng (loitering), 182
 lubberde, 36
 luske, 16, 59
 magistrall, 19
 marshal of the field, or, of the camp, 168
 mass-mongers, 316
 mast (for master), 325
 miser (a wretch), 32
 modirwife, 24 note
 molspade, 37
 mother (applied to a grandmother), 313
 murian or morion, 168
 necname (nick name), 73
 nigromancie, 314
 nosseled, 218
 ostler of an inn, 100
 pelting, 36
 philopony, 16
 placard, 332
 place (text), 73, 77
 poll-axe, 161, 322
 poore-blind (purblind), or short-sighted? 240
 poulter, 331
 progeny (ancestry), 238
 promoter, 161

 wheras (*meaning* whereat), 336
 zowche, 54

II. Phrases.
 answer to the prick, 345
 Banbury glose, 105, 346
 bear in hand, 255
 black dog of Bungay, 51

GLOSSARIAL INDEX.

II. PHRASES—*continued.*
black guard, 50
Bonner paunch, 51
born in a happy hour, 258
a bow shot (distance), 350
as if the catt had lycked you cleane, 89
changing your tippet and turning your coat, 118
clean-fingered clergy, 24, 37
con you thanks, 157
corry favell, 159
crafty conveyaunce, 109
a craftie crowder, 109
Croydon complexion, 51
curry favour, 159
a desperate Dick desirous to die, 127, 346
desperate debts, 28, 298
a dog's life, 30
drunk as an ape, 337
turned his face to the wall, 35
two faces in one hood, 89, 100, 120
fawn friendship, 62
as he had fished so he should fowl, 102
no small fools, 343
gentle reader, 86, 89, 120, &c. 348
too good (too much) for him, 122, 137
hot gospeller, 159, 324
grown out of knowledge, 213
out of hand, 179
smell his stinking heart, 87
heavy friend, 207
you hide yourself among the bushes, 130
hucker mucker, 162
hunt and hawk (a country gentleman's occn-
  patiou) 36
the living God, 179, 336
the Lord liveth, 335, 350
whether he knew, 64
Marian persecution, 57
Mariana tempora, Title-page
to help up your market, 109
masking mass, 81
massing matter, 193
to make up your own mouth, 129

water his plants, 213
white son, 149

II. PHRASES—*continued.*
   white witches, 174
   as a ravening wolf greedy of his prey, 104 ;
     looking as the wolf doth for a lamb, 188
   world without end, 149
   it is a world to see, 109
   worth as many pence as there be shillings in
     a groat, 90
   not worth a fly, 267

III. PROVERBS.
   Of all treasure
   Cunning is the flower, 63
   He that wylle in courte dwell
   must corye favelle, 159
   He thatt wylle in courte abyde
   must cory favelle bake and syde, 159
   Scarborough warning, 199
   Such a master, such a servant, 201
   The blind doth eat many a fly, 202
   Fast bind, fast find, 205

IV. OATHS.
   by my faith, 337
   forsooth, 183, 188, 206, 270, 337, 350
   Godamercy, 15, 165
   by God's blood, 141, 178
   by God's body, 163
   God's passion, 179
   in the name of God ! (a form of assent) 135,194
   by the Lord's foot, 137
   Mary, 140, 163, 165, 257, 266, 272
   by mass, 141
   by the holy mass, 185
   by saint Saviour, 334

GENERAL INDEX.

A——, J. letter on Craumer's last hours, 229
Abetot, *see* Dabitote
Abingdon abbey, surrender of, 286
Adams, or Aldam, John, 43, 307, 310
Aldworth, Thomas, 95, 123
Alexander, keeper of Newgate, and James his son, 147
Allen, Robert, a prophesyer, 159, 172, 173, 326
Allerton, Ralphe, 337
Alley, William, 22
Allin, Rose, 65, 337
Allyngton, mr. 46
Ambrose Waterduke, a spirit, 334
Amport, 71
Anderson, sir John, 333
Anthony, Anthony, 305; journal of, xxvii
Antwerp, 212, 214; the English house, 216
Apostles' mass at St. Paul's, 288
Articles of religion, *see* Six Articles
Arundel, Henry Earl of, 136, 139, 140, 142, 143, 170
—— archbishop, 294
Aske's rebellion, 285
Askew, Anne, her family history, 299; her marriage, 300; the racking of, 303; entertained by Anne Hartipole, 313
Aslacton, 218, 238, 263
—— family of, 250
Asple hall, 9
Astrology, 327
Astronomy, science of, 173, 326, 327
Attenborough, 31
Auchier, sir Anthony, 335
Aungell, William, 35

Austhorpe
Ansty, or C
Aval s, *se*
Aylmer bı
  elm 267
  xix
Ayscough,
—— sir E
—— Elizab
—— sir Fr
—— Faith
—— Jane,
—— Ma
—— sir

Babingto
 masine,
Bacon, arm
—— Lady

GENERAL INDEX.

Bishops' book, the, 224, 248
Bishop's Stoke, 317
Black dog of Bungay, 51
Blagge, sir George, 41, 302, 306, 333
Blean forest, 266
Blenerhasset, arms, 6; Elizabeth, 4, 302; sir Thomas, 4; John, 5. 302
Blunte, mr. 208
Bocking, dr. Edward, 280, 281
Boleyne, queen Anne, 52, 297, 305; coronation of, 250; execution, 283
Bolles, Agnes, Lucy, 299; William, 28, 299
Bolton, John, 87, 90, 96
Bonner, bishop, 65, 138' 147, 295; his personal appearance, 51
Bonner's coal-house at the Marshalsea, 184
Bonville, Hester, sir William, 344
Books, built up in a wall, 171
Bostock, Lancelot, 291
Boulogne, 137, 148, 279
Bourn, sir John, 68, 134, 138, 139, 140, 142, 143
—— lady, 68
Bourne, Anthony, 68, 142
—— bishop Gilbert, 142, 287
Bourne, John, mayor of Reading, 126
Bowes, sir Martin, 40
—— sir Robert, 148
Bowls, playing at, 227
Bowyer, Robert, 90
Boxley, rood of, 286
Brahan, 315, 316
Bradford, John, 93, 145
Bray, Edmund lord, Elizabeth, 162, John lord, 170
Brentwood, 212
Brereton, Randle, 283
Brewster, William, 295
Brian, sir Robert, 334
Brigandine, 166
Briggs, Simon, 236, 341
Bright, dr. Timothy, 18
Bristol, 31
Brooke, *alias* Organmaker, Alice, Nicholas, Oliver, 62
—— Margaret, sir Richard, 143

Brooke, s
Brooks, J
Brown
Browne, 321, 3
—— sir
—— Ant
Bruss ls,
Bryd
—— sir R
—— sir T 342
Brysse (T
Brysto,
Brytty sea 84
Buckingh
Bulling las, Ric
Bungay
Burdett, C
Burghle
Bur

C

storation of the mass at, 227; prior's house burnt, 282; pri-

histo

C
C
C

C

Christchurch Twinham, 7
Christopherson, bishop, 3
Circulus Salamonis, 332
Cirencester, 89
Clarence, Lionel duke of, 344

GENERAL INDEX.

Clarke, master John, 293, 294
Clerke, John, a prophesier, 314, 332
Clink, the, 49
Clinton, lord, 168
Clopton, Elizabeth, Frances, 4
Cobham, George lord, 166
—— Thomas, 166; his capture, 168
—— sir William, 166
Codnor castle, 57
Colchester, 210, 295, 325, 336; a harbourer of heretics, 212
Cole, dr. Henry, 229
Common Prayer, Book of, 224, 225
Communion, a Protestant, disturbed at the accession of queen Mary, 178
Compter, in Wood-street, 146
Compton, near Winchester, 47
Concealed lands, commission for, 291
Conjurations, statute against, 330
Cooke, Anne, 313
—— sir Anthony, 146, 313
—— John, register of Winchester, 49
—— chaplain at Lincoln's inn, 58
Cope, Alan, 16
—— sir Anthony, 236
Cornelius Agrippa, 221
Cornwallis, arms and quarterings, 6; Edward, 5; Francis, 5, 7; sir John, 5; John, 7; Margaret, 4, 7; epitaph, 6; Mary, 7; Philip, 7; Richard, 5, 7; sir Thomas, 5; Thomas, 7
Cornwell, or Ansty, Thomas, 295
Corsley, 88
Cossyne, mr. 212
Cotton, Thomas, 189
Courtenay, Mary, sir William, 52
Coventry, 85, 163, 171
Coverdale, Miles, 295
Coxe, dr. 253
—— Leonard, 107, 108, 109, 122; letters patent granted to, 319
—— bp. Richard, 138, 236
—— William, 101, 109, 110
Craddock, John, 81
Cranmer, archbishop, 72; his lenity towards papists, 157, 246; the life and death of, 218—233;

his Coll
circumst
king Ed
last
his arms
anecdote
duct as
273;
in thr m
visitatio
on sain
read a
epistle t
letter to
boo
338; h
the H
Fathe s,
—— mrs.
—— Th
bishop)
Cran
Cres
Monume
Cressly, m
Creting

Dade, arms, 7

360   GENERAL INDEX.

Dyndee, 9
Dyott, sir, 293

Eagles, George, 211, 336
Easter, houselling at, 149
Edmondes, William, 90, 97, 99, 123, 124; his wife, 116
Edon, master, 293
Edward VI. duke of Somerset's appeal to, 80; false report of his death, 173; circumstances of Cranmer's signature to his will, 226; called "a poor child," 317; his worthy education, 317; his inquiry respecting St. George, 323; "Funeralles of," 324
Elizabeth, princess, 53, 136; sent a prisoner to Woodstock, 288; her praise as queen, 82
Elmsted, 211
Ely, of Brazenose, 229
Emerods, of silver or gold, 25
Englefield, *see* Inglefield
Erasmus, 219, 227, 283
Erith boat, 23
Essex, Thomas Crumwell, earl of, *see* Crumwell
Eton school, 239
Euer, Richard, 67, 315
Ewerby Thorpe, 300
Eyebright, the herb, 62

Fagot, carrying a, 20, 294
Fane, Henry, 94, *see* Vane
Farron, Laurence, 2
Fasterne park, 121
Fayre, maister, 306
Feasts, certain, prohibited, 285
Feerefilde, mr. 66
Ferrar, bp. Robert, 293
Ferrers, George, 163, 164, 166 *note*
—— Walter lord, 138
Finch, Katharine, sir William, 52
Fisher, bishop, execution of, 282
Fitzwilliam, Anne (lady), 312; Jane (lady), 313
FitzWilliam, sir William, 298
Fitzwilliams, lord, 56
Flanders lock, 101
Fleet prison, 143, 144, 172
Fleming, Abraham, 51

Fo d palace,
Ford, Willia
Fortescue s
Fortune te l
Foster Will
Foule, T
Foxe bisho
FOXE, John
  xi, xxi,
  desce
  veraci
  racter of
  xxii; m
  17 19 14
  59, xii· h
  numents,"
  Mart
  of Thoma
  omitted m
  tion that
  him in th
  preacher a
  wor

Hainault, *see* Henawd
Hales, Sir Christopher, 26 343
—— sir James, 265

GENERAL INDEX.

Hales, sir John, 236
Hall, mr. Robert, 323
Hals, *see* Hawes
Hampshire, opposed to Protestant doctrines, 315
Hampton, 100, 101
Hampton court, 173, 341
Hancock, Thomas, auto-biographical narrative of, 71—84; notes, 315; Gedeon, Sarah, 84
Hand-gun, 81
Harding, Thomas, 55, 56
Harley, bishop of Hereford, 85
Harpsfield, John, 47
—— Nicholas, 16
Harrow-on-the-Hill, 264
Harston, mr. Henry, 323
Hart, Anne, John, 341
Hartgills, murder of, xvi
Hartipole, Anne, 313; Richard, 314
Harvey, Henry, LL.D. 177
Harvye, Gerarde, 336
Harwich, 337
Hastings, sir Edward, 134, 143, 144
—— Henry lord, 134
Hatfield, Agnes, Laurence, 216
Hatton, sir Christopher, 323; sir William, 57
Havyland, William, 78
Hawes, or Hals, John, 298
Hawkes, Thomas, 163
Hawton, 9
Hayes, 264
Headborough, 104
Hearing, arms, 7
Heath, archbishop, 61, 158, 236, 245, 295
Hedingham castle, 35
Heigham, sir Clement, 206
Henawd, Mary of, 1, 35, 344, arms? 3
Henri d'Albret II. king of Navarre, 279
Henry VIII. 141, 148; anecdotes of, 25, 36, 42, 54; styled " the good king," 39; anecdotes of connected with Cranmer, 252, 253, 260; purposed to send his daughter Mary to the Tower, 259; his taking Otford and Knole, 266; visits Dover, 283; his picture painted with the bible defaced, 288

Herd, mr. 3
Hereford, W
Heretics kno ology, 33
Her'ng Jul
Hervey, Edm Joh , 333
atte-H t
Hickley, sir
Hicks, Hen
Highgate
Hilsey bish
Hilstal , 300
Hinchinbrok
Hoby, sir P
Holcro
—— sir Tho
Hollock, 150
Honne, mas
Hooper, bish 265
Horne, Chri
——

Laconicum, 57
Lambeth, 238, 248, 249, 2
—— bridge, 252
Lanam, or Latham, 302
Landerci, 132, 148, 169

362   GENERAL INDEX.

Lane, sir Robert, 114
Langporte, a black monk, 293
Lascelles, John, 41, 302, 306, 307, 310, 345
—— Mary, 43
Latham, or Lanam, 302
Latimer, bp. Hugh, 141, 223, 237, 298
Latin service, revival of the, 131
Lawney, Thomas, 276
Lawrance, Edmond, 188
Layton, dr. Richard, 282 bis, 284
Leader, sir Oliver, 196, 200, 204, 206; funeral of, 336
Leche street, at Worcester, 64
Lee, archbp. Edward, 220
—— Edward Dunne, 123
—— Ralph, 98, 110, 123
Legh, dr. Thomas, 253, 282
Leicester, Robert earl of, 51
Levyns, Christopher, 283
Limehouse, or Limehurst, 134, 140, 153, 156, 157, 210
Lincoln, 203
Lincoln's inn, 46, 58
Lincolnshire, rebellion in, 284, 285
Litany, English, 288
Little ease, 189
Littleton, master, 42
Lloyd, sir John, priest, 334
Lodge, sir Thomas, 298
London, dr. John, 34, 282
London, mode of election of members to parliament, 295; the city watch, 325; high price of wood, 150, 324
—— Allhallows Barking, 298; St. Bartholomew's, 295; hospital, 44, 182; St. Botulph's Bishopsgate, 294; Christ's hospital, 182; Charter house, 45; Coleman st. 171; Lion's key, 26, 345; Long lane by Smithfield, 96; Ludgate, watch at, 164, 324; St. Magnus church, 159; St. Margaret's Eastcheap, 23; St. Martin's Orgar, 23; St. Michael in the Ryal, 177; Montjoy house, 59; Newgate, 325; St. Pancras Soper lane, 177; St. Paul's church, exhibitions of agility from its steeple at the coronations of

Edward struck wi
ib ; the n
course, 1
mass, 28
ried pries
Northen,
51, 272,
hall, 40 ; S
heretics in
297 ; Stoc
Thomas's
Thomas o
tington co
Wood str
prison, Li
Tower
Longe, J an
Longland,
Lorraine ca
Loughborou
Louthe, arm
6 ; branch
Anne, 1, 4
Edm
E

Mortlake, 264

GENERAL INDEX.

Morwen, his verses on bishop Gardyner, 85
Morysin, sir Richard, 146
Mountjoy house, 59
Mouse, eating the host, question of, 40, 42
Mowntayne, Richard, 177
—— Thomas, the troubles of, 177—217, 335
Moyer, John, 87, 96 ; letter to Thomas Purye, 88, 95, 110
Moyle, sir Thomas, 137, 343
Moyne, arms and crest, 3, 6 ; sir John, sir William, 344
Mulso, arms, 2, 6 ; Anne, 1, 4, 35 ; Benet, 36 ; sir Edmund, 35 ; Thomas, 1 ; William, 4
Mummuth, *see* Monmouth
Mumpsimus, 141
Mylsent, Richard, 336

Names, instance of two *prænomina*, 123
Netherclief, Stephen, 100
Neville, sir Alexander, sir Anthony, 262 ; sir Edward, 152, 163 ; Frances, 152 ; Katharine, 163 ; Richard, Thomas, 262, 265
Nevynson, dr. Stephen, 339
Newbury, 29, 31, 85, 106, 118, 128, 334, 341
Newent, 69, 70
Newgate prison, 143 *et seq.*, 153, 165
Newman the ironmonger, 165 ; John, 337
Nicholson, Sygar, 203
Nicknames, satirical, 267, 350
Nine worthies, pageant of, 288
Non-residence of the clergy, 291
Norfolk, Thomas duke of, 5, 258, 276, 284, 314
Norris, Henry, 162, 283, 292
—— John, 162, 169
North, Edward lord, 264
Northampton, 120, 128
—— marquess of, 146, 322
Northumberland, John duke of, 134, 144, 158, 323 ; unpopularity of, 226 ; archbp. Cranmer's occupation with, 247; resident at Oxford, 266; letter to lord D
cation to,
Northwell,
Norwich, 3
Nottingham

Oakingha
Ochyne Ba
Ogle, Γ
Okyng, dr.
Opilio *see*
Organmake Nicholas,
Orleans, 8
Ormond, *se*
Osberton 2
Osiander
Otford, 266
Otterden 43
Owldıng T
Oxford, 15 232 · pr Mary at 85 ; card 2

364 GENERAL INDEX.

Poulet, lady Margaret, 79
Poynings, sir Thomas, 147
Poynter, mr. 157
Poyntz, sir Gabriel, Thomas, 235
Priests, required to put away their wives by the act of Six articles, 276; would have other men's wives, 35, 36, 276; " the old *Mumpsimus*," 141; only two left in Ipswich, 289; penance of married priests at St. Paul's, *ib.*
Proctor, James, 188
Promoters, 161, 213
Prophecies respecting Anne Boleyne, 52; on going a journey, 328, 347
Prophets, 331, 334
Protestants, 141; the first in Dorsetshire, 77; the first at Oxford, 293; in the city of London, 296, 298; at the court of Henry VIII. 311; concealed in Mary's reign, 149
Psalm, the 50th, used for divination, 332, 334
Purye, Thomas, 87, 88, 95, 110; letter to Foxe, 87; Katharine, 88
Puttenham, George, Rose, 52
Putto, of Colchester, 295
Pyttyes, parson, 186

Quynby, mr. 32; Anthony, *ib.*; Robert, 33

Rabetts, John, Mary, rev. Reginald, 7
Rack, the, 188
Racking of Anne Askew, 303
Radcliffe highway, 134
Radcliffe, sir Humphrey, 161, 168, 322
Radley, 293; John, 110
Rainsford, William, 162
—— sir John, 148
Ramsey abbey, 36, 148
Raner, Adam, 216
Raynold, dr. Thomas, 25
Read, Anne, sir William, 229
Reading, 334; the Bear, 104, 126; the Cardinal's hat, 99, 100; the cage, 114; the abbey, 96; royal palace and stables at, 86, ma
319
Rebeck, 14
Record, Ro
Rede,
Repps *al*
Reyno
Rich Hug
—— R c
307, 31
Richmond coun
Ridges, Jo
Rigby, Ric
Ring, sent 56, 256
Robarde ,
Robi 174
Rochester
Rochford,
Rogers Jo

Shaxton, bishop Nicho 223, 248, 306
Sheffield, Edmund lord ret, sir Robert, 57
Sheldon, William, 143
Shelley, William, 75

GENERAL INDEX.

Shepherd, Luke, 171, 325
Sherley, Jane, Ralph, 75
Shirley, sir Ralph, 132
Shoreditch, 28
Shotley, 5, 6
Shrewsbury, earl of, 9, 284
Shrift, on Shrove Tuesday, 287
Sieve and shears, divination by, 334
Singleton, 297
—— Harry, 100
Six Articles, the act of, 224; other notices of, 61, 62, 71, 276; Cranmer's opposition to, 237, 247
Skelton, father and son, 38; the host, 325
Skevington, sir William, 189
Skyppe, bishop John, 249
Smeaton, Mark, 283
Smith, Richard, S.T.P. 177; sir Thomas, 331
Smythe, vicar of Christchurch Twinham, 72
Somayne? arms, 3
Somer, Wylle, 318
Somerset, duke of, 76, 78, 80, 173, 323; connives at a conjuror being consulted, 331, 333
Somner, master, 293
Sonning, 319
Sorcery, 175, 333
Southampton, 74, 76
—— countess of, 312
Southo, 1, 292
Southwark, 210, 212
—— the Clink, 49
Southwell, sir Richard, 8, 44, 139, 140, 143, 166, 167, 187, 188
—— Richard, jun. 46
Spears, or men-at-arms, 321, 322
Speryne, see Perrins
Spilman, mr. 284
Spirits, invocation of, 330, 332, 334
Stafford, sir William, 322
Stafforton, mr. 323
Stephens, dr. 241
Stepney, 45, 59, 134, 157. 158, 160
Sternhold, Thomas, 48
Steward, of the church of Reading, 124; of the church of Worcester, 142

Steward, dr
Stilton 292
Stokisley bis 243, 298, anecdote tion of
Stoke Clare,
Stolen goods recovery, 3
Stonynge, T
Stop-galla
Story, mr 1
Stourton, A 47; Eliza Charles lo
Stove, or ud
Stratford on
Strype, his i xiii; chara
Stukeley, 38
Suffolk, Cha of, his dea
—— Henry

Udall, mr. 186; Nicholas 239, 293

GENERAL INDEX.

Uffculme, 82
Ulster, Lionel earl of, 1, 35
Underhill, Edward, biographical notice of, 132; his children, 133; his autobiographical anecdotes, 134—176; intimate with the duke of Northumberland, 144, 158; called the Hot-Gospeller, 160; his prayer, 175; verses, 176; his anecdote of King Edward and Saint George, 323
—— Guilford, 133, 153
Urmond, Jane, John, 303

Vachell, Thomas, 96
Vales, John, 161, 171, 214
Vane, lady Elizabeth, 90, 93, 95; her Psalms and Proverbs, 346; sir Ralph, 94, 321
Vanwylder, Edw., Margaret, 341
Vasternes, at Reading, 121
Vaughan, Cuthbert, 166
Verney, Edward, Francis, 171

Waad, Armigill, 314
Wackelyn, 186
Waddington, Richard, 313
Wadloe, 40, 47
Wainfleet, 300
Waldegrave, sir Edward, 95, 152
Walker, or Fuller, 66
Wallop, sir John, 148
Walsingham, custom of kissing on returning from, 37
Waltham abbey, 240
Walthamstow, 28
Warden pears, 34
—— abbey, 34, 35
Ware, and its inns, 192
Warham, archbp. 56, 221, 244; arms of, 250
Warren, W. 24
Warter, curate of St. Bride's, 188
Watch, the city, 324

Wattes, t e
  his daugh
Webb, mr. p
Welbeck, 30
Welch,
  128
Weldon, 333
Wentw
Westminste
Westo
  287
—— mr 28
—— the lut
Wesynham,
Wever, Ric
W

Yarmouth, 334
Yelverton, sir Christophe
Youle, Robert, 66
Young, archbp. Thomas,
Yownge, lusty, 158

Zealand, 211
Zouche, George, 52—5
  John, 52, 57; Margare
Zuinglian faction, 155

Westminster: Printed by J. B. Nichols and Sons, 25, Parliament Street.

REPORT OF THE COUNCIL
OF
THE CAMDEN SOCIETY.
ELECTED 2nd MAY, 1859.

The Council of the Camden Society, elected on the 2nd of May, 1859, refer with satisfaction to the Report of the Auditors for proof of the continued welfare of the Society.

The Council have to report the death during the past year of the following Members of the Society—

EDWARD NELSON ALEXANDER, Esq. F.S.A.
F. R. ATKINSON, Esq.
JOHN BRIGHT, Esq. M.D.
The Rev. D. C. DELAFOSSE, M.A.
The Right Hon. the EARL DE GREY, F.S.A.
WILLIAM RICHARD HAMILTON, Esq. F.R.S., F.S.A.
PHILIP AUGUSTUS HANROTT, Esq. F.S.A.
JAMES MAITLAND HOG, Esq.
BISHOP MALTBY.
The LORD MURRAY.
Sir GEORGE T. STAUNTON, Bart.
LORD P. JAMES CRICHTON STUART, M.P.

some of its oldest and most honoured members, that year has not been without compensation in the addition made to the number of Public Institutions now enrolled on the List of Subscribers.

The Library of King's College, Cambridge, and the Chetham Library, Manchester, have recently joined the Society; while the interest taken in its objects by our Transatlantic brethren is shown by the fact that no less than five American Libraries have just been added to the List of Members.

The Council venture to suggest that the friends of the Society cannot more surely promote its usefulness and secure its permanence than by doing whatever is in their power to bring its claims under the notice not only of all lovers of history, but also of all corporate or associated bodies which possess libraries.

The following Works have been issued since the last General Meeting:—

I. The Camden Miscellany, Volume the Fourth, containing: 1. A London Chronicle in the reigns of Henry VII. and Henry VIII.; 2. The Childe of Bristow, a Poem by John Lydgate; 3. Expenses of the Judges of Assize riding the Western and Oxford Circuits, temp. Elizabeth; 4. The Incredulity of St. Thomas, one of the Corpus Christi Plays at York; 5. Sir Edward Lake's Interview with Charles the First; 6 Letters of Pope to Atterbury when in the Tower of London; 7. Supplementary Note on the Jesuits' College at Clerkenwell.

This Volume, which belongs to the subscription of the past year, has been found fully equal to its predecessors in the variety and interest of its several papers. The Miscellanies are generally approved, and the Council will have pleasure in receiving valuable *short* papers suitable for a Fifth Volume. Some such are already in hand.

II. The Journals of Richard Symonds, an Officer in the Royal Army, temp. Charles I. Edited by CHARLES EDWARD LONG, Esq. M.A.

A Volume full of interest to the Historical Student, as well as abounding in materials of great value to the Genealogist and Topographer.

III. Original Papers illustrative of the Life and Writings of John Milton, now first published from MSS. in the State Paper Office. Edited by W. D. HAMILTON, Esq.

The name of Milton would justify and vindicate the publication of any volume of papers in which his hand could be traced. The present volume, publishing various new Latin letters written by him for the government of the day. It contains also the papers which explain the nature of the pecuniary dealings between himself and the Powell family, many of them now published for the first time, and the whole now also for the first time thrown into one entire series.

The last published volume, which has only just been issued to the Members, is—

IV. Letters of George Lord Carew, afterwards Earl of Totnes, to Sir Thomas Roe. Edited by JOHN MACLEAN, Esq. F.S.A.

a volume full of gossip about the notables of the time, and containing many interesting particulars of the Court and Courtiers of James the First.

The Council would close its account of its stewardship by again calling attention to the services which the Camden Society has rendered to Historical Literature. The Council have shown that, by a careful disposition of the funds at their command, and by an equally careful selection of books for publication, the Society is able to do good service to Historical Literature, and to maintain its reputation as a valuable auxiliary to the Historical Student.

By order of the Council,

JOHN BRUCE, Director.
WILLIAM J. THOMS, Secretary.

April 18, 1860.

REPORT OF THE AUDITORS.

We, the Auditors appointed to audit the Accounts of the Camden Society, [that the] Society, that the Treasurer has exhibited to us an account of the Receip[ts and] [Exp]enditure from the 1st of April, 1859, to the 31st of March, 1860, and t[hat we have] examined the said accounts, with the vouchers relating thereto, and find th[em to] [b]e correct and satisfactory.

Receipts.	£.	s	d.				
[B]alance of last year's account..	129	1	2	P[a]id f[or]			?
[Recei]ved on account of Members				Mis[cellaneous]		......	18
[who]se Subscriptions were in ar-				The li[...]		".....	4
[rea]r at the last Audit..	109	0	0				
[The l]ike on account of Subscrip-							
[tio]ns due 1st May last (1859) ..	335	0	0			......	[ ]
[Ditto] on account of Subscriptions					"		[ ]
[due] 1st May next..	7	0	0			......	[ ]
[A y]ear's dividend on £1016 3s. 1d.						......	[ ]
[3 p]er Cent. Consols, standing in						......	[ ]
[the] names of the Trustees of the							
[Soc]iety, deducting Income Tax..	29	6	10			......	[ ]
[Sa]le of Publications of past years	28	12	0				
				"		c.....	
						......	
						......	
					By Balance.............		
	£638	0	0				

And we, the Auditors, further state, that the Treasurer has reported to u[s that over] and above the present balance of £96 3s. 7d. there are outstanding variou[s subscrip]tions of Foreign Members, and of Members resident at a distance from L[ondon, whi]ch the Treasurer sees no reason to doubt will shortly be received.

Henry Stone Smit[h.]